When Deborah Met Jael

When Deborah Met Jael

Lesbian Biblical Hermeneutics

Deryn Guest

scm press

© Deryn Guest 2005

British Library Cataloguing in Publication data

A catalogue record for this book is available
from the British Library

0 334 02958 9

First published in 2005 by SCM Press
9–17 St Albans Place, London N1 0NX

www.scm-canterburypress.co.uk

SCM Press is a division of
SCM-Canterbury Press Ltd

Typeset in Albertina by Regent Typesetting
Printed and bound in Great Britain by
William Clowes Ltd, Beccles, Suffolk

Contents

Acknowledgements and thanks   vii

Part 1 Identifying the 'Lesbian' in Lesbian Hermeneutics   1

Introduction   3
1 Who is the lesbian in a lesbian-identified hermeneutic?   9
2 Lesbian-identified hermeneutics in context   59

Part 2 Guiding Principles for Lesbian-Identified Hermeneutics   105

Introduction   107
3 Resistance: commitment to a hermeneutic of hetero-suspicion   111
4 Rupture: commitment to the disruption of sex-gender binaries   157
5 Reclamation: commitment to strategies of appropriation   195
6 Re-engagement: commitment to making a difference   231

Conclusions   269
Bibliography   271
Subject Index   297
Name Index   301
Bible References Index   305

Acknowledgements and thanks

For commissioning this publication I would like to thank Anna Hardman. Her initial confidence in the project was much appreciated. When Barbara Laing took up the position that Anna vacated, I found myself working with another supportive editor who dealt with all my queries with patience and efficiency – many thanks.

I am grateful to the University of Birmingham for granting sabbatical leave for two terms, enabling me to work on this project. Thanks also to my colleagues in the department of theology, especially Isabel, who commented on a lengthy draft, regularly offered valuable advice and access to her personal library, for dealing patiently with my numerous queries as and when required, and for the welcome tea breaks when the going got tough. Such friends bear no responsibility for any errors that appear in the publication. Appreciation must be extended to the students of the first 'Que[e]rying Theology' module at Birmingham. I was pleased to have the opportunity to share with them ideas expressed in this publication and I am grateful for the critical suggestions and insights that were forthcoming in class discussions and in their assignments.

I must also extend gratitude to friends both within and outside the university who took an interest in my work and were encouraging and optimistic about the project even when I wasn't – Rachel, Sharada, Pam, Charlie, Helen and Jilly – many thanks to you all.

A beaming grin to my children, Tom and Jenny, who have lived through the effects that writing a book inevitably produces. If one includes thinking time, this book has been ten years in the making and that followed fairly closely on from a time-consuming PhD. Tom and Jenny thus grew up with a somewhat unconventional mother whose mind was usually engrossed in the contents of books rather than saucepans and I am grateful for their resilience when faced with sparsely stocked fridge-freezers and cupboards, and for their willingness to make do with 'whatever you can find' throughout the years.

Acknowledgements and thanks

Finally to Fiona, for reading umpteen drafts of all chapters without ever complaining, for being a keen critic, for unbounded enthusiasm in the project, and for being the most dependable, loving and supportive partner one could ever wish for – my heartfelt appreciation.

Part 1

Identifying the 'Lesbian' in Lesbian Hermeneutics

Introduction

In my adolescence I knew there were women called lesbians, because my perceptive but somewhat discomforted mother once handed me some kind of Christian booklet on 'being a teenager'. It contained a paragraph on 'crushes' where girls mistakenly focus their desire on someone of their own sex – a teacher, a school friend – before making the step into the full 'maturity' of heterosexuality. I remember how the word 'lesbian' was reserved for women who never made that step and who were tragically doomed to an unfulfilled life. As a young teenager I had never met any such women and harboured no expectations of meeting one (the only recognizable feature would appear to be a woman of extreme doleful and tragic demeanour, and although several acquaintances matched such a description I thought it highly unlikely that all these women could be 'lesbians', especially since many of them were married). However, contrary to my mother's probable intentions, I was glad to hear about these women because it was at least a relief to know that there were other women out there who were attracted to members of their own sex and that there was a word to describe them, even if that word was somewhat unpalatable.

I expect that I was given this booklet because of my apparent lesbian potential. Growing up in the 1960s I was undoubtedly demonstrating many of the characteristics that had come to be associated with lesbians: a definite preference for clothing predominantly assigned to boys (how else could one comfortably go adventuring with one's friends?); a preference for toys and activities predominantly assigned to boys (action men always had better outfits and gear than Sindy dolls and besides, action men were jointed at the ankles and wrists); a partiality for active sports and anything that involved a football; a disdain for anything pink, frilly, flowery, lacy or with ribbon-attachments. As will be discussed in Chapter 1, these are precisely the manifestations of gender nonconformity that had been identified by the European and American sexologists as marking the women they categorized as lesbian.

In my mother's view, such lesbian potential was definitely not to be encouraged: a sentiment endorsed by the instruction of the religious denomination into which I was born. I was a third-generation Salvationist, taken along to the local corps as a baby, but choosing this as my confessional home when I became first a junior soldier and later, at the age of 15, a senior soldier. Nurtured in a religious context that bore no few similarities to the environment so hilariously, but astutely, described by Jeanette Winterson in *Oranges Are Not the Only Fruit*, I was encouraged to have a negative view of same-sex relations. Not that they were talked about; heterosexuality being the expected norm, lesbian or gay choices never cropped up in Sunday school or youth fellowship discussions. Although I have a vivid early memory of being dismayed when a Sunday school mate told me that I couldn't grow up and marry the girl I had just named because you have to marry a boy, my astonishment was quickly subdued in the realization that this was indeed what was expected. When working through the lessons required for entering into senior soldiership, the regulations confirming that expectation came to light: no one can become a uniformed senior soldier of the Salvation Army if they enjoy same-sex sexual relations. If I was to make the commitment to soldiership and fulfil a calling to Salvation Army officership, I had to promise to uphold such regulations. In due course, I married, went to the Salvation Army training college and, after two years' training, was commissioned an officer in 1984. I was appointed to a corps in Manchester during which time I gave birth to my two children. As the reader will realize, this situation was not destined to last. There were many complex reasons that contributed to my resignation from Salvation Army officership in 1987, but one of these was the inability to stand by a regulation that I could no longer accept and continue with a marriage that was unravelling. My story is not unlike many other women's stories who try to conform to the expectations of their family and religion, but eventually have to resist in order to preserve their integrity and dignity.

I tell this story not because it grants this publication any authority, nor to win the reader's sympathy, but in order to indicate some of the specifics of my location. Several years after the experiences had passed, having entered higher education and eventually securing a lecturing position, I decided to embark upon this project. But it seemed a grandiose project to say the least: Who was I to try to define the principles and strategies of a lesbian hermeneutic? How could the principles and strategies that are proposed in this publication be of relevance outside my immediate context? I am acutely aware that any attempt to define a lesbian-identified hermeneutic will inevitably be partial and subject to blind spots. The brief account of my story does at least let the reader know something of my context and they can draw their own conclusions about how such a context may have motivated and influenced my findings. Although I would now refer to myself as postchristian, I retain a keen interest in the way my own and other Christian and Jewish organizations negotiate the presence of lesbians in their pews. I wonder what differences, if any, the presence of women priests and rabbis may make. I am concerned for religious young people who continue to be faced with difficult dilemmas when trying to reconcile their sexual selves with the demands of their confessional homes. The Salvationist in me has never completely disappeared – the concern for justice, for theological integrity, for the well-being of others that compelled me into ministry, continues to drive my work. The reader should therefore not be surprised to find that one of the principles of a lesbian hermeneutic, in my view, is that it should be committed to making a difference.

The book is organized into two major parts. Part 1 consists of two chapters. Chapter 1 examines the problematic word 'lesbian' and attempts to define who, or what positionality, it might incorporate. Here, the reader will find reference to the work of the sexologists and the theories that produced the now stereotypical concept of the lesbian as woman suffering from gender nonconformity. However, it moves on from those discussions to the concept of political lesbianism within second-wave feminism and from there to the impact of queer theory on lesbian and gay studies. The chapter concludes with an explanation of why this publication prefers the phrase 'lesbian-identified hermeneutic' and why it continues with this terminology rather than that of queer.

Hermeneutical principles are always marked by the context in which they are produced and Chapter 2 discusses the various ways in which lesbians find themselves positioned and subsequently oppressed, depending upon the specific context in which they live. It opens with an illustrative tour of non-Transatlantic contexts where, in some cases, the criminalization of same-sex relationships has led to state-sanctioned oppression of lesbian-identified individuals. In other contexts the oppressive factor is silence which has its own deadly effects. In a second section this chapter concentrates on the situation in England, demonstrating how a wide range of civil discrimination and stigmatization continues to prevail. The chapter closes with an exploration of the ways in which Christian discourse has contributed to and sustained the criminalization and civil discrimination discussed in the previous sections.

Part 2 identifies four principles for a lesbian-identified hermeneutic.

These four principles are not separate, stand-alone ideas, but each is meant to interact with the others in a holistic manner. Readers who wish to move quickly to the strategies for interpreting scripture could begin here, but I would suggest that the groundwork laid in Part 1 is necessary if the rationale for the principles and strategies is to be appreciated. Chapter 3 identifies the first principle – that of resistance to the effects of silence and erasure that have characterized lesbian history. Taking to task the common (mis)conception that there are 'no lesbians in the Bible', it examines the textual strategies that have rendered female homoeroticism all but invisible before offering suggestions as to how these strategies might be disrupted. Chapter 4 deals with the second principle – the commitment to rupturing sex/gender categories. It examines the way in which religious institutional discourse draws upon selected texts to enforce a hetero–homosexual binary that appears to be ordained by God. Three strategies for dealing with this problem are identified before the chapter closes with an explanation of why I believe it is vital not only to continue engaging with the 'texts of terror' debate but to deepen and widen the discussion. The principle of reclamation is discussed in Chapter 5; a chapter which examines the usefulness of queer theory and its application to scripture. It demonstrates how the scriptures contain elements that come alive to lesbian and gay-identified readers and how those scriptures can be interpreted in ways not conventionally explored. The final chapter explains why the lesbian-hermeneutic advocated in this publication is committed to making a difference. It calls for academics to recognize and address the effects and consequences of their exegesis for contemporary contexts. It confronts the one issue that is probably of the most fundamental importance, yet is so often elided in debates, that of scriptural authority. In my view, the battle for the Bible that continues to swing to and fro is founded on the protagonists' earnest belief that their method of interpretation is the most appropriate and that they are upholding the will of God. Yet, despite their opposing agenda, one soon discovers that the debaters use similar tools and strategies, claim similar authorities and attempt to occupy the same theological high ground, i.e. the right to claim scriptural and divine support for one's beliefs. Ultimately, the discussion needs to move away from what individual texts may or may not mean, and place the focus on where authority resides. Commitment to making a difference means getting involved in this debate and this chapter accordingly considers how lesbian and gay-identified and queer readers position themselves vis-à-vis the scriptures. The final section of this chapter puts forward my own view that a lesbian-identified hermeneutics would find a welcoming and thriving home in the *métissage* – an umbrella space for those committed to social, political, economic and religious justice and transformation.

Throughout the publication all scriptural references follow the New Standard Revised Version unless otherwise stated.

1

Who is the lesbian in a lesbian-identified hermeneutic?

The European sexologists, who were busy constructing the lesbian at the turn of the twentieth century, could hardly have conceived how their efforts would contribute to the emergence of a lesbian subject within a matter of a few decades. Originally the object of scrutiny, she has become the scrutinizer, not only of her own experience but of how that experience has been shaped by social, political, legal and religious discourses. This is reflected in the explosion of lesbian studies within the academy during the past few decades. One cannot say that this new lesbian perspective is well-represented but, comparatively speaking (with say 50 years ago and certainly beyond that), lesbian studies have certainly made their mark in the arts and humanities with recent sorties into new areas such as geography, law, biology and information technology.[1] However, in all these fertile areas of potential research, this lesbian subject is often to be found stumbling over her own feet before she can begin the work before her. The stumbling block is the very word 'lesbian'. Precisely what is a 'lesbian' and what is a 'lesbian perspective'? Lynn Pearce (1996, p. 229) recounts how students in her class are often forestalled in their efforts to answer essays on some aspect of lesbian criticism precisely because they have become entirely entangled in the question of who or what a lesbian might be. This is not a problem limited to students alone; it has beset the academic world far more widely. Both Pearce and several other writers express doubts about even beginning to undertake 'lesbian' projects, when the definition of the very word 'lesbian' continues to evade resolution to the satisfaction of all interested parties. Sally Munt, editor of *New Lesbian Criticism* published in 1992, confesses in her introduction that she had reservations about undertaking the project at all given the

---

1 For a review of how various disciplines have been modified by such forays, see Griffin and Andermahr (1997).

current criticisms of identity politics. Lynn Pearce's opening sentences to her essay on lesbian criticism similarly express an awareness that her essay will be outdated before the book is published given the 'epistemological freefall' taking place in the wake of postmodern trends (1996, p. 227). Such qualms are endemic within contemporary studies, even as this discipline comes of age. These qualms have been further exacerbated now that the usefulness of retaining a lesbian identity has been so profoundly challenged by the expanding area of queer studies.

Marilyn Farwell (1996) helpfully identifies three 'critical moments' in theorizing lesbian subjectivity in the western context. First, there was the role played by the discourse of late nineteenth-century and early twentieth-century sexologists who put scholarly weight behind existing representations of the lesbian as a mannish woman by their theories of inversion.[2] Second, the concept of the lesbian continuum in the early 1970s opened up the possibility that women could align politically with/as lesbians regardless of sexual practice. Third, the advent of late twentieth-century postmodern discourse and contemporary queer theory challenged the ontological basis of any 'lesbian' identity and questioned radically the usefulness of continuing with such a label. These major developments have certainly informed the ways in which a lesbian signifier is defined and applied. This chapter is thus organized around those three critical moments exploring how different understandings of the lesbian signifier have repercussions for any notions of a 'lesbian sensibility' and 'lesbian perspective'. In each section, the ramification for a lesbian reading of scripture will be addressed, indicating who the 'lesbian' might be who would apply such readings. The chapter concludes with an explanation of why this publication prefers the phrase 'lesbian-identified hermeneutic' and why it continues with this terminology rather than that of queer.

---

2 Lisa Duggan's work on the trials of Alice Mitchell convincingly demonstrates that the sexologists were not constructing anything new in their case studies; their 'radical innovation' lies in the new subjectivity the lesbian now embodied: 'She came to see herself as an erotic subject – as a woman whose desire for women was felt as a fundamental component of her sense of self, marking her as erotically different from most other women' (2003, p. 73). Jennifer Terry also notes that the creation of the sexual deviant was not entirely dependent on medical discourse for its enunciation since lesbian and gay subcultural practices may have overlapped to some extent with the pathologizing discourse (1991, p. 72 n. 4). See further Jackson (1994).

Innate Lesbianism and Lesbian Sensibility in the Discourse of the Sexologists

Contemporary understandings of 'lesbian' have been substantially informed by the medical discourse of the European sexologists during the late nineteenth and early twentieth centuries. Both the word and the concept of lesbian as a 'certain kind of woman' pre-dates their work,[3] but the attempt to define and identify the characteristics of lesbian women as a *species* was undertaken with new-found fervour at the turn of the twentieth century. Although there were diverse theories, for several sexologists the lesbian was best described as a congenital invert; born biologically female but possessing the emotions, desires and preferences traditionally the preserve of the male.[4]

Inversion was thought to be a visibly marked condition. Physically, the lesbian was variously described as possessing well-developed muscles, a masculine type of larynx, and although some (Havelock Ellis, 1936) dismissed such claims, thought to be in possession of a lengthy clitoris.[5]

---

3 Bernadette Brooten suggests that the earliest use of the word 'lesbian' to denote 'a woman erotically orientated toward other women' comes from Arethas' medieval (c. 914 AD) commentary on Clement of Alexandria (scholion to *Paidagōgos* 3.3.21.3) which equates *tribades, hetairistriai* and *lesbiai*. She concludes: 'All of these nouns demonstrate that people in the ancient Mediterranean had the concept of an erotic orientation with respect to women' (1996, p. 5), though whether the women themselves thought of themselves in these terms is not clear. Dating the recognition of women who love women as belonging to a recognizable 'type' in the modern world is more debatable. Certainly the diaries of Anne Lister (1791–1840) reveal a woman who can recognize herself and like-minded individuals as belonging to an identifiable group, and representations of women who pursue and love women can be found in Renaissance literature. Emma Donoghue (1993) argues that the 1736 reference to 'lesbian' in William King's *The Toast* (by which King unleashes smear attacks on the widowed Duchess of Newburgh), has distinctly modern connotations. However, whether such references do have any direct traceable connection with sexological constructions of lesbian as a species in the early twentieth century is a controversial issue that continues to provoke scholarly debate.

4 For an examination of such theories circulating in America between 1870–1900, see Gibson (1997), Chauncey (1982–3), Katz (1976). For useful extracts of primary sources, consult Part II of Katz (1983) and for extracts relating to lesbians in particular, see chapter 3 of Oram and Turnbull (2001).

5 In 1883 Dr James G. Kiernan reported that a woman of Belvidere, Illinois was in possession of a two and a half inch clitoris when erect (see Katz 1983, p. 195). Such claims have a long history; Brooten (1996), for example, demonstrates how Greek and Roman sources masculinized female homoeroticism and portrayed the *tribade* as a sexually aggressive woman. These sources fixated on the idea of women being able to penetrate other women. The distinction between imaginative representations of sexually active women and descriptions of what we would now term intersex features requires further investigation.

Behaviourally, she was likely to prefer clothing and work/leisure activities traditionally associated with men, and enjoy 'masculine' habits such as cigar smoking. Richard von Krafft-Ebing's comments on the appearance of Miss X provide illustration:

> Man's hat, short hair, spectacles, gentleman's cravat and a sort of coat of male cut covering her woman's dress. She had coarse male features, a rough and rather deep voice, and with the exception of the bosom and female contour of the pelvis, looked more like a man in woman's clothing than like a woman . . .
>
> I incidentally discovered that as a child she had a fondness for horses and masculine pastimes, but never took any interest in feminine occupations. (cited in Katz 1983, p. 207)

Sexually, her objects of desire were members of her own sex and, being considered to be in possession of a heightened sex drive, she was likely to take the active sexual role in pursuing women and engaging in love-making activities including kissing, embracing, touching intimately and achieving orgasm.[6] In short, the congenital invert was a woman-who-ought-to-have-been-a-man; the reports of the sexologists often carrying references to their interviewee's desire to be such. Even though Ellis dismissed the idea that all 'mannish' women were necessarily inverts, he still sustained the perception of the lesbian as woman-who-acts-like-a-man, as his following description demonstrates:

> The brusque, energetic movements, the attitude of the arms, the direct speech, the inflections of the voice, the masculine straight-forwardness and sense of honor . . . will often suggest the underlying psychic abnormality to a keen observer. In the habits not only is there frequently a pronounced taste for smoking cigarettes, often found in quite feminine women, but also a decided taste and tolerance for cigars. There is also a dislike and sometimes incapacity for needlework and other domestic occupations, while there is often some capacity for athletics. (1936, p. 250)

---

6 See, for example, Karl von Westphal's (1869) case of Miss N who has sexual encounters with several women, or Havelock Ellis' (1895) account of Miss X's physical sexual intimacies.

Certainly, there is a narrowing of definition here. As Lisa Duggan (1998) rightly notes, to subsume all lesbians under the category of the masculine-like invert ignores the range of diverse alternatives for women such as the romantic friends model and, most notably, the women who chose as their partners those categorized as inverts. The sexologists seized only upon the image of the masculine invert, the one who was already visibly present in the world, whose appearance could easily be lampooned (see Katz 1983, pp. 313–14) but who, arguably, posed the most obvious threat given her presence as a visible rival to the male wooer.

While the sexologists narrowed the field, the idea of inversion was not without basis. For all the clear caricaturing that is going on here, there is evidence that gender nonconformity was keenly felt and lived out by some women. The diary musings of Anne Lister (1791–1840), written long before the diagnostic notes of the sexologists, repeatedly refer to her 'masculine' traits. She speaks, for example, of her deep-toned voice and manly conversational style (Whitbread 1992a, p. 116), her possession of the 'civility of a well-bred gentleman' (1992a, p. 120), her 'manner of walking' (1992a, p. 155), her 'manly feelings' (1992a, p. 267), the way in which she once 'Twirled my watch about, conscious of occasionally bordering on a rather gentleman-ly sort of style' (1992a, p. 330) – qualities she often refers to as oddities or singularities. She also describes how her contemporaries 'generally remark, as I pass along, how much I am like a man' (1992a, p. 48), how the Mackenzies 'thought I was a man & the Macks too had wondered. Mrs Barlow herself had thought at first I wished to imitate the manners of a gentleman but now she knows me better, it was not put on' (1992b, p. 37). This sense of gender nonconformity has continued to be a significant feature of lesbian auto-biography where tales of enjoying a tomboy childhood/youth are common. Indeed, as Kath Weston observes, it continues to play a large part in cultural expectations:

> Rather than ask whether anyone has ever spotted So-and-So kissing another woman, people are more likely to assess her gay potential based upon the timbre of her voice, the way she occupies space in a room, the boyish cut of her clothing, or her 'nontraditional' job . . . Lipstick lesbians aside, most popular representations still depict 'real' lesbians as masculinized women, assuming all the while that everyone agrees upon the meaning of 'masculine'. (1996, p. 7)

Refigured as gender play, nonconformity continues to feature strongly in the contemporary cultural productions of lesbian or queer artists, but this has come a long way from the initial observations of the sexologists for whom such gender nonconformity was evidence for an ontological condition.[7] Working within an ideological framework where woman–woman relations only made sense if one of the partners occupied an active, visible male role, the sustained attention of the sexologists on 'masculine' features is not surprising. Invert status was conferred only on those women who were the active initiators of same-sex relations. The women pursued, who usually conformed to 'feminine' expectations, were often not considered to be innate lesbians, nor were they inverted or perverted, but merely, it seems, seduced, or women with 'acquired' homosexuality (see Katz 1983, p. 144).

Although the sexologists are sometimes criticized for their crude stereotyping of lesbian women and for introducing a medical model of homosexuality as abnormality, their work did provide an apology for lesbian existence since the notion of inversion did not equate with sexual vice. Inversion was considered to be an innate condition which a woman did not choose and which therefore did not deserve censure and punishment. Indeed, in such apologies the lesbian could actually become an *admirable* figure. Edward Carpenter (1914), for example, upheld her fiery boldness, her frankness, her ability to use her masculine qualities to relate men to women, and vice versa (though she also possessed qualities of brusqueness and coarseness which, in his view, were defective elements). One woman who immediately latched on to the opportunity for a full apologia from the perspective of an invert was Marguerite 'John' Radclyffe Hall whose infamous 1928 novel – *The Well of Loneliness* – represents an apology for all inverts. It contained a foreword by Havelock Ellis and her main female character, Stephen Gordon, manifested the outward signs noted by him.

What then, would this mean for lesbian interpretation of biblical texts? Primarily, the discourse of some sexologists, particularly those promoting the idea of the congenital invert, constructed the notion of the lesbian who

---

7 Self-described as a gender terrorist ('anyone who consistently and intentionally subverts, destabilizes and challenges the binary gender system'), Del LaGrace Volcano's mission is: 'To uncover and dislodge the dis-ease(s) created by centuries of mandatory and violently enforced gender conformity' (Halberstam and Volcano 1999, p. 36). Volcano's photography, as would be expected, confounds gender expectations. For examples of such work see Halberstam and Volcano (1999) and Volcano (2000).

was born, not made. The particular traits that identified her as a species and that would, in due course, lend her a political identity, were innate: an outward manifestation of an inner determinism. There is an unchanging fixity about the signifier. She is not a woman in the process of becoming, but one who is contained by the lesbian category. Working within this definition, a lesbian reading would be one undertaken by a woman who is 'wired' to have certain characteristic traits, emotions and desires. Accordingly, she may have an inherently different viewing angle on texts, her sexual orientation influencing the way she writes, reads and thinks. Thus, Una Troubridge (1973), one of Radclyffe Hall's lovers, confirmed the latter's conviction that only one qualified by experience of inversion could write such a book as *The Well of Loneliness* and speak on behalf of all inverts.

If this were the case, a lesbian reading position would not be available to 'heterosexually wired' persons, but would be a meaning-producing perspective geared directly to one's homosexual orientation. The reader, in possession of an innate lesbian sensibility, would be able to write, read and respond to cultural productions in a way that was inherently different from heterosexual women.

Since lesbian and gay interpretations of scripture largely emerged post-1970, I have been unable to find any examples of a lesbian-identified approach to scripture that would be contemporaneous with the work of the sexologists. Probably one of the earliest writers, who was certainly influenced by the early twentieth-century constructions of the homosexual, was Derrick Sherwin Bailey. In 1955 he published *Homosexuality and the Western Christian Tradition* which contains an exegetical study of those scriptural references commonly thought to refer to homosexuality. It is notable for its commitment to the notion of the congenital invert, where (genuine) inversion is considered to be an inherent condition. Bailey, for example, differentiates between the true homosexual – 'the genuine homosexual condition, or *inversion*, as it is often termed, is something for which the subject was in no way to be held responsible; in itself, it is morally neutral' – and the pervert who is defined as 'a heterosexual who engages in homosexual practices' (1955, p. xi). And in his view, 'of the existence of the genuine, inherent invert there can be no possible doubt' (1955, p. xii). However, his publication does not consider how a 'homosexual' orientation might contribute to a distinctive writing or reading perspective. For this, we have to wait several years.

Notwithstanding, although she writes almost a century later than the sexologists and would not uphold their construction of 'the lesbian', certain parts of Nancy Wilson's work seem to be rooted in a concept of the essential

lesbian whose innate sensibility means that she has a natural ability to tune
into the characters and stories of the Bible that are part of her ancestry.
Wilson's unbounded confidence that 'our counterparts followed Moses
and Miriam in the Exodus, wandered in the wilderness, and walked with
Jesus by the Sea of Galilee' (1995, p. 112), her adventurous reclamation of the
eunuchs, the magi, Jesus, Lazarus, the Marys of Bethany, Paul and his male
friends and the female missionary couples to whom Paul refers, and her
ability to find in these figures hints of an alternative and marginal sexuality
that resonate with late twentieth-century lesbian and gay experience,
appears to be grounded in the dual concepts of lesbian essentialism and
lesbian sensibility. Essentialist approaches (discussed more fully in Chapter
3) affirm that there have always been women who were erotically attracted
to other women even though they may not have known themselves as
'lesbians'. Within such a framework, an attempt to reclaim these foresisters
from the Bible could be deemed an entirely appropriate endeavour. Indeed,
Wilson's book is called *Our Tribe* precisely because, in her view, all lesbians
belong to a cross-cultural, cross-time ancient 'tribal remnant' whose legacy
is so tangible that she speaks of 'several experiences of what I feel is something akin to lesbian and gay tribal memory' (1995, pp. 111–12). Hence in
the opening worship service at the National Council of Churches of Christ
where the Metropolitan Community Church's application for membership was being considered, she had a sense of tribal unity that upheld and
sustained her:

> Suddenly, I sensed *them* in the room: gay men and lesbians through the
> ages. In the churches, burned by the churches, persecuted by the churches,
> serving the churches, loving and hurting. *They* were there. They knew I
> was there. I had this overwhelming sense of a mystical communion of
> gay and lesbian saints . . . I wept for them and for us, for their longing,
> pain and shame, for their need even now for vindication and for a voice.
> (1995, p. 13)

Her semi-autobiographical book was never intended to be one that
ventured into the complexities of biblical hermeneutics and it would be
unfair to judge it on such a basis. Her book is written for a community who
have experienced the Bible as a weapon wielded against them. To have a
lesbian, gay, bisexual and transgender presence illuminated within its pages
is a liberating surprise. For the purpose of this section, what is noticeable is
the way in which Wilson's bold, provocative and conjectural outing of the
Bible seems to be guided by a lesbian sensibility innately wired up for the

recognition of certain signifiers. These signifiers are unlocked by entering into an imaginative rapport with the Bible in an approach that has much in common with the phenomenon colloquially referred to as one's 'gay-dar'. Popularly used to describe how lesbians recognize each other in public spaces, the idea of the gaydar permeates more critical discussions of the lesbian gaze insofar as the gaydar operates in the open, slippery spaces that are inevitably present in the gap between author/artist and the reader/audience. The gaydar renders the lesbian reader/viewer attentive to any action, image, word that speaks intentionally, or unintentionally, to their experience; and it facilitates gap-filling. Wilson's reading of biblical texts operates in a similar way as she seizes upon signifiers that carry contemporary resonance for her community. For example, the colours purple or lavender have a long association with lesbian and gay culture (Grahn 1984, pp. 6–8), and the reference to Lydia as seller of purple in Acts 16.11–15, 40 is enough to warrant the inclusion of this woman in 'our tribe' of ancestors. Such a claim, if it remains grounded within an essentialist framework, is not likely to win much critical support, though it may provide the starting point for a queer reading, as will be discussed in Chapter 5.

Although Wilson's work was not honed in an academic context, her basic approach does have some useful connections with more critical treatments of lesbian and gay sensibility. Film critic Vito Russo, for example, notes how the stigma that was attached to homosexuality necessarily constructed a lesbian or gay sensibility:

> Gay sensibility is largely a product of oppression, of the necessity to hide so well for so long. It is a ghetto sensibility, born of the need to develop and use a second sight that will translate silently what the world sees and what the actuality may be. It was gay sensibility that, for example, often enabled some lesbians and gay men to see at very early ages, even before they knew the words for what they were, something on the screen that they knew related to their lives in some way, without being able to put a finger on it. (1987, p. 92)

Sometimes film producers played deliberately to this emergent gay sensibility. Thus, when the prohibitive Hays code[8] was introduced, producers

---

8 The Hays code was a self-regulatory code of ethics created in 1930 by the Motion Picture Producers and Distributors of America under Will H. Hays. It came into effect in July 1934 and prevented producers from screening anything that might cross norms of 'good taste'. It specifically prescribed that the sanctity of the institution of marriage and the home should be upheld and sex perversion or any inference to it was strictly

had to resort to subtlety. Coded signifiers such as lavender, carnations, or the scent of gardenia were used to indicate a gay presence on screen. Driven underground, coded 'gay language' developed; shared between those in the know who would recognize these indicators and draw the required conclusions.

However, a lesbian or gay sensibility can also find resonances and meaning where such deliberately coded language is absent. Indeed, readers who identify as lesbians often testify to the greater satisfaction to be gleaned from reading straight texts aslant, rather than consuming cultural productions that come with an overtly lesbian label. What seems to be important is not the text itself, but the gaze that scans it, and the alluring experiences of transgressive reading. Alison Hennegan, an avid book reader as a child, describes how books repeatedly let her down, but as her 'chief companions' and 'most important source of knowledge', she was not able or willing to concede that books were of no use to her. Literature was therefore made to serve Hennegan's desires:

> Wherever I scented mutinous tendencies in an author, I helped them along a little by the creation of my own parallel text. And this was a liberty I felt as free to take with the Greats as with the Also-rans. Fanny Price was obviously never going to come to any good with Edmund so I gave her to Mary Crawford instead and ended *Mansfield Park* properly. Charlotte Lucas had to be saved from Mr Collins somehow and Elizabeth Bennet seemed to me the woman to do it . . .
>
> . . . *Our Mutual Friend* was so clearly improved and rang truer, if Eugene ended up with Mortimer, Lizzie with Bella. Miss Abbey, redoubtable publican of the Thameside Six Jolly Fellowship-Porters, is obviously a dyke and deserves a worthy lover. So I gave her one. Clearly Steerforth should live *and* have David Copperfield who's anyway been madly in love

---

forbidden (as was any representation of interracial sexual relations). In the wake of the Motion Picture Association of America's 1961 decision to 'consider approving such references in motion pictures if the allusion to sexual aberration was treated with care, discretion and restraint' (Russo 1987, p. 127), films with an explicitly homosexual content were shown, notably *A Taste of Honey* (1961) and *Victim* (1961). Later, the Supreme Court's decision concerning obscenity, and the action of civil liberties groups brought a sweeping revision to the code in 1966. The new code suggested restraint in treating sexual themes on the screen, rather than forbidding them outright. In 1968 a rating system was put into effect, classifying films according to their suitability for viewing by the young.

with him from that first moment in the playground. Thus should the world be ordered and thus I ordered it. (1988, pp. 174–5)

Such comments are representative of a wide body of testimony that lesbians can and do call upon a lesbian sensibility to resignify given signifiers, recontextualize cultural productions, and basically, read differently from heterosexuals. Nancy Wilson's approach, though uncritical and often seemingly naive, thus has some consistency with the position of acclaimed critic Sally Munt, who says

we are particularly adept at extracting our own meanings, at highlighting a text's latent content, at reading 'dialectically', at filling the gaps, at interpreting the narrative according to our introjected fictional fantasies, and at foregrounding the intertextuality of our identities. If we accept that language is unstable, then within its heterosexuality we must also be able to find its homosexual other. A lesbian reader's literary competence brings to the text a set of interpretative conventions for decoding and encoding which is rich in its own historical, cultural and linguistic specificity. (1992, p. xxi)

Munt's concept of lesbian sensibility is one grounded in an awareness of postmodern critical theory, discussed in the 'third critical moment' below, and that inevitably sets Munt's work in a different category from Wilson's. However, as we shall see in Chapter 5, this concept of lesbian sensibility and Wilson's rapport with certain scriptural figures and stories has a valued part to play within a lesbian-identified hermeneutic.

The Lesbian in All Women
Strategic definitions of lesbianism in the discourse of second-wave feminism

Although the sexologists' creation of a lesbian identity had its uses, it inevitably set lesbians apart from 'normal' women, and created the anxiety that one's friendships with women could be deemed 'lesbian' if one was not careful. 'What a shame that feminine friendships should be unnatural,' wrote Willa Cather to Louise Pound in 1892; while in 1895 Ruth Asmore warned readers of the *Ladies' Home Journal* of the dangers of forming romantic bonds with other women (Miller 1995, pp. 61–2). And if domestic friendships came under increasing scrutiny, how much more so did the pioneering activities and friendships of the first-wave feminists. The construction of the lesbian was considerably damaging for the fledgling women's movement especially when figures like Havelock Ellis claimed that the women's movement brings in its wake

> an increase in feminine criminality and in feminine insanity, which are being elevated towards the masculine standard. In connection with these we can scarcely be surprised to find an increase in homosexuality especially since congenital anomaly occurs with special frequency in women of high intelligence who . . . influence others. (1895, pp. 155–6)

The 'smear' of lesbianism significantly slowed the movement down:

> Those opposed to women's growing independence now could hurl, with credible support behind them, accusations of degeneracy at females who sought equality, and thereby scare them back to the hearth with fears of abnormality . . . Love between women was metamorphosed into a freakishness, and it was claimed that only those who had such an abnormality would want to change their subordinate status in any way. Hence, the sexologists frightened, or attempted to frighten, women away from feminism and from loving other women by demonstrating that both were abnormal and were generally linked together. (Faderman 1985, pp. 239–40)

This association between lesbianism and feminism continued to stalk second-wave feminism where it was most effective in splitting the ranks. Even though many of the women at the forefront of second-wave feminism were lesbians, lesbian women had to fight to overcome considerable resistance within a feminist movement afraid that association with lesbianism would prevent its own growth and acceptance.[9] Betty Friedan's infamous 1969 reference to lesbians as the 'lavender menace' offended many, and the National Organization of Women (NOW) lost many of its lesbian members in the late 1960s and 70s. Prominent among these deserters was Rita Mae Brown who co-founded, with five other women, a group based in New York known initially as the Lavender Menace, and later as Radicalesbians. The important document that the Radicalesbians would produce will be

---

9 A review of these antagonistic years from a lesbian perspective can be found in Abbot and Love (1972), Myron and Bunch (1975) and Echols (1989).

discussed shortly. In the meantime, it is important to note how the suggestion that 'those feminists are nothing but Lesbians' affected Black women. Described by Barbara Smith as possibly the 'most pernicious myth of all' (2000, p. xxxi), the association silenced Black lesbians in the newly emerging womanist movement. Fearful of being stigmatized not only as lesbians but simultaneously as 'a category totally alien from "decent" Black folks, i.e., not your sisters, mothers, daughters, aunts, and cousins, but bizarre outsiders like no one you know or *ever* knew' (Smith 2000, pp. xxxi–ii), Black women who loved other women feared to make their voices heard. Despite the fact that the second element of Alice Walker's much-quoted definition of womanism (Walker 1983, p. xi) specifically included women who love other women sexually, womanism developed in a context governed by a deliberate strategy of 'silence, secrecy, and a partially self-chosen invisibility [as] black women reformers promoted a public silence about sexuality which, it could be argued, continues to the present' (Hammonds 1994, p. 132).[10] To speak out in such a context was costly. Smith again:

> Black women . . . are not supposed to differ with each other. We may revel in our nonconformity vis-à-vis the world at large and any fool looking at us could tell how unique each of us is. But . . . a tacit assumption exists that we must be fundamentally alike and, at all costs, we must not disagree. (2000, p. xl)

Some Black women did find the courage to speak out. A collective of Black feminists who had been meeting together since 1974 published 'The Combahee River Collective Statement' in 1977. Their specific experiences of racism in addition to sexism and heterosexism meant that they accepted labels of feminist and lesbian but wished to maintain their solidarity with progressive Black men. They thus did 'not advocate the fractionalization that white women who are separatists demand' (Combahee River Collective 2000, p. 267) and spoke of the 'misguided notion that it is their [Black men's] maleness, per se – i.e., their biological maleness – that makes them

---

10 Renée Hill concurs and argues strongly for the inclusion of a lesbian perspective so crucial for a rounded womanist theology. 'The acts of black women in relationship, women-loving, between and among black women, are critical in the formation of any understanding of womanist spirituality . . . In positive nurturing relationships between black women, womanists can find models for mutuality, self-determination and self-love, all of which are important elements in liberation thought and praxis for black women, and for the black community in general' (1997, p. 149).

what they are' (2000, p. 269). Objecting to any kind of biological determinism, their statement explains how the stability provided for Black women by their economic and sexual arrangements cannot be blithely ignored when the 'psychological toll of being a Black woman' is taken into account (2000, p. 269). Their struggle against the racism of society in general, and within the feminist movement in particular, thus led to different emphases than those being made by Radicalesbians who, in 1970, had issued the document entitled 'The Woman-Identified-Woman' and disseminated it to those who had congregated at NOW's Second Congress to Unite Women (which had omitted lesbian women and their concerns from the conference's agenda). 'The Woman-Identified-Woman' paper famously identified the lesbian as 'the rage of *all women* condensed to the point of explosion' (emphasis added); and this political, rather than sexual, formulation emphasized the ways in which lesbianism can be an act of *political choice* rather than an innate orientation. The document did not ignore the sexuality of lesbian relationships (the authors refer to 'the primal commitment which includes sexual love'), but it prioritized the concept of woman-identification as a social-political choice through which all women can rid themselves of male-defined concepts of what it means to be 'a woman'. According to their manifesto women-identified women 'must be available and supportive to one another, give our commitment and our love, give the emotional support necessary to sustain this movement. Our energies must flow toward our sisters not backwards towards our oppressors' (Radicalesbians, 1997, p. 399). This document did not, however, take into account the ways in which Black women might be severely compromised by its calls for absolute female solidarity and their denouncements of women as 'collaborators' with heterosexual society would certainly have been an obstacle for Black women who stood in a position of critical loyalty with Black men. Black women in Britain would have found themselves in a similar bind when the Leeds Revolutionary Feminist Group published their paper 'Political Lesbianism: the case against heterosexuality' in 1979. It stated that all women who were opposed to patriarchy should opt for political lesbianism. Such women did not have to have sexual relations with other women to class themselves as lesbians, but it was expected that they would refrain from sexual relations with men.

However, the salient issue that is of most significance for this publication is the way these papers were broadening the definition of 'lesbian' to include women who did not share any notion of 'always being a lesbian'. Although this did not necessarily negate the concept of the innate lesbian, it shifted the ground from the rigidity of essentialism. To *choose* to identify as lesbian was to recognize how heterosexuality holds women in line and imposes a false consciousness, to shed inherited constructions of what it is to 'be a woman' and to commit oneself to relationships of solidarity and primacy with other women, refusing the stigma that keeps women from forming primary attachments with each other. This emphasis upon solidarity was particularly valuable given the stigmatism with which lesbianism had been associated. Rather than a smear on the women's movement, lesbianism was upheld and extolled as the way forward. The slogan 'Feminism is the theory, lesbianism is the practice' typified this move.

It was in this context that Adrienne Rich's groundbreaking article 'Compulsory Heterosexuality and Lesbian Existence' was published as a pamphlet in 1979. Her notion of a lesbian continuum would enhance the link that had been made between feminism and lesbianism still further. Her paper has been so influential that it merits some lengthy citations. In Rich's words, the lesbian continuum represents

> a range – through each woman's life and throughout history – of woman-identified experience, not simply the fact that a woman has had or consciously desired genital sexual experience with another woman. If we expand it to embrace many more forms of primary intensity between and among women, including the sharing of a rich inner life, the bonding against male tyranny, the giving and receiving of practical and political support, if we can hear in it such associations as *marriage resistance* and the 'haggard' behavior identified by Mary Daly . . . we begin to grasp breadths of female history and psychology which have lain out of reach as a consequence of limited, mostly clinical, definitions of *lesbianism*. (1987, pp. 51–2)

Women, said Rich, will move in and out of the lesbian continuum throughout their lives. It does not matter whether a woman does or has in the past, identified as a lesbian; it does not matter whether she 'does it' or 'did it'; this continuum embraces all women who have shared moments of 'primary intensity' with each other. Thus:

> We can . . . connect aspects of woman-identification as diverse as the impudent, intimate, girl friendships of eight or nine year olds and the banding together of those women of the twelfth and fifteenth centuries known as Beguines . . . It allows us to connect these women with the

more celebrated 'Lesbians' of the women's school around Sappho of the seventh century B.C., with the secret sororities and economic networks reported among African women, and with the Chinese marriage-resistance sisterhoods ... to connect and compare disparate individual instances of marriage resistance: for example, the strategies available to Emily Dickinson ... with the strategies available to Zora Neale Hurston. (1987, p. 55)

The reference to the specific networks deserves greater notice than it has been given. As we shall see below, one of the criticisms of the political lesbian movement in Britain and the United States was that it was largely a white, European, middle-class affair. Yet Rich did draw attention to the wide range of women's history that could be embraced by her notion of the continuum and she was inclusive of diverse contexts in her work. Moreover, her idea of the continuum could be applied to further diverse contexts. Taking just one example, it may well be that the female slave network described by Deborah Gray White could be seen in terms of the continuum. Although jealousies and competition for male attention could and did split female solidarity, White describes how women 'often worked in exclusively or predominantly female gangs. Thus women were put in one another's company for most of the day ... [and] their sense of womanhood was probably enhanced, their bonds to one another made stronger' (1987, p. 121). White reports how women chose to spend time with each other in non-working hours, lived in close quarters and socialized in ways that 'generated female cooperation and interdependence' and in ways that rendered slave owners unable to penetrate their private world (1987, p. 124). Barbara Omolade similarly speaks of the Black female self-reliance that ensued from oppression and more frankly of the fact that Black women 'often lived with women as both emotional and sexual companions' (1984, p. 372). It would be interesting to explore further how far the female slave network with its 'emotional sustenance' of women could be seen in terms of the lesbian continuum.

However, what needs to be noted in this section is how the question 'who is a lesbian' developed a much broader answer. The papers discussed above offer a strategic definition of 'lesbian' which can encompass a variety of women's primary relationships with one another. One of the obvious benefits of understanding lesbian in this way is that it enlarges the numbers of 'lesbian' subjects and issues thereby broadening what may count as falling under the 'lesbian' scope. More significantly, the reader does not have to be biologically wired to undertake a lesbian perspective, but can be adopting a strategic position of choice. The only caveat that Rich insisted upon was that women must examine their complicity with heterosexual privilege. Rich wanted to initiate within feminists a recognition that heterosexuality offers a position of privilege and potentially a site of complicity that must be questioned. She wanted 'feminists to find it less possible to read, write, or teach from a perspective of unexamined heterocentricity' (1987, p. 24).

Working with this definition, a lesbian reading a biblical text would theoretically be a reading position open to all women who are willing to engage critically with their own experiences of heterosexuality and the ways in which biblical texts operate in ways that uphold and maintain heteronormativity.[11] It would be geared towards highlighting instances where women's primary bonds with other women are found, exposing the forces that drive wedges between those bonds, and illuminating strategies of resistance. In terms of feminist, womanist and mujerista biblical criticism there is much work to be done in this regard, for while there are several publications on the status and role of women, much of the literature has investigated their lives in terms of their life-cycle as daughter, wife and mother. Even when the valorization of motherhood is being deconstructed, the founding heterosexual assumptions undergirding such images of women are rarely addressed. There has been very little consideration of anthropological, sociological and textual evidence that might indicate the presence of women who resisted their script due to their sexual preferences, women who preferred the company of and physical contact with, other women. The concept of the lesbian continuum would facilitate research that is not naively looking for 'lesbians in the Bible', but demonstrates the ways in which compulsory heterosexuality is maintained, and disrupts the scriptural picture that we have been given of a society consisting entirely of heterosexual women longing to bear (male) children for their husbands, as will be fully discussed in Chapter 3.

An example of how Rich's concept of the lesbian continuum has been used within biblical studies can be seen in Mary Rose D'Angelo's study of an Augustinian funerary relief featuring two women with their right hands clasped together. In the classical world, the handclasp is a gesture frequently read as an expression of marital fidelity, commitment and love. The fact that this relief had been re-cut in order to make one of the women appear male

---

11 Heteronormativity is helpfully defined by Corber and Valocchi as 'the set of norms that make heterosexuality seem natural or right and that organize homosexuality as its binary opposite' (2003, p. 4).

seems to indicate discomfort with the image of two women whose commitment to each other is cast in stone. This inspired D'Angelo 'to reflect on the relationships between women whose names are mentioned together in the New Testament and to ask whether they may not be relics of the silenced past of women's affective lives and relationships with each other' (1997, p. 444). She thus revisits the references to female partnerships in the Christian scriptures: Tryphaena and Tryphosa (Romans 16.12), Euodia and Syntyche (Philippians 4.2), Mary and Martha (John 11/Luke 10.38–42); and queries whether 'these partnerships reveal a commitment between women that, in the light of early Christian revision of sexual mores, can be seen as a sexual choice' (1997, p. 442). As D'Angelo acknowledges, any attempt to reclaim the figures on the relief and the female partnerships in the Bible as part of a lesbian ancestry is on shifting sand since one must beware of reading anachronistically; yet, the concept of the lesbian continuum offers D'Angelo a very useful heuristic tool for her research. While acknowledging that the funerary relief gives no evidence about the erotic life of the two women,

> What their handclasp announces is a commitment between women: not necessarily a commitment that is exclusive or primarily erotic in nature … This commitment may have involved a recreated familial relationship, a partnership in work, a religious commitment, or some combination of these.
>
> Such a commitment, however, might well be considered as belonging to the range of women-identification that Adrienne Rich describes as a lesbian continuum. (1997, pp. 443–4)

Similarly, the biblical texts only provide evidence that there were female partnerships and we will never know how or why these women organized their lives together.

Nevertheless, the case for a *possible* suppression of (or ignorance of) the nature of these women's partnerships is well-made. The enthusiastic speculation offered by Nancy Wilson is not present in D'Angelo's work. D'Angelo recognizes the need to make a case for any suggestion that relationships between Tryphaena and Tryphosa, Euodia and Syntyche, Mary and Martha could be considered 'lesbian' and knows it is highly unlikely that any evidence as to the nature of these women's friendships will be forthcoming. Even if it did, the understanding of women's relationships in the first century CE will not, by any means, be equivalent to our twenty-first-century understandings of lesbian relationships. Notwithstanding, the lesbian continuum provides a framework for cautious suggestions and gives her a useful means of breaking with heteronormative interpretation of biblical texts.

The lesbian continuum has also been used within theology. Mary Hunt's 'Feminist Theology of Friendship' speaks of lesbians as women who take their relationships with other women 'radically seriously', and of lesbian feminists as women who have chosen to define themselves not by their sexual object choices and practices, but by their commitments to women in radical 'female friendships'. Drawing on Rich's continuum, Hunt characterizes such friendships as 'mutual, community seeking, honest about sexuality, nonexclusive, flexible, and other-directed' (1994, p. 170). In her rehabilitation of the lesbian label, Hunt argues:

> it is important that *'lesbian'* not be forced to carry the symbolic freight of sexuality for all women. Instead, we can insist on our self-identity as friends in a culture which tells all of us to keep our distance from one another. Thus *lesbian* takes on a new meaning. It becomes paradigmatic of all types of friendships in a culture which provides precious few structures for women and men, men and men, women and women to relate to each other as friends without the corruption of such unions with partial, distorted notions of heterosexism. (1994, pp. 173–4)

It is true, the lesbian signifier can conjure anxiety because of its 'symbolic freight of sexuality'. The Lesbian History Group, established in 1984 by women who had belonged to the London Feminist History Group but were dissatisfied by the group's neglect of the lesbian aspect of women's lives, believed the anxiety surrounding the word lesbian derived from the 'belief that the term "lesbian" refers solely to a sexual practice, and not to a mode of life in which a woman's political, intellectual, emotional, social and sexual energies are focused in other women' (Lesbian History Group 1996, p. 6). They acknowledge the associated stigma:

> The word is perceived as an insult. It suggests abnormality: at worst a perversion, at best a pitiful handicap. There are even lesbians today who find it hard to speak directly of women in history as lesbians, so strong is the influence of the heterosexist culture we live in. (1996, p. 6)

Mary Hunt's opinion is that 'lesbian' is the only available word to signify the revolutionary force of women taking their friendships with other women radically seriously and a reorganization of the kind of relationships 'lesbian' embraces, enables women to reclaim and use a stigmatized word and reduce the anxiety. It helps to break down the homo–hetero binary, bringing the concept of lesbian into the realm meant to bespeak its 'other'. As will be discussed in Chapter 4, this is a useful strategy.

However, while Hunt is right that the lesbian label has historically divided women from each other, to redeem it by using it as an umbrella term for all women who take their female friendships radically seriously is problematic insofar as it deliberately marginalizes the one element that some might consider the most defining feature of lesbian existence: sexuality. Lesbian criticism outside biblical studies has long been challenging the dilution that the lesbian continuum brings in its wake.[12] This has particularly been seen in the reception of Lillian Faderman's work. In her acclaimed anthology of lesbian literature from the seventeenth century onwards, Faderman explores the passionate correspondence between women who shared what she terms 'romantic friendships'. She classes the literature in her anthology as 'lesbian' because these romantic friendships were 'not simply a "rehearsal" for heterosexuality but rather the most important relationship of their lives' (1995, p. 5). However, her chosen phrase 'romantic friendship' sweeps over the issue of erotic relationships quite purposefully. She is not unaware of the existence of women who wore male attire, used dildoes, actively pursued women and took women as wives, but such women may, in her view, simply have been engaging in general degenerate behaviour. Faderman contrasts this with the examples of correspondence that detail a passionate, 'pure', romantic friendship. This inevitably draws an unhelpful line between reprehensible women who engaged in sexual relations and gender nonconformity, and commendable women for whom sexual desire may have existed but was not acted upon. Moreover, it glosses over the evidence for the significant place of sexual desire and acts in those romantic relationships. Carroll Smith-Rosenberg's (1975) paper is often paired with Faderman's work, yet Smith-Rosenberg's research indicates quite clearly that the bonds between romantic friends in nineteenth-century America were often intense, physical and sensual. In a later radio programme she agreed that some of those women would have engaged in genital sex.[13]

---

12 Early responses can be found in Campbell (1980), Nestle (1981) and Ruehl (1983).

13 Smith-Rosenberg was interviewed in 1988 by Alison Laurie for the Lesbian Community Radio Programme, Wellington Access Radio. See Laurie's web article 'Female Friendships in Aotearoa/New Zealand – Close Friends or Lesbian Lovers?' that can be accessed via the Women's Worlds website at: http://www.skk.uit.no/WW99/proceedings/proceedings.html

There is also evidence for such intimacy between Black women. Karen V. Hansen's (1995) account of an erotic friendship between two African-American women in the mid-nineteenth century reveals how 'friendship' involved bed-sharing and physical appreciation of another woman's body. However, it is the diary records of Anne Lister (1791–1840) above all that reveal with truly astonishing frankness the physical activities that charged her 'romantic friendships' with Marianne (Mary) Lawton, Isabella Norcliffe, Anne Walker and the unfortunate Mrs Barlow. The letters that Anne wrote to Marianne certainly sound like the 'pure' letters of romantic friends that are discussed by Faderman. For example, Lister wrote to Marianne on 8 February 1821:

> I can live upon hope, forget that we grow older, & love you as warmly as ever. Yes, Mary, you cannot doubt the love of one who has waited for you so long & patiently. You can give me all of happiness I care for &, prest to the heart which I believe my own, caressed & treasured there, I will indeed be constant & never, from that moment, feel a wish or thought for any other than my wife. You shall have every smile & every breath of tenderness . . . (Whitbread 1992a, p. 145)

But the surrounding diary entries belie the 'purity' and platonic tone of this letter. For example, Anne regularly refers to giving and receiving 'kisses' (which Helena Whitbread believes to be her coded way of describing orgasm) and there are several references to her 'kissing' activity with Marianne.[14] Lister is hardly constant, despite her pledges to the contrary. The amorous Anne regularly shared 'kisses' with Isabella Norcliffe (Tib)[15] and on 5 December 1820 we find her in the bedroom of Anne Belcombe, who permits Anne to kiss her breasts, with Anne put off further exploration only by the fact that 'neither she nor her room seemed very sweet to my nose' (Whitbread 1992a, p. 139). In 1824 during a stay in France she encounters Mrs Barlow and undertakes a lengthy dalliance with her that includes French kissing, passionate embraces, fondling her breasts and grubbling – Anne's none too pleasant sounding term for handling/rubbing her partner's petticoat-covered vaginal area.[16]

Lister also ponders what kind of relationship was enjoyed by the

---

14 See the diary entries for 18 March 1819, 9 February 1820, 10 April 1820, 23 July 1821, 13 July 1822, 14 September 1823, 20 and 22 July 1824 in Whitbread (1992a).

15 See the diary entries for 26 October 1821, 25 November 1822 and 14 December 1822 in Whitbread (1992a).

16 See for example the entries for 11 and 15 November 1824 in Whitbread (1992b).

celebrated Ladies of Llangollen (Lady Eleanor Butler and Sarah Ponsonby), who caused a scandal by eloping to Plas Newydd, Wales in 1790 and subsequently lived together for over 50 years. During her tour of North Wales, on 23 July 1822, Lister managed to call upon the two women. Her verdict after her visit is that

> I cannot help thinking surely it [the Ladies' relationship] was not platonic. Heaven forgive me, but I look within myself & doubt. I feel the infirmity of our nature and hesitate to pronounce such attachments uncemented by something more tender still than friendship. (Whitbread 1992a, p. 210)

Whatever the actual state of affairs may have been between these women, Lister's own passionate relationships and her suspicions indicate that Faderman's distinction between pure 'romantic friendships' and sexually charged relations cannot so easily be upheld. To some extent, it depends what we mean by 'sexual'. If only penetration counted as 'having sex' then women might have engaged in what would today be classed as 'lesbian sex' without it being deemed as such, and without any sense of untoward immorality. Lister is aware that the 'scrapes' into which she gets herself may have a negative impact upon her reputation if any affair were to be revealed in the papers. She is also very careful to veil her own knowledge of women's sexual relationships with each other and to feign ignorance even when in the full flight of dalliance with one of her friends.[17] Nevertheless, her diaries reveal no guilty conscience for her physically intimate relations with Tib, Marianne and Mrs Barlow. She continues to describe her regular church attendance without any suggestion that her conduct unbecomes the Christian woman or any feelings that she might be unworthy to take the sacrament. The only occasions where pangs of conscience are recorded occur after Marianne marries Charles Lawton. This complicates the relationship between Anne and Marianne, with Anne (despite encouraging the union) claiming that Marianne has prostituted herself for the security of 'carriage and jointure'. She bemoans and regrets her part in the engagement in typical overwrought style: 'I have acted very foolishly & wickedly. Oh that I may repent & turn me from my sin. Lord, forgive & help me' (1992a, p. 57). After the marriage, Anne continues to share 'kisses' with Marianne but now speaks of the 'criminality' of their relationship. This criminality lies not in female homoeroticism, but in the fact that Anne now lies with another man's wife. Clearly it is adultery that is the sin, not the same sex

---

17 See the entries for 20 and 25 October 1824 in Whitbread (1992b), for example.

relationship per se. Moreover, in Lister's view, any unnaturalness on her part would be manifest only if she married a man. Her love for women is entirely consistent with her 'nature' and masculine identity.

The diaries make it clear that women's relationships could be physical and while not wanting to insist that the lesbian signifier must *always* indicate women who engage in sexual relations with women, Catherine Stimpson is right to state that we must maintain some aspect of erotic drive in a definition of lesbian, for 'carnality distinguishes it from gestures of political sympathy for homosexuals and from affectionate friendships in which women enjoy each other, support each other, and commingle their sense of identity and well-being' (1981, p. 364). After all, why should qualities such as 'strength, independence and resistance' be seen as innately lesbian? To be sure, the continuum 'has the virtue of . . . suggesting interconnections among the various ways in which women bond together', yet it also threatens to eliminate anything distinguishably meaningful for the word 'lesbian' (Zimmerman 1985, p. 184). I am acutely aware that insisting upon a strong carnal element may have its pitfalls, not least since foregrounding sexuality may be uncomfortable for some Black lesbians given the historical association white slave owners and colonialists constructed between Black women and excessive sexual appetites.[18] An approach that pushes sex to the fore could easily reify that association. This is particularly the case when the middle-class, sex-free 'pure' romantic friendships of the eighteenth and nineteenth centuries can so easily be offset against Black sexualized working-class lesbians. Black women have to contend with the fact that the air of purity that attaches itself to white middle-class families has historically been at the expense of stigmatizing African-American families and relationships as being deviant. As Patricia Hill Collins says, 'Black "whores" make white "virgins" possible' (2002, p. 203). On the other hand, reaction against the caricatures of the 'Jezebel' and 'brood whore' has led to Black lesbians being condemned (at worst) or silenced (at best) in an overcompensating strategy.[19] In response, Black lesbian writers have not shied away from writing about the significance of their sexual relationships and the

---

18 On the caricature of Black sexual excesses as represented by European colonizers see Fanon (1967). For an account of how the stereotyped images of the Jezebel and the Mammy shaped white perspectives of Black women, see chapter 1 of White (1987). On the way this has contributed to homophobic attitudes within the Black churches, see Douglas (1999, pp. 31–59).

19 On the ways in which Black women have responded to their stereotyped images in ways that have intentionally silenced discussion of Black women's sexuality, see Simson (1984), Hine (1989), Giddings (1992), Higginbotham (1992), Carby (1992) and Brown (1992).

empowering nature of those sexual practices. Indeed, Evelynn Hammonds argues that the work of Black lesbians is vital if Black women's sexuality is to come out of its partially self-imposed closet. For example, Audre Lorde's insistence on declaring her sexual choices and writing on the empowering nature of the erotic

> suggests that black lesbian sexualities can be read as one expression of the reclamation of the despised black female body. Therefore, the works of Lorde and other black lesbian writers, because they foreground the very aspects of black female sexuality which are submerged – that is, female desire and agency – are critical to our theorizing of black female sexualities. (Hammonds 1994, p. 137)

I therefore maintain the importance of foregrounding a strong carnal element in any definition of 'lesbian' and do so for at least three major reasons. First, concepts of political lesbianism are in danger of glossing over the oppression, stigma and persecution faced by women who *do* make an erotic choice and are prepared to make this publicly visible. Sheila Jeffreys summarizes this well:

> Lesbianism cannot be subsumed beneath the good feelings of hand-holding sisterhood . . . I don't accept Adrienne Rich's idea of the lesbian continuum whereby all women's friendships with women are some shade or graduation of lesbianism. Women who simply have 'best friends' who are women share neither lesbian oppression nor lesbian experience. So long as we keep the definition of lesbianism open enough to include heterosexual women who love their women friends, it will be hard to articulate what is specific about the experience and oppression of lesbians and to develop the strength to fight compulsory heterosexuality and the invisibility of lesbians. (1984, p. 26)

Joan Nestle also criticizes the idea that the continuum that would pull feminists and lesbians together in a common cause with shared interests for it overlooks the specificity of her lesbian experience:

> If we [lesbians and straight feminists] are to be comrades in the days of battle ahead, it is essential that we clear the air between us . . . I think the phrase, *every woman is a potential Lesbian*, is no longer useful. It trivializes my own history and the history of a community I was part of just as

it trivializes the history of individual straight women. It once served a rhetorical purpose of carrying the discussion of Lesbian-feminism into more respectable places, but all my fifties knowledge tells me that my sexual journey was not a rhetorical device . . .

We must stand together, realizing the complexity of our histories, both personal and social, choosing when we can tolerate each other's company and when we cannot. We must never pretend to be experts on each other's lives, never belittle the deep differences that do exist or pretend that we do not see the places of exposed pain. (1987, pp. 114–15)[20]

Rich conceded in an afterword that one of the problems with her concept of the lesbian continuum was indeed that it could be used by women 'as a safe way to describe their felt connections with women, without having to share in the risks and threats of lesbian existence' (1987, p. 74). Chapter 2 considers further the nature of the oppression faced by lesbian women on account of their sexual choices and it will become clear that the signifier must make a bold reference to women whose sexual attraction to other women is physically manifested in order to avoid rendering them, and their particular experiences of oppression, invisible.

Second, preserving and visibly upholding the sexual dimension of the lesbian signifier is important politically. In my view, contemporary society will have less difficulty allowing the word 'lesbian' to signify women's serious friendships with one another since it is their mutual, exclusive, no-need-of-men *sexual* choice that upsets utterly the alignment between sex, gender and sexuality and remains taboo. Contrarily, Jeffreys argues that the sexual activity of lesbians is not the threat: 'if it were, then it would not be the stock in trade of brothels and men's pornography' (1984, p. 27). Perhaps it is the case that the idea of lesbian sex has turned more men on than off, but on the other hand, the resolute determination to keep penalties for lesbian genital activities off the statute books in England testifies to a real anxiety surrounding the issue. Annabel Faraday's review of proposals to legislate against lesbians reveals how such attempts were resisted for fear of advertising the thinkability of *sexual* relations between women. Concluding that these 'acts of official silencing demonstrate the extent to which lesbian existence threatened patriarchal dictates embodied in the law' (1988, p. 16), her article touches on the reason why lesbian sex *is* a threatening taboo.

---

20 For further criticisms along these lines, see also Ferguson, Zita and Addelson (1981), Wendy Clark (1987).

Women who choose to give their erotic passion to other women are removing themselves from their availability to men, from the institution of wifery and, to some extent, from the institution of motherhood.[21] Jeffrey's opinion is not surprising given that her examples derive from the world of pornography where feminine women perform with women directly for the pleasure of male voyeurs. Naturally, this is not threatening because it is devoid of any accompanying feminist politics. Within male discourse, the intolerable, much satirized lesbian is always the 'mannish' lesbian who takes for herself the prerogatives and privileges that are normally assigned to men, including taking an active sexual role without any deference to gender and sex norms. This is hardly the kind of woman usually pictured within the pornography largely consumed by male heterosexuals. If, as Chris Weedon (1999, p. 59) argues, a *significant* number of women were to 'refuse to serve men's needs', any apparent indifference to lesbianism would soon be shaken off. Therefore the lesbian signifier should not be diluted of its sexual features but enriched by its power to fright, to provoke anxiety, to disturb and unsettle. It is the sexual dimension of the word, *combined with* the radical commitment to women and the threat that *many* women will choose lesbianism, which gives it that power. Hence, we cannot afford a marginal-ization or silencing of sex and we should not be too quick to soften the most taboo aspect of the signifier by brushing its sexual dimension under the (friendship) carpet. 'Sexuality' says Joan Nestle

> is not a limiting force but a whole world in itself that feeds the fires of all our other accomplishments. Many of us are just beginning to understand the possibilities of erotic choice and self-creation. It is this open declara-tion of our sexual selves that moralists and governments have tried to silence. They know that a Lesbian celebrating her desire is a symbol of the possibility of social change for all women. (1987, p. 108)

Third, the definition of lesbian needs to feature sexual expression if there is to be any real breakthrough from the oppression of lesbians within religious settings. The next chapter will demonstrate how Jewish and Christian posi-tional statements routinely distinguish between the 'sinner' and the 'sin'. While the former can be treated compassionately, and maintain a place within her religious community, this is usually only on the basis that she

---

21 For the larger part of the twentieth century any woman following a 'lesbian path' would have probably thought she was surrendering, willingly or unwillingly, the opportunity to become or remain a mother. This is no longer the case given the rise of artificial insemination and the reform of adoption law.

remains celibate. Such a position is strongly refuted by lesbian, bisexual and gay-identified Jews and Christians.

The above discussion does not mean that I insist the lesbian signifier must *always* indicate sexual activity between women, for this would be too limiting. One can have strong erotic feelings for women and yet choose to be celibate throughout life. Rather, it is intended to make it very clear that we should not be distracted from adopting a definition that features a bold reference to the carnal dimension of lesbian relationships. Mary Hunt's (1994, p. 172) claim that women's sexual object choice and practices are no one else's business is, to some extent, right and the freedom *not* to discuss one's sex life publicly should be upheld. But, to revive an old slogan, while sexual practice is one of the major obstacles to being accepted within one's religious community, the private remains the political. Lesbians will not receive social justice until they are free to be themselves, and that has to include the freedom to be sexual should they so wish.

Apart from the issue of sexuality, there remains one other major problem with using the lesbian continuum as a primary tool of engagement. This lies in its unreserved commitment to the category of woman. Both second-wave feminism and the lesbian feminist movements of the 1970s onwards achieved much by making one's female identity the rallying point for action and the focus of community ethos. However, the rapid gains made by second-wave feminism came at a cost. In hindsight, the totalitarian tendency to bring all women within its net and speak in one voice inevitably glossed over or forcibly repressed the diverse voices and experiences of the women it claimed to represent.[22] Moreover, the tendency to valorize women was problematic. For all that the Radicalesbian Manifesto encouraged its readers to break out of the imposed notions of what a woman is and find their authentic selves, the rallying point was precisely one's identity as women. Similarly, it was the potential of shared 'womanness', the sense of 'being-in-it-together' that informed and sustained the notion of the lesbian continuum. However, a contemporary of Adrienne Rich introduced an approach that contains foreshadows of what was to come in the postmodern climate.

---

22 In the 1980s there were strong reactions from those who criticized the ways in which feminism had not accounted for racial, class and sexual differences among women. See the statement of the Combahee River Collective (2000 [originally published in 1979]), hooks (1981), Hull, Scott and Smith (1982), Smith (2000), Moraga and Anzaldúa (1981) and Lorde (1984) for contributions from women of colour. See Balka and Rose (1989) for an anthology that considers the implications of class, colour, sexual orientation in the context of being Jewish.

In 1978 the materialist feminist Monique Wittig presented her paper 'The Straight Mind' to the Modern Languages Association's annual conference. Her paper argued that there is 'no such thing as being-woman or being-man' (1992, p. 29) and that the categories of 'man' and 'woman' are not ontological givens but products of the straight mind. Of course, feminists before Wittig knew that one was scripted and socially moulded to become a woman, but for Wittig, this renders the category itself irredeemable. Wittig therefore resists all attempts to reclaim and extol the virtues of being a woman because the 'woman is wonderful' concept merely takes what the oppressor has given and valorizes it without fighting the category itself which, for Wittig, has no essential biological core. The way of escape from this apparent impasse for 'women' is provided by the critical insights and activism of lesbians, who, because they refuse to submit to the heterosexual relations that require 'men' and 'women', stand outside of those constructions and provide the practical 'living proof' that there is no natural state of womanhood:

> Lesbianism is the only concept I know of which is beyond the categories of sex (woman and man), because the designated subject (lesbian) is *not* a woman, either economically, or politically, or ideologically. For what makes a woman is a specific social relation to a man, a relation that we have previously called servitude, a relation which implies personal and physical obligation as well as economic obligation . . . a relation which lesbians escape by refusing to become or to stay heterosexual. (1992, p. 20)

Lesbians, she argued, will never have to face the question 'what is a woman' because 'it would be incorrect to say that lesbians associate, make love, live with women, for "woman" has meaning only in heterosexual systems of thought and heterosexual economic systems. Lesbians are not women' (1992, p. 32).

For Wittig, this escape route is open to all people who can choose lesbianism. As with Rich's continuum, one does not have to be biologically wired to 'be' a lesbian; the word now signifies a space that can be occupied by those who have taken themselves out of the heterosexual sex-gender system. But Wittig's work is more radical than that of Rich. Rich's call to explore critically the ways in which women's primary bonds with other women are broken may help break the grip of compulsory heterosexuality, but the continuum itself, with its emphasis upon female solidarity does not sufficiently challenge the actual sex binary of male–female. For Wittig the critical struggle is about undoing the male–female categories altogether. Thus, for any work to carry the lesbian label, it must disrupt and transcend sex and gender categories. Future critics such as Barbara Hammer (1994), Teresa de Lauretis (1994) and Lynn Pearce (1996) would thus explain why cultural products produced by lesbians, scripted by lesbians and with overt lesbian content are not radical or innovative enough to be hailed as 'lesbian' unless the actresses, their activities, their roles break with hetero-normativity. Lynn Pearce thus claims that Alice Walker's *The Color Purple* puts so 'very little pressure ... on the text's primary heterosexual economy [that] the fact that this is a novel which "features" a lesbian relationship does not mean that it is, in the last analysis, a very lesbian text' (1996, p. 245). Lesbian cultural productions must break the script, the social contract, the heterosexual imperative in ways that render the product impossible to assimilate.

Wittig's approach was bold and innovative. The 1978 audience's stunned silence to her claim that lesbians are not women indicated, says Louise Turcotte (in her foreword to the 1992 collection of Wittig's essays), the radicality of Wittig's vision of that time; a vision carried through in her essay 'The Category of Sex', where she makes it clear that the fight is to make the apparent 'givenness' of the sexes visible as a social construct:

> we must destroy the sexes as a sociological reality if we want to start to exist. The category of sex is the category that ordains slavery for women, and it works, specifically, as it did for black slaves, through an operation of reduction, by taking the part for the whole (color, sex) through which the whole human group has to pass as through a screen ... The 'declaration' of 'color' is now considered discriminatory. But that does not hold true for the 'declaration' of 'sex' which not even women dream of abolishing ... I say: it is about time to do so. (1992, p. 8)

However, Wittig has her critics. Some have argued that her notion of the lesbian is prone to the same problems as the notion of 'woman's experience' which usually meant white, American and European, middle-class, often heterosexual experience and that, for all her exposure of the *constructed* nature of sex and gender identities, she is, paradoxically, prone to essentialism. Pam Morris, for example, states: 'By claiming "lesbians are not women", she seems to construct an acultural, totalising, even mythic, lesbian identity which cannot account for the real differences of race, class, politics and so on existing among actual lesbians' (1993, pp. 172–3). Morris knows that the construction of a positive identity is vital for political group consciousness and activism, but in her view Wittig's construction of the lesbian pays insufficient attention to the vast cultural, economic, national and individual differences of women who claim, or are positioned, within this category. This inability of the word 'lesbian' to bear the full weight of everyone's experiences is strongly echoed in postmodern discourse, as discussed further below.

Marilyn Farwell neatly suggests that Wittig's position seems to be that of an 'anti-essentialist postmodernist with essentialist moments' (1996, p. 96). Her 'essentialist moments' lie in her commitment to the lesbian subject that she has moved to centre stage in order to deconstruct 'man' and 'woman' differentiation. However, as Farwell goes on to say, this is not necessarily a flaw in her position if one sees this as a *strategic* essentialism, a place to stand in order to undertake the deconstruction.

> Rather than resolving the binary essentialism/nonessentialism, I would prefer to let the two positions remain problematically intertwined, leaving essentialism as inescapable in our thinking as nonessentialism and thus leaving gender an issue with which we must contend. Wittig becomes a primary example of a postmodern thinker who cannot escape categories nor, it seems, does she try. (1996, p. 97)

Farwell also remains unhappy with moves that would break down the fragile solidarity that feminism has thus far won. Having argued that to be a lesbian is to have a *positional*, not an ontological status, she points out that such a position is one of *sameness* to, not difference from, other women. However, we anticipate here the developments of the 'third critical moment' and the postmodern discourse of recent decades concerning sex, gender and sexuality as seen most prominently in the work of queer theorists.

The Disappearing Lesbian Subject: Destabilizing Lesbian Identities in Queer Studies

As we move into the third critical moment we bring with us two major problems. First, although the gay liberation movements made it relatively easier to 'be' a lesbian, and to live out one's ascribed identity, that identity label inevitably excluded some women as boundaries were drawn and redrawn. Contests over who counts as a lesbian were never successfully resolved. Second, and perhaps more significantly, the labelling of identities as homosexual or heterosexual came to be seen as further examples of master's tools that will never destroy the master's house.[23] Homosexuality does not signify an autonomous domain completely outside of heterosexuality. Rather, what appears to be an 'outside' domain is really 'inside' a heterosexual economy that requires the marking of what-it-is-not in order to exist. Thus heterosexuality that is unmarked, normalized and idealized relies upon homosexuality that is marked as abnormal and/or deviant, to entrench itself. As Diana Fuss puts it:

> The homo in relation to the hetero, much like the feminine in relation to the masculine, operates as an indispensable interior exclusion – an outside which is inside territory, making the articulation of the latter possible, a transgression of the border which is necessary to constitute the border as such. (1991, p. 3)

The creation of an apparently 'outside' territory had its uses and although rupturing the homo–hetero binary was one of the aims of lesbian and gay activism, such vision was rather quickly dispelled in favour of adopting an ethnic minority model of group identity. 'Lesbian' and 'gay' communities solidified around those very labels as they adopted this ethnic minority model as a basis for human rights lobbying, thereby reifying the idea of a collective identity into which one can 'come out' and live authentically. This reclaimed 'outside' territory provided a useful place in which sexual outlaws could congregate, form subcultures, and use as a vantage point from which to evaluate and criticize heteronormativity. Since then, the sense of a collective identity has been strengthened through the bonding that ensues from political activism, and reverse discourse (gay is good), and nurtured through the emergence of lesbian and/or gay magazines, newspapers and websites, dedicated venues for meeting, various societies, community-specific insurance and legal services, therapists, holidays, bookstores. This has been empowering, good for self-esteem and politically effective. It also facilitated the emergence of lesbian and gay studies that formulated its own critical theories of analysis, that articulated lesbian and gay perspectives on a diverse range of issues, that began locating and writing its own histories.

---

23 Audre Lorde astutely observed that 'the master's tools will never dismantle the master's house' at the Second Sex conference in 1979. For the context of this statement, see Lorde (1981).

As such, the territory of the 'outside' did not seem such a bad place to be since it provided a seemingly free space to develop serious challenges to the heterosexual matrix.[24]

However, as a product of the binary thinking that created the homo–hetero divide, 'outside' will always be a permitted, accommodated space that necessarily permits a certain amount of discontent and challenge to the regulatory discourse of the heterosexual matrix. In order to maintain itself as a place of normalized privilege, heteronormativity needs the existence of a space containing *marginalized* and *stigmatized* persons. Early lesbian and gay studies, for the most part, recognized this and did not reify those categories uncritically but contested the content and meaning of the received 'lesbian' and 'homosexual' signifiers. Thus an early advocate of breaking the binary code was Dennis Altman who spoke of a future where there would be no homosexual or heterosexual categories which would mean we would no longer have to 'choose between an exclusively straight or exclusively gay world' (1971, p. 107). The categories of homosexual and heterosexual were being seen for what they are – limiting, narrow, tied into an imposed polarity. Jonathan Katz thus argued for a move beyond an easy reverse discourse since 'our words, concepts, responses, and lives are determined by our adversaries' (1983, p. 171). With foresight, he argued that we should 'consider what it would mean to transcend a sexual world-view which posits them and us – thinking our way beyond distinctions based on the biological sex of our erotic or affectional partners' (1983, p. 172). Such a move was for Katz in 1983 a 'dream', a 'utopian vision', but the early shifts made towards attaining that vision, that have been subsequently taken up in queer activism, have been effective. Sasha Roseneil notes, for instance, that we now live in a western world of heteroreflexivity rather than heteronormativity, where personal ads need to stipulate whether the advertiser is a 'heterosexual' male or female; where women's magazines occasionally encourage readers to be more imaginative than binary thinking has conventionally permitted; where straight-identified students in universities take an interest in lesbian and gay study courses; where television dramas and

---

24 The heterosexual matrix is Judith Butler's phrase for 'that grid of cultural intelligibility through which bodies, gender, and desires are naturalized' (Butler 1990, p. 151, n. 5). Within the heterosexual matrix the sexes are 'natural' states of being on to which we attach gender norms. Intelligible identities are those that adhere to these alignments and the boundary of the matrix is policed stringently in order to offset the anxiety that its borders might become contaminated. The 'outside' territory is created for those unintelligible persons who do not cohere with its alignments.

sitcoms are no longer always based on heterosexual families. In her view, 'heterosexuality is increasingly a conscious state which has to be produced, self-monitored, thought about, and, for some, defended, in relation to its other, in a way that was not necessary when heteronormativity was more secure' (2002, p. 35). She goes on to venture that, in Britain particularly, there is a tangible 'queering of popular culture, a valorizing of the sexually ambiguous, of that which transgresses rigid boundaries of gender' (2002, p. 36), and she demonstrates this by reference to dance culture, fashion magazines and television programming. For the young contemporary generation 'queer' has become trendy, aspirational and cool.

However, as indicated, while several lesbian and gay theorists were already moving in this direction (as had feminists), it has probably been the work of the 1990s queer activists and theorists who have taken up the disruption of binary codes with renewed fervour. In one of the early publications to articulate the new directions that queer theory would take up, Jennifer Terry demonstrates how researchers can break away from the problematic reification of categories. She advocates an approach that is situated within the dominant discourse, examining the ways in which it constructs its hegemonic account, how it operates, what it produces and how it establishes itself as 'truthful'. In reality, says Terry, we can do no other, for there is no fully 'outside' alternative discourse to draw upon; we cannot disentangle a free, coherent and autonomous lesbian or gay account outside the influences of the dominant discourse:

> a lesbian and gay history which hopes to find homosexuals totally free of the influences of pathologizing discourses would be an historio-graphic optical illusion. At best, we can map the techniques by which homosexuality has been marked as different and pathological, and then locate subversive resistances to this homophobia. (1991, p. 58)

So, rather than looking inward at our own experiences and stories and enunciating them, trying to do history in a way that concentrates on the people and events that the dominant history has repressed, the way to upset heteronormativity and break with the binary is via 'effective history' which 'exposes not the events and actors elided by traditional history, but instead lays bare the *processes* and *operations* by which these elisions occurred' (Terry 1991, p. 56 emphasis original). This will destabilize the hegemonic account by exposing the constructed, ideological nature of those very features that stabilize it. Applying such a method to scriptural hermeneutics would mean that a lesbian approach would not be looking for lesbians in the Bible in the sense of 'there's one' and 'there's another'. Rather, adoption of Terry's strategy would mean examining the processes and operations by which a textual heteronormative ideal is maintained and deviance constructed. It would explore the construction of boundaries, noting how these are policed, and looking for the shrapnel evidence of resistance.[25] The researcher would not have to 'be' lesbian or gay in any ontological sense, but able to adopt strategic positional stances. Terry, for example, sees herself as a mobile archivist, never situated as a neutral observer but always in the thick of things, able to occupy the different subject positions created by discourse and counter-discourse. These subject positions are places from which one can see 'not only how subjects are produced and policed, but how they are resistant and excessive to the very discourses from which they emerge' (1991, p. 57). This is not to deny the importance of the reverse discourse of the late twentieth century that has provided resistance to the dominant account. The difference is that this reverse discourse and its effects is not viewed as an authentic, pure, lesbian or gay perspective, but as the discourse of a deviant subject position inevitably coloured by the discourse that positions them as deviants in the first place.[26] Those who occupy deviant subject positions simultaneously occupy 'inside' and 'outside' positions:

> Subjects in deviant positions are required, as a matter of survival, to have the ability to see and know the rules of the center as well as those of the margins ... Deviant subjects are engaged in a *process* of living in a system of epistemic relay between authoritative knowledge and 'experience,' and between past and present. (Terry 1991, p. 70)

Deviant subjects, she says, thus have valuable experience of operating 'in relation to pathological representation on the one hand, and the social subjects called "lesbians" and "gay men" on the other ... watch[ing] from multiple and changing vantage points' (1991, pp. 70–1).

---

25 Terry likens 'effects' to pieces of shrapnel that scatter the site of a discursive battle. 'They are not to be forged into a new functioning story but remain as evidence of the violence of dominant discourses. They are traces of the unremitting and carefully crafted terms of hegemonic accounts that structure conditions of marginality for certain subjects who are marked as Others. Effects are deviant fragments which fall outside these accounts' (1991, p. 57).

26 The very terminology of 'subjects' is a decisive move away from the concept of 'selves'. The modernist concept of the essential self with a core identity as a natural given is abandoned in the postmodernist recognition that the self is a constructed idea; a provisional and shifting product shaped by discourse and behaviour.

Clearly the mobile archivist herself does not have to identify as lesbian. Indeed, unless it was made clear that the researcher was using the signifier as a heuristic tool, acknowledging the provisional and contextual nature of this label, it would probably be seen as a backward step. This is, therefore, a research strategy that is open to all who would critically engage with the structures and effects of dominant discourse.

As queer theory has evolved in the 1990s, this kind of approach has been developed further. As most introductions to queer theory indicate, queer necessarily resists any formal definition for, to remain 'queer', it ostensibly needs its roving brief, its flexibility to shape-shift in response to changing hegemonic discourses. Notwithstanding, queer theory consistently exhibits the characteristics of Terry's approach, squatting in the midst of hegemonic discourse in order to expose how normativity and truth claims are constructed and upheld and the existence of critical introductions to queer theory belie claims that it is an indefinable approach (see McKee, 1999). The application of such theory within biblical studies does herald new insights. Ken Stone's *Queer Commentary* contains a range of contributions demonstrating the various ways this might work. Characteristic features of these queer readings include attention to binary oppositions such as male/female, homo/hetero, dominance/submission, pleasure/pain. Two examples will illustrate the interesting effects such queer readings produce.

Lori Rowlett's contribution on the Samson and Delilah narrative launches straight into the themes typical of queer discourse – the breaking of normative gender roles, attention to active and passive sex roles, fetishism and the politics of bondage. She sees Delilah as a 'femme dominatrix' who teases and torments Samson the 'butch bottom', noting how 'the constant give and take between the two lovers resembles S/M role play', complete with ritual questions, hair fetishism and other power games (2001, p. 106). As Delilah provides the 'top' to Samson's 'bottom', so a parallel relationship can be drawn between YHWH and Israel, and between the Deuteronomistic Historian and the citizens of Jerusalem/Yehud (dependent upon when one dates the Deuteronomistic history). Analysis of these binaries exposes the Deuteronomist's attempt to impose a particular party political manifesto upon his generation, one where there is a rigid centralization of power in Jerusalem and one where the political regime is one of zealously upheld monotheism. His generation, however, is one that participates in religious diversity and has competing loyalties. By describing repeated cyclical patterns of monotheism and apostasy, where YHWH repeatedly exerts power to bring the people back into submission, he reiterates again and again the message: monotheism is rewarded and apostasy is punished. But in so doing he draws a disturbing portrait of the deity as one caught up in a cyclical game of deploying and relinquishing power, and Rowlett leaves us with the rather unsavoury image of the deity as sadistic player.

Roland Boer's attention to active/passive, dominant/submissive, pleasure/ pain binaries pervades his imaginary male-bonding session between YHWH, Moses, Freud, Sade, Sacher-Masoch, Lacan and Deleuze, held atop mount Sinai. Again, this paper explores how the deity's relationship with Israel is one that could be interpreted as characterized by sadomasochistic power games. In an intriguing paper Boer argues that the Israelites appear in the Hebrew Bible's storyworld as characters whose periods of faithfulness and unfaithfulness repeatedly indicate the desirability of deliberately disobeying the divine law since such disobedience evokes a period of suspense that inevitably follows before punishment is meted out (suspense being a major feature of sadomasochism game play). Thus in the garden of Eden and in repeated acts of disobedience such as the creation of the golden calf, punishment is something that is 'outwardly avoided but unconsciously wished for so that they might gain pleasure' (2001, p. 100).

In his formal response to the essays in *Queer Commentary* Daniel Spencer refers to Roland Boer's playfulness, nay 'naughtiness' (2001, p. 204). Certainly Boer's paper, as with queer essays more generally, is written in a controversial, provocative and bold style that transgresses established academic norms and expectations. He does handle his subject matter with a light, irreverent touch, so irreverent in places that some readers would undoubtedly find it offensive. And yet his article 'carries the reader along and rewards the reader's patience with several provocative insights about the biblical text, biblical religions and divine-human dynamics' (Spencer 2001, p. 204). Rowlett's article, as noted above, similarly illuminates the Samson and Delilah narrative in new and unexpected ways, and the S/M lens does appear to be merited: the desire to enter into arenas where there is potential risk and danger on a rising scale, the power game that involves submission to the dominatrix, the shaving of the head are key elements in S/M and are evidently present in Judges 13–16. Once enlightened, one is surprised that this has not been noticed before.[27] Another of the respondents says 'how can we now *not* see queer twists in the stories?' (Schneider 2001, p. 210). However, such insights may well be disturbing for some readers and the juxtaposition of discourse pertaining to sadomasochism and scripture will

---

27 Rowlett notes that Danna Fewell (1998) recognized the game play between Samson and Delilah, but Fewell did not take it as far as Rowlett has done.

undoubtedly offend religious scruples. Queer readings may, in fact, further the breach between those arguing for pro-lesbian and gay interpretations of scripture and those refuting them. Queer theorists, however, appear largely unperturbed by this prospect and have no qualms in using this discourse to illuminate scriptural texts. This is an issue that requires further thought and it will be discussed in Chapter 6. At present, let us consider how far a queer approach is open to anyone who can apply its strategies.

The term 'queer' carries an echo from earlier times when it was used as sneering insult and as such it does have a past as an identity label. However, it now sometimes functions as a recuperated umbrella signifier under which all gendernauts and sexual nonconformists can come together, strategically, in order to challenge heteronormativity. Although one does find writers who identify as 'queer' the idea of 'being queer' is something of a misnomer given that queer theory problematizes identity categories and labels.[28] Thus one 'is' queer only insofar as one contests the confining labels that have been applied, explores what creates and upholds such identities, and works towards the transformation of sex-gender binaries. Kathy Rudy puts it well: 'Being queer is not a matter of being gay, then, but rather of becoming committed to challenging that which is perceived as normal' (1996, p. 83).

The implications of this are significant. A lesbian reading of scripture, in light of the above comments, would appear to be grounded on rather shaky ground for it runs the risk of reifying an identity label that has been imposed in the interests of maintaining heteronormativity, furthering the apparent solidity of a fiction. This is acknowledged by Ken Stone who notes how queer theory's interest in challenging the heterosexual–homosexual binary will 'stand in tension with simplistic appeals to lesbian or gay identity – and hence in some tension, as well, with any simplistic appeal to a lesbian or gay "social location" for the purpose of biblical interpretation' (2001a, p. 24). As such, queer readings of scripture are potentially open to any persons who would apply the insights of queer theory and have relevant knowledge of contemporary critical theory on gender, sex and sexuality, or anyone who perceives that their marginalized or non-normative status could be usefully examined via the filter of queer theory. It would thus appear that it is time to move away from the idea of a lesbian hermeneutic and cast one's lot with

---

28 Queer is a positionality, says David Halperin. It is 'by definition *whatever* is at odds with the normal, the legitimate, the dominant. *There is nothing in particular to which it necessarily refers.* It is an identity without an essence. "Queer," then, demarcates not a positivity but a positionality *vis-à-vis* the normative' (1995, p. 62).

the burgeoning number of queer readings that have emerged within the last ten years. But there are a number of reasons why this is resisted.

First, there is justifiable concern that queer will turn out to be a critical tool that is insufficiently cognizant of the feminist criticism that precedes it and enabled its birth. At worst, the anxiety is that queer will not be gender neutral but will install a new universal masculinity at its heart.[29] Historically, such fear is not groundless. Given the low profile of women and their concerns in the Mattachine society, women broke away to form the Daughters of Bilitis in 1955. When gay liberation exploded in the 1970s, it was soon discovered that 'gay' would never prove to be an umbrella category. The anxiety that queer might follow suit and render lesbians and lesbian issues invisible once more, that it will not be sufficiently cognizant of feminist politics and the realities of the continued oppression of women, is not unfounded. Mary McIntosh, who offers a useful summary of how men and women treated each other with suspicion and hostility in the Gay Liberation Front and beyond, argues that queer theorists should not forget how heterosexuality is 'highly gendered'. Since this is so, 'our otherness and the forms and meanings of our dissidence are also gendered' (1993, p. 47). Her essay cautions feminists from an uncritical application of queer theory and encourages them to strive for gender awareness in queer theory. It is indeed the case that whereas some feminists demonstrate a readiness to engage with queer theory and use its critical tools, others are unwilling to be the ones 'expected to make all the running' in a context where one is 'disturbed by the degree of ignorance about feminism evinced by most male queer theorists' (Stevi Jackson 1999, p. 163). Queer theory may be very astute in destabilizing heterosexist norms, but when it comes to destabilizing the male dominance inherent in heterosexism the keen edge is sometimes found wanting. Moreover, the fact that some lesbians, especially lesbian feminists, are reluctant to abandon their solidarity and primary commitment to other women for what is still an uncertain future, is understandable. As Margaret Cruikshank says, 'I have fought too hard for the psychic freedom

---

29 Jeffreys (1994) is probably the most outspoken critic who, despite some misrepresentation of Judith Butler's work, nonetheless issues significant warnings against any ready assimilation. Farwell also fears that when gender is not a central, strategic component of theory, then there will always be the risk of constructing 'another universal male subject, more likely today to be the universal gay male subject'. She emphatically argues that gender 'is a category of interpretation ... that must be affirmed' (1996, p. 66). For further discussion from the early 1990s, published in the wake of queer theory, see Arlene Stein (1992), Smyth (1992, pp. 31–3), Castle (1993) and Grosz (1994). For more recent criticisms, see Heller (1997) and Jeffreys (2003).

to name myself as lesbian to disappear now under the queer rubric' (1996, p. xii).

Analysis of the contributions to *Queer Commentary* did not dispel the lurking suspicion that this will also be a weakness as queer theory is applied within biblical studies. Two of the three respondents to the essays in that publication were critical of the lack of any thoroughgoing engagement with feminist theory (Liew 2001, pp. 187–8, Schneider 2001, pp. 212–18). The latter was especially concerned about the reinscription of masculinity onto the divine which 'leaves contemporary women exegetes of all kinds, and queer women in particular, in an awkward (and all too familiar) position' (2001, p. 217). Schneider believes Boer's image of Yahweh as 'effete top, turning into a puppet for some kind of tormenter Ur-goddess' might have had something if it did not 'reinscribe a Victorianesque cult-of-femininity muteness on her' (2001, p. 221). She concludes:

> If queer readings of the Hebrew Bible are ever to help undo some of the patriarchal, racist, and kyriarchal biases of so many generations of commentary, teaching and theology, the further masculinization of the divine that emerges from these readings will have to be addressed. (2001, p. 221)

Liew combines his criticism of the insufficient attention to gender with the failure to follow through on racial and ethnic issues raised in the readings. He is 'thoroughly disappointed that *no* essay makes a "racy" attempt to look into the question of how sexuality can be racialized or ethnicity can be sexualized, even when the texts under examination (canonical or otherwise) beg for such an investigation' (2001, p. 189). This lack of investigation has been caused, he believes, by the centralization of sexuality which is tantamount to 'tunnel vision'. Thus Jennings' suggestion that feminist, class and other readings could supplement his queer reading reminds Liew of 'a "benign" form of multiculturalism that functions to assuage rather than address difference' (2001, p. 188). Liew would prefer it if queer theory developed a 'multifocal reading that attends simultaneously to sexuality, gender, class as well as race and ethnicity' (2001, p. 188).[30] Ten years previously, Gloria Anzaldúa had expressed concerns that issues of race were in danger

---

30 On concerns that queer theory is insufficiently attentive to issues of race and on the predominant whiteness of queer activism, see Smythe (1992), Charles (1993) and Barnard (1999). However, there are queer theorists who engage with the interaction of race, sex, gender and class with sexuality; see Corber and Valocchi (2003) and the essays in their volume. For an overview of the interaction of race and sexuality within queer theory, see Sullivan (2003, pp. 57–80).

of disappearing under a 'false unifying umbrella'; one that has the potential to homogenize and erase difference (1991, p. 250).

Second, while it is true that the revolutionary ideals of lesbian and gay liberation movements did not come to fruition (insofar as the sex, gender and sexuality alignment was not fundamentally breached), 'queer' does not have to assimilate that latter field as if it were entirely bankrupt. There need not be a wholesale move to queer terminology if our definition of 'lesbian' can be organized in such a way that resists the rigidity of sexual identity labels. Speaking of more recent lesbian history writing, Wilton notes that the term is capable of providing a pluralist picture of lesbianism which contests any 'narrow and demonised discursive structurations of lesbianism deployed by and in the interest of, the heteropatriarchy' (1995a, p. 65). It can expose mechanisms of suppression, elision, and the effects of resistance in much the same manner as Jennifer Terry (1991) advocates while resisting erasure and promoting the survival of 'lesbian' interests. While there may always be the danger that such writing will reify a lesbian identity, it may well be a price that has to be paid given the practicalities of living in a world that continues to use the lesbian label to stigmatize and demonize, that has continually kept such persons from connecting with their history, and that suppresses information about women's feelings for other women while elevating information about women's feelings for men through processes of bowdlerization and erasure.[31]

This leads us into the third concern that queer theory (as opposed to the engaged queer activism of groups such as ACT-UP or Outrage!), with its resistance to identity-reinforcement, will not sufficiently engage with the contemporary grassroots concerns. As Steven Seidman (1993) and Cindy Patton (1993) both have noted, queer theory tends to be good at posing problems, but not so astute in proposing effective practical solutions. It would be wrong to say that queer does not have a political conscience. The work its theorists are doing is in the vanguard of cultural criticism and, in the long term, may help to bring about real change of the kind envisaged by the early gay liberation movement. However, given the real grassroots situation of contemporary anti-lesbian oppression (discussed further in Chapter 2), we need an approach that will engage practically and politically in the here and now.

When turning to queer readings of scripture, the level of political engagement here is worryingly low. While some contributors to *Queer Commentary*

---

31 For several good examples of such processes of bowdlerization and erasure, see Lesbian History Group (1996) and see further below, pp 116–17.

demonstrate the relevance of their work for contemporary politics (notably Carden, West and Stone), others leave it for readers to see the relevance of the work and apply it. Remaining engaged in political and ecclesial discourse on these issues is vital for the well-being of lesbian, gay, bisexual and transgender (LGBT)-identified persons, and when one is involved in such engagement, identity labels – however contested – remain part of the discourse. Later in this publication, I will be arguing that lesbian-identified hermeneutics could find a useful home in Elisabeth Schüssler Fiorenza's community of justice seekers – the *ekklēsia* of wo/men.[32] But at this point, it is relevant just to note how Fiorenza, while actively contesting the category of 'women', retains a firm foothold in the women's movement, privileging the women's movement as the primary grassroots centre from which she works in order to transform academic and ecclesial discourse. Such a hermeneutic priority demands a strategic commitment to people positioned as 'women' and particularly to those 'who live at the bottom of the kyriarchal pyramid and who struggle against multiplicative forms of oppression' (1994, p. 14). This means that one cannot yet relinquish the category of 'woman' for it serves as the primary community driving her approach to scripture. And just as Fiorenza speaks of 'a spirit of responsible global citizenship' (1994, p. 6) which challenges any use of Christology as a 'weapon in the hands of the powerful who use it to conservative, oppressive ends' (1994, p. 8), I will argue that the driving force of lesbian hermeneutics will be to challenge any wielding of scripture as a weapon for oppressive and dehumanizing purposes. In this task, the strategic and heuristic use of the lesbian category will remain necessary.

This will also help with the fourth concern that relates to the bafflement, unease, anxiety, pain, anger and loss that will ensue from an abandonment of 'lesbian' as an identity label. Given the supportive environment that lesbian and gay communities/studies provides, it is difficult for those who have found a home within lesbian and gay communities to consider abandoning

---

32 Fiorenza uses the form wo/men to 'draw to the attention of readers that those kyriarchal structures that determine women's lives and status also have an impact on men of subordinated races, classes, countries, and religions, albeit in a different way . . . "wo/men" seeks to communicate that wherever I speak of "wo/men" I mean not only to include *all women* but also to speak of oppressed and marginalized men. "Wo/men" must therefore be understood as an inclusive expression rather than an exclusive universalised gender term' (1994, p. 191, n. 1). She also uses it to draw attention to the fact that 'women's' experience is not universal. The new spelling 'seeks to indicate that women are not a unitary social group but rather are fragmented and fractured by structures of race, class, religion, heterosexuality, colonialism, age and health' (1994, pp. 24–5).

labels that have been so politically useful and personally empowering. When the ownership of the lesbian label represents a difficult, maybe traumatic rite of passage through which one has journeyed, the very contemplation of rejecting it might seem an undoing or even betrayal of personal history. Roseneil, for all her examples of the queering of heteronormativity, does not believe that we have yet witnessed the advent of the post-lesbian and gay era and part of the reason for this is that 'lesbians and gay men do not appear ready to collectively cede their hard-won sexual identities and many are firm believers in their difference (variously conceived as cultural, biological, psychological and/or genetic) from heterosexuals' (2002, p. 38). The resistance to queer theorists' call to undermine sexual categories and move beyond them is a good indicator of the hold lesbian and gay labels now exert for those who have found in them useful grounds for theory and activism. For lesbian-identified feminists in particular, it raises further fears of betraying one's commitment to women's issues. Judith Butler may well be right that sexed and gendered identities are not expressions of core or true selves, but rather the fictional consequences of discourses that produce them, combined with the compulsory performances of identity. Yet having relatively recently found strength to claim lesbian identities and be proud about the fact, being asked to leave this behind as a false consciousness understandably causes dismay.

As far as lesbian approaches to reading the Bible are concerned, these are so much in their infancy that there has hardly been an opportunity to articulate them, let alone object to their assimilation into queer commentary. The practice of applying a lesbian perspective to a biblical text is gradually emerging, but recent collections of essays have been published under the queer rubric without any lengthy evaluation of the potential differences between the two.[33] Such publications highlight the potential danger of lesbian-specific readings of biblical texts being swallowed up within queer readings before they have had time and space to be developed.

---

33 In addition to Ken Stone's *Queer Commentary*, publications that use 'queer' in their titles or subtitles include Comstock and Henking (1996), Goss and Strongheart (1997), Stuart (1997), Goss and West (2000), and Goss (2002), though this does not indicate that editors of these publications are not unaware of the difficulties involved in moving towards queer terminology. Goss clearly indicates how queer theory can alienate some gays and lesbians who dislike its derogatory connotations and its confrontational tactics; how it can erase the voices of lesbians, African-Americans, Hispanic, Asian and 'other ethnic identities' and how it can deny the oppression experienced by specifically identified individuals (1996, p. 12). Notwithstanding, he is robustly confident that queer strategies within theology can be inclusive.

Who is the lesbian in a lesbian-identified hermeneutic?

In her practical reflection on how and where she can usefully locate herself and her work in the changing domains of the academy where queer is rapidly becoming a respectable face for the lesbian and gay studies of old, Bonnie Zimmerman strongly resists any 'premature merging' of lesbian studies with queer: 'We have hardly, in our mere two or three decades of self-conscious existence, so thoroughly established the lesbian subject that we can now blithely discard her' (1996, p. 274). I concur with her anxiety that if a lesbian-feminist discourse is shunted into the new forward-looking domain of queer theory, it runs the risk of being assimilated

> without any recognition or citation of sources, the vilification of our values and continued existence, and the appalling misrepresentation and ahistorical construction of the past twenty years. To counter this, lesbian feminists need to reinsert ourselves into the debates in a forceful and intellectually impeccable way. That, to me, is the most important work facing lesbian-identified scholars today. (1996, p. 274)

Zimmerman can see the usefulness of coalition building but not if it is at the expense of losing lesbian studies' room of its own. In taking a position that is broadly adopted in this publication, she says

> lesbian and/or lesbian/gay/queer/sexuality studies will develop best if each constituency maintains some healthy and sceptical distance, engages in open and critical dialogue, and acknowledges both the similarities and the differences, the congruencies and the contradictions, among our multiple points of view. (1996, p. 274)

A final concern is that queer will prove to be an elitist discourse, hardly accessible to the lay person or in touch with the lived realities of grassroots communities (see Escoffier, 1990 and Malinowitz, 1993). Despite the argument that complex ideas require complex terminology, some feminists have long upheld a commitment to the communities they seek to represent and to present their ideas in ways that are accessible to such communities. Thus when Adrienne Rich published her vision of the 'woman-centred university' its defining features included non-hierarchy and an orientation to grassroots communities. It would create connections between women within the university and those without, and would draw upon 'the special experience of nonacademic women ... the grandmothers, the high-school dropouts, the professionals, the artists, the political women, the housewives' (1980, p. 145).

51

Zimmerman reissues the call to action that resists any elitism:

> We need to maintain or, more accurately restore the links between academic lesbian feminism and lesbian communities. We need always to listen to the voices of women who do not necessarily speak in the dialects of high theory and modish ideas. This is particularly important if lesbian studies is to reflect our very visible diversity of race, class, physical ability, age, and personal history – diversity that is not yet and may never be fully evident within the academy. Moreover, we need to ask how we can make our scholarship and criticism useful, not only to ourselves as we climb the academic ladders of success. (1996, p. 274)

For these five reasons a wholesale move to a queer hermeneutic is resisted. However, this is certainly not to say that queer theory does not have its uses and the role it can play in the interpretation of scripture is upheld and explored further in Chapter 5.

The third critical moment has provided a timely challenge to preceding lesbian and gay studies. Although it would be misleading to imply that such studies had neglected the importance of rupturing sex and gender binaries, the advent of queer politics and theory did bring a new visibility to that issue. There has been the reminder that although the adoption of a lesbian identity is still a transgressive act, it arguably complies with the cultural imperative to identify as a marginalized sexual subject. Embracing a lesbian identity can lend support to the idea that hetero and homosexual are stable identities to which one is oriented. Adopting a lesbian identity may thus be a brave act of independence from sex-gender norms, but it simultaneously risks solidifying the lesbian label and thereby, paradoxically, endorsing normative heterosexuality. Moreover, the continued use of lesbian and gay labels can be reductionist, narrowing the diverse speaking positions from which opposition to heteronormativity may be articulated. This 'results in the unnecessary and inaccurate labelling of many people practising non-heteronormative erotics as either lesbian or gay . . . stemming the productive proliferation of anti-heteronormative stances that ground themselves in alternative, emergent or subcultural discourses' (Cover, 2002). Not only reductionist, the regimentation of lesbian and gay communities can be oppressive for those who, for whatever reason, fall outside the hetero–homo binary. In Cover's view, in order for the binary to be ultimately discredited, binary-based sexual terminology has to be abandoned while, presumably in the short term, the binary should be used only 'in the most strategic ways, only with care, and only under a sense of ethics derived through arguments of performativity, post-structuralism and difference' (Cover, 2002). Such concerns have to be carefully considered. Nevertheless, this publication heeds Zimmerman's call to develop lesbian studies in its own right and seeks to find a voice for a specifically lesbian approach to biblical interpretation, despite the fact that such a move seems to run against current trends. This means that some way of dealing with the problems identified has to be found. Specifically, how does one solve the problem of representation and how does one avoid reifying the category of lesbian?

Conclusion
Why a 'Lesbian-Identified Hermeneutic'

It is the case that identity categories will inevitably exclude as they include. Feminist theory is yet to negotiate a fully workable and acceptable-to-all way to embrace radical plurality while holding onto the category of 'woman'. Lesbian critical theory faces the same challenge for it has become abundantly clear that the label cannot contain all the peoples it purports to represent. To its credit, while lesbian theory and study projects of the last quarter of the twentieth century predominantly derive from white Euro-American, middle-class contexts, there has been a keen consciousness of the need to hear from the different experiences of women living in diverse locations, women of working-class backgrounds, women of different racial heritage, for example. This is largely thanks to the work of the Black, Chicana, Jewish, third world and working-class women who made early vital contributions to lesbian studies, undertaking valuable research within diverse communities and challenging any emerging tendency to speak of the lesbian as fixed, unitary subject.[34] Nevertheless, representation has been a problem. Laura Gowing, for example, rightly notes how Faderman's work

---

34 See, for example, the essays on racism and classism in Gibbs and Bennett (1980). For the analysis of the experiences of a working-class, Jewish fem in the 1950s, see the work of Nestle (1987, 1993). For contributions from third world and/or women of colour in the United States see Moraga and Anzaldúa (1981). There was also willingness to move beyond established norms of research in order to listen to the voices of lesbians not usually represented within academic discourse, as indicated in the work of Moraga and Anzaldúa (1981) and later in the editors' willingness to delay the 1993 volume of *Signs* 'in order to incorporate better the work of lesbians of color and non-academic scholarship' (McNaron, Anzaldúa, Arguëlles and Kennedy 1993, p. 758). For a discussion of this input, see Garber (2001).

concentrated on the lives of white, middle-class women, effectively erasing the 'experiences of black women and working women, and of the quite different understandings of friendship, sex, and bodily closeness that might obtain outside the world of white middle-class women' (1997, p. 62). And there have been some long-lasting dog-fights. Contests for the public face of lesbianism dominated the sex wars, fought between those who thought certain features of lesbian dress and behaviour were deleterious to the feminist cause and those who found such criticism puritanical and unnecessarily censorial. Working-class lesbians insisted upon their right to diverse sexual practices and objected to the 'Lesbian Sex Police' (Wilton 1996, pp. 7–8) who told lesbians how to regulate their love lives. Indeed, the working-class voices of women like Joan Nestle and Audre Lorde fought against the censorious criticisms of some lesbian feminists (who felt that some lesbians were letting the side down) and emphatically insisted that 'lesbian' carry the right to signify women's sexual passions for each other – however that was manifested.[35] As a result, some lesbians found their allegiances best served by the gay liberation movement rather than the feminist and womanist movements.

There remain contests and anxiety over who this signifier can represent: 'Can a male-to-female transsexual join a lesbian collective? Is a "political lesbian" a "real" one? What do we call a repressed married woman who lusts for her girlfriends but dies wondering?' (Malinowitz 1996, p. 263). Thus, questions of who the lesbian signifier includes, questions of lesbian 'authenticity', the contesting of the boundaries put around the label, all inevitably threatened to disrupt and fragment any fixed or unified concept of 'lesbian'. Such challenges demonstrate the striking thought 'that sexual orientation may not constitute sufficient grounds for commonality among lesbians' (Jagose 1996, p. 67).

I cannot envisage being able to broaden the scope of the lesbian category so that it can fully represent the diverse realities of lived experience. Definitions will always be limiting and the urge to police the boundaries probably inevitable, but lesbian critical theory has not been ignorant of this problem. On the contrary, Harriet Malinowitz (1996) traces the

---

35 For further discussion of the sex wars, see Vance (1984), Rich (1986), Hunt (1990), Echols (1984), Hollibaugh and Moraga (1984), Duggan and Hunter (1995). For an account of the clash between lesbian feminists, who were predominantly Anglo, educated and middle-class and the bar lesbians, many of whom were lesbians of colour from poor and working-class backgrounds, see Franzen (1993).

acknowledgement of difference and recognition that 'we' cannot be used unproblematically back to Audre Lorde's view that difference should never be tolerated in a never-ending diluting of category labels. Tolerance, said Lorde, is 'the grossest reformism' (1981, p. 99). Acknowledgement of difference, however, sparks creativity, creates awareness and facilitates attempts to 'make common cause with those other identified as outside the structures, in order to define and seek a world in which we can all flourish' (1981, p. 99). As Malinowitz points out, there are obviously significant differences between the postmodern theories of difference and the comments of Lorde, but Lorde's work remains an early indicator that there were clear antecedents to queer theory in the lesbian and feminist work of previous decades. The fact that a signifier cannot contain all the peoples it claims to represent is not a reason for giving up entirely on the signifier. It is a problem, but it is a problem to be worked through in ongoing debate. There is bound to be real conflict among potential constituent members, but as Shane Phelan argues, these need not necessarily be 'cause for despair but grounds for continued rearticulation' (1993, p. 783). In her useful article, Phelan concludes that we

> should not refuse the specifity and reality of lesbian experience; neither should we reify our experience into an identity and history so stable that no one can speak to it besides other lesbians who agree on that particular description of their experience. Our politics ... must consist of continued patient and impatient struggle with ourselves and with those within and without our 'communities' who seek to 'fix' us ... We can afford neither assimilation into mainstream politics nor total withdrawal in search of the authentic community. (1993, p. 786)

I will argue below that an approach, alert to the issue of representation, aware of the fluidity and constructed nature of its own identity label, can use the insights of queer theory to develop its own agenda without abandoning the term 'lesbian' altogether. However, prior to that, the second problem – that of reifying the lesbian label – needs to be addressed.

It is certainly the case that lesbian critical theory runs the risk of solidifying the lesbian signifier. However, it has not ignored this problem but, particularly within the last two decades of the twentieth century, has actively addressed this issue. Phelan notes the new developments that would enable theorists to retain 'lesbian' as a meaningful category while working 'against reification of lesbians, toward views of lesbianism as a critical site of gender deconstruction rather than as a unitary experience with a singular political meaning' (1993, p. 766). Phelan makes a convincing case for introducing the changes necessary to avoid reification of the identity label, while keeping faith with lesbian studies as a subject in its own right. This avoids any head-long rush to embrace and be assimilated into 'queer'.

That there were indeed such changes afoot is reflected in the title of Sally Munt's 1992 collection of essays *New Lesbian Criticism*. In her introduction, Munt acknowledged some of her doubts and reservations about publishing such a volume, specifically referring to the dangers of reifying the 'lesbian' category and of reproducing essentialist notions (1992, p. xv). Yet she also recognized the important role that identity politics plays. She concluded that there was still a place for taking an identity and claiming a space for 'lesbian criticism' given that the contemporary climate remains one of homophobia and invisibility (1992, p. xvii). Notably, like Munt, Phelan does not entirely abandon 'lesbian' as a category of identity because the hostile environments in which we live 'require that we base common action in the provisional stability of categories of identity, even as we challenge them' (1993, p. 779). In the next chapter I also argue that the global context of oppression against lesbian-identified people requires a hermeneutic that is ethically responsible and that 'lesbian' is a label worth retaining in this effort.

Munt's reference to *New* lesbian criticism helpfully indicates that there is something distinctive about this version of lesbian theory. In the past, feminists have similarly articulated changes in emphasis and theory by referring to first, second and third waves. While this terminology recognizes chronological moments of renewed engagements, it also reflects new foci, new critical theories and self-critical reflection upon its own past. Although Phelan does not use this phrase, *New* lesbian theory could be adopted to describe an approach that recognizes there is no universal 'deep meaning and truth of lesbianism' (Phelan 1993, p. 772); and recognizes 'lesbian' is a critical stance from which the dominant discourse can be evaluated, but knows that this stance operates within the system rather than standing outside it. The *New* lesbian criticism therefore recognizes the provisional and contextual nature of identity labels and is committed to exercising caution and humility when using such identities. Phelan, therefore, advocates entering the public domain not as persons with some 'eternal identity but as those who *continue to become* lesbians – people occupying provisional subject positions in heterosexual society . . . articulating our lives, interpreting and reinterpreting them in ways that link us to others' (1993, p. 779 emphasis added). Later she adds: 'I may insist on my lesbian identity not because I believe myself to be "really" lesbian, but because my relationship to that category (whatever that relationship may be) importantly structures my life' (1993, p. 782). This resonates with Judith Butler's articulation of her own position, for while refuting attempts to totalize her identity in one word such as lesbian, she confirms, 'This is not to say that I will not appear at political occasions under the sign of lesbian, but that I would like to have it permanently unclear what that sign signifies' (1991, p. 14).

In the light of the above discussion, it is clear that the issue centres not so much upon 'who is a lesbian reader' as 'what constitutes a lesbian reading/writing position?' Thus, for the purposes of this publication, the phrase 'lesbian-identified' has been selected. 'Lesbian' is retained because I believe it still has value for highlighting the concerns of a particularly situated constituency of readers who speak from a stigmatized place and who know what it feels like to be positioned as a deviant subject. Although the 'outside' space is always 'inside' the organization of heteronormativity, the sense of not belonging, of not desiring to follow the compulsory heterosexual script, distances one from it and facilitates a keen, heightened awareness of the features that contribute to, police and maintain the inside/outside, heterosexual/homosexual binary. Accordingly, while cautious of any claims to innate experiential knowledge, it remains the case that those who have occupied deviant subject positions, who have swum strongly against the tide of hegemonic expectations, often have an advantageous perspective. It is unlikely that this constituency could constitute an international community, for as Ann Ferguson so astutely observes, any attempt to construct an international culture may very well result in an imperialist imposition of western 'notions of the proper values for a lesbian culture of resistance onto other societies' (1990, p. 64). To avoid this, she advocates 'the construction of international lesbian, feminist and gay liberation *movements* which develop a radical democratic form for promoting the development of indigenous national and local lesbian, feminist and gay oppositional cultures in their particular locales, social classes and racial and ethnic groups' (1990, p. 64). So, while this publication aims to define and situate a lesbian approach to biblical interpretation it can only be the product of a specific cultural moment and a single author who is a white, British, lesbian feminist-identified, able-bodied, middle-aged person of working-class origins brought up in an evangelical tradition. Its perspective is inevitably limited and will rightly provoke evaluative criticism, further negotiation, and widening of its parameters.

The 'identified' portion of 'lesbian-identified hermeneutic' points to the fact that dominant discourses have historically identified and positioned women as lesbians, regardless of their own self-understandings. But it simultaneously points to the reverse discourse that this initiates from women who choose willingly to identify as lesbians (always acknowledging that such counter-discourse can never free itself from its entanglement with the dominant discourse in any authentic 'outside' pure form). Importantly, it is also meant to indicate that 'lesbian' is not a fixed state, but a perpetually unclear signifier that carries a diversity of different identifications depending upon who is doing the positioning. It was tempting to use scare quotes to achieve this instability, but this would be cumbersome. When Valerie Traub uses the terms lesbian or lesbianism she italicizes them to 'remind readers of their epistemological inadequacy, psychological coarseness, and historical contingency' (2002, p. 16). Hopefully the addition of '-identified' will be sufficient to achieve the same purpose.

2

Lesbian-identified hermeneutics in context

No biblical hermeneutic emerges from a vacuum; on the contrary, hermeneutical principles are always marked by the context in which they are produced. The dominant historical critical approach to interpreting biblical texts that held sway in the nineteenth and twentieth centuries, for example, is now widely seen as a product of the western context of enlightenment, permeated with its interests, norms, values and ideologies. Historical critical approaches are thus 'readings' despite the fact that they are often not overtly labelled as such. More recent approaches to reading scripture that proclaim their advocacy, such as Black or feminist approaches, are more open about the fact that they are grounded in specific contexts. Black interpretations of scripture have their context in early responses to slavery, the civil rights movement of the mid-twentieth century and the continuing struggle for equality. Feminist interpretations have appeared in 'waves' that coincide with the first, second and postfeminist secular movements. Lesbian-identified interpretations of biblical texts also bear an overt label and, as with Black and feminist readings, have materialized during a period marked by protest and activism. The Stonewall riot of 1969 is etched into gay and lesbian history because this was when a handful of people fought back. There are debates about exactly what happened but the basic features were that there was a police raid (a common event in the 1950s and 60s, which meant verbal and often physical abuse for those arrested) at the Stonewall Inn, Christopher Street, in the heart of Greenwich Village. As police attempted to manhandle drag queens and at least one butch lesbian into the police van, the latter fought back and hostile onlookers erupted into action, with the throwing of coins, beer bottles and stones. The police retreated into the bar where they were hemmed in and some members of the crowd tried to set light to the pub. The small-scale but significant riot continued until it was quelled in the early morning. Yet the hostile atmosphere continued for the next two days as crowds congregated again and resisted attempts by the police to break them up. This event spurred the emergence of groups such as the Gay Liberation Front that were more overtly active than their predecessors (the Homophile movement, the Mattachine Society and Daughters of Bilitis), and is celebrated in the annual pride marches around the world that began in 1970.[36]

Gay and lesbian studies emerging in Transatlantic contexts post-1970 are grounded in this period of protest. Finding a voice and room for oneself after decades of being variably objectified as deviant, sick, perverted, sinful individuals was hugely important. In a context where there existed a wide range of civil discrimination that stigmatized and marginalized gay and lesbian-identified people, where gay-bashing was a potential threat to be faced, where 'faggot' jokes and threats were an uncriticized staple of movie scripts, fighting for gay and lesbian rights became a prime objective. It is in this, largely Transatlantic context, that lesbian-identified readings of scripture are beginning to emerge. They are accordingly marked by western understandings of sex and gender, by the lived experiences of those who have been positioned as, or self-identify as, lesbians in those contexts and by the methods of activism prevailing in those cultures.

However, being identified as lesbian has different meanings and consequences depending upon where one lives, and is always mediated through additional filters such as one's racial and ethnic identity, age, religion, class and so forth. Indeed, the very use of the word 'lesbian' is problematic since its use is rejected in some contexts, and even in contexts where it is utilized, it certainly does not carry equivalent connotations. Accordingly, what one means by 'lesbian' will always have to be carefully considered without making any Eurocentric assumptions of its signification. Thus, the term 'lesbian' is rejected by Astrid Roemer, an Afro-Surinamese poet-novelist, who believes it is an outsider's term used to categorize practices that do not necessarily conform to its connotations. The Mati culture, experienced within the Afro-Surinamese context, is one where a woman can enjoy special relationships with another woman, but where marriage and childbearing within a simultaneous heterosexual relationship is not unusual. In her view, Mati-ism preserves a more African terminology than the Afro-American 'black lesbian' terminology which, in her view, has been unduly influenced by western ideas. (Roemer's views and her discussion with Audre Lorde can be found in Wekker, 1993.) A similar resistance to the 'lesbian' label can be found within Asian contexts. This is made very clear in Sullivan and Jackson's (2001) collection of essays on *Gay and Lesbian Asia*,

---

36 For further information, see Duberman (1993) and Martin (1993).

where not only is its non-transferability explained but also why there is local resistance to the term. In Thailand, for example, 'female erotic cultures have trenchantly resisted the dominant English label for female homoeroticism, *lesbian*, instead appropriating and adapting the terms *tomboy* to *tom*, and *lady* to *dee*, to reflect the gendering of female same-sex relations' (2001, p. 17). Jackson also notes that the avoidance of the word 'lesbian' derives from its use in describing pornography produced for male audiences, and because it is 'understood as representing woman-centred relationships in overly sexualised terms, with many Thai women who love women preferring to imagine their relationships in emotional rather than explicitly erotic terms' (2001, p. 23 n. 5). Chou Wah-Shan only uses the word 'lesbian' when referring to westerners, preferring 'People who are erotically attracted to People of the Same Sex' (PEPS) to speak of pre-twentieth-century Chinese society and *tongzhi* when referring to contemporary Chinese people (2001, p. 27).[37]

Consideration of these regional differences, when combined with Peter Drucker's caution that Euro-American labels do not correspond with indigenous sexual categories in the so-called Third World (2000, pp. 1–15), provokes the question of whether 'lesbian-identified' is the best phrase to have used in this publication. This is a question that also confronted Blackwood and Wieringa as they commenced their investigation of same-sex relations across a variety of cultures. They acknowledge 'the problem of misrecognition and ethnocentrism that use of the term "lesbian" occasions' (not least its inability to include transgendered females who do not wish to identify as women or as lesbians). They are also well aware that 'those who prefer to maintain the "walls of silence" they have built around themselves' have to be respected, since their continued existence 'may at times rest on their not being associated with the word "lesbian"' (1999, pp. 21, 28). Nevertheless, they conclude that the visibility the term grants to women's issues and its continued political usefulness outweigh its problems. As noted at the close of Chapter 1, I too have decided to stay with 'lesbian-identified' since

---

37 *Tongzhi* translates the Soviet communist term 'comrade'. *Tong* literally means 'same/homo' while *zhi* can mean 'goal', 'spirit' or 'orientation'. Chou finds this a useful term for disrupting of the homo–hetero binary since it doesn't invoke a boundary between those who love the same and the opposite sex. She likens it to the force that 'queer' has in the West 'but whereas queer politics confronts the mainstream by appropriating a formerly derogatory label *Tongzhi* harmonizes social relationships by taking the most sacred title from the mainstream culture. It is an indigenous strategy of proclaiming one's sexual identity by appropriating rather than denying one's familial-cultural identity' (Chou 2001, p. 28).

I am writing from a western perspective, since this is the term commonly used in international discourse and because I believe there is still sufficient common association with the term to merit its usefulness.

However, there is no intention to ignore the use of alternative terms in accordance with local formulations and an acute awareness that, as a western term, it is laden with associations to white western culture that are very problematic for emergent postcolonial societies. This is an issue that will, no doubt, provoke controversy and require further consideration. What can be agreed, however, is that because of the multiple ways in which 'lesbianism' is negotiated, there cannot be any monolithic lesbian hermeneutic with fixed principles and strategies. Rather, each country and region will need to develop its own particular terminology and interpretational strategies in the light of their specific experiences. Therefore, this publication cannot determine a lesbian-identified hermeneutic that can be applied universally and remain constant. It has to be seen as the product of a specific contextual moment, grounded primarily within a British context and inevitably reflecting the context-specific perspective of a white, able-bodied, working-class, educationally privileged, lesbian-identified lecturer. It is a starting point; an opening for discussion. But it has to begin somewhere, and in an attempt to appreciate how the lived realities in a variety of contexts might inform the principles and strategies of a lesbian-identified hermeneutic, this chapter takes a broad overview of how those lived realities can differ. Although lesbian-identified persons suffer from widespread discrimination, harassment and serious violence in Transatlantic contexts (from where the vast majority of LGBT/Q[38] readings of scripture have emerged), the penalties imposed on a criminalized homosexuality in other countries and the risks lesbian-identified women face in those contexts is often far more systematic and extreme. A responsible approach must take account of this wider global context in order to suggest principles and subsequently strategies that might be effective in the harshest of situations and hopefully be of value to those living in such contexts as they develop their own distinctive strategies.

I recognize that some lesbian-identified people may go through their entire lives without ever having experienced overt hostility and who may

---

38 LGBT/Q is shorthand for lesbian, gay, bisexual, transgendered and queer. I have chosen to separate Q with a slash in order to indicate that 'queer' is a term that calls the previous identity labels into question. Although queer can be used as an umbrella term for sexual outlaws, dissidents and their allies, queer upsets the homo–hetero binary and resists stable LGBT categories.

find the data in this chapter concentrates too heavily upon the experiences of those who have not had such good fortune. The chapter may also be criticized for concentrating so much on contexts of oppression that it constructs lesbian-identified persons as victims. As I note at the end of the chapter, this is not necessarily the case. While there are victims – victims of random shootings, brutal beatings, gang rape and victims of the routine discriminatory practices, the petty humiliations that wear one down – there are the survivors who continue with their lives and nurture such qualities as hardiness. However, it is important to document the different ways in which lesbian-identified persons situated in different regions of the globe are subject to discrimination and hostility if a lesbian-identified hermeneutic is to retain its connection with diverse grassroots communities and shoulder its ethical responsibilities. This chapter accordingly explores a range of contexts where some of the people positioned as lesbians suffer oppression ranging from potential execution to the routine discriminations and stigma faced on a daily basis. It is not within the remit of this section to cover the full range of discriminatory and punitive practices that are applied across the world. A variety of organizations are committed to documenting instances of such practices and providing up-to-date reports which can be consulted for further information.[39] It is limited to an illustrative tour of non-Transatlantic contexts where, in some cases, the criminalization of same-sex relationships has led to state-sanctioned oppression of lesbian-identified individuals. It will consider in particular how the 'heterosexualization' of Africa features in the anti-colonial rhetoric of some prominent African politicians and how this marks the lesbian not only as an affront to public decency but also as a betrayer of her nation's authentic heritage.[40] The focus upon Africa is important since it provides an informative backdrop for later discussion of how the Black churches negotiate texts that

---

39 Organizations such as Amnesty International, the Lesbian and Gay Immigration Rights Task Force, the International Lesbian and Gay Association, the National Gay and Lesbian Task Force, Queer Resources Directory, Behind the Mask (lesbian and gay affairs in Africa) maintain websites with relevant, detailed documentation. For a review of the global context, see West and Green (1997) and Donnelly (2003).

40 This heterosexualization of Africa is not something new. Bleys (1996) indicates how it suited the purposes of abolitionist colonizers to present African (heterosexual) humanity as something worthy of protection. Presenting Africa as a heterosexual continent simultaneously facilitated the denigration of homosexuality within the mother-country by indicating that even 'black savages' do not engage in such practices.

appear to condemn homosexuality. In order to demonstrate the brutality faced by lesbian-identified women when they have been arrested, the discussion will move to Romania and the well-publicized experience of Mariana Cetiner. Finally, in order to demonstrate the effect that sheer silence can exert, this section will close with a consideration of Asian contexts where same-sex relations are not outlawed, but neither are they acknowledged. Far from indicating an absence of oppression such determined silence has its own particularly negative effects upon those who seek primary relationships with members of their own sex.

The second section of this chapter narrows the focus to my own country. Despite the fact that laws criminalizing homosexuality were repealed in 1967 and that substantial progress has been made since, it is still the case that there is a wide range of continuing civil discrimination and stigmatization. The review of the English situation by West and Wöelke (1997) suggests that for lesbian/gay-identified people today it is 'the best of times and the worst of times' (1997, p. 212). Persistent lobbying over the past 40 years has borne considerable fruit: the lifting of the ban on gays in the military, the equalization of the age of consent for gay men, the introduction of a new Sexual Offences Bill which treats homosexual and heterosexual public sex equally, the availability of partnership registration schemes and most recently civil partnership law, the repeal of Section 28 and the adoption of the European directive to protect people from discrimination on the grounds of sexual orientation. These advances, together with the open and positive ways in which lesbian and gay topics can now be addressed in the media, the relatively easy accessibility of lesbian and gay venues, magazines, travel agencies, directories of services and so forth, are all indicative of the 'best of times'. However, the authors note that 'things have not gone so far that same-sex couples are likely to be seen holding hands or kissing in public as heterosexuals might'; that 'a majority of the population remain intolerant'; that religious groups, such as the Courage Trust, 'which has an ideological commitment to "treatment" to convert homosexuals into God-fearing Christian heterosexuals' continue to exist; and that surveys reveal significant levels of violent attack against gays and lesbians (West and Wöelke 1997, p. 212, 214). They conclude by pointing to the growth of religious fundamentalism in England and the USA, and end on the following rather chilling note:

Berlin in the 1930s, before the Nazis took over, was a city renowned for its permissiveness, but that did not prevent gay men and women from being later rounded up and put into concentration camps along with Jews and other despised minorities. (1997, p. 218)

The chapter will close with a third section exploring the ways in which Christian discourse has contributed to and sustained the criminalization and civil discrimination discussed in the previous sections. It is important to note that the general oppression of lesbian-identified people is often constructed and sustained by adherence to seemingly implacable scriptural texts that condemn same-sex behaviour. The development of a lesbian-identified approach to these scriptures in particular remains vital and potentially has positive social and political consequences if such approaches were to win widespread support.

The data in this and the previous section is likely to be quickly outdated. Nevertheless, it remains important to document this material for it is in direct response to such history that lesbian-identified readings of scripture have evolved. This chapter thus grounds the principles and strategies that are outlined in subsequent chapters.

Life in the Margins: Outside the Transatlantic Context

At the time of writing, the International Lesbian and Gay Organization (ILGA) listed 42 countries where homosexual acts are illegal and, apart from one or two uncertain cases, lesbians are explicitly included in that legislation.[41] Those arrested are liable to a range of penalties, which can include execution, particularly in those countries where Sharí'a law prevails.[42] However, imprisonment is more likely to be prescribed with sentences ranging from ten days to 20 years, depending upon the country,

---

41 In Africa: Angola, Benin, Burundi, Cameroon, Cape Verde, Djibputi, Ethiopia, Guinea Conakry, Liberia, Libya, Malawi, Mauritania, Mauritius, Morocco, Senegal, Sudan, Swaziland, Togo and Tunisia. In Asia/the Pacific: Afghanistan, Bangladesh, Brunei, Pakistan, the Solomon Islands and Western Samoa. In Europe: the Chechen Republic. In the Americas: Barbados, Grenada, Nicaragua, Puerto Rico, Saint Lucia, Trinidad and Tobago. In the Middle East: Bahrain, Iran, Lebanon, Oman, Qatar, Saudi Arabia, Syria, United Arab Emirates and Yemen.

42 According to the International Lesbian and Gay Association, countries where homosexual acts remain subject to the death penalty include Mauritania, Sudan, Afghanistan, Pakistan, the Chechen Republic, Iran, Saudi Arabia, Yemen and possibly the United Arab Emirates (source: http://www.ilga.info/Information/Legal_survey/ Summary%20information/death_penalty_for_homosexual_act.htm

plus fines. This official state-sanctioned treatment is, however, only one level of the oppression faced. Being held for trial and subsequent imprisonment can bring its own additional terrors of unofficial torture and rape. And, in regions where the rhetoric of government and religious authorities is virulently anti-gay/lesbian,[43] this can indirectly lead to rapes, beatings and murders in regions where perpetrators can act with relative impunity. The Amnesty International report *Crimes of Hate, Conspiracy of Silence. Torture and Ill-Treatment Based on Sexual Identity* is clear:

> Around the world, lesbians, gay men and bisexual and transgender people are imprisoned under laws which police the bedroom and criminalize a kiss; they are tortured to extract confessions of 'deviance' and raped to 'cure' them of it; they are killed by 'death squads' in societies which view them as *'desechables'* – disposable garbage. (ACT 40/016/2001)

The wording of the various laws used within the 42 countries where homosexuality is overtly criminalized reveals that, in several cases, homosexuality is associated with predatory behaviour. In such cases, laws exist to protect the vulnerable from unwanted sexual advances. Thus the punishments that exist are almost unanimously increased when a minor is involved, or where intimidation, trickery, coercion or violence has been used. In these cases, mutual consenting relationships are not at issue, and such laws are consistent with developments in Transatlantic contexts where male rape is recognized as a crime, and where violence and abuse within lesbian communities is beginning to be documented.[44] Criminalizing sexual abuse in this way is welcome. Yet these laws stand side by side with laws that prohibit *consenting* acts between women with penalties ranging from ten days' to ten years' imprisonment. The greater penalty for same-sex acts that have used coercion or violence, trickery or fraud (up to 20 years' imprisonment) indicates awareness of the difference, but it is disturbing to find consenting mutual relations on the same continuum.

The laws are predicated upon a narrow definition of lesbian as one who

---

43 Following Celia Kitzinger (1996) I have deliberately avoided using the word homophobic. Its psychological connotations imply that homophobia is a sickness, and that homophobes can therefore be indulged and defence lawyers have been known to use 'homosexual panic' as justification for the murder of gay men. On such cases, see Tomsen (1998), Bendall and Leach (1995), Mouzos and Thompson (2000). My alternative is to refer to *anti-lesbian/gay* attitudes, discourses and behaviours.

44 The Criminal Justice and Public Order Act 1994 amended the category of rape to include non-consensual vaginal and anal intercourse in England and Wales.

commits *acts*; specifically as one who has sexual relations with another woman. Thus, in some countries, women are prosecuted under sodomy laws (for example, Tunisian Article 230 prescribes imprisonment of up to three years for acts of sodomy between consenting adults, *both* men and women; while Nicaraguan Article 204 defines a sodomist as 'anyone who induces, promotes, propagandizes or practises in scandalous form sexual intercourse between persons of the same sex'). However, sodomy laws are not the sole basis for criminalization. Several countries criminalize on the basis of provoking public outrage. Thus, Algerian Article 333 speaks of 'an act against nature with an individual of the same sex' as an 'outrage to public decency'. In Cape Verde lesbians can be punished for violating Section 391 of the Penal Code that prohibits 'assaults on public or personal decency'. In Guinea Conakry laws relating to 'public indecency' (defined as 'any intentional act committed publicly and likely to offend the decency and the moral sentiments of those who are its inadvertent witnesses'), can be used to convict. Closely linked is Angola's wording of 'against public morality'; while the Penal Code of the Solomon Islands, particularly Section 155, prohibits acts of 'gross indecency' and since 1989 specifically includes lesbian relations under that rubric. In several cases, this language of public outrage is combined with the presentation of the lesbian as one who acts 'against nature' (Algeria, Cape Verde, Guinea Conakry, Morocco, Senegal, Bangladesh, Pakistan), 'unnaturally' (Malawi), 'deviantly' (Liberia) or with 'serious indecency' (Trinidad and Tobago).[45]

These legal traditions, in many cases, date back to periods of colonization. But, in an irony that has not gone unnoticed, this colonial heritage has been turned back upon the colonizing nations themselves as 'homosexuality' becomes a rallying point around which the decadence and pollution of the colonizing power can be distinguished from an indigenous non-homosexual culture. The representation of homosexuality as alien, the 'other' to the authentic self, is occurring most vehemently within countries that are working through the aftermath of the struggle for independence from colonial rule.

President Mugabe has probably been the most frankly outspoken. The charismatic figure of the president, together with his eminently quotable views, has ensured plenty of media coverage. In one of his most infamous

---

45 References in this paragraph are derived from the International Lesbian and Gay Association: http://www.ilga.info/Information/legal_survey/Summary%20informa tion/countries_where_same_sex_acts%20illegal.htm

speeches, his address to the International Book Fair in Harare on 1 August 1995, he declared:

> I find it extremely outrageous and repugnant to my human conscience that such immoral and repulsive organisations, like those of homosexuals who offend against the law of nature and the morals and religious beliefs espoused by our society, should have any advocates in our midst and elsewhere in the world. (West and Green 1997, p. 43)

Just ten days later, on 11 August, the president included this statement in his address to ZANU-PF Women's League:

> [Homosexuality] is unnatural and there is no question ever of allowing these people to behave worse than dogs and pigs ... What we are being persuaded to accept is sub-animal behaviour and we will never allow it here. If you see people in your area parading themselves as Lesbians and Gays, arrest them and hand them over to the police. (West and Green 1997, p. 52)

A week later, having incurred the wrath of 70 American congressmen who sent the president a letter criticizing his views, Mugabe provided one of his most oft-quoted statements: 'Let the Americans keep their sodomy, bestiality, stupid and foolish ways to themselves, out of Zimbabwe. We don't want these practices here. Let them be gay in the United States, Europe and elsewhere. They shall be sad people here' (Dunton and Palmberg 1996, p. 13).

One month later, in a Parliamentary Debate on 'Homosexualism [*sic*] and Lesbianism' (6 September 1995), Border Gezi reiterated the government's rhetoric:

> I would like to ask ... that police should be on the lookout and look for homosexuals and lesbians. They should take them and put them some-where they can never be seen because we cannot mix with such people. They will tarnish our image. We should look for ways of keeping these people separate from those who are normal. (West and Green 1997, p. 43)

The outspoken vitriolic of President Mugabe and his ministers quickly spread to nearby countries such as Namibia, Zambia and Uganda where there have been further calls for the elimination of homosexuality. In 1995, shortly after the International Book Fair speech by Mugabe, Namibian finance minister Helmut Angula's three-part article in *Namibian* (10, 17 and 24 November) entitled 'Homosexuality Is a Mental Disorder Which

Can Be Cured' emphasized that homosexuality was to be considered both unnatural and unAfrican. Just over a year later, on 30 January 1997, the Namibian secretary for information and publicity, Alpheus Naruseb, said that SWAPO (the South West African People's Organization) would not allow individuals with 'alien practices' such as homosexuality to destroy the social fabric of the country, adding

> It should be noted that most of the ardent supporters of this [sic] perverts are Europeans who imagine themselves to be the bulwark of civilisation and enlightenment. They are not only appropriating foreign ideas in our society but also destroying the local culture by hiding behind the facade of the very democracy and human right we have created.[46]

In 1998 the home affairs minister, Jerry Ekandjo, reinforced the view that 'gay rights can never qualify as human rights. They are wrongly claimed because it is inimical to true Namibian culture, African culture and religion. They should be classified as human wrongs which must rank as sin against society and God' (Maletsky, 1998). On 2 October 2000, he reportedly encouraged 700 newly graduated police officers to 'eliminate gays and lesbians from the face of Namibia'.[47] This comment was endorsed when the President of Namibia, Sam Nujoma, speaking to University of Namibia students on 19 March 2001, said: 'the Republic of Namibia does not allow homosexuality, lesbianism here. Police are ordered to arrest you, and deport you [i.e. in the case of foreigners or non-citizens] and imprison you.' His comment was endorsed by members of Nujoma's cabinet who have made statements that homosexuals should be 'eliminated' from Namibian society.[48] And in a direct acknowledgement of the anticolonial interest of his stance, Nujoma's address to a SWAPO rally in the same year included the words:

> The enemy is still trying to come back with sinister manoeuvres and tricks called lesbians and homosexuality and globalisation. These are all madness and they claim to be Christians ... They colonised us and now they claim human rights when we condemn and reject them. In Namibia there will be no lesbian and homosexual left. (Maletsky 2001)

---

46 All quotations from Alpheus Naruseb can be accessed at: http://www.mask.org. za/SECTIONS/AfricaPerCountry/ABC/namibia/namibia_035.htm

47 See the Human Right Watch paper 'More than a Name: State-Sponsored Homophobia and its Consequences in Southern Africa' which can be accessed at: http://www.hrw.org/reports/2003/safrica/

48 http://www.amnestyusa.org/stoptorture/lgbt/nambia.html

As the 'More than a Name' paper notes (Human Rights Watch 2003, pp. 29–33), the government's statements are not necessarily supported in all quarters of Namibian society, but organizations that try to provide space and help for gay and lesbian-identified individuals, do so in the knowledge that reprisals may follow. It is also recognized that the government's encouragement of a culture of intolerance means that the country remains a dangerous place for such individuals.

In Uganda, during September 1999, President Yoweri Museveni responded to the coverage of an alleged 'gay wedding' in his country by calling upon the police 'to look for homosexuals, lock them up and charge them'. Amnesty International's report details the devastating effects this had upon five gay and lesbian human rights defenders who had formed a group (Right Companions) in October 1999. While meeting to discuss a strategy in the wake of the President's statement, eight armed men burst into the room and arrested them. Black cloths were tied on their heads and they were taken to different detention centres. In her statement to Amnesty International, 'Christine' reports that she was stripped, beaten and raped by at least two of the guards before she passed out. The one other woman was beaten, stripped, sexually and physically abused and threatened with gang rape. Although the five were released two weeks later, they all fled the country.[49] Gillian Rodgerson's recent article (2003) reports a further incident. In December 2000 two young female Ugandans were dragged from their bed by four men and taken to face the local council. They were allegedly stripped, assaulted and verbally abused before being expelled from the village of Najjanankumbi for their 'immoral' conduct. One of these women, who had supported an opposition politician, was subsequently picked up by the police and taken into custody where she was repeatedly beaten and gang-raped. Having escaped the country, her appeal for asylum has been refused by the British government on the grounds that she could return to Uganda and live quietly; a view rejected by 'Florence' who reasons that 'she cannot hide anymore, and certainly could never endure a marriage of convenience to a man' (Rodgerson 2003, p. 25). Such occurrences are not common but they promote a climate of anxiety and fear. Current news emerging from Uganda reveals that, despite the severe personal risks involved, a largely Christian (but open to Muslim concerns) lesbian and gay organization named Musla-Uganda has emerged to fight for the human rights of LGBT-identified people. Established in the Makere University but

---

49 http://www.amnestyusa.org/stoptorture/lgbt/uganda.html

open to all who will join, their literature confirms the general climate of hostility, speaking of harassment and dismissal from the work place, organized mob violence in the countryside, being generally regarded as 'misfortunes' by family clan and tribe, rejection from the church and mosque and living in 'total fear of constant attacks in estates, schools/colleges or communities' (personal communication, 19 September 2003).

In Nigeria, a country that criminalizes (male) homosexuality, the International Gay and Lesbian Human Rights Commission confirmed reports of the rape at gunpoint of four Nigerian lesbians who had been seeking refuge in a feminist centre in Calabar in September 1994. *Behind the Mask* reports that this came just days after one of the women published an article on lesbianism tracing the advent of Nigerian lesbianism and condemning previous attacks against the centre.[50] On the one hand, these documented rapes may indicate exceptional, ad hoc examples of violence against lesbian-identified persons that become cause célèbres precisely because of their out-of-the-ordinary occurrence. On the other hand, they may well indicate the tip of the iceberg of many other such violations within Nigeria.

Reflecting on these various statements and incidents across Africa, it becomes very clear that there is a connection between the issue of homosexuality and the aftermath of liberation from colonial rule. In the simultaneous desire to resist western interference and return to (or, more accurately, recreate) indigenous ways of life, anti-homosexuality rhetoric has become a touchstone for traditional values. Homosexuality thus becomes an entirely foreign phenomenon, a 'white' disease, a scourge on African soil, to be uprooted and eliminated in the process of purging the continent of all immoral, exploitative and unwanted colonial influence. Accordingly, homosexuality has been proclaimed as an abomination that runs 'against all the norms of African society and culture' (Zimbabwe's president, Robert Mugabe).[51] It is an unnatural behavioural disorder that is 'alien to African culture' (Namibian finance minister, Helmut Angula).[52] It runs 'against African tradition and biblical teachings' (Kenya's president,

---

50 http://www.mask.org.za/SECTIONS/AfricaPerCountry/ABC/nigeria/nigeria_02.htm

51 http://www.ilga.info/Information/Legal_survey/africa/supporting%20files/gays_are_main_evil.htm

52 http://www.ilga.info/Information/Legal_survey/africa/namibia.htm

Daniel arap Moi).[53] It 'is the deepest level of depravity. It is unbiblical and abnormal' and should not be allowed to take root on African soil (Zambia's president, Frederick Chiluba).[54]

The connection between postcolonial nation-building and the issue of homosexuality is helpfully explored in Margrete Aarmo's case study of Zimbabwe. Her essay contextualizes the statements from Mugabe, demonstrating how he uses significant dates and locations to reinforce his heterosexualization of Zimbabwean national culture. For example, he chooses the Zimbabwean International Book Fair to make a public denunciation of the GALZ (Gays and Lesbians of Zimbabwe) lobbying and support group that had been established at the turn of the 1990s. As Aarmo notes, the book fair is 'a big and prestigious event' for the nation and it offered a celebrated public platform to announce his views. As for the 11 August 'worse than pigs' speech, this was delivered on Heroes Day, a significant date which celebrates the memory of the freedom fighters who died in the Zimbabwean liberation war. The people who heard the speech had gathered at Heroes Acre where the fighters had been buried. As Aarmo comments, 'Mugabe thus deployed a black, national symbol, the Heroes Acre, in the construction of a distinction between those who belong to the nation and those who do not "fit in," the homosexuals' (1999, p. 262). She later adds that the logic represented in this speech is as follows: 'animals represent fertility and symbolize the natural order of things, while gays represent infertility, which symbolizes danger and death' (1999, p. 266). In Mugabe's view, authentic Zimbabwean society is a heterosexual, patrilineal society that invests much in the family and production of children. He is attempting to reinforce this view in a context of rapid change and economic difficulty and in a country where there are ethnic and class divisions. Thus, as Aarmo notes, Mugabe's denunciations have to be set within his

> growing need for a unifying identity that goes beyond all immediate and internal politic, economic, and social crises and divisions among people of different classes and ethnic groups. Where there is no homogenous national identity, it must be 'invented'. Notions of culture become a powerful means to this end … To produce meaning, the culture and the nation must appear as a whole, as a 'we.' This can only be done by establishing an other, a 'they' … the boundaries of the nation must be clear …

---

53 http://www.ilga.info/Information/Legal_survey/africa/kenya.htm

54 http://www.mask.org.za/SECTIONS/AfricaPerCountry/ABC/all%20africa/all%20africa_4.htm

Nationalism is an ideology that requires a reified, essentialist notion of culture in order to establish the boundary between 'us' and 'them.' The promotion of cultural homogeneity is an ideological project . . . What is crucial is that people are made to believe that they 'have' a culture, which is distinctly different from other people's cultures. (1999, pp. 267–8)

Since Aarmo's article was published, Mugabe has been increasingly vehement. Shunned by western governments, he used his 2002 election campaign to speak of a homosexual conspiracy against his country. As his denouncements become ever more strident it is important to recognize that Mugabe's heterosexualization of Zimbabwe has to be viewed in the context of postcolonial nation-building. In a situation where traditional masculinity and femininity is being firmly endorsed, individuals who break out of that collective duty will always be seen as national traitors who do not conform to the collective values. 'They thus serve as the "perfect other" in a context where definitions of culture seem to be crucial for the construction of the modern Zimbabwean national identity' (Aarmo 1999, p. 276).

To some extent, the claim that homosexuality is an import from the West is an accurate summary of the situation. Homosexuality, as it came to be defined in late nineteenth-century Europe and North America, is a modern western phenomenon. To the extent that gay, lesbian, bisexual and transgender support groups are emerging in non-western countries, adopting these labels and using the methods of political action honed in British and American contexts, homosexuality could justly be said to be a western import. Thus, Marc Epprecht can say of the Zimbabwean situation:

There was no such thing as a homosexual identity until recently (Zimbabwe's first black lesbian only came out in 1993, for example). Even today, open gays and lesbians probably number no more than several hundred in a country of twelve or more million. (1998, p. 649)

However, Epprecht also distances himself from the 'dangerous myth' that 'Zimbabwean Africans are exclusively heterosexual by nature' since the presence of 'sexually intimate relations between males can be attested in Zimbabwe from time immemorial' (1998, pp. 650, 631). The point is that these 'sexually intimate relations' are not simply to be understood as cultural variations of a lengthy, global and universal LGBT ancestry. Rather, such relations need to be understood within the organization of the specific social, political and religious context of precolonial Zimbabwean history where the hetero–homosexual binary that has typified western ideas during the last century is not applicable. In precolonial Zimbabwe same-sex relations could occur within the largely homosocial groupings which

> created conditions for widespread homosexual 'play' . . . erotic touching between same-sex friends of the same age was considered quite normal and in no way threatening to future heterosexual relations. Indeed, homosexual sex play was often regarded as appropriate 'training' for future heterosexual marriage, preferable to heterosexual mixing that could result in illegitimate pregnancies and political complications. (Epprecht 2000, p. 16)

These relations were not considered the product of white influence but were part and parcel of social life. However, in all these cases, same-sex relations were not permitted to interfere with the imperative to marry and procreate. Children provided a necessary labour force for the family and also were an investment against one's old age. This 'political economy of heterosexuality', as Epprecht terms it, meant that non-procreative sex was frowned upon, if and when it was even recognized, for when 'sex' is understood narrowly as male–female penetrative intercourse for the purposes of procreation, same-sex activities hardly count as 'sex'. Same-sex relations do, however, attract disapproval when they are exclusively preferred or pursued and they then may be subject to coercive force. Resisting girls, for example, are kidnapped in order to force them into marriages and Epprecht cites cases of 'forced and violent sexual intercourse with recalcitrant girls . . . condoned by family or community' (1998, pp. 634–5). The only (rare) cases where same-sex relations appear to have been acknowledged and permitted in defiance to the procreative imperative occur in cases of spirit-possession. Thus a woman claiming to be possessed by a male ancestor, could 'legitimately marry another woman, could remain unattached, and could dress and behave as a man' (Epprecht 2000, p. 17). Nevertheless, the possibility that the woman's claim could be countered by another diviner meant that not all women would be successful in their bid to live in this way. Aarmo (1999) concurs; it is more likely that they would be forced into a heterosexual relationship, or expelled from the extended family and forced to eke out an existence in a hostile climate as best they could.

Thus, although it is appropriate to resist naive claims that there has always been a homosexual presence in Zimbabwe, it is also appropriate to resist any claims that Zimbabwe has always been heterosexual. Both terms – homosexual and heterosexual – are so loaded with ideas of distinct sexual identity and orientation that their applicability outside the contexts in which they originated is highly questionable. Nevertheless, the heterosexualization of Zimbabwe that is currently going on actively represses any past history of same-sex relationships and vigorously promotes anti-homosexual attitudes as it constructs a particular image of the Zimbabwean male and female. This rhetoric has to be understood in the wider context of Zimbabwe's colonial past. In Epprecht's view, colonial rule emasculated African men, treating them as 'boys' while white males possessed the prerogatives of manhood. The traditional signifiers of masculinity (the acquisition of land, a submissive wife and subsequent children) were kept from the African male for years longer than it would traditionally have taken. In fact, colonial bureaucracy and land shortages meant that the boyhood stage became, for some men, a permanent condition. This inferior positioning vis-à-vis the white male colonists was exacerbated by the assertiveness of town women who exercised 'a degree of independence from men, including the ability to control and deploy their sexuality, which mocked customary expectations of masculinity' (Epprecht 1998, p. 641). Such assaults on the masculinity of the Zimbabwean male helped create the atmosphere for anti-colonial rebellion and the subsequent period of nationalist struggle witnessed the effects of African masculinity being reasserted. Rape crime increased dramatically and the space for tolerating (albeit negatively) indigenous forms of male–male relationships (such as mine marriages) decreased. Mugabe's denunciation of homosexuality is inherently part of this endeavour to idealize a national patriarchal culture and construct a Black Nationalist society that defines itself as staunchly heterosexual.

The struggle for independence hardened a pre-existent bias against non-procreative relationships and motivated the positioning of lesbian-identified people as unnatural, indecent, scandalous figures of public disgrace who act contrary to 'normal' women. This not only constructs and sustains heteronormativity, but explicitly endorses widespread anti-lesbian sentiment and action among the general population. Thus, the widely publicized pronouncements by leading figures of the Zimbabwean government, noted above, leave the way clear for aggressive behaviour by the police force and hostile elements within the country generally, though the extent to which such aggression is actually carried out upon lesbian-identified members of the population with any regularity is difficult to ascertain.

Overall, it is clear that in certain parts of Africa there is a general hostility towards any manifestation of same-sex desire and a firm rejection of any activism on the part of lesbian and gay-identified citizens. It is relatively easy to give the impression that there is rampant persecution and oppression of lesbian-identified women in certain parts of Africa, but this would be to overstate the situation. The general political climate of hostility certainly facilitates oppression and it is evident that there have been individual experiences of that hostility, but this is not necessarily tantamount to widespread persecution. Before moving on to a different part of the globe, it is important to recognize that South Africa is, conversely, the first country to have enshrined the rights of sexual minorities. In May 1996, sexual orientation was included in its list of human markers that can no longer legally provide a basis for discrimination (the other areas included race, gender, sex, pregnancy, marital status, ethnic or social origin, colour, age, disability, religion, conscience, belief, culture, language and birth). This constitutional commitment was strengthened by the ANC's 1997 resolution that equality for lesbian and gay people should be actively *pursued* in areas of employment, family and youth. It was strengthened still further by the October 1998 declaration of the Constitutional Court of South Africa, that the crimes of sodomy and Section 20A of the Sexual Offences Act were unconstitutional. The reason given for this declaration is worth noting. Such laws were said to adversely affect the 'dignity, personhood and identity' of lesbian and gay people; a statement which echoes the South African Constitution that upholds the dignity and self-worth of all people, regardless of their sexual orientation. Thus, while the situation seems to be particularly dire in certain parts of Africa, there are also pioneering efforts being made to secure the safety and dignity of lesbian-identified people which should be recognized and applauded.

There are several other areas of the globe that use state legislation to criminalize lesbian-identified individuals and turn a blind eye to the further harassment that occurs when they are imprisoned. Romania's application to join the European Union brought Article 200 of their 1968 Penal Code under the spotlight. Under pressure from the Council of Europe, this Article was revised in 1996. Whereas same-sex relations had been punishable by imprisonment of between one and five years, the 1996 'concession' amended the wording to refer only to acts 'committed in public' or 'causing public scandal'. However, additions made to the fifth paragraph which criminalized anyone 'inciting or encouraging a person to the practice of sexual relations between persons of the same sex, as well as propaganda or association or any other act of proselytism' in effect meant that acts in private were still forbidden, particularly in a context where private life was hardly existent. This fifth paragraph rendered any bar or place where lesbians could gather illegal, the registration of formal lesbian organizations illegal, magazines, publications, public marching or public events banned. Deputy Emil Popescu made the position clear in June 1997: 'If a lesbian were to go out in the streets dressed to protest, it is not certain she would get away alive. This law exists to protect her from doing so' (Human Rights Watch and the International Gay and Lesbian Human Rights Commission [HRW&IGLHRC] 1998). The report of the HRW&IGLHRC further noted that arrests continued to be made under the new version of Article 200 and criticized the ongoing

> climate of legalized intolerance. Officials, whether in police stations, prisons, courtrooms, or hospitals, are routinely encouraged to regard gays and lesbians as persons without rights. Once arrested, those accused of violating Article 200 are routinely beaten by police, and while in detention are targeted by other inmates for sexual abuse, with the tolerance and even encouragement of guards. Throughout Romania, meeting places of lesbians and gays, as well as the few organizations that have attempted to form, exist, if at all, under the continual threat of legal harassment. And it is widely accepted that a legitimate national purpose is served by eradicating homosexuality completely from public view. (HRW&IGLHRC 1998)

The case of Mariana Cetiner exemplifies the above comment. Arrested in October 1995 for 'attempting to seduce another woman', she spent seven months in jail before being indicted, during which time Cetiner reports that she was beaten and insulted by her prison guards. The HRW&IGLHRC's report records a visit to Mariana Cetiner in Tirgsor penitentiary where

> The conversation was supervised by two guards who seemed determined to threaten Cetiner. She was able to communicate briefly in English, before guards stopped her. She said an officer had beaten her the day before, because she tried to file a complaint: 'He handcuffed me and pulled me out of my cell by the hair. I have much to say but it is forbidden. When you leave, I will have big problems.' (HRW&IGLHRC 1998)

The report also draws upon an interview by Scott Long and Bogdan Voicu with Cetiner, at Tirgsor Penitentiary, July 1997. It notes that 'Cetiner had a large bruise on her right thigh, and her knee was bandaged. She attempted to show another bruise, on her side, but was afraid in the guards' presence.' Amnesty International were later to report that when she complained, she was 'handcuffed to a radiator and made to stand for 11 hours "in a position like Jesus Christ" without food' and that her request to see a doctor resulted in a ten-day period of solitary confinement (ACT 40/016/2001). Amnesty International reports that such treatment is particularly prone to be dealt out to those whose choices demonstrate some autonomy over their own bodies. Such autonomy is punished by rape, severe beatings or torture within prisons or such state institutions, with impunity.

Despite this situation the Bucharest Acceptance Group did form in 1994 and was officially registered in 1996 as a non-governmental organization, after being advised to delete all references to sexual minorities or homosexuality. Thanks to its lobbying efforts and the human rights efforts required from those countries wishing to join the European Union, there has been a remarkable recent turn of events. In June 2000, the Chamber of Deputies voted to repeal Article 200 and on 31 August 2000 Romania passed an anti-discrimination law which included sexual orientation among its protected categories, backed with substantial fines and lawsuits for those tempted to test the new legislation. In accordance with such law, Article 200 was repealed in February 2002, against strong representations from the Orthodox Church to keep this law on Romania's statute books. How far this was a measure designed solely to get Romania into the European Union rather than a genuine progressive move by the government carrying the support of the largely Orthodox population, remains to be seen.

Pressure from the European Union is a significant factor in producing such change in the legal situation for lesbian-identified people in this region of the globe. Estonia and Lithuania also repealed criminalizing laws as they prepared to become members of the Union. Only three candidate countries – Cyprus, Hungary and Bulgaria – continue to have discriminatory laws on their books. And yet while prospective nations are expected to clean up their legislation in respect to the human rights of sexual minorities, the finger has recently and rightly pointed at the double standards of existing members such as the UK. For while laws criminalizing homosexuality were repealed in 1967, the UK is tarnished with the reputation of having the 'most repressive legal situation of any country in Western Europe other than Cyprus'.[55] This will be discussed further in the third section of this chapter.

Before closing this section it is important to note that the effects produced by state-sponsored criminalization of same-sex relations can be present even when there are no specific laws that relate to homosexuality at all. One might think that such a situation indicates an absence of oppression, but any consideration of the situation in Asian countries reveals otherwise.

---

55 http://www.ilga.info/Information/Legal_survey/europe/United_Kingdom.htm

In several Asian countries consensual same-sex relations and acts are not outlawed, but neither are they discussed. This tangible silence is not indicative of a benevolent accepting attitude but rather indicates disapproval for relationships that threaten the strong emphasis upon marital and family life that characterizes countries such as Japan, China and Korea. In these societies the family is the predominant means of social organization and there is a compelling social imperative to marry and settle into harmonious family life.

In Japan, for example, the silence surrounding same-sex relationships is enshrined in law which defines sexual conduct solely in terms of male–female acts; same-sex activities (*seikou-ruji-koui*) do not equate and are not recognized as authentic sexual relations. In such an environment the silence indicates implicit censure. Thus in his visit to the Japanese Association for the Lesbian and Gay Movement, OCCUR, ILGA co-ordinator Andy Quan reported that there remains a 'widespread disapproval' and although this is 'definitely different from the violent forms that homophobia takes in other countries' it stigmatizes those who choose same-sex relationships.[56]

In Korea, where again there are no specific laws prohibiting homosexuality, but where there is a deeply felt obligation to marry and settle into a family life, same-sex relationships are also subject to disapproval. As Seo Dong-Jin says: 'In modern Korean society . . . homosexuality does not seem to be "that love whose name one dare not utter" but rather "that love whose name does not refer to anything"' (2001, p. 66). Trying to write about homosexuality in Korea, he says, is like trying to 'bring to light some wispy phantom that I only know through its effects' (2001, p. 66). In fact, the primary effects that enable its existence to be felt at all are those of pain and deep unhappiness, fear and anxiety. Seo believes the emphasis upon a different familial culture might be overemphasized but nevertheless confirms that in Korea, the fear that people have results less from 'society's hatred and prejudice' and more from the 'anxiety and stress that would result from the breaking of their familial bond' (2001, p. 77).

In China, the pressure to marry means that homosexuality is neither supported nor accepted even while it is periodically discreetly tolerated. During China's recent history, particularly since 1949, there have been cases of arrest and imprisonment.[57] During the Republican period, western

---

56 http://www.ilga.info/Information/asia_pacific/visit_by_ilga_coordinator_to_ Jap.htm. For further information on the situation in Japan, see Pinkerton and Abramson (1997).

57 Arrests on the charge of 'hooliganism' (Article 106 of the Criminal Law of the

notions of homosexuality as an aberration engaged Chinese intellectual thought and led to the adoption of the western mental illness model. During these years people would be sent to 'labor reform camps, prisons, or clinics for electric therapy, or even executed in extreme cases' (Chou 2001, p. 31). Although there are no sanctions explicitly against homosexuality, its very absence from public discourse in China has been the problem. When Fang-Fu Ruan pseudonymously published an article on homosexuality in a widely circulated health magazine and later in the (Chinese) *Reader's Digest*, he received a mailbag from readers hugely relieved to have read his work and expressing their sense of isolation and desperation, with 15 of the 56 correspondents mentioning suicide attempts. With no education about same-sex relations, no cultural images, many Chinese men and women live lives that have been guilt-ridden.

Organizations for sexual minorities are emerging in Japan, China and Korea and there is a growing awareness of a wider lesbian and gay community through access to the Internet and higher education, which is available to the young middle class in particular. However, among the working classes or older population who do not have such access, there is a tendency to avoid the growing subculture of a lesbian community. Seo notes that the young *kkirikkiri* group is largely ignored by the older, less well-educated women who have viewed their own same-sex leanings as 'a shameful desire that constantly hounds them' (2001, p. 76). In Japan there are the beginnings of a more open and political life; OCCUR organizes contact groups, festivals and conferences and there are gay bars, discos and magazines (mostly for men).[58] However, the political activities that have been part of western gay and lesbian liberation, based on an individualism and sexual identity, do not sit comfortably with Japanese understandings of humanity and its social relations and it is highly questionable whether such activities are the

---

People's Republic of China) are no longer regular occurrences, but the climate of fear and enforced silence remains. As Ruan puts it: 'silence, especially a silence based on repression and enforced ignorance, must not be mistaken for approval or tolerance. When public figures do speak out on homosexuality, it is usually to condemn it' (1997, p. 63).

58 However, Andy Quan's research found that most of the women of Sapporo chose to meet separately from the Hokkaido Sexual Minorities Association. One couple explained that their priority was to 'get together to enjoy each other's company rather than organize any events'. One reason was that they were simply too tired to do so given their social familial commitments. They also considered the men of the Association 'too political'. Source: http://www.ilga.org/Information/asia_pacific/visit_by_ilga_coordinator_to_Jap.htm.

best way forward in this and other Asian societies. Indeed the sixth point of the manifesto that emerged from the Chinese *Tongzhi* Conference held in December 1996 was that the confrontational politics that have been operative in the West 'may not be the best way of achieving *tongzhi* liberation in the family-centred community oriented Chinese societies which stress the importance of social harmony'.[59]

In conclusion, the above discussion has demonstrated that a wide range of laws are used to criminalize same-sex relationships and even in situations where there are no specific laws, a climate of oppressive silence prevails. The oppression of lesbian-identified persons takes on different shapes according to the context in which one lives. Resistance will also take the form of tactics that are appropriate to the individual context. What is right for America and Europe may not be right for African or Asian countries. Postcolonial critiques of Eurocentric presumptions should prevent westerners from making easy equations or imposing political action that has worked in those situations upon other cultures. However, it should not hinder collaboration. A responsible lesbian-identified hermeneutic will deprivilege western-centralized ideas on sex and gender categories and on methods of resisting heteronormativity. It will recognize how a Transatlantic history of lesbian and gay resistance to the medical and sinful models of their societies is a *local* history and reaction. It will recognize that if one is to help rather than hinder the process of resistance, practitioners 'must be able to participate in recovering histories that are not their own and to share in lives within which their own aspirations may be irrelevant' (Jackson 2001, p. 22). It needs to identify ways of working collaboratively that do not reproduce western hegemony.

Life in the Margins: The UK Context

In countries where criminalizing laws have largely been repealed, lesbian-identified people continue to face the effects of routine civil discrimination and anti-lesbian attitudes. This was made abundantly clear at the National Lesbian Conference held in Atlanta, Georgia in 1991, where 3,000 attendant lesbians were greeted with Urvashi Vaid's summary of the realities of discrimination facing lesbian-identified people in the current social context:

59 http://www.ilga.info/Information/Legal_survey/Asia_Pacific/supporting%20 files/manifesto_of_the_1996_chinese_to.htm

- To be lesbian today means to face loss of our jobs, loss of housing, denial of public accommodation, loss of custody, loss of visitation simply because of our sexual orientation.
- To be lesbian today means to face violence as a queer and violence as a woman.
- To be lesbian today means to have no safety for the families we have created, to face the loss of our children and our loved ones, to have no status for our committed relationships.
- To be lesbian today means to be invisible ... hidden from a world whose sight is monochromatic and patriarchal, hidden even when we are out and powerful, by a world that is obsessed with the relationships between men ...
- To be lesbian today means to work in social change movements ... that still ghettoize the multiple issues of discrimination that we face and that still tokenize us or put our concerns and voices on the back burner.
- To be lesbian today is to have, until very recently, absolutely no images in mainstream culture of out, proud, powerful, strong, independent women.
- To be lesbian today is to live in a society that identifies and defines us only through our relation (or lack thereof) to men – lesbians are masculine, men-haters, the sexual fantasies of straight men.
- To be lesbian today is to face multiple systems of oppression – to face homophobia, sexism, racism, ageism, ableism, economic injustice – to face a variety of systems of oppression *all at once*, with the type of oppression changing depending on who we are, but the fact of oppression remaining constant. (1997, p. 799)

The list may surprise some readers, particularly the fact that this social context relates to the USA in the 1990s and not some unenlightened age of the distant past. They could partly be forgiven for believing that such days are gone given the growing tolerance and acceptance of gay and lesbian-identified people. Certainly, it is no longer a foregone conclusion that all lesbian-identified persons will experience abuse, violence, stress or negative health issues as a result of being positioned as such. Moreover, lesbian-identified women have largely escaped specific targeting in the UK, despite several attempts.[60] However, published studies indicate that 'the realities

---

60 Faderman (1985) identified a dozen court cases prior to 1900. Faraday (1988) has described the parliamentary considerations about whether to criminalize lesbianism in 1921, and subsequent debates in 1937 and 1956. There were clearly desires to regulate and possibly eradicate it, but these desires were hamstrung by the equal desire not

of discrimination' Vaid listed in 1991 remain in force, both in the USA context and in the UK. For this section of the chapter, the focus will primarily relate to my own British context and the introduction of two pieces of legislation: one relating to civil partnerships and the other to employment equality. These examples are useful for illustrating the historical effects of civil discrimination and, particularly in the next section, for analysing the ways in which the lesbian is being identified and positioned in competing discourses, primarily those of the government and the Christian Institute.

In the summer of 2001 Stonewall (an all-party political lobbying group) asked Lord Lester if he would consider introducing a private member's bill in the House of Lords on civil partnership registration. On 9 January 2002, the bill, the joint initiative of the Odysseus Trust and Stonewall, was read in the House of Lords. It was given a second reading on 25 January 2002 whereupon Lord Lester dropped the bill in the wake of the government's commitment to set up a review of the issue. In due course, a consultation document was published by the Women and Equality Unit of the Department of Trade and Industry in June 2003 entitled 'Civil Partnership. A Framework for the Legal Recognition of Same-Sex Couples'.[61]

A by-product of this paper was its useful identification of the discriminatory atmosphere prevailing in England and Wales. It demonstrated clearly how women in same-sex relationships have not been able to secure a guaranteed stable future in terms of inheritance, tenancy, pension and next-of-kin rights. Tenancy rights, more secure as a result of the 2002 *Ghaidan v Mendoza* case, have historically been insecure. Surviving partners who were not the direct rentee have been evicted from council properties. The government's paper recognizes this in its proposal that registered partners be given the right to succeed. Pension wishes have not always been upheld. Some companies allow their clients to nominate a recipient for their pension in the event of death, but whether the nomination will be honoured is left entirely in the hands of the company. There is no guarantee that one's wishes will be upheld. The lack of next-of-kin status has a number of effects. One is that visitation rights in hospitals can be contested

---

to advertise the possibility of women's same-sex relationships. One place where lesbianism remained criminalized until January 2000 was in the armed services. For further information, see Crane (1992).

61 The paper can be accessed at http://www.womenandequalityunit.gov.uk/research/civ_par_con.pdf

by staff insisting on spouses only, a particularly distressing occurrence for gay men in the wake of AIDS.

Furthermore, a same-sex partner would not necessarily have any rights in the event of their partner's mental illness. The Mental Health Act 1983 indicates that the partner must have been living with the patient for five years if she is to take precedence over actual relatives, but that this can never be precedence over an existing spouse. An application for power of attorney can be made to the Court of Protection, but 'the partner's relatives have to be notified and can challenge the arrangement' (West and Wöelke 1997, p. 207). Overall, the proposals recognized that 'some people have faced particular difficulties after the death of a same-sex partner, either due to social attitudes or because the relationship was not recognized in law' (Women and Equality Unit 2003, p. 52). This rather tamely conceded that lesbians have been positioned as inferior citizens whose choices were not worthy of recognition. Lord Lester was not so tame when he commended his bill to the Lords. 'Gay people' he argued

> have notoriously experienced cruel treatment after their partners have died, especially if they died intestate, when members of the family of the deceased partner, refusing to accept the relationship, have taken over the home and the property which the partners have shared in common for many years.
>
> (Lords Hansard, 25 January 2002, col. 1693)

The key point underlying his original bill was that the legal position of same-sex partners was not only inferior but 'not recognised as a family status at all' (Lords Hansard, 25 January 2002, col. 1692). The refusal to acknowledge same-sex partners (and their children) as a family had been enshrined in law in 1988 during a decade of increased anti-gay/lesbian discourse encouraged by the right-wing press, a conservative government and certain segments of the Church, all amid the outbreak of AIDS. Despite the street protests in London and Manchester, resistance from lesbians who abseiled into the House of Lords from the public gallery and who chained themselves to Sue Lawley's desk on the six o' clock news, Section 28 of the Local Government Act became law on 24 May 1988. It was finally repealed, very quietly, on 18 November 2003. But between those dates Section 28 came to be seen as a particularly invidious law in its 'remarkable denial of the reality of thousands of parents' and children's lives' and in making 'prejudice against homosexuality newly respectable' (Weeks 1977, pp. 61–2). It made it an offence for local authorities to 'intentionally promote homosexuality', publish material with the 'intention of promoting homosexuality', or to 'promote the teaching in any maintained school of the acceptability of homosexuality as a pretended family relationship'.[62] There is a stark contrast between this language and the foreword to the civil partnership proposals by Jacqui Smith MP. Smith refers to 'same-sex couples living in stable and committed partnerships . . . living in exactly the same way as any other family' (Women and Equality Unit 2003, p. 9). In government rhetoric, lesbian-identified people have thus moved from 'pretended family' to equal family status within 15 years.

It will take time for this progressive move to undo the effects of the 1988 derogatory and stigmatizing language of Section 28. The lack of recognition of same-sex families impinged upon and penalized lesbian-identified people in a variety of ways that the new partnership proposals made evident. The 'Rights and Responsibilities' section of those proposals revealed a range of discriminatory treatment in the areas of immigration, elections, giving evidence in court, making financial decisions on behalf of adults with mental incapacity, prison visiting, hospital visiting and medical care, protection from domestic violence, adoption, parental responsibilities, income-related benefits, dependency increases, state pensions and life insurance. This is in addition to the issues that arise upon the death of one's partner including tenancy succession, intestacy, inheritance, survivor pensions, compensation in areas of fatal accidents and criminal injuries, post-mortems and organ retention, inquests/burials and registering the death of one's partner, some of which has been discussed above. Overall, as Lord Rennard rightly pointed out during the second reading of the Lester's Civil Partnership Bill in the Lords on 25 January 2003, it is fundamentally a matter of respect. 'The registration of a civil partnership is the best way . . . of saying that there should be mutual respect for couples who make a significant commitment to each other' (Lords Hansard, 25 January 2002, col. 1727).

The proposals for civil partnerships did not, however, indicate the range of discriminatory experiences that lesbian-identified persons have faced in the working environment as a result of a legal situation that offered them little acknowledgement or protection of human rights. It was possible to be fired from one's job because of one's sexuality. In a celebrated case from 1974, Tony Whitehead was filmed kissing his boyfriend goodbye at Brighton

---

62 The full wording of the legislation can be accessed at: http://www.legislation. hmso.gov.uk/acts/acts1988/Ukpga_19880009_en_5.htm

station. He was sacked by his employers, British Home Stores. As recently as 1984 conservative MP David Waddington suggested it was 'crankish' to object to someone losing their job because they were gay. In the past decade or so, some employers chose to incorporate anti-discriminatory wording into their equal opportunity policies, but this has been an option rather than a requirement or expectation. In fact, writing in the 1990s, the International Lesbian and Gay Association (ILGA) noted how the precedents set by the Employment Appeals Tribunal have established 'that it can be reasonable for a lesbian or gay man to be dismissed because of public prejudice, the prejudice of other workers in the company or because their job requires them to work with children'.[63] Draft regulations for protection against sex orientation discrimination were circulated for consultation during 2003 and again these proposals made evident the widespread opportunities for discrimination on the basis of one's sexual preferences, opportunities confirmed by a range of surveys conducted over the past ten years.

For example, in the Social and Community Planning Research (SCPR) report compiled by Snape, Thompson and Chetwynd on discrimination against gay men and lesbians in Britain, more than half the lesbian and gay-identified people sampled believed that some employers would refuse jobs or would sack them (1995, p. 18), and there were fears that applications to work in certain spheres would be rejected if their sexual choices were made known. Sure enough, among the 619 heterosexual-identified people sampled there was a 'substantial minority' (over two-fifths) opposing certain career options for gay men: 'teaching at primary or secondary schools; working in the civil service with access to defence secrets; serving as a prison officer; or supervising in youth clubs' (1995, p. 72), with almost a quarter stating that 'homosexual people should be banned from working with children' (1995, p. ix). The report indicated less opposition to lesbians 'but at least around a third of heterosexuals still opposed lesbians working in most of these areas' (1995, p. 72). It concluded that 'many heterosexuals are quite frank about the fact that they would treat homosexuals less favourably than others, and this was the case across a range of situations, confirming the prevalence of prejudice and discriminatory behaviour towards gay men and lesbians' (1995, p. 74).[64] Such opinions surprisingly sit side by side with the

---

63 http://www.ilga.info/Information/legal_survey/europe/United_Kingdom.htm

64 These opinions are supported by numerous discussions in the UK lesbian magazine *Diva* where readers debate how far it is possible to be out in certain careers, most notably teaching and the police force.

fact that two-thirds of the heterosexual-identified interviewees approved of anti-discriminatory legislation – a contradictory situation noted also by Gregory Herek (1998) who notes that the relationship between anti-lesbian/gay thought and behaviour is not necessarily coherent: people's expressed beliefs can run counter to their actions.

The fears of the lesbian and gay-identified interviewees in the SCPR report also resonate with the *actual* experiences of discrimination: 21 per cent reported harassment at work, 8 per cent had been refused promotion and 6 per cent had not been able to pursue the career of their choice. Although Snape et al note that these figures are not 'startlingly high' they rightly remind readers of the need to take into account the ways in which 'people are having to alter their lives to avoid discrimination' which 'is a form of discrimination in its own right' (1995, p. 44). Such figures are reinforced by a number of other studies. The 1995 investigation into the employment experiences of lesbian and gay men, commissioned by Stonewall, indicated that

> 68 per cent of the sample was not 'out' at work because they feared the consequences. There were clearly good reasons for this fear as 48 per cent had been harassed in the workplace because of their sexuality and 8 per cent had lost their jobs because they were homosexual. (Dunne 1997, p. 173)

The SCPR report indicates three ways in which the respondents tackled such discrimination: by secrecy, by restricting public behaviour and by identifying safe(r) environments. On secrecy, some respondents were clearly willing to go to extreme measures to hide their sexuality, booking single rather than requesting double rooms in hotels, attending functions as a single person rather than with their partner, avoiding places associated with gays and lesbians, being silent when homosexuality is discussed, hiding any gay literature or pictures in their home when heterosexual people visit. Some said they would flirt or go out with people of the opposite sex to throw people off the scent, pretend that their same-sex relations are platonic, and feign disgust at homosexuality in order to deflect attention away from themselves and allay suspicions. This could even go as far as getting married for the sake of appearances (1995, pp. 53–4). 'Passing', as it is known, is a survival strategy in a hostile world, motivated by real fear of 'losing custody of children; rejection by friends and family; losing jobs; not being promoted; damaging relationships with clients; blackmail; and potential allegations of child abuse against those working with children' (1995, p. 50). These fears are not without substance. Secrecy, however, is not always a healthy way to tackle discrimination. Enforced suppression of knowledge and emotion can induce physical and psychological symptoms, as has been noted in a range of studies.[65]

Restricting public behaviour is linked to secrecy. Even among the 'out' population, not all are prepared to exhibit their relationships completely freely. There is substantial testimony to a self-enforced restriction of public affection. The in-depth SCPR interviews revealed how people refrained from displays of affection such as kissing or holding hands with their partner. The *Count Me In*[66] Brighton and Hove survey, conducted in 2000 by Spectrum in order to discover the personal, social and community needs of local LGBT people, also found that in a town known for its lesbian and gay population, 66 per cent of respondents deliberately avoided showing public affection for fear of safety. The high figure is not surprising since 60 per cent of respondents had actually experienced abuse, harassment or violence outside the home, with over half listing their sexual orientation as being related to that experience. The 2002 report from Manchester's *First Service* survey[67] on 'relationships, sex, and health among lesbian and bisexual women' found that practically half of all respondents would not show affection to their partner in public for fear of consequences. When asked to itemize what consequences they feared, 29.5 per cent of the respondents mentioned physical assault, 32.9 per cent verbal abuse, 19.9 per cent negative reactions such as 'staring', 'gawking', 'intimidating looks and comments' and 'disapproval', 13.5 per cent noted unspecified abuse while 13.2 per cent mentioned discrimination from employers or neighbours resulting in negative effects upon their children if found out, or possible job loss. The compilers of the report concluded that 'the avoidance of same sex affection is an everyday occurrence for many women' and that 'the fear of homophobic verbal or physical assault and the knowledge that it happens can be

---

65 For an overview of the costs of daily concealment for lesbians in corporate occupations, see Hall (1986); and for a consideration of the 'minority stress' caused by the negative life events that can afflict lesbian-identified women, such as being fired, losing one's home, or one's children and the daily hassles that contribute to such stress, see DiPlacido (1998).

66 The findings of this survey can be accessed at http://www.spectrumbrighton. com/countmein/index.htm

67 The findings of this survey can be accessed at http://www.sigmaresearch.org.uk/ downloads/report02a.pdf

extremely effective as an inhibitor of affection in public between same sex couples' (Henderson et al, 2002, pp. 17, 18). The 2003 *Beyond Barriers* survey[68] of LGBT people in Scotland found that 68 per cent of respondents had, at some time in their life, been verbally abused or threatened by someone who had assumed they were lesbian, gay, bisexual or transgendered. Such abuse had occurred mainly in the streets and it is a problem that is not going away: 35 per cent had experienced this hostility in the past year (2002); 23 per cent had been physically assaulted (the targets of these assaults was more likely to be male and transgender respondents). Such assaults had taken place mainly in the streets but also at school/university or outside a gay venue. The report's compilers note that 'these disturbing statistics are compounded by the under-reporting of these incidents to the police' (Morgan and Bell 2003, p. 43). Such testimonies explain, to some extent, the last strategy, that of finding safe environments.

Socializing with friends in homes or lesbian-friendly venues and segregating this from work and blood-family lives appears to be fairly common. In the SCPR survey around 'a fifth of respondents would look for accommodation in areas where they knew that other homosexuals lived' (Snape et al 1995, pp. 54–5), and some moved to other parts of the country to be near other gays and lesbians. Segregation may go as far as looking for specifically gay-friendly holidays, hotels, hairdressers and painters and decorators. 'This was not necessarily because of fear of violence or abuse but rather because of a desire to avoid the potential hassle of having to cope with discriminatory views' (Snape et al 1995, p. 55).

These strategies indicate clearly how the absence of anti-discriminatory law has led to a climate of justified anxiety for many lesbian-identified individuals. Working in environments where there has been little or no protection against anti-lesbian jokes or comments, dealing with the eternal question of whether or not to come out, the stressors of self-concealment and/or emotional inhibition, inevitably takes its toll. Maggie Magee and Diana C. Miller rightly speak of the everydayness of repeated coming out declarations, but they are also right to point out how 'revealing a lesbian identity or relationship can turn an ordinarily conversational moment into something extra-ordinary' (1995, p. 99) when one never knows for sure what the reaction will be. Certainly, it is often just easier to fall in with the majority and be silent about one's own relationships. It is this sheer unpredictability

---

68 The findings of this survey can be accessed at http://www.beyondbarriers.org.uk/docs/First_Out_PDF-Report.pdf

that gay and lesbian-identified people face in their everyday life that can be so disabling. As Tamsin Wilton says

> One of the hardest things for lesbians and gay men to live with is unpredictability. There is no way of knowing when you get up in a morning whether today will be one of those days when everyone you meet returns your smile, or whether you and your partner will be spat at in the street. (2000, p. 6)

In view of all this, the implementation of the Employment Equality (Sexual Orientation) Regulations at the end of 2003 has been vital; offering legal protection against harassment, victimization, direct and indirect discrimination in the workplace and in applying and training for work. It does not, however, protect lesbian-identified people from the abuse that occurs outside of the workplace.

In conclusion to this section, it has been seen that lesbian-identified persons in England and Wales have faced routine civil discrimination combined with fears of ad hoc violence. This environment is not as unremittingly harsh and the penalties not so severe as those facing state-sponsored criminalization of their life choices in other parts of the world. But, as one contributor to the counselling book *Pink Therapy* puts it: 'Lesbians, gay men and bisexuals spend every day of their lives knowing that some sections of society wish they did not exist' (Davies 1996, p. 54). The effects of living in such an environment can be manifested in low self-esteem, depression, drug abuse, alcoholism, self-harm and ultimately suicide. Notwithstanding, it is important to note before closing this section that lesbian-identified people are not necessarily victims. They can be fighters and survivors. For all the documentation on how physical and mental health problems ensue from one's criminalized and stigmatized positioning, Joanne DiPlacido (working within an American context) points to various studies indicating how the psychological adjustment of lesbians are no different, on average, from that of heterosexuals (Gonsiorek, 1991), that there are actual advantages to be found (Garnets and Kimmel, 1993), and argues that the situation can foster qualities such as 'hardiness', defined as 'the ability to face the situations with feelings of challenge, control and commitment' (DiPlacido 1998, p. 144).

Life in the Margins: The Religious Sponsorship of Discrimination

Finally, we turn to the ways in which certain strands of religious discourse, mainly Christian in this discussion, have contributed to this climate of oppression by supporting the criminalization of lesbian-identified people and by hindering progressive attempts to remedy instances of civil discrimination.

It is not always possible to distinguish between genuine anti-lesbian/gay religious discourse and governmental appropriation of a religious discourse to support their agenda. Thus it was in a *state*-sponsored Zimbabwean newspaper in which this advertisement appeared in 1997: 'CRUSADE AGAINST RAPISTS AND HOMOSEXUALS. God commands the death of sexual perverts. Our culture and traditional justice system condemns them to death. Our religion condemns them to death' (Donnelly 2003, pp. 230–1). In Kenya, during September 1999, it was the president, Daniel arap Moi, who denounced homosexuality as a 'scourge' on the grounds that it was against African tradition and biblical teachings: 'It is not right that a man should go with another man, or a woman with another woman. It is against African tradition and biblical teachings. I will not shy from warning Kenyans against the dangers'.[69] In Namibia, President Sam Nujoma grounded his call for discrimination against sexual minorities in the workplace in the claim that homosexuality is against God's will and is 'the devil at work'. [70] When President Museveni called upon the public to search actively for homosexuals, lock them up and charge them, at the opening of a 1999 meeting on Reproductive Health, he called upon the Bible for legitimation saying: 'the Bible spells it out clearly that God created Adam and Eve as wives and husbands, but not men to marry men'.[71] In Zambia, President Frederick Chiluba used the 1998 Independent Anniversary Thanksgiving and Rededication Service at the Cathedral of the Holy Cross in Lusaka to claim: 'Homosexuality is the deepest level of depravity. It is unbiblical and abnormal.'[72]

---

69 http://www.ilga.info/Information/Legal_survey/africa/kenya.htm

70 See Keith Boykin's report 'Black Homophobia Contributes to Persecution of GLBT Africans' at http://www.mask.org.za/SECTIONS/AfricaPerCountry/ABC/all%20africa/all%20africa_7.htm

71 http://www.ilga.info/Information/Legal_survey/africa/supporting%20files/gays_are_main_evil.htm

72 http://www.ilga.info/Information/Legal_survey/africa/supporting%20files/zambia__the_birth_of_a_movement.htm. Chris McGreal's report for ILGA notes that such attacks, presenting homosexuality as a by-product of colonization, serve to

It is certainly not the case that all religious leaders and members would unequivocally support the vitriolic rhetoric of their politicians. On the other hand, it is abundantly evident that there *has* been a sustained opposition from religious figures and institutions to any political attempts to provide basic human rights for lesbian and gay-identified people. Jack Donnelly (2003, p. 230) notes how it was religious leaders who called for the execution of two men in India who had attempted to celebrate a public marriage, when the maximum punishment for the arrested men would have been life-imprisonment. He notes how religious leaders in Petaling Jaya, Selangor State, Malaysia supported and encouraged local vigilante groups to hunt out the lesbian and gay-identified people in their neighbourhoods. He also notes how representatives of the Church in Africa have been vehemently opposed to any slackening of discriminatory precedents. In Uganda for example, the Church has actively resisted the attempts of gay and lesbian members of their churches to form supportive networks. *Behind the Mask* reports that leaders of Uganda's house of bishops have called upon the government to deny the application of *Integrity Uganda* to become a registered society, describing the organization as 'unbiblical and inhuman' and simply a front for decadent US gays and lesbians. Alfred Zulu, President of the Zambia Independent Monitoring Team, has noted the encouragement of the religious right in ensuring the exclusion of gay and lesbian society in Zambia. In Zimbabwe, the Church has been known to support the provocative statements of President Robert Mugabe. When the World Council of Churches met for the eighth general assembly in Harare 1998, local churches opposed the Gay and Lesbians of Zimbabwe (GALZ)'s request to be present for the public discussion period. Two years prior, Anglican Bishop Jonathan Siyachitema, president of the hosting Zimbabwe Council of Churches (ZCC), at a press conference announcing the forthcoming event, said, 'We are not going to allow, as a Christian body, gays in our council and destroy that which we cherish: our culture.' When it became clear that the Anglican lay Ecumenical Support Services *were* prepared to sponsor GALZ's application, this bishop whipped up press support for his stance, stressing the opposition of the ZCC: 'We feel that Zimbabweans should not be coerced into a practice that is alien to them.' And in overt support of Mugabe's opinions, the Evangelical Fellowship of

---

galvanize opinion around a common scapegoat and thereby deflect attention from the countries' problems. See http://www.ilga.info/Information/Legal_survey/africa/ supporting%20files/gays_are_main_evil.htm

Zimbabwe declared that they were ashamed to find that it is the 'politicians ... who have to preach to the church that homosexuality is wrong'. Such accounts evidence the religious sponsorship of discriminatory practice against homosexuals and the close links that can be forged between Church and state.[73]

Both Aarmo (1999) and Epprecht (1998) argue that there is a significant interlink between Church and state in Zimbabwe. Both religious leaders and politicians have joined forces and taken the common line that

> homosexual behaviour is 'un-African,' a foreign 'disease' that was introduced by white settlers and that is now principally spread by foreign tourists and ambassadors. This belief underlies recent state and church rhetoric about expunging homosexuals from the body politic and returning [to] 'traditional' family values. (Epprecht 1998, p. 632)

Epprecht later adds: 'Christian church leaders are *at the forefront* of the demonstration in support of [Mugabe's] stance' and that the

> 1997 crusade against rapists and homosexuals was announced by Bible thumper Michael Mawema. His call for castration, public whippings and stoning to death of convicted 'perverts' were all justified by reference to Corinthians, Leviticus and spurious 'scientific studies' from the West. (Epprecht 1998, p. 647)

This, all within a context where 'some of the fastest growing "churches" are fundamentalist sects that propagate both anti-feminist and explicitly homophobic translations of the Bible imported from the United States' (Epprecht 1998, p. 647). Elsewhere in the world, it often seems to be the case that for each step of progress made secularly, there is a backlash religiously. As sodomy laws began to be repealed across the United States, as the English Houses of Commons and Lords debated progressive legislation such as the equalization of the age of consent, the lifting of the ban on gays and lesbians in the military, permitting same-sex couples to adopt or foster, and repealing Section 28, the religious right have mobilized swift counter-campaigns to inform and arm their governmental representatives with data upon which they can mount opposition to proposed legislation.

The opposition to secular advances is particularly evident now that

---

73 Cited in the Human Rights Watch paper 'The Spread of Homophobic Rhetoric in Southern Africa'. This can be accessed at http://www.hrw.org/reports/2003/safrica/safriglhrc0303-02.htm

legislation for civil registered partnerships has begun to appear more widely. In Brazil, where the Civil Registered Partnerships Bill which would grant inheritance, pensions, health benefits, tax benefits, social benefits and immigration rights to same-sex couples was approved by a Special Parliamentary Committee in 1996, there was strong resistance from the Catholic Church as the bill moved through the parliament. The head of the national bishops' conference declared the bill immoral and in violation of God's law.[74] In England and Wales the Civil Partnership Bill has similarly been staunchly opposed by the Christian Institute whose 2002 paper described the bill as 'wrong and misconceived', promoting 'counterfeit marriage'.[75] The Christian Institute also published documents to counter the government's employment equality regulations discussed further below.[76] These are not insignificant documents. They provide data for the purposes of parliamentary opposition to reform. In the House of Lords debate on Lord Lester's Bill on Civil Partnership, Lord Lester clearly discovers towards the end of the debate that some of the members had received the 'Counterfeit Marriages' briefing (Lords Hansard, 25 January 2002, col. 1743), and the effect of the Institute's document can clearly be seen in the discussion.[77] Its influence was also later detected in the amendment to the government's subsequent bill at the report stage in July 2004. Effectively halting the progress of this legislation, the amendment proposed that the law should be extended to cover family members who live together on a long-term basis – such as a daughter caring for an elderly mother. Participants to the discussion effectively reproduced the examples provided by the Christian Institute. Despite Lord Alli's reminder that 'This Bill is about same-sex

---

74 http://www.lgirtf.org/newsletters/Spring97/6.html

75 The paper 'Counterfeit Marriage: How "Civil Partnerships" Devalue the Currency of Marriage' prepared by Hart, Calvert, Dobson and Woodward is available online at http://www.christian.org.uk/pdfpublications/counterfeit-marriage.pdf

76 Their summary document 'Squeezing Churches Into a Secular Mould. How Planned Government Employment Laws Threaten Religious Liberty' was published in December 2002 and is available online at http://www.christian.org.uk/pdfpublications/employ_regs_leaflet_dec2002.pdf. This was followed in January 2003 by 'Implementing the EU Employment Directive' produced by Ian Leigh and Colin Hart which is available at http://www.christian.org.uk/directive2003/seminar.pdf

77 The statistics provided on pages 5 and 26 of the Institute's paper and the Institute's main claim that civil partnerships will undermine marriage were repeatedly reflected in the Lords debate (see, for example, the comments of the Lord Bishop of Winchester, Lords Hansard, 25 January 2002, Col. 1704). There are several further examples of how the Institute's paper had an influential role in the discussion.

couples whose relationships are completely different from those of siblings' and his suspicion that Baroness O'Caithain's amendment 'is a fig leaf to disguise her opposition to the Bill' (Lords Hansard, 24 July 2004, col. 1369, 1370), the amendment was agreed by 148 votes to 130. While Stonewall is sympathetic to a revision of tax law for such relationships, the organization points out that this is a separate issue requiring a family and domestic partnership bill.

As an influential organization, it is worthwhile noting how the two papers from the Christian Institute position 'homosexuals'. In the 'Counterfeit Marriage' document, the contrast between its language and that of the government's paper is stark. The Institute steadfastly resists referring to same-sex couples as families while Jacqui Smith's foreword to the government paper readily does so:

> There are thousands of same-sex couples living in stable and committed partnerships. These relationships span many years with couples looking after each other, caring for their loved ones and actively participating in society; in fact, living in exactly the same way as any other family. They are our families, our friends, our colleagues and our neighbours. (Women and Equality Unit 2003, p. 9)

She concludes:

> I believe there will be a day when same-sex couples don't have to struggle to have their partnerships and their families recognized.
> I am confident that our plans for civil partnership registration will be an important step towards bringing that day closer. (Women and Equality Unit 2003, p. 9)

The government paper presents lesbian couples as people prepared to make a 'very strong commitment to each other . . . agreeing to support each other financially and emotionally throughout their lives' (Women and Equality Unit 2003, p. 30). It recognizes, realistically, that this is not always going to be achieved and caters for irretrievable breakdown by suggesting that divorce can be sought after one year of partnership (with the consent of both parties, five years without such consent). Significantly, the government's proposals do not get tangled in issues of sexual activity. The language is only of 'long term, stable relationships' (2003, p. 10) with 'rights and responsibilities' (2003, p. 11). There is nothing about defining same-sex couples by reference to the sex life of the partners whatsoever. The proposals do, therefore, incorporate lifelong friends who have chosen to live together celibately and those choosing to enter into civil partnerships need not have any assumptions made about their sex lives. In this respect, the government's proposals cater for a range of relationships in ways that would be consistent with Rich's lesbian continuum of same-sex friendships that may or may not be genitally expressed.

The Christian Institute, on the other hand, places its emphasis squarely on the temporary and unstable nature of same-sex relationships. Rather than the language of 'family' we have the language of 'liaisons' and 'the hop-on-hop-off merry-go-round of cohabitations' which constructs same-sex relationships as transient, easily dissolved unions. Their report uses selective articles to demonstrate how gay writers themselves have argued that complete monogamy may not be desirable or possible to sustain. It cites, for example, Andrew Sullivan's *Virtually Normal* where he says that in gay partnerships 'there is more likely to be greater understanding of the need for extramarital outlets between two men than between a woman and a man' (1996, p. 202). While it seems that the Institute has gay men in view here rather than lesbians, there is no reference to the long-term relationships between women noted in some texts and articles.[78] The report reserves 'true love' as a characteristic only of heterosexual marriage; the implication being at best that same-sex couples cannot aspire to such love, at worst it implies that same-sex 'liaisons' are the product of lesser, more dubious motivations.[79] The Christian Institute also misrepresented Lord Lester's bill insofar as it emphasizes the *sexually active* nature of same-sex relationships, something that both the bill and the subsequent consultation paper specifically avoid. The Institute's paper does later concede that 'The Bill does not require sexual relationships as such, but merely six months of

---

78 Rochelle Klinger's summary of 11 studies on 50 or more lesbian-identified couples indicated that the 'mean longevity' of relationships was two to five years, but the full range was between one and 34 years and the figures were compromised by the impossibility of obtaining a representative sample due to 'homophobia and fear of disclosure' and the study's class and race bias (Klinger 1996, p. 33). For discussions of long-term relationships see Taverner (2001, pp. 10–13), Johnson (1990) and Holmlund (1999).

79 It may be that this is what was in the mind of Lord Bishop of Guildford when he supported the fact that civil partnership at least acknowledged 'relationships based on love and friendship' rather than 'the shallow or abusive relationships based on power, expediency or pecuniary gain' (Lords Hansard, 25 January 2002, col. 1721).

living together under the same roof, by two individuals who are not closely related' (2002a, p. 23), but the dogged determination to define same-sex couples as sexually active results in the statement that 'registration will probably be perceived as a statement of sexuality, and therefore avoided by routine house-sharers' (2002, p. 23). In the parliamentary debate on his bill, Lester's response was to re-emphasize the actual position:

> My Bill in no way depends on there being a sexual relationship for the civil partnership to be able to operate. I hope that that is clear. It is true that we have been cautious in excluding close members of the family from the civil partnership ... partly because we were concerned that people might think that we were promoting, for example, incestuous relationships and partly because of the problems of multiple partners – if there are many brothers and sisters, how does one pick out who will be the civil partner? How will one stop them from squabbling with one another and how will one stop abuse? (Lords Hansard, 25 January 2002, col. 1745)

The Institute's reluctance to recognize that companionate same-sex relations can come under civil partnership legislation is telling. As noted above, the government proposals are, probably unconsciously, quite in accordance with Rich's lesbian continuum insofar as companionate relationships are catered for in the legislation. In so doing it implies that the lesbian label can be broad and incorporate a range of relationships that do not necessarily include physical expressions of love and affection. The Institute, however, narrows the definition of lesbian to one who commits sexual acts, strongly objecting that two old ladies who had lived together for 40 years would have to 'pretend to be lesbians to benefit from the changes'. The Christian Institute is forced into this position because it is caught in the Church's distinction between the 'sinner' and the 'sin', where a compassionate and welcoming attitude of lesbian-identified people exists simultaneously with the condemnation and rejection of their sexual practices. On the one hand, the 'compassionate' line enables the Church to distance itself from any actions that could be categorized as homophobic or as encouraging homophobia. For example, the Roman Catholic Church deplores the ways in which 'homosexual persons have been and are the object of violent malice in speech or in action' and advocates 'condemnation from the Church's pastors wherever it occurs'.[80] Similarly, the Church of England's *Issues in*

---

80 Congregation for the Doctrine of the Faith, 'Letter to the Bishops of the Catholic Church on the Pastoral Care of Homosexual Persons', October 1986, point 10.

Human Sexuality (1991) calls upon Christians to reject all forms of hatred of homosexual people and to protect those who are victimized. Such compassionate positions also include strong statements concerning the dignity and worth of lesbian-identified people. The Roman Catholic 1986 Letter to the Bishops speaks of respect for the 'intrinsic dignity of each person' and the later document 'Considerations Regarding Proposals to Give Legal Recognition to Unions Between Homosexual Persons' states that men and women with homosexual tendencies 'must be accepted with respect, compassion and sensitivity. Every sign of unjust discrimination in their regard should be avoided'.[81]

However, this talk of intrinsic dignity is severely compromised by the Church's resistance to secular legislation that seeks to enshrine that dignity with a series of rights. In response to the spread of civil partnership schemes across the world, the Vatican has issued a paper calling upon every Catholic politician to vote against such proposals since 'to vote in favour of a law so harmful to the common good is gravely immoral' and if legislation is already in force, the Catholic politician must oppose it and strive to repeal the law. It is rather disturbing to read the letter's expectation that when 'civil legislation is introduced to protect behavior to which no one has any conceivable right', then one should not be surprised if 'irrational and violent reactions increase'.[82] Dignity, it seems, is a right reserved only for lesbians who remain in the allotted space: Lesbians who are celibate, who accept that they are 'objectively disordered', that their acts 'go against the natural moral law', 'do not proceed from a genuine affective and sexual complimentarity' and can 'under no circumstances' be approved; who thus do not deserve those rights automatically available to heterosexuals.[83]

This paradoxical approach is often unconvincingly referred to as 'loving the sinner and hating the sin' and is worth a brief digression to note how this much-vaunted 'compassionate' stance is the velvet glove that tries to soften and disguise the reality of the iron fist. In my own tradition, the Salvation Army positions the lesbian in essentialist terms as one who has a 'disposi-

---

81 Congregation for the Doctrine of the Faith, 'Considerations Regarding Proposals to Give Legal Recognition to Unions Between Homosexual Persons', June 2003. Available at: http://www.vatican.va/roman_curia/congregations/cfaith/documents/rc_con_cfaith_doc_19861001_homosexual-persons_en.html

82 Congregation for the Doctrine of the Faith, 'Considerations Regarding Proposals to Give Legal Recognition to Unions Between Homosexual Persons', June 2003.

83 Congregation for the Doctrine of the Faith, 'Considerations Regarding Proposals to Give Legal Recognition to Unions Between Homosexual Persons', June 2003, point 4.

tion' that cannot be rectified at will. As such she should not bear any blame for having such a disposition. Indeed, the Salvation Army's positional statement opposes any 'victimization of persons on the grounds of sexual orientation and recognizes the social and emotional stress and the loneliness borne by many who are homosexual'. And lest this talk of isolation and stress paints too negative a picture, their positional statement affirms that 'same-sex friendships can be enriching, Christ-honouring relationships'.[84] All good news for the well-loved 'sinner', it seems. What of the 'sin'? The 'sin' is identified as 'genitally expressed' behaviour and is clearly denounced: 'whilst we are not responsible for what we are; we are accountable for what we do; and homosexual conduct, like heterosexual conduct, is controllable and may be morally evaluated therefore in the light of scriptural teaching'. On this basis, the Salvation Army will not formally allow any practising lesbian to be a Salvation Army soldier.[85] However, a careful reading of the positional statement makes it clear that she surrenders far more than soldiership: the lesbian who continues to engage in genitally expressed love for another woman is positioned as a rebel who does not yield to Christ's lordship, and who will be held morally accountable for her actions. The severity of this accountability is made clear in the statement's emphasis upon the role of scriptural teaching, which prescribes exclusion from God's kingdom. Evidently, she loses both soldiership and her soul. Notably, the Salvation Army's standpoint, like that of the Church at large, rests entirely upon its interpretation of, and commitment to, a handful of texts that appear to condemn same-sex activity. Paralysed by fear of transgressing these scriptural injunctions, its back is pinned to the wall. This inescapable hurdle undoes the welcoming and accepting words, and the Army, as with other Christian denominations, is enmeshed in this double bind, and all the loving words in the world will not render the dogged condemnation any less oppressive.

Meanwhile, the 'don't ask, don't tell' policy enforces its lesbian-identified members to be secretive about an important aspect of their lives. It means that a range of conversational subjects, usually the most common subjects enjoyed by many heterosexuals, are now out of bounds. Tolerance and

---

84 The Salvation Army's positional statement is available online at: http://www.salvationarmy.org.uk/en/Library/masic/Homosexuality.htm

85 Informally it is a different matter which gives rise to a compassionate, but hypocritical, situation that is certainly not peculiar to the Salvation Army. Comstock's conversations with various pastors and academics involved in the Black Churches in America reveal that the 'don't ask, don't tell' policy is abundantly alive there also.

acceptance thus comes at considerable cost. 'Don't ask, don't tell' actually translates as don't tell us about your anniversaries, your relationship joys and problems, your joint endeavours; don't show any public affection for each other, don't expect joint invitations, don't expect your religious community to honour your commitment to each other. All the basic fundamentals of life that heterosexuals enjoy as a matter of course become at best privileges, and at worst, examples of flaunting one's sexuality. Tolerance is a concession and the trade-off is gaining an artificial acceptance at the cost of invisibility. The problem is that invisibility reinforces the very heteronormativity that needs to be challenged and has damaging consequences for the individual forced to live a double life. It is invidious that 'Honesty and openness are not rewarded by the churches whereas deceit and secrecy are' (LGCM 2000, p. 7), especially when the Jewish and Christian scriptures themselves promote embodied spiritual wholeness.

Returning now to the Christian Institute's positioning of the lesbian, it can be seen that in addition to constructing same-sex relationships as sexually active, non-monogamous merry-go-round liaisons that are not good for children and not repositories of 'true love', the Christian Institute positions lesbians as a tiny proportion of society (claiming same-sex house-holds represent only 0.2 per cent of all households), and in language very reminiscent of Section 28 speaks of how the bill legalizes counterfeit unions and undermines marriage. Simultaneously, marriage is constructed as a public, monogamous commitment for life, biologically ordained in terms of gender: 'Marriage is not an arbitrary construct; it is an "honourable estate" based on the different, complementary nature of men and women – and how they refine, support, encourage, and complete one another' (2002a, p. 7). 'Children are conceived through heterosexual intercourse. The most basic unit of society – the family – is based on biology not ideo-logy. Children need a father and a mother to nurture them. We are made that way' (2002a, p. 9). Marriage is part of 'the natural moral order' (thus Genesis 2.24 is endorsed by Jesus in Matthew 19.4–5), part of the 'corner-stone of society' and 'the primary carrier of values': 'It is in married families that values are most effectively passed down through the generations. It is where children learn right from wrong and where they learn to get along with others and control their own selfish impulses' (2002a, p. 7). The construction of marriage thus implicitly positions same-sex couples not only as non-monogamous transitory arrangements but as immoral unions where values cannot be transmitted which stand in contradiction to the intention of God.

This is not the place to point out the several flaws in the Christian Institute's position. The significance for this chapter lies in the obstacle that the Institute has placed on the path of reform by positioning lesbians in such a negative and unfair light. And as we now move on to the Christian Institute's response to the employment equality regulations, it will be seen that this hindrance continues, together with the preoccupation with narrowly defining lesbians in terms of their sexual activities. In fact, this preoccupation comes even more to the fore.

One of the Institute's main objections to the employment equality regulations was the government's 'ambiguous' definition of sexual orientation; said to be ambiguous because the regulations do not stipulate whether sexual orientation refers simply to attraction or incorporates sexual conduct. For the Institute, such a distinction 'is crucial for Christians' since 'There are many Christian organisations that would employ *celibate* faithful believers who experience sexual attraction to the same sex. But many would not employ someone who is a practising homosexual' (2003, pp. 20, 21). In the original government proposals, it would not have been possible for an employer to uphold such a distinction since the regulations cover indirect discrimination. For example, an employer might make a decision not to hire a *practising* lesbian, arguing that while they had no problem with sexual orientation per se they could only employ those who were celibate. But requiring a lesbian to abstain from sexual conduct puts her and her group at a disadvantage compared to other people, which constitutes indirect discrimination. The Christian Institute thus argued for specific wording so that churches can 'state that they are seeking to employ people who are either sexually celibate or married', a requirement which would 'discriminate equally against homosexuals, heterosexuals and bisexuals'.[86] The report openly concedes that the 'requirements to be married *indirectly discriminate* against homosexuals since they cannot marry' (emphasis added), and expresses no qualms about such discrimination. Ultimately, the final wording of the regulations, which came into force on 1 December

---

86 Looking for aspects of the regulations that can be used to serve this interest, the Institute noted that the government's final paragraph of article 4 stated that individuals working for churches can be required 'to act in good faith and with loyalty to the organisation's ethos'. Seizing on the verb 'act', the Institute said 'religious bodies can argue that they have no objection to employing someone who experiences a same-sex attraction or bisexual attraction, provided they are either celibate or married' (2003, p. 34). This illustrates again the Institute's wish to distinguish between a non-practising 'orientation' and active sexual practices.

2003, gave ground. Discrimination on grounds of sexual orientation can be exercised when 'employment is for purposes of an organized religion' and where the employer stipulates that a specific sexual orientation is required 'because of the nature of the employment and the context in which it is carried out, so as to avoid conflicting with the strongly held religious convictions of a significant number of the religion's followers'.[87]

Overall, these two papers from the Christian Institute provide illustration of the more general findings of the Commission on Christian Homophobia. The Commission's terms of reference were first: 'to investigate and issue a Report on incidents involving discrimination and the abuse of human rights where the victims are lesbian/gay, and when the reason is "justified" by invoking Church/Christian tradition' and second: 'to provide good practice guidelines, and recommendations for the eradication of "Christian homophobia"' (LGCM 2000, p. 4). The first phase of the Commission's work was completed between October 1999 and October 2000, culminating in the publication of a significant report published by the Lesbian and Gay Christian Movement in 2000. The Commission achieved its aims and the report documents the existence of

> Christian homophobia in the areas of employment, ordination, access to church premises, censorship, fostering and adoption, exorcism, expulsion from church membership, deficient equal opportunities policies, and church attempts to gain exemption from crucial sections of human rights legislation – all of them areas which are immeasurably damaging to the integrity, the probity and the honourable status of any Christian church. (LGCM 2000, p. 4)

In more detail: its first key finding was that 'the majority of homophobic abuse suffered by gay men and lesbians in the UK is supported by the words and actions of the Christian churches' (2000, p. 6). The report later adds that for '*every* area of gay law reform in the last three years the government has been forced to introduce compromising amendments or guidelines suggested by the Christian Right' (2000, p. 17). Accordingly, the third key finding is

> That the Christian churches in the UK have had a disproportionate influence on legislation affecting gays and lesbians and have, at every turn, tried to frustrate the will of parliament, defy the international con-

---

87 The full wording of The Employment Equality (Sexual Orientation) Regulations 2003 is accessible at http://www.hmso.gov.uk/si/si2003/20031661.htm

sensus on human rights, and to gain exemptions for themselves from the fair and equal treatment of lesbians and gay men. (LGCM 2000, p. 6)

And the fourth states: 'That in their methods and organization, conservative Christian groups in this country now amount to a "Christian Right" similar to that which has been active in the US for some years' (LGCM 2000, p. 6).

It makes depressing reading. The effects of this religious opposition upon lesbian-identified people within Christian faith communities are very damaging indeed. The eighth and ninth of the 11 key findings of the Commission on Christian Homophobia state that 'lesbian and gay church members are being expelled from congregations, lesbian and gay groups have been refused the use of church premises, church run welfare and housing organisations have specifically excluded gay men and lesbians', and that 'sermons and Christian resource material supporting gay men and lesbians have been censored or destroyed, and that young people in church youth groups and other Christian settings are being indoctrinated into homophobia' (LGCM 2000, p. 6). As a result of such experiences it is of no surprise that some congregants have felt compelled to move to a different branch or denomination, while others have abandoned their religious heritage altogether. When oppression is legitimated by the very scriptures to which one gives allegiance there is inevitably a sense of radical dissonance. Linda McFarlane's review of the experiences of lesbians, gay men and bisexuals in the mental health services reveals that attempts to be Christian, Jewish or Muslim *and* lesbian, gay or bisexual, lead to very discomforting experience of living double lives or having split personalities (1998, pp. 22–5). In the literature dealing with health and well-being for lesbians and gays there is usually a significant proportion of space devoted to ways in which religion has been a damaging influence. Several gay-affirmative books on raising self-esteem, on counselling, or aiding spiritual well-being, contain chapters on counteracting the effects of one's religious upbringing. The dissonance is so strong that it can threaten to force individuals down two equally distressing paths: either stay with one's religious faith, live a life of enforced celibacy or secrecy and bear the severe consequences – or leave. Certainly, abandoning one's faith could be seen as a liberative option. Turning one's back on an apparently oppressive deity, scriptures and condemnatory community could be applauded as an affirming, positive action. However, such drastic action can nevertheless leave its scars and insofar as such a decision may lead a person to abandon the idea of faith and religious life in toto, it impoverishes individuals further, forcing them to choose, sometimes from a very young age between the integration of their self and sexuality and the god presented to them by church, family, culture. Put quite simply, either God goes or the person goes. This huge conflict creates a spiritual lacuna. The therapist working psychospiritually is engaged in guiding the client back to themselves. (Lynch 1996, pp. 203–4)

Conclusion

This chapter has demonstrated that to self-identify as lesbian or to be positioned as such has substantial consequences. I have spent time documenting the diverse nature of those consequences so that readers can have some understanding of the circumstances in which a lesbian-hermeneutic has emerged and in which it is grounded. However, there is a more direct relevance: much of the opposition to same-sex relationships is grounded in scriptural texts. Fearful and righteously indignant about progressive legislation that appears to be ignoring the divine plan for humanity, the religious right are able to present themselves as the guardians of scriptural truth, as the embattled and beleaguered defenders of God's revealed intentions for humankind, the custodians of the 'true' Christianity. The Christian Institute stakes its interest in such a guardianship role when it entitles its summary leaflet 'Squeezing Churches Into a Secular Mould. How Planned Government Employment Laws Threaten Religious Liberty'. The deliberate echo of J. B. Phillips' translation of Romans 12.2 demonstrates the Institute's commitment to stand firm, even if isolated, against a rising tide of secularism. Having lived and worked within a staunchly evangelical organization, I understand this 'backs to the wall' attitude and the genuine anxiety that such legislation provokes. But this only underscores the importance of biblical hermeneutics. At the root of all the dissent and anger stand the Jewish and Christian scriptures. These scriptures, while extolling the primary virtue of loving one's neighbour as oneself, contain a handful of verses that appear to condemn lesbian and gay-identified persons together with an introductory prologue, in Genesis 1–3, that ordains the creation of male and female for the complementary purposes of marriage and procreation. For as long as these scriptures, read uncritically, continue to carry authoritative weight for Jews and Christians, there will be a corresponding opposition to practising same-sex relations. In the light of this situation, a lesbian-identified hermeneutic is vital.

Part 2

Guiding Principles for
Lesbian-Identified Hermeneutics

Introduction

The variety of approaches to scripture emerging in the late twentieth century has demonstrated how well-known texts can yield different and surprising interpretations when the interpretational framework of enquiry is differently angled. Feminists and womanists have done sterling work; shedding light on the role and status of scriptural women, asking new questions, modifying and challenging existing methodologies, raising issues not traditionally incorporated within historical critical exegesis.[88] However, almost the entirety of this work has taken place within a heterocentric frame of reference; one that assumes the heterosexuality of the scriptural women themselves and one that appears to presuppose a heterosexual academic community, since lesbian-related concerns and issues have hardly been given a sentence until very recently. A hermeneutic of suspicion has certainly been operating to ensure that we recognize and expose how the images of scriptural women are inauthentic, stereotyped and caricatured, serving as they do the needs of an andocentric and patriarchal society. It has operated to ensure that we are suspicious of the history of reception where scholars and preachers alike have tended to reinforce those images uncritically and thereby added further damaging layers. Reading against the grain, *mujeristas*, womanists and feminists have taken up reading positions that unpick the narrator's strategies of persuasion, of manipulation, so that the values and ideologies incorporated into the text are exposed rather than absorbed. Yet, for all this good work, the framework of enquiry has remained predominantly heterocentric.

---

88 For review articles on feminist interpretation of Hebrew scriptures, see Anderson (1991), Bach (1993), Exum (1995, 2000), Hackett (1987), Reinhartz (1997), Sakenfeld (1982, 1985). On feminist interpretation for both Hebrew and Christian scriptures, see McKay (1997), Milne (1997), and the collection of essays in Collins (1985) and Russell (1985). For womanist interpretation, see Grant (1989), Martin (1999) and Weems (1988, 1991). For review essays on postcolonial interpretation, see Dube (2000, 2001) and West and Dube (2000).

There are a handful of notable exceptions. Exum's essay on Ruth and Naomi in *Plotted Shot and Painted* examines how the relationship between the two women is renegotiated in Calderon's painting which foregrounds two people in an embrace, possibly Ruth and Boaz, possibly Ruth and Naomi. I remember vividly Exum's reading of this paper at a conference for the Society of Old Testament Study (SOTS). As we all filed into the lecture theatre that evening, Calderon's painting was projected large scale onto the back wall. The erotic pose of the two figures immediately captured (my) attention but I was even more surprised when the possibility of this being indeed a romantic, if not erotic, embrace between a young Ruth and Naomi became a key focus of the paper. The specific paper itself was engaging but I was more intrigued by the general fact that lesbian critical studies had found their way into a SOTS conference. Curiously much of the question-and-answer session that followed centred on the plant to the left of the two figures . . .

Elisabeth Schüssler Fiorenza has repeatedly noted that heterosexism is one of the multiplicative oppressions faced by women and although her interpretations of specific texts do not, as far as I am aware, consider a lesbian-identified perspective, she has encouraged her readers to recognize that such a perspective is very important for some women. In *But She Said* she locates the *ekklēsia* as an umbrella frame of reference within which a range of interpretational strategies can operate and which provides a home for polyglot discourses. She writes:

> Such discourses must render those women who have remained invisible even in feminist discourses visible again. By insisting in its own discourses on the *theoretical* invisibility and difference, for instance, of black, poor, colonial, lesbian, or working women, feminist theory and theology make it clear that 'women' do not have a unitary essence but represent a historical multiplicity not only as a group but also as individuals. Feminist discourse must also take care not to portray one group of women, e.g., lesbians, as monolithic, essentialist, and undifferentiated with no competing interests, values, and conflicts. (1992, p. 131)[89]

This move away from any essentialist location of feminist interpretation is also present in Esther Fuchs' engaging introduction to her study of *Sexual Politics in the Biblical Narrative*. She confesses her nervousness about using a hegemonic 'we' in feminist discourse and mentions sexual orientation as

---

89 See also Fiorenza (1994, pp. 10, 13, 24–5).

one of the differences between women along with race and class (2000, p. 18, n. 23). It is just a brief footnote but, in an important discussion, it is there. The discomfort that Fuchs experiences with speaking of 'we' is also a key issue in Alice Bach's (1993) review essay on feminist biblical criticism as it approached the new millennium. Bach fears that there is a rather unhealthy homogeneity within feminist criticism and warns against the possibility of it becoming normative rather than challenging. When she writes, 'I suspect that every woman, scholar and activist, has multiple relationships with chosen audiences' (1993, p. 193), the implication is that the multiple voices that should permeate feminist biblical criticism are not being raised, or more likely, heard.

In Chapter 1 I argued that lesbian-allied readings or straight-critical readings are welcome and there is much useful work that could be undertaken by scholars already working within the area of feminist, womanist and *mujerista* biblical studies. Bearing in mind the previous chapter's summary of the nature and scale of oppression that lesbian-identified people face in non-western contexts, it is actually vital that allied readings come to the fore, for in the words of Colombian human rights defender, Juan Pablo Ordonez,

> the defence of human rights of homosexuals solely by homosexuals is impossible – or at best, places them in imminent peril of their lives. The struggle must be taken up by outsiders, gay or straight people, who are not themselves the victims of this hostile society. (Amnesty International, 1999)

However, I also concluded that lesbian-identified critics are probably best positioned to begin this work. Lesbian-identified critics who have experienced the routine invisibility of their perspectives have a vantage point and are more equipped to see the gaps and the potential for new avenues of study. Their hetero-suspicion is already well rehearsed and they are in a greater sense of readiness to challenge assumptions, put new questions to the text, apply new methodologies and thereby usefully broaden feminist agendas.

When considering the principles and strategies that might guide a lesbian-identified reading position in this second part of the book, it is important to remember the findings of the first part: that we move into the third millennium with many countries still determinedly upholding laws that criminalize same-sex relationships, with global discrimination in existence, and with the implementation of legislation to protect the basic human rights (not 'special' rights) of lesbian-identified people being hampered and opposed by religious forces. A lesbian-identified approach to scripture is grounded in these lived realities and is committed to changing the way scriptural texts are used to maintain the climate of oppression.

The four following chapters identify principles that could inform and direct an overall frame of reference for lesbian-identified hermeneutics. Within this framework a diverse range of reading methods and strategies can co-exist. The principles, which are not to be read as progressive linear movements but rather as interweaving commitments, are as follows:

1 Resistance: commitment to a hermeneutic of hetero-suspicion
2 Rupture: commitment to the disruption of sex-gender binaries
3 Reclamation: commitment to strategies of appropriation
4 Re-engagement: commitment to making a difference

3

Resistance: commitment to a hermeneutic of hetero-suspicion

Arguably, the single most pressing obstacle to any kind of lesbian-identified critical study is invisibility. Numerous book titles reflect the intangible nature of the subject matter. Terry Castle's *The Apparitional Lesbian*, for instance, demonstrates how the lesbian is a ghostly figure that haunts the scenes of history, the pages of literature and the screens of our cinemas but is never permitted to manifest herself fully. Duberman, Vicinus and Chauncey's *Hidden from History* resists the repression and marginalization that has troubled the field, containing essays that are representative of the reclamation work done in the 1980s. Despite the controversial debate such work arouses (and contributors to *Hidden from History* address these issues), reclamation of the past is a major dimension of secular lesbian and gay studies. In *Lesbian Studies: Setting an Agenda*, Tamsin Wilton notably places 'affirmation' at the top of her syllabus, describing it as salvage activity – making visible the glossed over, the suppressed, the neglected and bringing the presence of those excluded figures and voices into the public domain, resisting the various strategies of marginalization and erasure.

Researchers have already covered a variety of periods and contexts from twentieth-century contexts, back through time and through various geographical settings to Bronze Age Mesopotamia. Inevitably such work raises significant questions about terminology and methodology. The debate that has arisen between so-called essentialists and social constructionists has dominated lesbian and gay studies during the past three decades and its issues inevitably affect projects such as this. Accordingly, this chapter commences with an introductory section on the problem of invisibility, tracing how resistance to the erasure of female homo-eroticism has emerged in secular lesbian-identified studies and noting the critical arguments such work provokes. It discusses the consequences a social constructionist position has for a study that deals primarily with

111

ancient texts and the social world that produced them. This informs a second section focused on the storyworld of the scriptures and the hetero-patriarchal framework in which it is located, a framework that has rendered female homoeroticism all but invisible despite the injunctions against same-sex activity between males. The third section identifies the textual strategies that have contributed to this erasure by obscuring and suppressing female homoeroticism, and considers how these strategies might be disrupted.

Resisting the Erasure of Female Homoeroticism

I have lost count of the number of times I have read stories from people who are now lesbian and/or queer-identified who spent their adolescence searching for literature that would speak to their experiences. A few representative examples will illustrate the point:

Judy Grahn, born in 1940 in Chicago, recounts her 'utter isolation at sixteen, when I looked up *Lesbian* in the dictionary, having no one to ask about such things, terrified, elated, painfully self-aware and grateful it was there at all' (1984, p. xii). She recalls going to a Washington DC library, aged 21, to read about lesbians only to experience the following disturbing event:

> The books on such a subject, I was told by indignant, terrified librarians unable to say aloud the word *homosexual*, were locked away. They showed me a wire cage where the 'special' books were kept in a jail for books. Only professors, doctors, psychiatrists, and lawyers for the criminally insane could see them, check them out, hold them in their hands. (1984, p. xi)[90]

Lillian Faderman, also born in 1940 and brought up in the Bronx, tells how, as a teenager in 1956, 'I began to consider myself a lesbian. Almost as soon as I claimed that identity . . . I looked around for literary representations that would help explain me to myself' (1995, p. vii). But at high school, there were no hints where such literature could be found and at college, as an English literature undergraduate, she only learned of lesbian literature

---

90 James Carmichael notes that 'novels with a homoerotic theme, such as Radclyffe Hall's *The Well of Loneliness* (1928), were usually available only upon request from the public librarian. Library catalog subject headings and classification schemes placed homosexuality with "sexual perversions" or "criminal behaviour," or for more progressive and sympathetic titles, "mental illness" and its analogs' (1998, p. 1).

'in an Abnormal Psych class, where *The Well of Loneliness* was mentioned'. Even when a postgraduate student

> I never had a professor who mentioned the world 'lesbian' or acknowledged that love between women had ever been a subject of literary focus. In 1967 I received a PhD in English without the slightest notion that lesbian literature had a rich history and that many of the writers I admired ... had contributed to that history'. (1995, p. vii)

As she later comments, literature *was* there, but women were either oblivious to it, alienated from it (due to the denial of its existence and the elevation of male relationships with women while trivializing female friendships), or not able to decode it: 'It is much easier to explain her [Louisa May Alcott] female characters' expressions of passionate intensity about each other as a manifestation of overblown Victorian rhetoric rather than the author's intention to convey same-sex love' (1995, p. 441).

Unfortunately, the overt literature that was accessible for those persistent enough to search for it (and brave enough to take it to the cashier), was not exactly positive. Lee Lynch, born in 1945, describes her adolescent years as 'driven, searching for my nourishment like a starveling, grabbing at any crumb that looked, tasted, or smelled digestible' (1990, p. 42). She recalls how the discovery of lesbian pulp fiction, characterized by such titles as *Odd Girl, Twisted Sisters, Twilight Lovers, We Walk in the Shadows, The Evil Friendship, The Twilight Lust, Odd Girl Out, Another Kind of Love* and *Whisper their Love*, was a lifeline.[91] Such fiction, once secured, was not readily let out of the clutches of the owner: 'Ann Bannon's books were so well loved I never even read one until much later. Some treasures were so priceless no one would lend them' (1990, p. 43). But she recognizes now that their images of tragic lesbians who led shadowy, murky existences were doing more harm than good:

> At last, lesbians! I devoured the books, loved the characters, identified completely. This was a mistake. These books, while validating because they acknowledge the existence of lesbians by portraying us, destroyed any incipient pride I might have had in my true fairy self. Titles like *Queer Patterns*, *The Evil Friendship*, and *The Sex Between* were instant signals of gay

---

91 For analysis of the portrayal of lesbians in these novels, see Zimet (1999), Stryker (2001, pp. 49–72, which also includes colour reproductions of the original covers); and for a study of the front-cover depictions of lesbians, see Sova (1998).

books. The characters were more miserable than Sartre's, and despised as well. (1990, p. 40)

But Lynch, like several others, found something intangibly resonant, something often more inspiring, in the chance discoveries of literature that was to all intents and purposes 'straight', but nevertheless spoke to her experience:

> It is amazing how unerring a kid with a variant eye can be . . . Katherine Hume wasn't uncloseted for years, nor were Edna St Vincent Millay, Mary Renault, or Virginia Woolf, but they felt variant to me . . .
>   . . . I found poets, Charlotte Mew and H. D., for example, before the gay scholars had at them. I could have taught a course in gay lit. by the time I hit college.
>   . . . Success depended on a vigilant desperation. I *had* to find reflections of myself to be assured that I was a valuable human being and not alone in the world. (1990, pp. 41–2)

Alison Hennegan likewise speaks of 'her' Greeks; sources that had virtually no women's voices, but which spoke of a world where heterosexuality was not the inevitable destiny of all humans. The fact that the same-sex bonds were all between men did not matter since, in part

> I spent at least half my adolescence 'being male' inside my own head . . . I never for one moment thought I was a man nor wished to be. But somehow I had to find a way of thinking of myself which included the possibility of desiring women. (1988, p. 170)

Thus it was that she could identify with and appreciate Achilles' grief when Patroclus died, for what she was looking for primarily were 'strong and passionate emotions which bound human beings to members of their own sex rather than to the other' (1988, p. 170).

These testimonies reveal a longing for literature that contained themes, characters and storylines that represented the reader's own experience of same-sex desire; and frustration that such literature was not easily accessible. In hindsight, some of these teenagers of the 1950s suggest that the struggle to find amenable literature had its merits in terms of character formation and learning the skills of reading aslant. However, it demonstrates how each woman had to embark upon her own individual journey with virtually no community support, little library help, no existing reviews of available titles. These women, together with those who collect, categorize and store the material collated in several archives around the world, have spent their lives educating their own and future generations, but their personal struggles to overcome their sense of isolation evident in their descriptions of avid searches for meaningful literature, are testimony to the way in which this topic of women's relationships with women is buried, untold, screened by heterocentric assumption and expectation. But this struggle was one that was already being recycled.

In a previous generation Virginia Woolf bemoaned the absence of literature that dealt seriously and at length with the subject of women's relationships with women. In the fifth chapter of *A Room of One's Own*, Woolf has the narrator consider a fictional text (entitled *Life's Adventures* by Mary Carmichael) that contained the sentence 'Chloe liked Olivia'. As her narrator leads up to this point Woolf has her abruptly break off the flow of the sentence and ask:

> Are there no men present? Do you promise me that behind that red curtain over there the figure of Sir Chartres Biron is not concealed? We are all women you assure me? Then I may tell you that the very next words I read were these – 'Chloe liked Olivia . . . ' Do not start. Do not blush. Let us admit in the privacy of our own society that these things sometimes happen. Sometimes women do like women.
>
> 'Chloe liked Olivia,' I read. And then it struck me how immense a change was there. Chloe liked Olivia perhaps for the first time in literature. (1929, p. 123)

The narrator goes on to decry the way in which fictional women have always appeared in relation to the men in their lives. And 'how small a part of a woman's life is that', she adds (1929, p. 124). The complexities of women's lives and relationships outside that male-oriented framework are neglected. Imagining literature that would take seriously the fact that 'Chloe liked Olivia' and be willing to explore the world of women, she says that such literature would 'light a torch in that vast chamber where nobody has yet been' where at present it is 'all half lights and profound shadows' (1929, p. 126). It might 'catch those unrecorded gestures, those unsaid or half-said words, which form themselves, no more palpably than the shadows of moths on the ceiling, when women are alone, unlit by the capricious and coloured light of the other sex' (1929, p. 127).

Some 66 years later, in a book whose title calls attention to Virginia Woolf's reference, Faderman writes:

> Woolf was predicting what must have seemed all but impossible in her day: a non-medical literature that would unmask the subject of love between women. *She was not aware, apparently, that there had already been such a literature in the centuries before Krafft-Ebing and Freud* ... works about female-female relationships that preceded her and that her era had forgotten or lacked the knowledge to decode. (1995, p. viii emphasis added)

Faderman thus calls attention to the frustrating cycle of finding and losing one's voice and history. Lillian Faderman, Lee Lynch, Virginia Woolf, all at some time in their lives found themselves looking for a body of literature that spoke meaningfully and substantially about the subject of women's relationships and desire. But just as the intellectual thought and practical activities of women fall quickly into obscurity so that new generations have to 'find' their history and be re-educated in wave after wave of feminist study, the topic of women's relationships with each other is repeatedly lost, obscured, suppressed and/or erased, so that generations of young people growing up in the first decades of the twenty-first century *still* feel as if they are the only one and have sparse knowledge of the rich history that has been researched and published during the past century. The letters written to the editor of *Diva*, expressing relief and joy to have found such a magazine and to have discovered that they are not alone, indicate how the situation of recycling continues: 'Thanks for producing such an excellent magazine,' says Lisa Pascoe of Portsmouth. 'I came out last November and *Diva* really made me feel part of something good. It's nice to know you're not completely alone in the world' (*Diva*, October 1999, p. 4). Karen similarly expresses her thanks for relieving the isolation:

> I just wanted to let you know how great it is to have a gay magazine to read. I'm 16, and until a few weeks ago thought I was the only gay girl in the whole world ... It's so great to know that I'm not alone, and the attitude my mum has is not the same as everyone else. (*Diva*, July 1998, p. 4)

In her article 'Who Hid Lesbian History', Faderman notes how biographers have repeatedly ignored or discounted their subject's relationship with women through bowdlerization, deliberate avoidance of the obvious, and the 'heterosexualization' of women's biographies by emphasizing, or

116

even inventing, relationships with men. Thus William Godwin's *Memoirs of Mary Wollstonecraft* interprets Wollstonecraft's depression not in terms of her passion for Fanny Blood, but as due to her mad love for the Rev. Joshua Waterhouse, despite lack of evidence for any such intense love. The letters and papers of Emily Dickinson have been purged of reference to her love for Susan Gilbert. Dickinson's niece, Martha Dickinson Bianchi, 'felt compelled to hide what her aunt expressed without self-consciousness' (Faderman 1982, p. 118), as can be seen in a comparison of Bianchi's (1924) edition of Dickinson's letters with that of T. Johnson and T. Ward (1958). There are many other such examples of the erasure of same-sex passions by families and publishers who hotly contest the 'lesbian' content of a deceased family member's letters, diaries and/or other papers, declaring this an unwarranted imposition upon innocent correspondence.[92]

Academics have also played their role and some scholars, such as Rictor Norton (1997, 2003), are frustrated by the theoretical straitjacket that has been imposed around the subject, contesting what can and cannot be the subject of 'lesbian' critical studies. When Faderman published *Chloe Plus Olivia* subtitled *An Anthology of Lesbian Literature from the Seventeenth Century to the Present*, she acknowledged that she used the lesbian label broadly and anachronistically since women of the seventeenth to the nineteenth centuries 'would have recognized themselves instead as belonging to other categories with which they were familiar, and which do not exist today' (1995, p. viii). Her justification for inclusion was that their writing 'contributes meaningfully to an illustration of the various genres in which love between women has been treated' (1995, p. xii). Her defence reflects the pressure on all academics to justify any use of the term 'lesbian' outside its use from the late nineteenth century onwards.

The scholarly debate is usually framed around the categories of social constructionism and essentialism. Broadly speaking, those who have implied that sexual orientation is an inherent biological drive existing independently of social forces and argued that what is now predominantly referred to as lesbian desire can be found *invariably* in most cultures and periods, are cast into the essentialist camp. Those who believe that sexuality is constructed by contextual social forces and argue that the 'lesbian' as we know her today is a specific construction of the late nineteenth century, who does not have any direct link with female homoeroticism as expressed in other

---

92 For a range of examples, see the essays by the Lesbian History Group (1996), Edwards (1995) and Cook (1979).

cultures and at other times, occupy the social constructionist ground. Thus the social constructionist David Halperin argues that 'sexuality does not refer to some positive physical property . . . that exists independently of culture; it does not rightly denote some common aspect or attribute of bodies. Unlike sex, which is a natural fact, sexuality is a cultural production: it represents the *appropriation* of the human body and of its erogenous zones by an ideological discourse. Far from reflecting a purely natural and uninterrupted recognition of some familiar facts about us, sexuality represents a peculiar turn in conceptualizing, experiencing, and institutionalizing human nature, a turn that . . . makes the transition to modernity in northern and western Europe' (1990. p. 25). He later adds:

> Instead of attempting to trace the history of 'homosexuality' as if it were a *thing*, therefore, we might more profitably analyze how the significance of same-sex sexual contacts has been variously constructed over time by members of human living-groups . . . The sort of history that will result from this procedure will no longer be gay history as John Boswell tends to conceptualize it (i.e., as the history of gay people), but it will not fail to be gay history in a different, and perhaps more relevant, sense: for it will be history written from the perspective of contemporary gay interests. (1990, p. 29)

Given Judith Butler's (1990) interrogation of the category of 'sex', Halperin is over-optimistic when he refers to it as a 'natural fact'. Nevertheless, the quotation does helpfully offer a social constructionist view of sexuality.[93]

Social constructionism emerged as an antidote to the popular 'we are everywhere' slogan that emerged in the aftermath of the Stonewall riot when self-identifying lesbians and gays came out of the closet in greater numbers than ever before to mobilize as a community. A surge of interest in locating a gay and lesbian heritage put that slogan into the past tense – 'we were everywhere' – as early attempts were made to make visible the presence

---

93 Social constructionist perspectives are informed by Berger and Luckmann (1966) and labelling theory within sociology. Early essays that pioneered the social constructionist perspective include McIntosh (1968), Plummer (1975), Weeks (1977), Foucault (1978), Padgug (1979) and the contributors to Plummer (1981) and Chauncey (1984). For debate on social constructionist and essentialist perspectives, see Epstein (1987), and the essays in Altman et al (1989), Duberman et al (1990), Stein (1992) and Seidman (1996). Application of a social constructionist perspective, as seen in the documentation of how lesbian and gay identities developed in specific contexts and periods can be found, for example, in Altman (1982) and Katz (1983).

of lesbians and gay men in different periods and cultures. Popular books of lists were published indicating that great geniuses from the past such as Plato, Sappho, Michelangelo, Leonardo da Vinci, William Shakespeare, Alfred Lord Tennyson, Benjamin Britten, André Gide, Emily Dickinson, etc. belonged to a gay ancestry.[94] Writers like Judy Grahn (1984) embarked upon the project of tracing a continuous history that would offer her readers a long, rich cultural tradition. At the time, the slogan and projects like these were politically useful. If one can demonstrate that same-sex relationships permeate societies cross-culturally and throughout time, and that some of the greatest figures of western civilization were 'gay' or 'lesbian', then this undermines accusations that such relationships are unnatural, sick or sinful.

However, as scholars began researching 'gay' and 'lesbian' history in the wake of early gay liberation politics (c. 1970 onwards), what became clear was that although same-sex activities are indeed a cross-cultural observable fact, homoerotic behaviour is not a uniform, universal phenomenon but something that has to be assessed in terms of the context in which it is found. Accordingly, social constructionists distanced themselves from popular publications of the mid to late twentieth century that had promoted the 'we are everywhere' belief, grounded in a so-called essentialist perspective.[95] Jeffrey Weeks, for example, argues that while same-sex behaviour 'has existed in a variety of different cultures' as 'an ineradicable part of human sexual possibilities', attitudes towards it are 'wholly specific and have varied enormously across different cultures and through various historical periods'. It is, accordingly, 'no longer possible to talk of the possibility of a universalistic history of homosexual behavior' (1996, p. 42). Likewise, David Halperin, in an influential publication *One Hundred Years of Homosexuality*, cautioned: 'It may well be that homosexuality properly speaking has no history of its own outside the West or much before the beginning of our century' (1990, p. 18). Thus, any suggestion that a 'homo-

---

94 See, for example, Garde (1964), Rutledge (1987, 1989), Richards (1990), Fletcher and Saks (1990).

95 The essentialist position has largely been constructed by social constructionism, and to some extent its ground is occupied by the proverbial straw man. However, this does not necessarily indicate that the idea of 'essentialism' is vacuous. Vance (1989) suggests that the essentialist perspective, like a heterosexist perspective, has not been in the business of naming or exploring itself. It has been an unmarked category, part of the dominant hegemony, that attracts attention and labelling only in the wake of alternative ideas.

sexual person', i.e. one who self-identified and who was acknowledged by others as a distinctive sexual category with a particular innate orientation, had a pre-nineteenth-century history was criticized. A social construction-ist perspective accordingly calls into question any reclamation of figures from the past as belonging to a 'gay' or 'lesbian' ancestry.[96] As Eric Savoy neatly puts it:

> Social-constructionist scholarship has effectively and necessarily short-circuited the desire to colonize the historical field in the name of an already problematic, contemporary 'gay identity' by questioning what might count as 'historical presence', by extension, thoroughly disrupting the illusion of a *coherent* trans-historical homosexual subjectivity. (1994, p. 131)

This academic debate does not limit one's research to the late nineteenth century onwards; what it does mean is that if one is investigating different culture and time periods, then terminology has to be clearly defined and anachronism avoided. It would be considered naive to look for 'lesbians' in the social worlds that produced the scriptures, if, by using that term, one is imagining that there is any kind of direct chronological link between women's relations in those worlds and twenty-first-century CE notions of 'lesbians'. Our understanding of 'lesbian' identities is culturally con-tingent and ideologically loaded and, as such, the 'lesbian' category can-not be applied transculturally and transhistorically. However, while there is no direct ancestry to be found in the scriptures (in terms of an invari-able lesbian consciousness that connects 'us' with 'them'), this does not mean that the phenomenon of female homoeroticism was non-existent, or that lesbian-identified people of the twenty-first century must consider themselves entirely cut off from a perceived past. While the work of social constructionists can give the impression that there is a 'no lesbians before 1900' school of thought, as Terry Castle puts it (1993, pp. 8–10), they are not suggesting that women's relationships with women are solely a modern concept. It is clearly acknowledged that same-sex relations have existed in the majority of cultures in all time periods, but they are organized and understood in culturally specific ways that may differ considerably from modern relations and have to be understood on their own terms.

It is not just an issue of semantics, of saying let us not use the word 'lesbian'

---

96 For further details consult Halperin's (1990) essays, some of which respond to John Boswell's work on 'gay history'. See also the debate among Boswell, Halperin and Padgug in Duberman et al (1990).

for pre-nineteenth-century and/or non-western contexts, but not rule out the likelihood that such women experienced desire for members of their own sex. Such a manoeuvre does not adequately address the question of whether sexual desire itself can be posited for a culture where what counts as 'sex' may be different and when 'sexuality' may not be seen as an inherent part of one's identity. Historical research requires a more sophisticated strategy, of which Valerie Traub's work is a good example.

Traub uses a 'lesbian-affirmative analytic, one that begins with the assumption of the worth and variety of female emotional and physical ties, and moves from there to explore the ways such ties are portrayed' (2002, p. 13). Such emotional and physical premodern ties may be manifest in 'caresses, kisses, bodily penetration, and passionate verbal addresses expressing longing, loss, devotion, frustration, pleasure and pain' (2002, p. 13). However, she draws a firm distinction between these premodern relationships and our contemporary understanding and use of the lesbian signifier. The representations of female homoeroticism she finds

> do not provide clear antecedents or stable historical ground for contemporary *lesbian* identities . . . my book does not push the birth of the *lesbian* back in time but, rather, pluralizes the notion of origins, multiplies sites of emergence, and traces various strands of influence. (2002, p. 27)

Consequently, Traub deliberately resists 'the temptation to make historical inquiry culminate in a politics of identity'. She is aware of the importance of identity politics in the contemporary world but also is aware that such politics can 'operate as a stranglehold, limiting the questions one asks and thus the answers one finds', reducing the examination of homoeroticism 'to the critical equivalent of "Look there! Look, there's another one!"' But this is to 'effectively quarantine individuals from complex and interdependent systems of erotic affect and practice (not the least of which is heterosexuality) as well as isolate erotic systems from other social formations, such as race' (Traub 2002, p. 27).

So, Traub is not looking for lesbians in the seventeenth century, but is rather exploring

> what it means for women to inhabit specific categories of representation at particular moments in time . . . I have striven not to recover the *lesbian* as a being with a discreet original and stable meaning, but rather to examine the conditions of intelligibility whereby female-female intimacies gain, or fail to gain, cultural signification. (2002, p. 28)

Accordingly, when she does use the terms lesbian or lesbianism she italicizes them to 'remind readers of their epistemological inadequacy, psychological coarseness, and historical contingency' (2002, p. 16). In their stead she prefers 'homoeroticism' since, despite being

> cumbersome and etymologically predicated on gender sameness, [it] conveys a more fluid and contingent sense of erotic affect than either 'lesbian' or 'homosexual' . . . homoeroticism retains the necessary strangeness and historical contiguity between early modern and contemporary forms of desire. (2002, p. 16)

This chapter will likewise use the terminology of female homoeroticism for discussing women's relationships in the ancient world. It does not attempt to use homoerotic as a way of referring to latent lesbianism. Rather, it needs to be understood as a deliberate attempt to steer clear of modern ideas of the lesbian as a specific sexual identity. It is intended to create a gap between what has been understood in early twenty-first-century western contexts as 'sexual' and the range of activities that can be more broadly encompassed by 'erotic'. Homoerotic

> suggests the possibility of desire without consummation, turns our gaze away from genital sexuality, and inscribes a more expansive field of relationships than does 'homosexual' . . . 'homoerotic' better tallies with the nature of our evidence about women's lives in antiquity. (Rabinowitz 2002a, p. 3)

Rabinowitz accordingly imagines a 'spectrum' of relationships between women from the homosocial to the homoerotic, not to indicate a straight line of progression from one to the other, but to 'delineate a range of women's relationships . . . instead of extracting one aspect (the physically sexual) for consideration' (2002a, p. 4).

This might imply that the high value placed upon sexual activity in Chapter 1's definition of 'lesbian' is difficult to maintain. Not only would it be impossible to determine the precise sexual activities of ancient women, but it would run the risk of imposing modern ideas of lesbian-identified relationships upon a different context and age. But, Rabinowitz is not ruling out the likelihood that women of the ancient world enjoyed sexual relations, she is recommending caution. Rabinowitz rightly points out that 'having sex' has historically been construed, in western discourse, in terms of (vaginal) penetration which is 'not consistent with much of the evidence from antiquity about women's relations to women' (2002a, p. 3). The probability that women enjoyed physical relationships with each other is not ruled out; rather she is suggesting that intimate relations between women should be thought of as encompassing a far broader range of activities than penetration alone.[97] Accordingly, 'sex' may be taking a back seat in this chapter, but it is not disappearing from view. Resistance to phallocentric semantics and resistance to imposing modern expressions of 'lesbian sex' upon a different context necessitates a broader vista, one where women may quite feasibly have marital relations with husbands, but where their affinities to women remain primary, as in Mati-culture described in the previous chapter.

Rabinowitz reminds her readers that even when using broad terminology, information about women's relationships with women in the ancient world will be difficult to obtain. The task is difficult due to the lack of interest or knowledge about women's erotic lives and concomitant scarcity of sources. It is exacerbated further by the fact that representations of women's relations in the ancient world are hardly authentic, embedded as they are 'in discourses of invective, satire, and insult' (Rabinowitz 2002a, p. 2). When it comes to the ancient Jewish and early Christian communities and their scriptures, source material is certainly more difficult to locate. The next section considers the effect that this has had in rendering female homo-eroticism all but invisible in the history of scriptural interpretation.

Resistance to the Androcentric and Heteropatriarchal Framework of the Storyworld and its History of Interpretation

Hermeneutics of suspicion have been integral to all liberation readings of scripture whether they be feminist, womanist, *mujerista*, postcolonial or any other engaged mode of interpretation. The practice of a hermeneutic of suspicion calls to attention not only the fact that texts are permeated by ideological perspectives and norms that distort their representation of the past, but that the history of reception has been similarly permeated with Eurocentric and androcentric philosophical and theological presuppositions and perspectives. Accordingly, the methods and tools of

---

97 One issue that recurs in Blackwood and Wieringa's (1999) collection of essays is what 'having sex' actually means. When physical acts of intimacy between women, including mutual masturbation, have no specific connotation as 'sexual' in, say, African countries, then those who one may wish to include under the rubric of 'lesbian' are either excluded, or exclude themselves because the label is thought to signify sexual relations. For an engaging essay on the (non)vocabulary of lesbian sex, see Frye (1990).

academic study that have prevailed until recently may have been suited to certain researchers and research tasks but they do not possess the universal application that was once thought. Thus, feminists found that the recognized tools and methods of biblical enquiry meant that women who entered the discipline of biblical studies 'could not do so on their own terms but only by adopting an androcentric conceptual framework and perspective that acknowledged women's experience and intellectual questions only peripherally or not at all' (Fiorenza 1985, p. 46). For Fiorenza, feminist study begins when the agreed-upon basis of research is disrupted, when the partiality and androcentrism of existing methods is challenged and when a new paradigm of enquiry is operational so that feminist critics are free to articulate their own questions.

A hermeneutic of *hetero*-suspicion is a specifically refined version of such feminist hermeneutics of suspicion. It draws critically upon the insights and principles that have already been established while appreciating the contribution that new lesbian critical studies can offer. But while it is grounded in a feminist framework it necessarily challenges and broadens that framework just as womanist and *mujerista* insights continue to do. By exposing the way in which the hetero-patriarchal bias of both text and the history of interpretation has operated, a lesbian-identified approach demonstrates an area of neglect in existing research, as will become evident in this and the following chapters.

Commitment to a hermeneutic of hetero-suspicion means that the researcher is resistant to the presentation of any storyworld where female homoerotic relations are virtually absent and seeks to problematize that apparent absence. And in those few cases where the possibility of female homoeroticism *is* raised, a hermeneutic of hetero-suspicion is resistant to the portrayal of such relationships as unnatural, sinful or 'other'. First, let us turn to the issue of absence.

In Shelly Roberts' humorous *Rules of Lesbian Living*, she writes, 'It can't be a sin. We are not even *in* the Bible' (1996, p. 164). This is a common assumption. While same-sex acts between men are mentioned on a number of occasions in the Hebrew and Christian scriptures, there is only one (disputed) reference to female homoeroticism, that of Romans 1.26.[98] Too easily, lack of references is equated with lack of existence, thereby leading to the circular

---

98 This has not prevented lesbian-identified persons being included in legislation that draws on wider scriptural condemnation of male same-sex activity. Donald Wold (1998) wants to include women in the condemnation since he believes this is the intention of the text.

argument readily found elsewhere.[99] It becomes all too easy to assume that female homoeroticism either did not exist in the communities that produced the Hebrew and Christian scriptures or, if it did exist, that the chances of locating it are seriously beleaguered by the lack of interest of the writers of history and the concomitant lack of any recorded evidence. However, there is evidence that female homoeroticism was not unknown in surrounding cultures. As far as the ancient Near Eastern world is concerned it is true that there are hardly any references, but there are at least two possible sources as noted by Pope and Nissinen. M. H. Pope (1976) refers to a Ugaritic text where Baal spits in the assembly of the gods because of the conduct of the servant girls at a banquet. The behaviour of these girls is said to be shameful and lewd (*btt, tdmm*) but nothing further is revealed. Second, Martti Nissinen (1998, pp. 35–6) notes an omen that says when a (male) dog mounts another then women will copulate. Not terribly clear references, but if J. Bottéro and P. Petschow are right to conclude that in the Assyrian world 'affaires de femmes' belonged to an 'autonomous world where men had no authority' (in Nissinen 1998, p. 151, n. 113), then the absence of sources does not indicate lack of presence but rather neglect or ignorance of a social reality. As for the Hebrew scriptures, the one text that was later taken as a reference to female homoeroticism is Leviticus 18.3 where Moses instructs the Israelites to avoid the activities of the Egyptians and the Canaanites. Whether the writer of this passage had in mind the female marriages that early commentators describe is not known. What is significant is the way in which those commentators identify such acts as belonging to other cultures. There is a fuller discussion of this passage in the next chapter and for our present purposes it is sufficient to note that in its debatable acknowledgement of female homoeroticism, it is seen as something foreign, an activity that marks such cultures off from the Israelite culture. Thus, in the Hebrew scriptures, as Shelly Roberts jokes, there do not appear to be any 'lesbians'. This absence has been reified in the commentarial history, with hardly any writers prepared to state, as Milgrom refreshingly does, that lesbianism 'was prevalent' and that 'Lesbians existed and flourished', within the

---

99 Consider Rabinowitz's (2002b) discussion of the Attic red-figure Apollodorus kylix from Tarquinia depicting a sitting woman resting one hand on a standing woman's thigh while her other touches the standing woman's genital region. Boardman and La Rocca (1975, p. 110) argue that this cannot depict an erotic relationship since there are no examples of this phenomenon in Attic vase painting. While the exact meaning of this representation is debatable, the circularity of an argument that rules out eroticism on the basis of uniqueness is evident.

Israelite community (2000, pp. 1568, 1786–7, though his use of the lesbian label needs to be read with caution).

As noted above, the one text where female homoerotic relations seem to be in view is Romans 1.26, a letter written in a time and context where sources relating to female homoeroticism are far more prevalent. In Bernadette Brooten's groundbreaking study of the context of Paul's indictment, she notes a range of such sources. They are problematic insofar as they are largely records of how men viewed female eroticism. She therefore exercises caution when considering the visual representation of female homoeroticism on various vessels and cites Kilmer's caution that they most likely represent the fantasies of men (1996, p. 59; Kilmer 1993, p. 30). Certainly it may be that some of these are titillating representations meant to satisfy male tastes but, as Rabinowitz (2002b) demonstrates, it is very difficult to be sure of who used such vessels and what the scenes would have meant to the ancient viewer. Then, as now, what one sees depends upon the eye of the beholder.

Brooten's investigation of several Greek erotic spells from Egypt reveals a number of spells containing the names of women who wished to attract other women. Cast in a 'highly formulaic language' Brooten believes they are more informative of 'cultural ideology than about individual women's lives' (1996, p. 73), but nevertheless these aspects

> do provide evidence that: (1) actual historical women in this period desired erotic attachments to other women and were willing to go to some lengths to consummate these relationships; (2) some nonelite women from Upper Egypt . . . experienced homoerotic desire; and (3) some social support for woman-woman relationships must have existed for those women who commissioned the spells, at the minimum on the part of the scribes who composed them. (1996, p. 76)

They are thus useful for indicating the reality of women's attraction to other women to which the textual sources, including Paul's letter to the Romans, may be reacting.

Her study of the astrological literature reveals further references to female homoeroticism; in fact this body of literature 'contains more references to female homoeroticism than any other type of literature in the Roman world' (1996, p. 115). It depicts female homoeroticism in negative terms as gender transgression, positioning the *tribade* as a masculine active woman who pursues other women. This is despite the evident belief that people born under certain planetary configurations were destined to have certain erotic inclinations: 'Because of a particular configuration of the stars, a girl would be born as a *tribas, virago, fricatrix,* or *crissatrix*; the stars, then, determined a woman's erotic inclinations for the duration of her life' (1996, p. 140). It seems reasonable to suppose that for these ancient astrologers, some of whom would have been contemporaries of Paul (Dorotheos of Sidon, at least), certain versions of female homoeroticism were recognized and could be spoken of in terms of a known category (1996, p. 116).

Her further analysis of literature relating to medical treatments suggests that same-sex activities could be associated with a particular lifelong identity type. The literature is informed by its context, viewing 'normal' female sexuality in passive terms and associating any active sexual pursuits with masculinity. The categories of active and passive, masculine and female, thus take precedence over our modern heterosexual–homosexual binary. *Tribades*, acting outside their gender norms, were thus conceived to be mentally ill, driven to their pursuits. As is regularly the case, the women pursued by the *tribade* are not the focus of attention and are not portrayed as diseased. Treatments for the *tribade* include mind control or surgical clitoridectomy for those women deemed to be in possession of an overly large clitoris imagined to be capable of penetration. The scientific interest in female homoeroticism thus has early origins and this literature represents early attempts to define, categorize and control love between women.

Overall, Brooten finds that the phenomenon of female homoeroticism is well-attested, though mostly in negative terms. Despite some tolerance of female unions, attested in Iamblichos and Lucian, women who pursued women had to live with the disapproval and scathing portrayals of male writers that may well have led to general social disapproval and of potential surgical reprisals.

Compared with the variety of sources discussed by Brooten, the scriptures have very little to say on the subject. But far from being a matter for celebration, as Shelly Roberts intimates, this virtual silence should itself be a matter for investigation and explanation. A range of explanations have already been forthcoming. Saul Olyan (1996) concludes that women were not included in the Levitical condemnation of same-sex acts since their activities did not involve the potential mingling of semen with excrement and therefore do not transgress purity boundaries. In Pope's view the absence was 'doubtless due in large measure to belief in the sanctity of semen (1976, p. 417). Likewise, Milgrom (1993) suggests that since semen is not involved in women's relationships there is no symbolic loss of life and therefore no prohibition needed. Nissinen (1998, p. 43) suggests that it was a non-issue since it was inconceivable to think of women in an active role in a sexual act and did not involve any loss of 'manly honor', thus it presented no challenge to male dominance.[100] Alternatively, the division of space into gendered homosocial spheres meant that men simply had little or no knowledge of women's intimate lives (Greenberg 1988, p. 19; Brooten 1996, p. 62).

Acknowledging the absence is a step in the right direction since it calls attention to the erasure. However, explanations that women's relationships were simply not of sufficient interest or significance to bear mentioning tend to reify that absence. It may be that the (male) producers of scriptures *were* completely ignorant of the existence of female homoeroticism within what was likely to be a largely sexually segregated world of women. It may be that female homoeroticism *was* known but was tolerated because no semen was involved. Alternatively it may be that the silence is due to the desire not to draw attention to such behaviour.

Although scriptural texts largely give the impression that female homo-eroticism was not an issue worthy of recognition, a view reinforced by commentators, a hermeneutic of hetero-suspicion questions whether the absence actually marks a presence that has been, consciously or uncon-sciously, driven deeply underground into the realm of the unspeakable. Noting Donald West's view that 'Lesbians owe their immunity from arrest and imprisonment to the masculine pride of legislative authorities who tend to resist the public admission that many women prefer to bestow their sexual favours elsewhere' (1969, pp. 14–15), Mariner comments that the rabbis may have been 'similarly considerate of the male ego, both their own and the ego of those for whom they legislated' (1995, p. 84). Given the way in which the scriptures present its versions of the heterosexual imperative, it is not unreasonable to suggest that female homoeroticism has been suppressed, not because it was a matter of little or no importance, but because its very thinkability would be so disruptive to the sex-gender system enjoined in Genesis 1–3.

Certainly for Adrienne Rich it is the naturalization of men's access to women and the restriction of other ways of relating that lies at the heart of the oppression of women:

---

100 Nissinen's belief that women would not be positioned in an active sex role is undermined by Jael's actions as described in Judges 5.24–27. The encounter between her and Sisera has been persuasively described as an active seduction and penetration of the feminized Sisera by a masculinized Jael. See Niditch (1989) and Fewell and Gunn (1990).

when we look hard and clearly at the extent and elaboration of measures designed to keep women within a male sexual purlieu, it becomes an inescapable question whether the issue feminists have to address is not simple 'gender inequality', not the domination of culture by males, nor more 'taboos against homosexuality,' *but the enforcement of heterosexuality for women as a means of assuring male right of physical, economical and emotional access.* One of the many means of enforcement is, of course, the rendering invisible of lesbian possibility, an engulfed continent, which rises fragmentedly into view from time to time only to become submerged again. (1987, pp. 49–50, emphasis added)

Noting Rich's caution that 'the physical passion of woman for woman which is central to lesbian existence ... has been, precisely, the most violently erased fact of female experience' (1987, p. 57), a hermeneutic of hetero-suspicion counters erasure by centralizing 'forms of primary intensity between and among women, including the sharing of a rich inner life, the bonding against male tyranny, the giving and receiving of practical and political support' (1987, p. 51). Thus, in ancient situations where women were thrown together as co-wives or concubines of men, as is frequently described in scripture, a lesbian-identified hermeneutic is open to the realistic possibility, if not likelihood, that it is the women who 'make life endurable for each other, give physical affection without causing pain, share, advise, and stick by each other' (1987, p. 62). Readings that centralize such relationships accordingly have a significant place in lesbian-identified hermeneutics and will offset the erasure.

Conversely, a hermeneutic of hetero-suspicion needs to consider the ways in which 'the enforcement of heterosexuality for women' is engineered within the scriptures and the ways in which the 'engulfed continent' of lesbian possibilities is submerged. Comments such as this, by Alice Bach, are therefore deserving of further consideration:

When women try to form communities, they do not fare well. Dinah goes out to visit the women of the land (Gen. 34) and is raped by Shechem. After wandering the hills with her female companions, the daughter of Jephthah returns home to be sacrificed (Judg. 11). Leah and Rachel gnaw at each other, more eager to possess Jacob than to share female commonality. (1993, p. 194)

Such stories indicate the narrator's recognition that women had common ground with each other, yet that female bonding is represented in the context of doom and/or competitiveness. Questions need to be asked of texts that punish potential female solidarity in such ways. A hermeneutic of hetero-suspicion will thus explore the strategies used by narrators to offset any idea that women could co-operate in order to thwart the demands of Israel's sexual economy, investigate the ways in which such a notion is driven underground, resulting in the erasure of female homoeroticism, and offer a robust challenge to such strategies.

Exploration of the Strategies Used to Obscure and Suppress Evidence of Female Homoeroticism

Female homoeroticism is most effectively erased when sexism and hetero-sexism are made to appear normative. This naturalizes a state of affairs where women are positioned as inferior beings whose highest good is to follow their innate desire to service male (sexual) requirements. The naturalization of male–female relations and the suppression of female–female relations in the scriptures are aided by a number of textual emphases: the valorization of motherhood, imaging women as competitive rivals, injunctions to comply with notions of gender complementarity; combined with textual admonitions that 'other' and condemn same-sex activities. Not only do these emphases and admonitions naturalize sexism and heterosexism, but they present both as God's ordained will for humanity. These strategies may, or may not, have been consciously deployed to prevent women finding in each other an alternative social world, but whatever the case, a lesbian-identified hermeneutic has a responsibility to counter them. The admonitions that 'other' and condemn same-sex activities will be discussed further in the next chapter; this section focuses on the valorization of motherhood, the images of women as competitive rivals, and the injunctions to comply with notions of gender complementarity.

The valorization of motherhood

Before embarking upon this section, it is important to note Meyers' caution about uncritically assuming that ancient women in Israel were restricted to domestic life. She argues that the nineteenth-century, western concept of the 'stay-at-home full-time wife-and-mother' has coloured our perception of ancient women's lives. Due to this perception, biblical scholarship emerging in the nineteenth century and indeed much of twentieth-century feminist biblical scholarship has suffered from a blindspot preventing our recognition of the important role that female networks and roles played in the community life of the Iron Age. The problem is that the interpreter's nineteenth and twentieth-century interpretive context, combined with the scriptural valorization of the role of wife and mother and lack of interest in women's broader roles and lives, has 'made it difficult to see women as other than subservient wife-mothers' (1999c, p. 113) and in fact encouraged a reification of those narrowed roles. In view of this, the focus upon the valorization of motherhood in this section must beware of falling into the same trap. It does so by pointing out, in due course, the different avenues that may have been open to women. However, Meyers does concede that Hebrew scripture usually represents the perspectives of 'high status males' (1999c, p. 111) who were 'relatively silent about women's activities in general and their corporate behaviour in particular' (1999c, p. 111). This silence, when considered in conjunction with the evident emphasis upon female duties as wives and mothers, does produce a valorization of motherhood that plays a crucial role in the naturalization of the heterosexual imperative.[101]

Channelling women into the roles of wife and mother is facilitated by a number of textual strategies. Motherhood is presented as the most positive role a woman can fulfil, one that will earn her respect and prestige. Thus, in the decalogue, mothers will be honoured, as fathers are honoured. In Proverbs there are injunctions to heed to the teaching of the mother and to give her due respect. Proverbs 30.17 suggests that anyone who scorns to obey a mother should have their eyes pecked out by the ravens of the valley and eaten by the vultures. Images of Israel's matriarchs competing for the attention of husbands and desperate to bear children also contribute significantly. Good women, often mothers or mothers-to-be, can be rewarded by being given a hymn of praise to sing. Hannah, who fulfils the heteropatriarchal ideological agenda in her longing for a child to the extent that she will surrender him to the Lord once weaned, is a useful example. In the first ten verses of 1 Samuel 2 she gives thanks to a deity who reverses the fortunes of the barren, the poor and the oppressed. This psalm would later serve as a model for the Magnificat in Luke 1.46–55. The sentiment of such hymns of praise has sometimes been highlighted by feminists, who latch on to the spirit of liberation thought to pervade them. However, this fails to

---

101 For further treatments of the valorization of motherhood in the Hebrew scriptures, see Bird (1974), Brenner (1985 especially chapter 9), Exum (1993), Fuchs (2000).

recognize the problematic nature of the songs: their rewarding of obedience, of dutiful adherence to the heterosexual imperative, their endorsement of the sex-gender economy. Women like Hannah are scripted characters in a male play. Operating as the male director's puppets, these women never speak or act with their own genuine voices and the image of such women longing for motherhood needs to be resisted.

In using the story and song of Hannah as an intertext, the author of Luke's Gospel valorizes again the ideal of a woman dedicated to the institution of motherhood no matter what the personal cost. He also reinforces the view that shame and distress would 'naturally' be experienced by barren women. Images of barrenness as a stigmatized and shameful condition, arguably a sign of divine displeasure since fertility was considered to be the gift of the Lord, encourage readers to take on this damaging view.[102] The rhetoric is strong, especially when the narrator populates his storyworld with female characters who are taunted by their rivals. Hannah, for example, is imaged as a woman desperate to secure her own fertility to avoid the shame and jibes of her peers. And in what was clearly intended to be one of the worst fates that can be bestowed upon a woman, Michal is punished when the narrator has David refuse to share her bed any longer, thereby robbing her of future children and heirs to the throne (2 Samuel 6.23). The rhetoric of these narratives encourages readers to associate women with an ardent desire for children which thereby ensures their co-operation in the sex-gender system.

Athalya Brenner agrees that the Hebrew scriptures present women as being innately desirous of having children, particularly sons, depict women as 'prepared to go to any lengths' to achieve this, and have virtually no images of women actively resisting motherhood (1997, pp. 56–7).[103] But for Brenner it is specifically the biblical *insistence that this is so* that belies a different state of affairs in reality, for if women concurred with this diagnosis why the need for the injunctions of Genesis and the idealization of motherhood?

---

102 For reflections on the impact of the image of the barren woman in scripture upon Jewish women, see Callaway (1986) and Cardin (1999).

103 Exum, however, believes that a mother's sense of outrage can be detected in the text, if not at the patriarchal system itself then at their lot in life: 'However subdued their protest may now appear in the text, each of the matriarchs at some point says something particularly revealing of the evil effects patriarchal constraints have on women. In these submerged strains of women's voices we can uncover evidence of patriarchy's uneasiness and guilt with regard to its treatment of women' (1993, p. 141).

One way this strategy can be resisted is by asking what it really would have meant to have been a woman in Israelite society, to be owned by a shared husband, expected to endure multiple pregnancies in the face of adverse circumstances. Brenner's work contains an interesting discussion of the burials at En Gedi which, despite the site report's typical lack of interest in gender issues, can be harnessed to indicate the health status of women. The skeletal remains indicate that women died younger than their male counterparts. Left to draw her own diagnosis as to why this should be, Brenner concludes that childbearing would have been a major contributing factor. For the women in ancient Israel, childbirth meant enhanced status and security in old age and another pair of hands for the labour force, but at a cost to their own health and longevity. So while the Hebrew Bible insists that women yearned for children, their pro-life stance was in reality a 'pro-early death choice' (1997, p. 68).

Given this situation it is at least possible that, for practical reasons alone, not all women longed for children. And for those women whose primary affinities and desires were directed towards their female companions, marriage and motherhood may have been thought of as particularly undesirable and onerous. Such a scenario is included in the fictional reconstruction of Dinah's story in Anita Diamant's *The Red Tent*. In her retelling, Diamant develops the character of Zilpah. An ardent worshipper of the Goddess, Zilpah looks forward to motherhood insofar as she may have a daughter to teach. But she has no desire for a husband and has to be commanded to go to Jacob's tent:

> Bilhah offered to put henna on Zilpah's hands, but she set her mouth and refused. That night she walked slowly to Jacob's tent, where he lay with her and knew her. Zilpah took no pleasure from Jacob's touch. 'I did what was required of me.' She said, with such a tone that no one dared ask her to say more. (2001, p. 57)

Diamant does not explain Zilpah's reluctance in terms of her desire for women, but leaves the narrative open for this possibility. Thus a reader alert to the gap sees in Zilpah's desire to rid herself of Jacob's attentions as soon as possible, her commitment to the Goddess and her independent spirit, indications of such desires. Diamant's development of Zilpah's character as a worshipper of the Goddess is interesting. Commitment to a hermeneutic of hetero-suspicion makes readers alert to the ways in which women might have historically sought to resist their 'biological destiny' as wives and mothers, perhaps by entering into religious life. Again, although feminist studies have been very helpful in documenting the roles that women could have in the cult, there has been scant consideration of the possibility that some of these roles offered opportunities both for female bonding and for deliberate resistance of the heterosexual imperative. Some, however, have offered tantalizing glimpses. Phyllis Bird's essay on women's place in the cult, for example, highlights how women were probably restricted to domestic roles, limited to such duties as 'the weaving and sewing of vestments, hangings and other textiles for cultic use; the preparation of cultic meals or foods used in the ritual; and the cleaning of cultic vessels, furniture, and quarters' (1987, p. 406). Yet, she also notes that where women are primarily restricted to the private domestic sphere, they may well find other outlets for their skills and devotions, creatively developing the cult in their own way:

> Local shrines, saints and spirits, home rituals in the company of other women (often with women ritual leaders), the making and paying of vows (often by holding feasts), life-cycle rites . . . appear better suited to women's spiritual and emotional needs and the patterns of their lives rather than the rituals of the central sanctuary, the great pilgrimages and assemblies, and the liturgical calendar of the agricultural year. (1987, p. 401)[104]

We rarely find any record of such activities in the scriptures themselves, but Bird takes what *is* there as the basis for her portrayal of women making their own way in the company of other women. In her recognition that some of the blank slots of women's history may be filled with data deriving from cross-cultural anthropological studies, further research may shed light on the importance of women *for each other* in this context.[105] It is intriguing to note Bird's further suggestion that some women might have had their 'rebellious moments' and escaped their procreative destiny by choosing (in so far as that was possible) a sacral life:

> Women may take vows that are costly and undertake forbidden pilgrimages as actions of rebellion or flight from oppressive household

---

104 See Gerstenberger (1996, 2002) for further reconstruction of the leading role of women in the household religious practice of ancient Israel.

105 It may be, for instance, that Carol Meyers' (1991, 1999a, 1999b) archaeomusicological study of female performers will be helpful in identifying a specific religious activity in which such bonding could occur. Her suggestion of an all-female group of drummers meeting to compose and rehearse, provides a space wherein relations could be formed, solidarity reinforced and sense of self-worth encouraged.

responsibilities and restrictions. As religiously sanctioned actions they may offer limited relief to women whose options for action were often severely circumscribed. (1987, p. 410)

Meyers, noting the sacral alternatives for the women in the surrounding culture who would not marry, speaks of the roles of priestesses who served the female deities, the female temple cult prostitutes, and refers to others, such as the *naditu* women, who 'refrained from sexuality and marriage by entering a sort of convent existence' (1978, pp. 93–4). Her theory is that such women were escaping from the risks and rigours involved with childbirth and/or securing economic stability. Maybe so, but the possibility that these were avenues pursued by women for whom the heterosexual imperative was itself an oppression, is not a considered option. Meyers finds it 'hard to reconstruct the social motivations for such a choice' (1978, pp. 93–4), but to a lesbian-identified researcher other motivations for making such a choice come readily into view. Religious life has often provided alternative spaces for women, who choose to escape the heterosexual imperative. As John Boswell notes:

Celibate religious life offered women escape from the consequences of marriage – for example, having to sleep with a husband and bear children, which might not only be unwanted but even life-threatening. It afforded both genders a means of avoiding stereotypical gender roles. Women could exercise power in religious communities, among other women, without being subordinated to the male head of a household ... women could become literate and learned, an opportunity rare for their sex outside religious communities after the decline of Rome.

It is reasonable, under these circumstances, to believe that the priesthood and religious communities would have exercised a particular appeal for gay people ... Indeed, lesbian and gay people would hardly have needed a spiritual motivation to join a same-sex community of equals. Joining a religious community from about 500 C.E. to about 1300 was probably the surest way of meeting other gay people. (1994b, p. 365)

While being wary of making unwarranted connections between the ancient and the contemporary society, or of any transhistorical lesbian identity, it is interesting that in our modern society more and more women are testifying that their entry into religious institutions such as the convent is a way of avoiding heterosexist expectations, noting how religious avenues can provide places of solidarity, refuge and joy for women-identified women.[106] It does not seem unreasonable to imagine that ancient women also found relief within cultic spaces and activities, the *naditu* women, called to attention by Meyers, being an interesting case in point.

The institutional life of the *naditu* in the old Babylonian cities of Sippar and Nippur (records are known from c.1880–1550 BCE), offered primarily upper-class women the opportunity to dedicate their lives to the deity (Marduk, Šamaš, Aja). Little is known of their religious duties other than their responsibilities for daily offerings and observance of festivals, but source material from Sippar offers over 500 texts detailing their extraordinary economic freedom to conduct business transactions including 'sale, lease, loan, inheritance, adoption and lawsuits in connection with the latter two' (Jeyes 1983, p. 261). Dedicated to their deity, the *naditus* of Marduk could marry but were expected to remain childless, whereas those of Šamaš did not marry. These lived with other *naditus* in the walled *gagûm* ('the Locked House' translated by Jeyes as the 'cloister'). They shared this cloister with between 100 and 200 other *naditus* and a female staff including weavers, millers and cooks.[107] There may have been a leadership role within the cloister since one text mentions a 'mother of the *naditus*' (Harris 1963, pp. 141–2), but there is no further evidence of such a figure or role.

It is commonly presumed that daughters had little choice in their destinies since they appear to have been dedicated to this institution at birth: thus names of *naditus* included Amat-Šamaš ('the servant girl of Šamaš') or Erišti-Aja ('Aja's desire') (Jeyes 1983, p. 263). If this was the case then the idea of women *choosing* this independent lifestyle among other women lacks conviction. However, it is possible that these names were conferred upon the women at initiation. While Harris and Jeyes think this is unlikely, saying there is no evidence for a change of name initiation ceremony, the silence is not proof. In fact, Elizabeth Stone claims that the initiation of *naditus* at Sippar 'involved a ritual in which a change of name occurred' which was 'not evidenced at Nippur' (1982, p. 57). It may be that some women were destined for a religious life at the behest of their fathers, but one cannot rule out the possibility that some women may have actively pursued life as a *naditu*, perhaps as a way of escaping the otherwise inevitable destiny of marriage and motherhood and in order to live in an all-female community.

---

106 On the occurrence of same-sex relationships within religious life, past and present, see for example, Curb and Manahan (1985), Boswell (1994a) and Raymond (1991, pp. 73–114).

107 In later references to the cloister there is mention of a male administrative staff.

Once within the cloister it seems that the women enjoyed mutually supporting relationships. Jeyes claims, 'There is some evidence that the *naditus*
cooperated in their business life inasmuch as they tended to own and buy
up land next to each other ... A field could be jointly owned by two *naditus* and probably joint arrangements were made for such things as trans-
port of produce' (1983, p. 271). Of interest is the practice whereby a *naditu*
adopted a younger woman as her carer and potential inheritor of property.
In return for care in her old age, respectful treatment, and performance of
the monthly offering on her behalf if necessary, the adoptee could obtain
'an inheritance such as a house within the cloister' (1983, p. 270). There were
cases where the *naditu* bequeathed self-earned property to an adoptee who
was not a blood relative which 'gave rise to some bitterly contested court
cases' (Jeyes 1983, p. 271; Harris 1969, pp. 138ff), indicating perhaps the primary affinities of a *naditu* for her adoptive heir. Frustratingly the adoption
records at Nippur were badly damaged and the significance of this practice
is thus largely left to the imagination. Overall, it is apparent that 'the cloister provided status, mutual support, social security and, exceptional for the
society in which they lived, a measure of financial and therefore also personal freedom' (Jeyes 1983, p. 272).

Whether there was any scope for Israelite women to escape from the wife/
mother destiny altogether by entering into religious life is unclear. Certainly
the Hebrew scriptures do not make any reference to the availability of any
similar cloistered life for women. However, now that archaeological inscriptions indicate its integral place in Israelite worship, the renewed interest
in the cult of Asherah may reveal possibilities not currently envisaged.[108]
Apart from this possibility for which there is currently no evidence, there
are virtually no examples of formal Jewish women's groups in late antiquity,
with the exception of Philo's first-century reference to a group of male and
female (segregated) monastics living on the shores of Lake Mareotis, outside Alexandria. The women, referred to as *therapeutrides*, are described
in exalted terms by Philo's *De vita contemplativa* as a group of mostly aged
virgins and celibates, dedicated to a life of seclusion that involved the study
of scripture, prayer and the composition of hymns and psalms.[109] According to Philo's account, the women did not have much opportunity for a
communal life since they lived separately except for a communal sabbath

---

108 On the inscriptions concerning YHWH and Asherah see, for example, Dever
(1984), Freedman (1987), Binger (1997), Hadley (2000). On the potential role of women
in the Asherah cult, see Ackerman (1993, 1998), Bird (1987), Gerstenberger (1996, 2002),
Meyers (1991, 1999a, 1999b).

109 For a translation of Philo's study, see Colson (1941) volume 9, pp. 104–71.

gathering and an annual feast, which Kraemer (1989, p. 345) believes to be Shavuot. If Philo's comments are accurate then, as Kraemer comments, this minimizes the likelihood of strong interpersonal ties between the women. Yet, given that the pool from which a group of highly educated, wealthy women could be drawn is likely to be small, she does say 'perhaps it would not be unreasonable to assume some prior social contacts' (1989, p. 366). This offers the narrowest of glimpses into the possibility that women who already had ties of some sort chose to enter a life of contemplation together and thereby evade intimacy with men and motherhood. However, one has to bear in mind that this is Philo's version and we do not have any access to the women's stories at all. Indeed, the question of whether Philo wrote this tract at all or whether it is a later account informed by Christian monasticism is debated, as is the question of whether Philo describes a real community or an idealized idea.[110] Kraemer believes there are sufficient indicators to attest the account's authenticity and speaks of 'the reasonable assumption . . . that a Jewish monastic community of women and men existed on the shores of Lake Mareotis in the first century' (1989, p. 348). The references to their ability to pursue scriptural study with a fervour equal to that of the *therapeutae* may be indicative of a highly educated collective of women who had the financial resources to choose this lifestyle. They were all single. Philo speaks of wives but never of husbands. As Kraemer comments:

> Those who adopted the contemplative life did not leave husbands behind because the women who became contemplative monastics did not have husbands to leave – either because they never had them or because they waited until they no longer had husbands to take up such a life. (1989, p. 352)

As such, this group does fall into the kind of community envisaged by Rich, whose lesbian continuum, as mentioned in Chapter 1, includes 'the banding together of those women of the twelfth and fifteenth centuries known as Beguines . . . the more celebrated "Lesbians" of the women's school around Sappho of the seventh century BC' (1987, p. 55) and so forth. The possibility that women were attracted to this movement specifically to be with other women is not directly addressed by Kraemer, though she does suggest that women may have been attracted due to the community's provision of a 'refuge from a world critical of childlessness' (1989, p. 363), among other things (such as the 'appeal of the philosophical life' – 1989, p. 366).

---

110 For sources that deal with these queries, see Kraemer (1989, p. 347, nn. 19, 20).

There was probably greater access to avenues of religious services that could provide refuge from marriage in Greco-Roman periods when virginity/celibacy was advocated as a higher form of spiritual life. Permeated by an eschatological worldview, the early Jesus and subsequent house church movements envisioned a new world order where conventional gendered roles could be overcome. Thus it was that during the first cèntury CE, female missionaries could work in pairs apparently without reference to any male relatives. The possibilities that such pairs of women chose to be together as life companions in their Christian services has already been raised by Wilson, who wonders whether the apparent bias against marriage allowed for a greater preponderance of leaders who were same-sex oriented. She suggests that the partnerships between Tryphaena and Tryphosa (Romans 16.17) and Euodia and Syntyche (Philippians 4.2) can be reconsidered in the light of Rich's lesbian continuum (1995, pp. 162–3), citing the work of Mary D'Angelo whose article on 'Women Partners in the New Testament' was discussed in Chapter 1. Groups such as the Orders of virgins and widows provided a context for women-only communities whose members were taken out of expectations of marriage and childbirth. Celibacy was a realistic option in the early Church and women had the opportunity to live in sex-segregated communities and thereby reject marriage. Notions of celibacy, of course, would have been tied to prevailing notions of sex. As discussed above, this means that celibacy was most likely interpreted as abstinence from male penetration. But it does not necessarily rule out various forms of women–women intimacy.

To summarize thus far: a lesbian-identified hermeneutic of suspicion disrupts the valorization of motherhood by countering with consideration of the harsh realities of multiple pregnancies and their effects on women's life and health and by exploring ways that women might have deliberately avoided the institution, perhaps in some cases via escape into religious life. However, one should not be too quick to cut women off from motherhood per se; what is being resisted here is the rhetoric that marriage to men and childbearing is what *all* women *inevitably* desired and the tyrannous way in which women have been pushed into these roles. Another way in which the valorization of motherhood can be disrupted is by reclaiming it for lesbian-identified women as opposed to resisting it, as the following discussion demonstrates.

Modern lesbian-identified women have had a particularly complex relationship with motherhood. Historically, those who already had children from their previous relationships often lost custody of those children in divorce cases, simply because of their decision to live openly and honestly. Being forced to choose between the woman one loves and one's children, or not even being granted that choice, must have been/be devastating. In such cases, scriptural texts that mourn the loss/absence of children, such as the image of Rachel wailing for her children and refusing to be comforted since they are no more, evocatively invoked by Jeremiah 31.15, could feasibly find new resonances for these readers. Another text that could speak to the experience of having to choose between being a mother and being another woman's partner is that of Ruth. Celena Duncan, in her midrash written from a bisexual perspective, suggests that in her vow to Naomi and her determination to cleave to her, Ruth was 'relinquishing the one thing by which a woman's worth, value, accomplishment and purpose were measured: her ability to bear children, in particular sons . . . Her love for Naomi superseded her procreative responsibilities'. In so doing, Duncan suggests Ruth was choosing 'what would provide her the greatest emotional and spiritual health and well-being' (2000, p. 95).

This choice no longer confronts western lesbian-identified individuals in the same starkness. Despite the negative press that has accompanied the fight for joint adoption regulations and the use of self-insemination procedures, lesbian-identified couples have demonstrated that their sexual choices and motherhood are not mutually exclusive categories. Hadar Dubowsky's account of choosing to inseminate from a sperm donor is a good example of how contemporary Jewish couples are organizing their own families. And as the insemination process dragged on through a number of failed attempts, Dubowsky called to mind the scriptures, in particular the story of Hannah. 'Okay,' says Dubowsky, 'so there are some feminist issues around Hannah, but I was desperate for some kind of role model, some kind of context to frame my experience' (2002, p. 48).

Lesbian-identified studies have also spotted the resonance that the book of Ruth might have for these women also. Mona West uses it as an 'Example of Procreative Strategies for Queers', claiming Ruth as a queer ancestor by virtue of the fact that 'she provides us with an example of self-determination, refusing to accept a marginalized status based on heterosexist, patriarchal definitions of marriage, family, and procreation' (1997, p. 54). In West's reading of this text, Ruth and Naomi's relationship is foregrounded, understood as one which runs against the status quo, which finds in the empathetic Boaz a contributor of economic stability which allows the women to fulfil their commitment to each other. In their unusual triangular relationship West finds a parallel to the alliances between lesbians and gay men, suggesting that the arrangement between Ruth, Naomi and Boaz are analogous to the way families of choice have been created by LGBT people.

On the other hand, another aspect of lesbian-identified women's complex relationship with motherhood is the historical stigma such women have faced for choosing to renounce their procreative potential *and being happy with their decision*. In the twentieth century, lesbianism was variably associated with the spinster, the feminist, the bluestocking: any independent women who preferred their own and the company of other women at the expense of the children they might have produced. Their independent spirit was caricatured in cartoons, criticized as unnatural, and stigmatized by the negative connotations of terms like 'spinster' or 'maiden aunt'. Some of these women were probably never desirous of children and have had to put up with the jibes not only of society, but of family members who continue to encourage relationships with a range of male candidates and pass well-intentioned but reproachful comments about the lack of grandchildren. The pressure to conform has been experienced particularly strongly within some African-American circles. Beverley Green (1996) notes how investment in the belief that one's culture can be put on a more secure and continued footing via a high birth rate can lead to antagonism against any persons who choose not to participate. This can encourage the belief that lesbian and gay-identified people of colour are threats to the society's survival and perpetuate a historical association between homosexuality and death. Pressure to conform is also keenly felt in Jewish families. Alan Unterman writes that failure to marry and procreate is 'not merely an avoidance of a positive commandment, it is akin to communal treason', and he goes on to speak of the 'vast burden of guilt' shouldered by gay Jews (1995, pp. 68, 69–70). In such cases, the stigma directed towards barren women in the scriptures may strike evocative echoes with contemporary readers. The scriptures have presented the barren woman as one grieving over her condition, but it does not have to be assumed that all women without children found this to be unbearable; what was unbearable was the provocation of those around her. It is possible, then, that contemporary readers can associate with these figures without having to endorse the supposed grief and guilt or the concomitant attempts to comply with the system as conveyed by the scriptural characters. I believe that lesbian-identified readings of scripture could provide some interesting applications of these narratives.

In all these cases, a lesbian-identified reading position produces unexpected resonances. The valorization of motherhood in the scriptures can be both resisted and reclaimed by being read in unexpected ways by unanticipated audiences (such readings are explored further in Chapter 5). As will be seen, the principle of resistance can combine with the principle of reclamation to disturb the way in which the valorization of marriage and motherhood erases female homoeroticism, thereby creating a multi-headed approach to this issue.

Images of women as competitive rivals

A second major strategy used to obscure and suppress the reality of female homoeroticism lies in the images of women as competitive rivals, since such images erase knowledge of women's affection and love for each other and suppress awareness of the ways in which they could act co-operatively. The legacy of the Deuteronomistic Historian in particular is one where women's relationships that, apart from some notable exceptions, are at best marked by disinterest ('Women do not often interact or speak to one another in the Bible', Exum 1996, p. 96).[111] At worst, their relationships are characterized by unattractive jealous rivalry and competition, with cattiness, and generally bitchy behaviour especially characterizing the relationships between mothers and would-be mothers.[112] Thus the relationship between Rachel and Leah, or Hannah and Peninnah, is portrayed as entirely wrapped up with procreation; their function in life being to provide their husbands with children, preferably sons, and their status being almost entirely dependent upon their success in that venture. As wives and prospective mothers, any sense of their own erotic desire is quickly suppressed.

If the portrayals of the text are read uncritically then it is all too easily agreed that women did naturally compete with each other to be breeders of good sons, were jealous of their husband's other wives (especially if they gave birth at a better rate and to more sons than they themselves) and certainly had no feelings of eroticism or even warmth for each other. Thus, Gale Yee, when discussing how a woman would be expected to leave her own immediate family to join her husband's household, writes: 'Her new household could sometimes be a hostile environment, particularly if

---

111 Exceptions would include the narratives relating to Ruth and Naomi, the range of female co-operation present in the opening chapters of Exodus where Moses' mother, the Egyptian princess and the latter's female servants act in concert to thwart the will of Pharaoh, and the co-operative daughters of Lot.

112 Only when mothers jointly face an outside danger do we find a spirit of co-operation; see Brenner (1985, pp. 94ff).

co-wives were present. Co-wives often vied for their husband's attention and the resultant status it could bring' (2003, p. 38).[113] It is likely that such rivalries did occur among Israelite women, but the images promote the idea that animosity was a characteristic feature of female relationships. Such images must be read critically for they undoubtedly serve a heteronormative point of view.

Thus, Lillian Klein (1994) rightly points out that the portrayal of Hannah and Peninnah competing for Elkanah's sexual attention acts as a sop to the male ego. More significantly, she notes how this imaging of women may be a means of suppressing the threat of female solidarity: 'The implicit traditional interpretation of women as jealous of each other . . . suggests, perhaps, the magnitude of the threat of female bonding to the patriarchal system' (1994, p. 92). But what if wives were not jealous, asks Klein? What if, on the contrary, they felt affection and sympathy for their husband's co-wives? What if the women turned to each other for comfort and consolation, 'even closing rank as women against the male Other' (1994, p. 85)? A lesbian-identified paradigm which queries not so much the dynamics of male–female relationships as it does their *primacy*, takes such questions and explores the likelihood of women's love and affection for one another, their common support, the preference of some to be in the company of each other rather than with their husbands.

For evidence of this, the scriptural sources offer little help. For all that there may be queer elements within the narratives that can be developed (as argued in Chapter 5), it is a social-scientific approach that offers useful insights for a principle of resistance. For example, Lila Abu-Lughod's (1993) ethnographical study of a small Awlad 'Ali Bedouin community on the northwest coast of Egypt, reveals that hostility can exist between co-wives but so can love and support. In her brief section on co-wives she tells the story of Gateefa's eleventh labour and the way she was supported by Azza and Safiyya – the co-wives of her husband. At the time when her labour was due, Azza sought out Gateefa, took her by the arm, comforting her and leading her to the chosen birthing room. She held Gateefa from behind while her sister-in-law held her from the front as the labour began. After the birth Azza washed Gateefa's bloodied clothes, dressed her in clean clothes, gave her food and brought requisite items for the new baby before sitting

---

113 However, Yee later draws upon a number of anthropological studies that demonstrate how women could co-operate in order to resist male authority and control (see 2003, pp. 49–50 and the sources cited).

with her and with the women who came to visit. At this point Abu-Lughod notices something important:

> The two co-wives, sitting cross-legged on the freshly laid bedding, their knees almost touching, and the tiny swaddled infant lying between them, looked long at each other. In that movement I saw something about these two women that I had not grasped before, although I had known them for many years. Despite their difficulties with each other – and they had many – there was between them a closeness and dependency, perhaps as women who give birth . . . perhaps as women bound together by sharing a household, daily life, and a history. Fourteen years of shared history made for a bond, even if life together was often tense. (1993, p. 90)

Such work troubles the scriptural implication that women, co-wives in particular, were always at enmity with each other. Drawing on a wide range of ethnographies of Middle Eastern societies Yee indicates how a sex-segregated world provides opportunities for female bonding and support rather than hostile competitiveness. In fact a sex-segregated world might be seen as a blessing, maintained to some extent at women's own request. In such contexts, women draw strength from each other and co-operate in a range of mutually supporting activities:

> Within their sexual segregated world, women can use secrets and silences to their advantage, colluding to keep knowledge of socially unacceptable behaviour from their spouses. Conversely, they can gossip about their husbands and spread stories about them, bringing shame to the patriline. They can skilfully manipulate their husbands verbally. They can steal from their husbands. They can oppose and stonewall marriages arranged by their male relatives. They can crudely poke fun at masculine shortcomings with sexually irreverent discourse. They can socialize their children about the fickleness of their fathers and use their sons covertly to achieve their aims. They can practice sorcery . . . nag incessantly or become shrewish and quarrelsome . . . refuse to cook or have anything to do with domestic or agricultural tasks. Finally, they can exploit their men sexually, by refusing sexual intercourse with them. (2003, p. 49)

Yee's summary combines insights from a wide range of sources which discuss women's strategies in quite different contexts. [114] Some of these are now dated and Carol Meyers (1999c) cautions against any overemphasis upon a hierarchical rating of the public over the private sphere that studies on sex-segregation sometimes imply. New social science research suggests that premodern community life is rarely organized along hierarchical gendered lines and indicates that women were involved in supradomestic activities that took the significance of their work into the public realm. [115] However, although these studies are blurring the hypothetical borders between private and public, it remains the case that in Iron Age village life, the labour tasks assigned to women and the adjoining clusters of village houses

> meant that Israelite women had more access to each other than men did to other men. Many repetitive household activities performed by women, such as certain food preparation tasks, would have been done in each other's company. Such regular and intimate contact creates familiarity; and the shared tasks, problems and experiences create a sense of identity. Familiarity and identity foster the solidarity of the women of a community – the neighbourhood associations visible in the Bible. (Meyers 1999c, p. 122)

Ethnographical studies, drawn upon by Meyers and Yee, place those scriptural images of quarrelling, competitive women in a different light. In the hands of a male narrator these behaviours contribute to the symbolic portrayal of women as the dangerous 'other': manipulative, scheming, adversarial, competitive and bitchy. Read from a feminist perspective such tactics can be read as 'diagnostics of power'. [116] As Yee puts it: 'The conflict-indicating behaviour of women reveals them as actors within an androcentric society, exercising power and manipulating and subverting its structures' (2003, p. 52). Read from a lesbian-identified feminist perspective, these 'weapons of the weak' might also have included finding support, solace, sexual satisfaction and a sense of solidarity in the arms

---

114 Yee's sources include Abu-Lughod (1985, 1990), Nelson (1974), Brison (1992), Rogers (1975), Lamphere (1974), Harding (1975), Dwyer (1978), Michaelson and Goldschmidt (1971), Udobata (1988), Wolf (1974), Moore (1989), Friedl (1967) and Rosaldo (1980).

115 Meyers' references to such studies include March and Taqqu (1986), Helly and Reverby (1992), Sharistanian (1987) and Rosaldo (1980).

116 The phrase 'diagnostics of power' derives from Collier (1974).

of female partners, facilitated by the sexually segregated space available to women.[117] It thus expands the realm of the thinkable and, in bringing female homoeroticism into the light, counters the expurgation of this 'most violently erased face of female experience' (Rich 1987, p. 57). Of course, these are the stories that are not told, the scenes that are not made visible, the relationships that are erased. But when one reconsiders the scriptures in the light of a lesbian-identified perspective, it is evident that there are elements that have the potential to destabilize this unhappy representation: notably the fleeting glimpses of the ways in which women engage in acts of co-operation and collusion in order to resist male authority and control. Part of the task of the second principle (commitment to reclamation) would be to consider ways in which these lost scenarios might be reconstructed, as explored further in Chapter 5.

Injunctions to sex-gender complementarity

While the emphases on women as competitive rivals and portraying motherhood as the highest good for all women are major ways in which female homoeroticism has been obscured, there is a more overt means of suppression: the presentation of gender-sex complementarity as God-ordained.

In Genesis 1.27–28 humanity is imaged as complementary male and female sexes which are commanded to 'be fruitful and multiply'. In 2.24 after describing the creation of Eve, the narrator writes, 'Therefore a man leaves his father and his mother and clings to his wife, and they become one flesh'. And in 3.16 the deity proclaims that the woman shall desire her husband, despite his exercise of power over her. These influential lines of the opening book of Jewish and Christian Bibles create a heteronormative atmosphere against which the remainder of the scriptures have traditionally been read. Thus, in the rhetoric of both politicians and church representatives, instead of argument there is often recourse to the jingle 'God made Adam and Eve, not Adam and Steve', as the Genesis text continues to

---

117 This is not to say that historically some women did not enter into competitive hostilities. There are always those who disassociate themselves from other women and their efforts to find mutual solidarity. As Exum notes, 'Women "sell out" all the time in patriarchy. To gain an advantage for themselves they cooperate with the oppressor. A third way patriarchy controls women is by dividing women into respectable women and disreputable women, and thus . . . making gender solidarity impossible' (1993, p. 90).

be a bulwark of contemporary religious resistance to challenges raised by issues such as civil partnership legislation.

Certainly, Genesis 1–3 is a foundational text. It not only enshrines the heterosexual contract but also buttresses the valorization of marriage and motherhood, structures male–female complementarity and locates hetero-sexuality as a self-defining characteristic of God's chosen people. It not only stands authoritatively at the head of the Hebrew scriptures but lies at the heart of subsequent structuring of the Christian community along sex-gender axes. Despite the fact that Paul was prepared to renegotiate gender norms given the eschatological context in which he worked, his new-found ordering of humanity 'in Christ' where there famously is no male or female, Jew or Greek, slave or freeperson, was undermined by the adoption of the household code which prescribed compliance to 'traditional' sex-gender conventions. The Jewish heritage of Genesis 1–3 together with the adoption of the Greco-Roman household code appears to have brought potential radical sex-gender revolutions to an early end.

Feminist critics have tackled Genesis 1–3 in a variety of ways, recognizing that its image of Eve/Everywoman has been extremely damaging for women throughout the centuries. Some, such as Trible (1978) try to argue that the text itself is not oppressive, only its history of interpretation. Others, such as Daly (1986) reject the text as irretrievably irredeemable. Few, however, have provided a thoroughgoing criticism of the heterosexual imperative enshrined in 3.16, and some have, perhaps unintentionally, reified it. Carol Meyers, for example, believes that the supposed Yahwist account of creation can be cast in a more positive light if we understand the social background for the scriptural injunctions.[118] In her view, the text has its origins in a time when the proto-Israelites belonged to a frontier society in the highlands of Canaan (twelfth to tenth centuries BCE) when the family would need as many hands as it could breed in order to survive. In such a precarious environment there was a strong call for women to 'do their duty'. Yee provides a rather different scenario. She also places the origins of the text with the proto-Israelite society in the highlands of Canaan, but at a time when a move from a familial mode of production to a native-tributary mode of produc-

---

118 The hypothesis that Genesis 1–3 can be divided between a priestly narrative and a Yahwist narrative is widely upheld, as is the view that the Yahwist account is earlier, dating back to the tenth century BCE. However, there are notable dissenters and this early date has been challenged. See Gunn (1978), van Seters (1983), Lemche (1988, pp. 41–58, 1993, 1994). If the narrative is not as old as Meyers believes, there is an inevitable consequence for her overall thesis.

tion was being made. In order to break the lineage bond and induce loyalty to the state, the rhetoric of the text privileges the marital bond. Thus for Yee, by stipulating that a man leaves his household and cleaves to his wife (not his wife's clan) the text inculcates a sense of small nuclear units, weakening the claims of clans/lineages and strengthening the allegiance of the nuclear unit to the state. Ordaining this union by divine word 'Genesis 2.23–4 can be seen as part of the state's sexual agenda in its ideological control over its populace' (Yee 2003, p. 71). As for 3.16's insistence that a woman will direct her (sexual) desire towards her husband, Yee claims this too can be seen as state rhetoric designed to emphasize women's primary social role (childbearing) and to ensure the legitimacy of her children through one paternal line. The husband's rule over her mimics that of the king's over the people.

Both Yee and Meyers recognize the compulsion of the text; the coercing of women into this childbearing role. However, Meyers' view that a woman will not experience her husband's exercise of power over her as oppressive because she experiences (sexual) desire for him, reads the Genesis text uncritically. One only has the narrator's word for it that 'woman' (a mythical universal woman) experiences such desire. What if some (real) women do not? Meyers' scenario does not account for that possibility. On the contrary, her work emphasizes only the likelihood of the ancient woman's lack of enthusiasm to bear children repeatedly in a world where medical technology and pain relief as we know it today were not available and death in childbirth probably frequent. Her assessment that the divine injunction was needed to overcome the reluctance of women to embark upon multiple pregnancies when it was a social and economic necessity that she do so, is credible. Her conclusion that 'Motherhood . . . was to be encouraged as being in the national interest (1988, p. 116) is credible. The view that 'because she experiences desire and yearning for the man, such male control would not be experienced as oppressive' (1988, p. 116), strains that credibility. This is one of those occasions when the heterocentrism of feminist studies has failed to take account of a lesbian-identified perspective and not recognized how this imperative is a major strategy for obscuring and suppressing any visibility of female homoeroticism. The alignment of sex, gender and sexuality in Genesis 1–3 is thus allowed to establish a storyworld where heteronormativity prevails, where any other possible ordering of human society is disavowed and any objection to it suppressed by divine fiat.

The influence that this scriptural text has exerted cannot be overstated, particularly for those with allegiances to Judaism and Christianity. Rebecca

Alpert notes how Genesis 1–3 has been foundational for an enduring Jewish commitment to the notion of male–female complementarity (1992, p. 363–4). It has also had enduring influence within Christianity. Chapter 2 noted how church positional statements on homosexuality draw on scripture in order to justify opposition to same-sex relations and drew upon my own tradition of the Salvation Army. While this organization is not exactly a representative of mainstream Christianity, its positional statement on homosexuality has strong links with those of other denominations. Its first paragraph, for example, refers to the 'truths' of Genesis 1.27 and 2.23–24; specifically that God differentiated humanity into male and female sexes, from which it can be construed that 'sexual union leading to a one-flesh relationship is intended to be between male and female' (citing Genesis 2.23–24) and that this complementary union is the basis of the family unit. Thus, the Salvation Army's oppositional stance to practising same-sex rela- tionships is grounded in the biblical indication 'that God's intention for mankind is that society should be ordered on the basis of lifelong, legally sanctioned, heterosexual unions'. It uses this perspective to define 'family' as a unit that complies with the heterosexual contract. The Salvation Army is by no means alone in the way it buttresses its position by references to selected verses within Genesis 1–3. Key verses such as Genesis 1.27 and 2.24 undergird virtually all Christian discussion of same-sex relations. Although not usually numbered among the texts of terror, the influence and impact of selected verses from Genesis 1–3 makes them worthy of a place.

And yet, even in the unlikely text of Genesis 1–3, the key verses that prescribe gender complementarity and the ordering of male–female relations have their queer elements that disrupt the heterocentric rhetoric. For instance, a lesbian-identified reading may well notice, not without humour, how the instruction that Eve's desire will be for her husband is contained with the *punishments and curses* meted out in verses 14–19. Thus, talk of desire for a husband, desire that outweighs the reluctance to be ruled over, does not appear to have been a feature of the Eden society. Moreover, a lesbian-identified reading notes that a woman's sexual drive has to be specifically directed towards a male object, *and* by ordination of a deity. Consider Marilyn Frye's point:

> There is so much pressure on women to be heterosexual, and this pressure is so pervasive and so completely denied, that I think heterosexuality cannot come naturally to many women; I think that widespread hetero- sexuality among women is a highly artificial product of the patriarchy ...

I think that most women have to be coerced into heterosexuality. (1982, p. 196)

Genesis 3.16's insistence that a woman's desire must be for her husband is a very early, but influential, example of such pressure. Why does the male object of Eve's desire need to be so clearly and unambiguously stipulated? Could it be that it is because there is so little to be gained by complying with the sex-gender system that women might justifiably walk away from it? Alpert (1997, p. 25) and Stone (2000) both note how this implies that women's desire could easily stray into other channels if not strongly circumscribed. Thus Genesis, for all the bolstering support it gives for the obligatory heterosexual contract, has its queer features. In Stone's words:

> the text seems to display a certain amount of insecurity about the woman's desire for the man, having to insist upon that desire as something that God ordains while also recognizing that it is a consequence of her rebellion . . . Moreover, this statement about the woman's heterosexual desire is followed immediately by the infamous recognition that, from now on, her husband will 'rule' over her. The conjunction of these two statements almost makes it sound as if the text recognizes, as Wittig, that women might have good reasons for refusing to submit to the terms of the heterosexual contract, so the text has to insist upon the installation of heterosexual desire as a guarantee of such submission. (2000, p. 64)

Stone's reading problematizes attempts to use these verses of Genesis for unequivocal scriptural support of the heterosexual contract. His queering of the text deliberately emphasizes the tensions and contradictions within it:

> What I am trying to argue is that the biblical contributions to the heterosexual contract, though clearly present and certainly visible in the Genesis creation accounts, are less secure than many contemporary readers wish to admit. One legitimate and important strategy of queer 'resistance reading' of the Bible (though not, of course, the only one) is therefore to expose this insecurity in Genesis and elsewhere . . . If we are able to contest what Butler calls 'the regulatory fiction of heterosexual coherence' by showing that the rhetorical foundations of this fiction – including the supposed biblical foundations – are never so coherent as we have been led to believe, we may open up spaces for the production of

alternative, queer subjects of religious and theological discourse. (2000, pp. 67–68 citing Butler 1990, p. 36)

Christian scriptures that endorse the notion of sex-complementarity can also be contested. In her article 'Camping Around the Canon' Elizabeth Stuart discusses laughter as a means of subversion and survival, offsetting the terrorizing way in which texts are used by conservative religious denominations. Taking a portion from the Christian scriptures which has similarly been used to undergird the heterosexual imperative and gender conformity she describes how the serious pronouncements of Ephesians 5. 21–33, heard so often as a 'heteropatriarchal and colonial manifesto for the ordering of male/female relationships' at weddings, used to produce within her bodily reactions of wincing or churning with anger. This was until she heard Gerard Loughlin's unpublished reading of the passage which points out the difference an unanticipated readerly audience can have. The idea that lesbian-identified readers could consider themselves called to act as Christ, to 'husband' their loved ones, enabled Stuart to experience an altogether different reaction to the text: one of laughter. Queer Christians, she argues, are ideally placed for subverting 'tragic' texts in this way since camp humour is at the heart of queer culture. She envisages a future where readers have learned to divest themselves of the inherited training not to laugh at scripture:

Perhaps there will be a Stonewall-type moment of laughter when queer Christians sitting in a cathedral hearing the intonement of Romans 1.26–7 one more time or one of the stories of biblical eunuchs or Jesus' words about marriage in heaven in Matthew 22 told 'straight' will begin to laugh, quietly at first but building to a crescendo that will sweep the queer world and disturb, disorder, and transform the straight church and its relationship with the biblical text. But learning to laugh at texts – to read them with camp humor communally and critically – must become an integral part of queer reading strategies if the Word is to be taken back. (2000, p. 31)

I enjoyed Stuart's article; it did indeed make me smile. However, the niggling thought that this kind of queer reclamation might be seen as a playful luxury that those living in a non-western context can ill afford, was not far away. When the context of oppression outlined in the preceding chapter is considered, such humour seems a little out of place when one's very liberty and safety are at stake. In addition, I am not yet convinced that such readings will be taken seriously by conservative and traditional religious leaders. These are two of the reasons why I believe there is still much to be done with the texts of terror that are widely used to support anti-lesbian and gay sentiment, as will be discussed further in the next chapter. However, the resistance that Stuart describes may well have its place in sustaining the spirits of these lesbian-identified readers who are living with the harsh realities of being a persecuted minority. Until their voices are heard more clearly, it is difficult to suggest what resistant strategies would be found most useful.

Other ways in which the scriptural injunctions to sex-gender complementarity can be resisted include highlighting those occasions where scriptural women choose instead an overt commitment to each other (as with Ruth and Naomi). Being prepared to imagine, to think creatively and openly about the likelihood of women's relations, even when they are not explicitly recorded in the text, is vital. For example, two women are mentioned in very close proximity to each other in Judges 4–5 who, despite being involved in the same literary storyworld and indeed, the same battle, never meet or speak to each other. One of these women has additionally suffered from the 'heterosexualization' process referred to in the first section of this chapter where an ambiguous pair of Hebrew words has been taken to indicate her husband. Deborah is described in Judges 4.5 as a prophetess and an *'ešet lappidōt*, invariably translated in English Bibles as 'wife of Lappidoth'. However *'ešet* could equally be translated as 'woman' and *lappidōt* as 'flames', as has been noted by Exum (1985b, p. 214), Gunn and Fewell (1990, p. 391; 1993, p. 59) and Bal (1988, p. 30). The feasibility of translating *'ešet lappidōt* as 'woman of flames' is aided by four factors.

First, Barry Webb has convincingly demonstrated that there is an abundant interplay of words, motifs and activities within the book and justified his case for a deep and rich coherence across the various constituent stories of Judges. Certain words provide both short and long-range connections within the narratives and *lappid* (which finds five of its 14 references in Judges), is one of those long-range connections (Webb 1987, p. 178). Hence, in a book where 'flame' seems to operate as a motif, it seems reasonable to believe that this plural noun is meant to be translated as 'flames'. Conversely, it is of course possible that the author could have selected a husband for Deborah with a name that suited his literary purposes; this cannot be ruled out. Perhaps the ambiguity was deliberate. However, if the next three points are taken into account, a more cumulative case can be argued.

Second, consider the word *'ešet* (woman/wife). In favour of preferring 'woman' rather than 'wife' stands the deliberate emphasis in Judges 4 on Deborah's identity as a woman. The Hebrew writer goes out of his way to emphasize Deborah's gender, literally saying, 'And Deborah, a woman, a prophetess, *'ešet lappidōt* she, she was judging Israel beneath the palm and she, she was sitting.' Robert Alter, whose comments bring this 'purposeful awkwardness' to our attention, writes: 'the stylistic bumpiness . . . is intended precisely to bump our sensibility as an audience. It is the rare exception and not the rule to have a prophetess rather than a prophet, a female rather than a male judge. A reversal of roles . . . will be at the heart of the story' (1992, p. 41). Translating *'ešet lappidōt* as 'woman of flames' rather than 'wife of Lappidoth' means that attention is not directed away from the emphasis upon the female sex to a male relative.

Third, Deborah is hailed in Judges 5 as a 'Mother in Israel'. Note that she is not the mother of any specific children, but a national Mother. If she is free to be hailed as such, then perhaps she was not considered anyone's specific wife or mother. However, this brings Judges 5, which is arguably an independent tradition, uncritically into the discussion of Chapter 4.

Fourth, the subsequent characterization of Deborah merits the 'woman of flames' translation. Deborah, for all that she is found 'sitting' beneath a palm, is a woman of action. She is portrayed as an independent prophetess who judged Israel. She summons Barak ('lightning' – an ironic name) to her presence and instructs him according to the word of the Lord. It is she who utters the imperatives while Barak is portrayed as the weaker, more reluctant, warrior. Faced with Deborah's 'Go!' his response, as translated by Alter is, 'If you will go with me, I will go, and if you won't go with me I won't go' (1992, p. 42). Commenting on this translation, Alter demonstrates the contrast between these two individuals: 'Barak in a paroxysm of hesitation, releases a stammering chain of go's, his going repeatedly conditional on Deborah's going, on her leading him by the hand all the way' (1992, p. 42). As I have argued elsewhere (Guest, 2003), Barak is portrayed as a comic slowcoach, full of hesitation, and compared to Deborah's fire, is a thoroughly wet fish. The 'woman of flames' thus stands as an eminently suitable contrast to the 'lightning streak' whose name is surely meant to be ironic.

Deborah, woman of flames, arguably independent of male relatives, is an extraordinary female image within the scriptures. One is immediately drawn to the possibilities that this character, with her gender non-conformity, offers promising material for a lesbian-identified hermeneutic.

However, it is vital to keep the hermeneutic of hetero-suspicion operative, especially where the text appears to be offering the very thing one wishes to see. First, Deborah exists within a literary storyworld where norms are deliberately topsy-turvy. As such, her out-of-character behaviour is already predetermined and serves the purposes of the author. Second, as Fewell and Gunn have pointed out, while she may threaten to subvert the norms of patriarchy (she is bold, orders men around, criticizes tribes, functions as both judge and prophet, does not remain behind the scenes), she is actually assimilated quite successfully and does little to challenge those norms effectively. Thus, in Judges 5, her earlier bossing of Barak is forgotten in a poem which celebrates their co-operation in battle. Deborah is praised as a Mother in Israel, 'who coerces her children to fight for what is rightfully theirs' (Fewell and Gunn, 1990, p. 402).

For Fewell and Gunn this acclamation of Deborah as Mother is problematic. It could be seen as an assimilation of her previous unexpected behaviour whereby the possibly subversive and disturbing glimpse of her as an independent, forceful military leader is accommodated into the patriarchal system as an oddity that worked for the good of Israel. Fewell and Gunn conclude that Deborah acts as a man's woman, constrained to function in stereotypically male ways – the way of violence and hardened hearts. She does not pioneer a path for woman carved through patriarchal territory, but performs a role that is prescribed and carefully contained: 'Deborah appears . . . trapped in the very value system which we imagine her to be subverting' (1990, p. 397). There may yet be a way of queering this text that overcomes the problems noted by Fewell and Gunn, but this remains to be seen. At present, in order to spring Deborah from her heteropatriarchal storyworld, one has to go beyond the usual boundaries of scholarly exegesis and enter the realm of the critical imagination, a realm where, for the first time, Deborah can meet her co-combatant – Jael. Such an encounter has never occurred before, not in scripture, nor in the commentarial tradition. However, in Sara Maitland's short story published in 1983 the two women at last meet. In her fictional retelling of their intertwined lives, one senses that they have known each other for many years. Maitland effectively disrupts the scriptural story to the extent where their (shared) victory cannot be so readily accommodated, where their friendship is a thing of fear and unnerving disquiet for their male peers. Here, the Song of Deborah never becomes one that men share. They may know a phrase or two, but it is never owned ('men never came to love and use it' – 1983, p. 1). The song, like the women it celebrates, disturbs the status quo, upsets the norms, and destabilizes even further the already upset order of things. This is what makes Maitland's reading such a valuable resource for the lesbian-identified reader. However, further discussion of how use of the critical imagination and Jewish midrash can be a valuable resource for a lesbian-identified hermeneutic must wait until Chapter 5.

Conclusion

The above discussion demonstrates how a lesbian-identified commitment to a hermeneutic of hetero-suspicion uses a variety of means to disrupt and resist the ways in which the scriptures are used to sustain heteronormativity. A hermeneutic of hetero-suspicion resists the 'no lesbians in the scriptures' assumption by exposing the strategies used to obscure and suppress any reference to female homoeroticism. It uses archaeological studies to explore the material lives of women, which can then be used to contest the valorized depiction of wifedom and motherhood. It draws upon historical and social-scientific research to explore the potential escape routes for women, using cross-cultural analogies where appropriate, to bring to light how women in the surrounding cultures of the ancient world, or in modern pre-industrial analogous societies, find ways of renegotiating their expected destinies. At times, it may well seem as if one is clutching at straws. Feminists often note how difficult it is to reconstruct women's lives given the poor resources available, how much more difficult it is to demonstrate that aspect of women's lives which is hardly ever documented – their love for each other. The above discussion demonstrates how useful the hermeneutic of hetero-suspicion is, but this principle needs to be combined with further principles if the awareness of female homoeroticism that has been prised open in this chapter is to be further expanded.

Notwithstanding, this chapter has indicated several avenues that await further research and, ultimately, the knowledge gained by these methods of historical reconstruction will contribute to the development of a fuller awareness of female homoeroticism so that the normalizing process at work within the scriptures is more easily identifiable, and collusion with it more readily resisted. When one has a broader, thicker awareness of women's worlds and is prepared to acknowledge that women experienced homoerotic desire for each other, then the absences of text are all the more glaring and the critical distance between the reader and the rhetoric of the text is all the greater. Commitment to a hermeneutic of hetero-suspicion unsettles the text by focusing upon its queerer elements and by welcoming the use of the critical imagination and midrash within biblical hermeneutics. All these strategies facilitate resistance.

4

Rupture: commitment to the disruption of sex-gender binaries

In a global context where lesbian-identified women find themselves at best marginalized, at worst criminalized members of society, it is tempting to ground lesbian-identified hermeneutics in one primary principle: a commitment to the absolute dignity and self-worth of the lesbian-identified person. Such a move would echo the progressive parliamentary moves made in South Africa. When its Constitutional Court declared, in October 1998, that the crimes of sodomy and Section 20A of the Sexual Offences Act were unconstitutional, the reason given was that such laws affect adversely the dignity, personhood and identity of lesbian and gay-identified people. It would also echo moves within biblical hermeneutics where reader-response interpretations and/or liberation theologies often privilege the dignity and experience of the relevant reading community. In early second-wave feminist hermeneutics, for example, the gold standard of judgement was the non-negotiable belief that women are possessors of full humanity, whose innate dignity should not be compromised, where women's experience and sense of integrity operated as the ultimate litmus test for the authority of scripture.[119] Rooted in the history of slavery and the ongoing experience that derives from the lived realities of existence, the Black readings of scripture that emerged in the second half of the twentieth century similarly asserted the dignity and self-worth of Black people.[120]

---

119 Ruether said the 'critical principle of feminist theology is the affirmation of a promotion of the full humanity of women. Whatever denies, diminishes, or distorts the full humanity of women is, therefore, to be appraised as not redemptive' (1985, p. 115). Margaret Farley claimed that scripture 'cannot be believed unless it rings true to our deepest capacity for truth and goodness. If it contradicts this, it is not to be believed. If it falsifies this, it cannot be accepted' (1985, p. 43).

120 On the connections between Black feminist thought and the lived realities of Black existence, see Collins (1991, pp. 3–40) and Smith (1982, p. 164). Famously, Howard

The priority in these and other liberation hermeneutics is the commitment to the reading community's life experiences and using these as a yardstick for measuring how far scriptural texts are revelatory or non-revelatory or, for non-confessional interpreters, how far scriptural texts are damaging to one's sense of personhood.

A lesbian-identified hermeneutic could likewise be one where one's sense of self-worth and one's experience of lived realities become the norm for evaluating scripture. This has already been suggested for lesbian-identified theology by Audre Lorde who, originally writing in 1984, encouraged her readers not to 'fear the *yes* within ourselves' and warned them of the dangers in locating authority anywhere else:

> When we live outside ourselves, and by that I mean on external directives only, rather than from internal knowledge and needs . . . then our lives are limited by external and alien forms. But when we begin to live from within outward, in touch with the power of the erotic within ourselves, and allowing that power to inform and illuminate our actions upon the world around us, then we begin to be responsible to ourselves in the deepest sense. For as we begin to recognize our deepest feelings, we begin to give up, of necessity, being satisfied with suffering, and self-negation, and with the numbness which so often seems like the only alternative in our society. Our acts against oppression become integral with self, motivated and powered from within. (1996, p. 110)

This is a view endorsed by Tim Koch (2001a) whose interpretative method is located in a correlation between the text and his own experience, rather than in what other people have to say about him and his relation to the scriptures. His views are discussed further in Chapter 5. However, if a lesbian-identified hermeneutic identifies innate dignity and the authority of experience as the fundamental criteria for interpretation, it could be in danger of essentializing and homogenizing 'lesbian experience', in danger of reifying a sexual category that will continue to divide one kind of woman from another and in danger of sustaining the homo–hetero binary that has funded the history of oppression.

Thurman's grandmother felt 'free to criticize and reject those portions and interpretations of the Bible that she felt insulted her innate sense of dignity as an African, a woman, and a human being, and she felt free to cling to those that she viewed as offering her inspiration as an enslaved woman and that portray, in her estimation, a God worth believing in. Her experience of reality became the norm for evaluating the contents of the Bible' (Weems 1991, p. 62).

Rupture: commitment to the disruption of sex-gender binaries

This problem of reifying problematic categories and binaries has already been faced by feminists. In *Theorizing Gender* Alsop, Fitzsimons and Lennon helpfully articulate the quandary: 'how do we challenge the structural and material inequalities that many women face if we do not operate on some basis at least with the category "woman", even if while utilizing the term we remain cognizant of its fictions and unstable foundation?' (2002, p. 232). Further: how does one 'reconcile the rejection of the binary male–female with a woman-based politics, and in so doing simultaneously deconstruct and claim the female identity?' (2002, p. 233). A lesbian-identified hermeneutic faces the same dilemma in slightly modified terms: how to reconcile the rejection of the homo–hetero binary with a lesbian-identified politics, and in so doing simultaneously deconstruct and reclaim a lesbian identity?

It appears contradictory to advocate the rupture of sex-gender binaries while holding to a specifically *lesbian*-identified interpretative position. However, as I argued in Chapter 1, a resolution can be found in heuristic or strategic use of the term 'lesbian'. This is not an appeal to so-called strategic essentialism. In fact, it is more accurate to speak of an appeal to strategic constructionism, for it involves, in Judith Butler's terms, having it 'permanently unclear what that sign ['lesbian'] signifies' (1991, p. 14). It is precisely the openness and 'becoming' of the signifier that renders it a (still) useful category to be decentred and destabilized, rearticulated and transformed so that it continues to provide a site for resistant agency. One of the impacts of queer theory is its reminder that although the adoption of a lesbian identity is still a transgressive act, it arguably complies with the cultural imperative to identify as an intelligible sexual subject. Normative heterosexuality depends upon people willingly adopting that marginalized half of the hetero–homo binary. Embracing a lesbian identity can thus lend support to the idea that hetero and homosexual are stable identities to which one is oriented. So despite the fact that adopting a lesbian identity is a brave act of independence from sex-gender norms, it simultaneously risks solidifying both the category (lesbian) and the binary (lesbian–straight) and thereby, ironically, endorsing normative heterosexuality. A lesbian-identified hermeneutic must remain acutely aware of this unfortunate paradox and be alert for ways of rupturing the homo–hetero binary and to the dangers of using hermeneutical strategies that perpetuate and cement rigid sex, gender and sexuality boundaries.

This does not mean that the notion of using experiential knowledge is to be cast aside rashly. While one needs to avoid making claims for an experiential knowledge that is essentially determined, it is still the case that those who have occupied marginalized subject positions have discourse horizons and insights not readily available to others. It is informative to see how Patricia Hill Collins works through the question of who can be a Black feminist. She too resists any definition that makes biological Blackness the determining essential quality from which Black consciousness derives since such definitions reify race as something 'fixed and immutable' and thereby cover over the ways in which racial categories are historically constructed. Such definitions mask the way meanings of race shift, and do not adequately deal with 'the crucial role of politics and ideology in shaping conceptions of race' (1991, p. 20). But this does not lead her to rule out the role of experience for the formation of Black feminist thought. On the contrary, Black feminist thought is the result of a particular vantage point, a 'unique angle of vision' that Black women gain by virtue of their position in society. In her words:

> our experiences as African-American women provide us with a unique standpoint on Black womanhood unavailable to other groups. It is more likely for Black women as members of an oppressed group to have critical insights into the condition of our own oppression than it is for those who live outside those structures. (1991, p. 33)

Black feminist thought thus 'consists of specialized knowledge created by African-American women which clarifies a standpoint of and for Black women. In other words, Black feminist thought encompasses theoretical interpretations of Black women's reality by those who live it' (Collins 1991 p. 22).

In like manner, a lesbian-identified hermeneutic will embrace the work of contributors whose consciousness has been sensitized by the lived realities of being positioned as 'a lesbian'. Coping with routine stigma and discrimination, with silence and invisibility, with threatened or actual rape and imprisonment, facilitates an acute awareness of the conspiracy of silence that obliterates 'lesbian' history and issues, a recognition of the processes of social control, a consciousness of the blind spots within feminist theory, insights into how religious institutions and discourse are implicated in discrimination and oppression, and so forth. As I argued in the opening chapter, one does not have to 'be' a lesbian in any ontological innate way to be able to interpret biblical texts from this position, but one does need both a discourse horizon and an understanding of what Rich calls the 'risks and threats of lesbian existence' (1987, p. 74). Yet because a lesbian-identified hermeneutic is aware of the ways in which sexual categories have been historically constructed, aware of how the category has different meanings and significance attached to it depending upon a variety of factors (including one's geographical location, class, race, age, among others), and aware of the role of politics and ideology in shaping conceptions of sexuality, it will resist interpretational strategies that only serve to solidify the category. A commitment to uphold the absolute dignity and self-worth of the lesbian-identified person could have precisely that unfortunate effect.

Notwithstanding, I am very aware that in contexts where people placed in the lesbian category are severely oppressed, the need for a hermeneutic which supports dignity and self-worth may be pressing, just as it was in the Transatlantic early gay liberation movements of the twentieth century. In her insightful review of early lesbian and gay theologies, Elizabeth Stuart demonstrates how the community's first theologians were largely committed to an essentialist understanding of sexual orientation as an innate biological destiny. This helped to offset the heritage of anti-lesbian/gay scriptural teaching. Early lesbian and gay theologies affirmed the distinctive spiritual gifts of the lesbian or gay-identified individual, affirmed sexual practice as celebration of spiritual experience and stressed the authority of innate authentic experience over traditional church teaching.[121] While those early approaches can now justifiably be criticized on a number of grounds, not least due to the way in which they reinforced sexual categories, I believe Stuart is overly critical in her assessment that they were 'brilliant' but ultimately 'bankrupt'. Stuart, however, chooses her words carefully:

> I do not wish to suggest that gay theology has been a mistake nor do I want to imply that it is completely redundant. Rather, what I want to suggest is that it has proved again and again that it cannot deliver what it has promised . . . It has failed to produce universally convincing reasons for the acceptance of lesbian and gay people and their relationships within the Church and society as a whole. (2003, p. 28)

Stuart's assessment paves the way for her advocacy of queer theology which she believes has the greater potential for upsetting the categories and moving beyond them. Whether queer theology will have the impact she

---

121 See, for example, Gearhart and Johnson (1974), Macourt (1977), McNeill (1976, 1996), Fortunato (1982), and to some extent the more recent work of Glaser (1990) and Wilson (1995).

anticipates remains to be seen. I suspect that Church and society as a whole may well have more problems with the radical and provocative features of a queer approach than it had with the old-style lesbian and gay theology, especially when one considers Goss's description of queer as confrontational and transgressive, something that 'produces transgressive gay/ lesbian bodies and voices to confront, antagonize, disrupt and overthrow the network of homophobic power relations' (1993, p. 56) or his portrayal of queer hermeneutics as the 'insurrection of the polymorphously perverse' which 'contradicts dominant cultural discourse and practice by deviating, inverting, distorting, reversing, and subverting . . . [which] involves a movement from inversion as a stage of resistance to flagrant transgression as rebellion' (1996, pp. 17–18).[122] This queering of Catholic Christianity, which will 'despoil its symbol system, theologies, and exclusion practices', is more likely to mean that Goss is considered a blasphemer rather than a redeemer. This does not mean that I advocate an assimilationist agenda. I do not. Queer theology, with its iconoclastic agenda, is a breath of fresh air. But the hope that queer theology, when it operates with such terminology, will provide a breakthrough for current Christian and Jewish religious debate, seems unrealistic to me.

Yet I empathize with Stuart's position. For someone who has engaged again and again with the Church, the frustration of seeing one's best efforts continually thwarted must be exhausting. One gains a glimpse of this in her telling scene where

> lesbian and gay people, their supporters and their opponents currently slump exhausted, having gone too many brutal rounds with one another, barely able now to muster the energy to raise two fingers at each other – never mind exchange a loving kiss. (2003, p. 3)

Such battle-weariness has no doubt contributed to the criticism of those early theologies. This is understandable; but perhaps it is too soon to sound the death knell for these apologetic approaches in toto, as she appears to acknowledge in her comment that gay theology is not 'completely redundant'.

Even in the UK, where LGBT community-building and queer activism

---

122 However, Goss does view such action as having a positive effect: 'Queering . . . inverts cultural symbols, perverts and disrupts valued theologies and church practices that are already spoiled for us. Queering imaginatively reconstructs theology, spirituality and church practices in new, inclusive configurations' (1998, p. 194).

has been developing over the past few decades, Pride gatherings are indicative of the need that still exists to *see* other lesbian-identified persons who look normal, nay attractive, positive and happy, who are unashamed, who live their lives openly and have productive lives. There is a thirst for representations of successful lesbians in art, in the music and film industries, in sport, in literature and so forth. And if this thirst is tangible in the UK it is not difficult to imagine the parched scenarios in other regions of the world where there is little or no access to any positive indigenous images, where the climate is one of vehement hostility to anything that threatens heteronormativity and where the struggle to make one's voice heard remains a perilous endeavour. In contexts where silencing or persecution drives any sources of community underground and where western images are demonized, there arguably remains a place for positive self-affirming, lesbian-identified theology and scriptural study. In a world where 'Lesbians and gay men are starved for words of life, for symbolic forms that wholeheartedly affirm their personhood' (Cherry and Sherwood 1995, p. xv), their collection of liturgies written to mark the transition points of a lesbian, bisexual or gay person's life, could have a much-needed positive impact.

Significantly, the move to queer theory is happening in western parts of the world where there has already been a 30-year history of lesbian and gay-identified theology (less so for biblical studies). Arguably, there was a need for this positive literature before one could be in a position to move beyond it. It seems to be the case that there is a stage through which all emancipatory movements move in order to articulate themselves. It is certainly difficult to envisage how queer theology or queer interpretations of scripture would have ever emerged without the prehistory of lesbian and gay activism and its resultant theological studies. The affirmation contained with those studies created a base on which to stand, a sense of community and support, and a confidence in one's own knowledge and experience despite the strong counter-messages that are culturally imposed. In time, there may well be a case for dropping a hermeneutical label that has the unfortunate habit of solidifying itself, but while lesbian-identified persons continue to be demonized, stigmatized and marginalized, and while queer readings fail to be sufficiently engaged with the situation in which lesbian-identified persons find themselves, affirmation of dignity and self-worth remains strategically important, particularly in non-western settings.

The way forward will be to hold the desirable disruption of sexual categories in dialectic tension with the strategic need to use the lesbian label as a political rallying point. In the British context in which I work,

I can appreciate the needfulness of making 'lesbian' a contested site so as to avoid solidification of the category itself. In this context, lesbian-identified approaches to scripture do ultimately need to recognize the provisional and contextual nature of their identity-laden label, be committed to exercising caution when using it and endeavour ultimately to resist the persuasive predilection to occupy it. However, the above discussion, particularly that of Chapter 2, makes me aware of the need to encourage a range of approaches and strategies to reading scriptural texts rather than any easy condemnation of certain readings as 'essentialist' or 'backward thinking'. Different situations call for different requirements.

With this in mind, this chapter looks especially at texts that continue to drive anti-lesbian/gay political and religious discourse in all parts of the world. When Church and state combine forces to condemn homosexuality, it is the ability to appeal to so-called texts of terror (Genesis 19; Leviticus 18.22, 20.13; Romans 1.18–32; 1 Corinthians 6.9; 1 Timothy 1.9–10), together with selected verses from Genesis 1–3, that facilitates their anti-lesbian/gay discourse and practice. These texts help political and religious leaders set homosexuals apart from heterosexuals, thereby encouraging the belief that a homo–hetero binary is already established within scripture, and that the homosexual element of that binary is therein denounced as sinful and unnatural. Accordingly, the following discussion first examines how contemporary religious discourse assumes and sustains the homo–hetero binary by grounding their positional statements upon a handful of scriptural texts. The second section investigates how the scriptures do contribute to the presentation of same-sex practices as belonging to the 'other', thereby giving the impression that the scriptures condemn 'homosexuality' and promote 'heterosexuality'. Three strategies for dealing with this problem are identified. A third section explains why it remains important to continue engaging with the 'texts of terror' debate. While there have been calls to abandon what has been seen as a no-win stalemate squabble, this chapter argues that the debate cannot be abandoned. Rather, given the significant role these texts continue to play in sustaining anti-lesbian legislation in non-western regions of the world, the debate needs to be deepened and widened.

Heterosexuals and Homosexuals in Christian Discourse

The scriptural condemnation of same-sex behaviour notably in Leviticus 18.22 and 20.13, combined with the apparent promotion of gender complementarity and male–female procreation in Genesis 1–3, has contributed significantly to assumptions that Jewish men and women are meant to be heterosexually oriented. Thus, when Evelyn Torton Beck was compiling the first edition of her then groundbreaking book *Nice Jewish Girls*, the reactions she received when answering queries about what she was working on included 'startled laughter and unmasked surprise bordering on disbelief' (1989, p. xv). Such reactions are entirely consistent with the fact that, for many, to speak of being both Jewish and gay or lesbian-identified represents an oxymoron. Thus, in her introductory article, which poses the question 'Why is this Book Different from all other Books?' she answers: 'Why? I'll tell you why. According to Jewish law, this book is written by people who do not exist' (1989, p. xv). They do not exist for, as Mark Solomon states: 'Homosexuality has always been for Jews the non-Jewish vice *par excellence*' (1995, p. 75). It is a behaviour that, since the writing of the Torah, has characterized the 'other' from which the good Israelite should distinguish him or herself.

A similar story is told within Christian circles: 'To many people both inside and outside the Christian churches, the name of the Lesbian and Gay Christian Movement is an oxymoron of a particularly scandalous and threatening kind' (Gill 1998, p. vi). In part 2 of his book, Gill includes extracts from the written testimonies of gay and lesbian-identified Christians, where the perceived anomaly of trying to live one's life as gay/lesbian *and* Christian is described. One member comments, for example, 'At first I thought that being gay and a Christian were two things that were never meant to go together' (1998, p. 112). The tension that many would-be lesbian or gay Christians have faced is so great that it has sometimes resulted in ill-health and in leaving the Church altogether. The dissonance is felt so keenly because Christian leaders have presented same-sex activities as very clearly denounced in scripture. To the lay Christian who has no ready access to scholarly debate concerning such texts, the evidence can seem incontrovertible.

Within the Black churches there has been an additional layer to deal with. Being gay/lesbian-identified can be deemed not only unchristian, but also a betrayal of authentic Black culture. Thus, although there clearly has been, and is, a lesbian and gay presence within American Black churches,

Comstock's (2001) research indicates how this presence has been tolerated only by its silence. This is consistent with Cathy Cohen's argument that being identified as straight has played an integral role in representation of 'true blackness' (2003, p. 47). She also indicates the significant influence of statements by African politicians where to be gay 'is to want to be white anyway, since we all know that there is no tradition of homosexuality in our African history' (2003, p. 53).

The idea that to identify as lesbian or gay is a betrayal of one's culture is also strong in those regions of the world where there has been a backlash against colonization and continued neo-colonial domination by Europe and America. This inevitably has knock-on effects for members of those cultures who wish to identify as Christian or Jewish *and* lesbian. In Asian contexts, as in African contexts, homosexuality is denounced as a practice associated with the colonizer from which the indigenous culture should be distinguished. When Christians living in such contexts attempt to confront the anti-lesbian position of their churches, they run the risk of being doubly denounced as 'homosexuals' *and* disloyal pawns of the decadent and invasive West.

This othering of homosexuality is built upon a far more ancient process of othering, already operational when the Jewish and Christian scriptures were being written. In the Hebrew scriptures, the community of Israel is presented as under dire threat of assimilation. It must distinguish itself from the culture of the surrounding neighbours if it is to remain in the land. Yet Israel is repeatedly portrayed as failing to uphold the separation, falling foul of the temptation to follow the practices of neighbours, in particular, the Canaanites. Thus, in the storyworld of the Deuteronomistic historian, the inability to fully conquer the land under Joshua accounts for physical co-existence with peoples left within the land (as is made clear in the summary of Judges 1). This leads to repeated periods of assimilation described in the subsequent chapters of Judges. The experiment with kingship, meant to ensure military security, but also to keep the Israelites from doing what was right in the eyes of the Lord rather than what was right in their own eyes (Judges 17.6; 21.25), failed to prevent repeated apostasy. Eventually and inevitably the threatened expulsion from the land happens. This is the basic storyline of the Hebrew scriptures from Genesis to 2 Kings.

It is relevant to note that, included among the whole host of forbidden activities covered in the books of the law, are the 'doings' of the land of Egypt. In Leviticus 18.3, the deity says to Moses, 'You shall not do as they do in the land of Egypt, where you dwelt, and you shall not do as they do in the land of Canaan, to which I am bringing you. You shall not walk in their statutes'. Leviticus 18.22 and 20.13 appear within a section introduced by these words and although 18.3 does not overtly speak about same-sex practices, this is a verse that has, as early as the second century CE, been used to denounce both male and female homoeroticism. Thus in the *Sifra*, the things that they 'do' in the lands of Egypt and Canaan include men marrying men and women marrying women (*Ahare Mot* 9.8). Such 'foreign' behaviour is clearly not to be mimicked by women within the Jewish community. The othering of same-sex behaviour is also an inherent feature of the Christian scriptures. Here, same-sex activities are included within lists of activities that divide people belonging to the kingdom of God from those who are excluded. There is more discussion of this process of othering in the next section; for now it has sufficiently indicated how the compilers of scripture distance themselves, and their communities, from any participation in same-sex practices. This is achieved by presenting such activities as being characteristic of the other, whether this be the Canaanites, the Egyptians, the Romans or the Corinthians. Same-sex activity is a foreign thing, something people do 'over there', something essentially alien. It is also achieved by overt condemnation and advocacy of harsh punishments for any insiders who do engage in such activities, including, in the case of Leviticus 20.13, the death penalty. This distancing or othering tactic has been highly successful, continuing some 20 centuries later to inform Jewish and Christian opposition to same-sex relationships.

Thus it is that these texts of terror, as they are often called, are the basis of religious positional statements on homosexuality. Historically, concentration on specific texts within Christian positional statements began a process of solidification in the 1950s. In the aftermath of a number of high-profile scandalous court cases[123] the government was pressed to consider legal reform and it did so by appointing the Wolfenden Committee in April 1954. Prompting the establishment of that Committee was the previous month's paper from the Moral Welfare Council of the Church of England entitled *The Problem of Homosexuality – An Interim Report*. This report,

---

123 In the UK in 1938 there had been 134 prosecutions for sodomy and bestiality, but by 1952 there had been 670. In 1938 there had been 822 prosecutions for attempted sodomy and indecent assault, which had risen to 3,087 by 1952. In 1938 there had been 320 prosecutions for gross indecency, but 1,686 cases were recorded for 1952 (see Hines 1990 for these figures, and for a broader discussion of the blackmail opportunities the law indirectly offered and its results, see Weeks 1977, pp. 156–67). The McCarthyism of the 1950s in the United States gave rise to a similar climate of suspicion and fear.

written by a group of Anglican clergy and doctors and intended for private circulation, recommended the decriminalization of same-sex acts (between men). A significant member of this Council was Derrick Sherwin Bailey, who had already published an essay entitled 'The Problem of Sexual Inversion' in 1952. The Moral Welfare Council's paper, with its call for law reform, influenced the report of the Council which, despite noting the immorality of any physical expression of homosexual desire, upheld Bailey's original call for law reform. The Council's report was considered by the members of the Wolfenden Committee and their subsequent recommendations eventually formed the basis for the passing of the 1967 Sexual Offences Act in Britain, which decriminalized same-sex acts between men (so long as they took place in private and that the consenting men were over the age of 21).

As noted, Bailey was an active participant in this development and it was his research project undertaken for the Church of England's Moral Welfare Council which singled out these significant scriptural texts. In his subsequent book *Homosexuality and the Western Christian Tradition*, published in 1955, he describes his remit as being 'to state as accurately and to examine as fully as possible the Bible and ecclesiastical attitudes to homosexual practice, and the contribution of Roman law and mediaeval thought to the views which are now current in the West' (1955, p. vii). Bailey was well aware of the implications of his research for legal reform and religious reform. While not completely exonerating the Church, he hoped to demonstrate how the homophobia of the Church had been prompted by its sincere (but misguided) belief that the scriptures called for the absolute condemnation of homosexuality.

It is Bailey who thus initiates the focus upon a collection of six texts that are used most often to denounce homosexuality (Genesis 19; Leviticus 18.22, 20.13; Romans 1.25–27; 1 Corinthians 6.9; 1 Timothy 1.10). He spends an entire chapter on Genesis 19, since the popular understanding that acts of sodomy were the reason for God's destruction of Sodom and Gomorrah had provided considerable fuel for criminalization. He demonstrates that the sin of Sodom has nothing to do with homosexuality, pointing out that it was not until the mid-first century CE, in the work of 2 Enoch (10.4 and 34.2) that such a connection takes place. The connection was subsequently taken up by Philo and Josephus, who in Bailey's view are responding to their Greco-Roman context and the practice of pederasty. The Christian Fathers strengthened this connection and, over the course of subsequent centuries, the association between homosexuality and sodomy became established. After demonstrating that such interpretations are unfounded,

Bailey expresses his earnest hope that 'we shall soon hear the last of Sodom and Gomorrah in connexion with homosexual practices' (1955, p. 155).

His second chapter commences with a study of the Levitical texts, noting how same-sex acts are associated with the 'doings' of the Canaanites and Egyptians. Noting the strategy of othering (though not using that terminology), Bailey describes this as 'a polemical exaggeration of heathen vice – designed to intensify Israel's sense of national "holiness"' (1955, p. 59). He concedes, however, that the writer sees male same-sex practices as 'peculiarly disreputable, and deserve exemplary punishment as unnatural indulgences, incompatible with the vocation and moral obligation of the People of God' (1955, p. 156). On Romans 1.25–27, 1 Corinthians 6.9 and 1 Timothy 1.10, Bailey also grants that there is a clear denunciation of the pederastic practices of the Hellenistic world and that the 'catamites and sodomites' referred to in 1 Corinthians 6.9 (his preferred translation) are to be understood as male perverts. He goes on to discuss further 'possible references' that relate to homosexuality (Revelation 21.8, 22.15), 'marginal references' (Wisdom 14.22ff), and cases where a 'homosexual interpretation [is] suggested by the language of the English Version' (Ephesians 5.12; Deuteronomy 23.17–18; and the references in 1 Kings to the *qadesh*). In his concluding summary he finds that the attitude of the scriptures to same-sex practices was one of firm disapproval. However, committed to sexologists' notion of the congenital invert, he undermines this disapproval by appeal to context:

> the Bible knows nothing of inversion as an inherited trait, or an inherent condition . . . and consequently regards all homosexual practices as evidence of perversion . . . St. Paul's words can only be understood in the sense which he himself would have attached to them, without introducing distinctions which he did not intend, and which would have been unintelligible to him. (1955, p. 38)

Paul, for Bailey, could not possibly have had in mind the 'genuine invert' (1955, p. 157). His final conclusion thus rests on the claim that

> the Christian tradition affords us little guidance, for it knows only one kind of homosexual behaviour – that which would be termed perversion; thus to one of the most perplexing ethical problems of our time it has at best but an indirect and dubious relevance. (1955, p. 169)

169

Bailey's apologetic work thus firmly reified the homo–hetero binary, claiming that the 'homosexual' has to be understood as a specific kind of person, different from heterosexuals. Nevertheless, his interest in the translation of Greek and Hebrew terms, his differentiation between authorial intention and later interpretation, his questioning of whether texts composed in an ancient context should continue to have relevance and authority for the twentieth century, set in motion a 50-year engagement with these texts that still continues. The interpretational tussle has raged to and fro and has begun to have an impact upon religious institutional discussion, as we shall see.

Within the Church of England, the initial impact of Bailey's work can be seen in the subsequent establishment of working committees set up to review the Church's thinking about homosexuality. Between 1970 and 1989 the Church received the reports of a Board of Social Responsibility (BSR) Working Party (1970), the 'Gloucester' report *Homosexual Relationships – A Contribution to Discussion* (1979) and the 'Osborne' report (1989) commissioned by the BSR for the House of Bishops. The Church, however, neither formally endorsed nor published these reports. Frustrated by the Church's lack of decisive policy, Tony Higton pushed the Church to make a clear declaration when General Synod debated his 1987 private member's motion calling for a return to 'Biblical standards of morality' among church leaders. Although his motion called for a wide-ranging discussion of sexuality, it was the issue of homosexuality that took media attention and grabbed the evangelical imagination. As the latest discussion document from the House of Bishops Group makes clear, Higton's motion has to be viewed in a context where the evangelical wing of the Church has grown stronger in a resurgence of conservative evangelicalism post World War Two. Under the leadership of men like John Stott and J. I. Packer, evangelicalism

> became a much more influential tradition . . . Evangelicals became increasingly committed to playing a full part in the national life of the Church of England, and in this context they have led the opposition to an acceptance of same-sex relationships by the Church. (Church of England House of Bishops 2003, pp. 28–9)

Higton, a leading member of the evangelical wing of the Church of England, was forcing the Church to make a clear stand against homosexuality since the majority of evangelicals 'remain convinced that, even when looked at in the light of the most up-to-date interpretative techniques, the

Bible still seems clear in its rejection of same-sex sexual activity, and for them this necessarily settles the matter' (Church of England House of Bishops 2003, p. 29). After debate and amendment, the final positional statement of the Church of England declared that homosexual genital acts fell short of the ideal of permanent married relationships and were therefore to be met with a call to repentance and the exercise of compassion.

Clearly, the efforts Bailey had expended had not convinced. However, the debate was not ended and a 48-page booklet entitled *Issues in Human Sexuality: A Statement by the House of Bishops of the General Synod of the Church of England* was produced in 1991. At the time of writing, this still represented the current position of the Church of England. Its various references to homosexuality continue to discuss issues already raised by Bailey. So, again, there is implicit recognition of the othering process evident in scripture where same-sex practices are associated with the Canaanites in order to construct a distinctive identity for Israel based on the holiness code (1991, pp. 8–9). There is also attention upon the distinction between consensual same-sex relationships in the modern world and the same-sex practices condemned in scriptures. Thus *Issues* poses the question: 'Did the ancient world recognise a class of people who were homosexual by orientation?' (1991, p. 12). The implication is that if it did not, then its statements about same-sex activity would not be relevant to modern-day gays and lesbians, as indeed Bailey had argued. *Issues* actually concludes that 'phenomena which today would be interpreted in terms of orientation *were* present and recognised' (emphasis added), but also adds that 'the modern concept of orientation has been developed against a background of genetic and psychological theory which was not available to the ancient world' (1991, p. 12). Thus on Genesis 19 *Issues* states:

> these stories simply are not relevant to the case, say, of two men or two women who find themselves deeply emotionally attracted to one another, and who wish to live together in a sexual relationship for mutual support in every area of their lives. The situations are too far apart in human terms for any ethical transfer to be made. (1991, pp. 14–15)

To its detriment, the statement also picks up (albeit critically) Bailey's insistence that homosexuality is a congenital condition that is basically unalterable. By 1991, there had been considerable further discussion regarding homosexuality as a lifestyle choice rather than an innate orientation, and the work of social constructionists was identifying good reasons for rejecting any idea of a fixed, universal, essential sexual identity; but the testimonies of gay and lesbian-identified persons still witnessed to the prevalence of the 'born that way' belief. Recognizing the uncertainty, *Issues* notes the 'general verdict' that sexual orientation 'cannot be said without qualification to be fixed and final', but also that it 'is in most instances strongly resistant to modification' (1991, p. 32). What is important to note is that the House of Bishops uses this belief to advocate a welcoming and accepting attitude towards its lesbian and gay-identified members (or 'homophiles' as it prefers to call them). The report calls upon the Church to provide homophiles with pastoral support and welcome them into congregations. It condemns homophobia, and instructs Christians to 'be active in protecting those who are victimised' (1991, p. 34). As Bailey (and the sexologists who had influenced him) recognized: an essentialist understanding of homosexuality as an innate orientation can be a useful platform for apologetics. But ultimately, the idea that sexual orientation is 'strongly resistant to modification' and the call for compassionate treatment of homophiles serve to reinforce the idea of the homo–hetero binary. Moreover, it still stigmatizes the homosexual element of that binary by calling for the homophile to restrict his or her sexual behaviour if possible and certainly if they are members of the clergy. Thus, while the report recognizes that the expression of one's love for one's partner in genital acts of intimacy can be experienced as the most natural extension of a deep and meaningful relationship, it claims that moral theology prevents acceptance of this where homosexuals are concerned. In moral theology what is 'natural' is not necessarily just what we find ourselves spontaneously doing, it refers to acts that 'are in harmony with the will of God as discernible from creation' (1991, p. 36).

Moreover, the will of God, as revealed in scripture, is apparently that heterosexuality is the norm and that the divine intention was for male–female complementarity. Thus, section 4.17 of *Issues* draws on selected verses from Genesis to stress the different roles of the man and woman in complementary relationship. *Issues* concludes that homophiles should exercise abstinence. There is a small get-out clause for the lay homophile because while the House of Bishops does not feel able to commend practising same-sex relationships, the bishops nonetheless do not reject those 'who are conscientiously convinced that this way of abstinence is not the best for them', who 'sincerely believe it is God's call to them' and there is the call for 'every congregation' to provide for their presence (1991, pp. 41–2). This grace is not, however, extended to the clergy, who 'cannot claim the liberty to enter into sexually active homophile relationships' (1991, p. 45).

Here, Comstock (1993) may well be right in his observation that resistance to ordaining lesbian and gay-identified people is a power issue: tolerating gays and lesbians in congregations is one thing, allowing them to be part of the decision-making process is another. The former is about acceptant tolerance, the latter is about equality.

Ultimately, *Issues* highlights the importance of living a holy and Christ-like life. But it notes that, where sexuality is concerned, it is difficult to say what constitutes holiness and Christ-likeness, especially when dealing with young Christians

> baptised, confirmed, communicant, converted and committed to per-
> sonal faith in Christ and to holiness in life . . . who find themselves to be
> attracted strongly and only to those of the same sex, and in their own
> conscientious judgement unable to attain inner peace or stability until
> that fact is accepted positively. (1991, p. 18)

Issues thus raises more questions than it answers. It swings between opinions – wanting desperately to offer a sincere word of compassion for lesbian and gay-identified church members while being seen to uphold and apply scriptural values. For all its recognition that the sex-gender systems pertinent to the social words of the scriptures have no direct lineage to contemporary lesbian, gay and heterosexual identities, it continues to use scriptural texts as the basis for its positional statement in a generally uncritical manner.

When Synod debated *Issues* in 1997 it was acknowledged (again) that this was not the last word on the subject and that there needed to be further ongoing discussion. As a means of stimulating that debate among the clergy and within congregations, the House of Bishops published *Some Issues in Human Sexuality: A Guide to the Debate* in 2003. For our purposes, it is relevant to note that section 1.2.25 *again* lists Genesis 19; Leviticus 18.22, 20.13, Deuteronomy 23.17–18; Romans 1.26–27; 1 Corinthians 6.9–10 and 1 Timothy 1.9–10 as the texts whereby 'homosexual activity has been consistently condemned within the Christian tradition' (2003, p. 14). Again there is the uncritical conjunction of a post-nineteenth-century term with specific connotations ('homosexuality') with ancient non-western scriptures. The *Guide* does go on to acknowledge John Boswell's argument 'that homosexual relationships have been tolerated in some periods of Church History and that provision was even made for the blessing of same-sex unions', but undermines this reference by noting that 'his controversial claim has not been widely accepted by historians' (2003, p. 14, citing Boswell's 1980, 1994a publications). So, almost 50 years on, the focus upon the 'texts of terror' provided by Bailey continues to represent the battleground upon which the war is fought, and these texts continue to provide the ammunition for those producers of church statements who would insist upon a literalist interpretation of these condemnations with little or no accommodation to current thinking on the construction of 'homosexuality'.

In the meantime, considerable time and energy has been expended on these texts.[124] Some 40 years after Bailey's 1955 publication, Daniel A. Helminiak, a Roman Catholic priest working in the United States, attempted to write a definite study of *What the Bible Really Says about Homosexuality* (1994), (not a very helpful title if one is attempting to break the connection between twentieth-century understandings of 'homosexuality' and the sex-gender systems operational in the social worlds reflected in the scriptures). It is worth noting this publication in some detail since it affords an opportunity to consider Roman Catholic positional statements on homosexuality.

Since 1981, Helminiak had lived in America's Bible Belt where he saw the Bible used as a tool to condone social, economic and legal oppression of contemporary lesbian and gay-identified people. The statements emerging from his Roman Catholic tradition were part of this oppressive climate. In the 1986 'Letter to the Bishops of the Catholic Church on the Pastoral Care of Homosexual Persons', the texts upon which the letter was founded predictably included Genesis 19 ('there can be no doubt of the moral judgement made there against homosexual relations'), Leviticus 18.22 and 20.13 ('excludes from the People of God those who behave in homosexual fashion'), 1 Corinthians 6.9 ('those who behave in a homosexual fashion ... shall not enter the Kingdom of God'), Romans 1.18–32 ('Paul uses homosexual behaviour as an example of the blindness which had overcome humankind ... Paul is at a loss to find a clearer example of this disharmony than homosexual relations'), and 1 Timothy 1.10 ('explicitly names as sinners those who engage in homosexual acts').[125]

Bailey had taken care to distinguish between the modern word 'homosexual' with its connotations of congenital orientation and the practices condemned in these texts. Catholic documents reconnected them with

---

124 For a useful overview and an estimation of the gains that have been won, see part 3 of Goss (2002).

125 This document can be accessed at: http://www.vatican.va/roman_curia/con gregations/cfaith/documents/rc_con_cfaith_doc_19861001_homosexual-persons_ en.html

vigour. The Congregation for the Doctrine of the Faith's 1975 'Declaration on Certain Questions Concerning Sexual Ethics' had advocated pastoral care and understanding for 'homosexuals who are definitively such because of some kind of innate instinct or a pathological constitution judged to be incurable'.[126] But it had also indicated that there was no 'moral justification' for their actions, since scripture

> does not of course permit us to conclude that all those who suffer from this anomaly are personally responsible for it, but it does attest to the fact that homosexual acts are intrinsically disordered and can in no case be approved of.

By 1986, this position had hardened: 'Although the particular inclination of the homosexual person is not a sin, it is a more or less strong tendency ordered toward an intrinsic moral evil; and thus the inclination itself must be seen as an objective disorder'. As for any ideas that scripture could not possibly have modern gay and lesbian relationships in mind, the Letter to the Bishops describes such views as 'gravely erroneous'.

Given the scriptural foundations of these Catholic documents, Helminiak's publication can be seen as an attempt to shake the ground upon which they stand. His sincere conviction that 'the Bible supplies no real basis for the condemnation of homosexuality' (1994, p. 14) drives the work. The wrath of God visited upon Sodom is demonstrated, again, to have nothing to do with the deity's horrified response to homosexual desire. Helminiak accepts that the story is about sexuality insofar as the men of Sodom attempt to 'know' Lot's visitors. But, in a move followed recently by Michael Carden (1999), he argues that this is an instance of male (heterosexual) rape, rather than homoerotic desire (1994, p. 38). Arguing that the text has to be understood in terms of its context, he focuses, like Bailey, upon the issue of inhospitality. The sin is 'abuse and offense against strangers. Insult to the traveler. Inhospitality to the needy. That is the point of the story understood in its own historical context' (1994, p. 39). The irony, that a modern-day equivalent of the situation would be the inhospitality experienced by lesbian and gay-identified people, is not lost on Helminiak:

> Lesbian women and gay men are just not allowed to fit in; they are made to be outsiders, foreigners in our society. They are disowned by their

---

126 This document can be accessed at: http://www.vatican.va/roman_curia/con gregations/cfaith/documents/rc_con_cfaith_doc_19751229_persona-humana_en.html

families, separated from their children, fired from their jobs, evicted from apartments and neighborhoods, insulted by public figures, beaten and killed on the streets. All this is done in the name of religion and supposed Judeo-Christian morality.

Such oppression is the very sin of which the people of Sodom were guilty . . . So those who oppress homosexuals because of the supposed 'sin of Sodom' may themselves be the real 'sodomites', as the Bible understands it. (1994, p. 41)

On the Levitical texts, he notes how Israel is being distinguished from its neighbouring Canaanites. Here, Helminiak draws on a now somewhat discredited scholarly tradition that reconstructed Canaanite religion largely on the basis of the scriptural texts, portraying it as a religion that involved orgiastic sexual rituals including temple prostitution.[127] Helminiak is more restrained in his treatment, just pointing out that those who draw on the Levitical texts have to bear in mind that they are derived from a context where cultic sex played a part in the religious life of Israel's neighbours and from which Israel distinguished itself. Insofar as homosexuality as a condition[128] is far removed from the issue of cultic sexuality, he concludes that 'the Levitical code is irrelevant for deciding whether gay sex is right or wrong. Though the Hebrew Testament certainly did forbid male homogenital activity, its reasons for forbidding it have no bearing on today's discussion' (1994, p. 47). Thus he concludes that 'it is a misuse of the Bible to quote Leviticus as an answer to today's ethical question, whether gay sex is right or wrong. Leviticus was not addressing this question' (1994, p. 53).

In chapter 7 he notes how the New American Bible's translation of *arsenokoitai* as 'practising homosexuals' in 1 Corinthians 6.9 was ideologically loaded: 'How amazing! A first-century text would now seem to teach exactly what Roman Catholicism began teaching only in the mid-1970s: to be homosexual is no fault, but to engage in homogenital acts is wrong'

---

127 Albright (1940) drew a firm line between the purity and distinctiveness of Israelite Yahwism over and against the practices of the Canaanite people, as did his student, Wright (1955). Such views informed the work of subsequent scholars such as Anderson (1966), Ringgren (1966), Fohrer (1973), Bright (1981) and Albertz (1992). However, the evidence that the Israelites and Canaanites share a common ancestry is compelling, as is the subsequent belief that the rhetoric against the Canaanites dates from a much later period. This is discussed more fully in the next section.

128 Helminiak's assumption is that sexual orientation is a given: 'The fact is that some people just happen to be homosexual' (1994, p. 19).

(1994, p. 87). However, his claim that 'nobody really knows' what the words *malakos* and *arsenokoitai* mean seems a little disingenuous. He suggests only that the references in 1 Corinthians 6.9 and 1 Timothy 1.9–10 are concerned with 'exploitative, lewd and wanton sex between men . . . This, then, and not male-male sex in general, is what these biblical texts oppose' (1994, p. 96). Again, this demonstrates a return to the now familiar claim that the Bible has little to say about contemporary gay and lesbian-identified relationships, a point he makes abundantly clear in his conclusion:

> If people would still seek to know outright if gay or lesbian sex in itself is good or evil, if homogenital acts *per se* are right or wrong, they will have to look somewhere else for an answer. For the fact of the matter is simple enough – the Bible never addresses that question. More than that, the Bible seems deliberately unconcerned about it. (1994, p. 109)

Between Bailey's and Helminiak's publications and subsequently, there has been a flurry of publications that attempt to demonstrate how these texts of terror have little relevance to our current debates about homosexuality. Contrarily, there have been publications by scholars who argue that they are of the utmost relevance. The arguments go back and forth and for all their posturing, none have been able to close the debate to the satisfaction of all. Not that permanent closure would ever be possible; interpretation is a continuing, developing process and the meaning of these texts cannot be fixed once and for all. The contested interpretations, the continuing scrapping over scripture only evidences the desire to stake one's claim to the Bible. As I have argued elsewhere (Guest, 2001), it is a fight for the high ground where one wins the right to interpret authoritatively and apply the implication of that interpretation to the current debate concerning the place of LGBT-identified persons within Christianity or Judaism. At stake is the right to claim scriptural authority for one's beliefs. Traces of the siege mentality are noticeable, for example, in Helminiak's work. The listing of the work of previous scholars (John Boswell, L. William Countryman, Robin Scroggs, David F. Wright, William L. Petersen, Victor P. Furnish), together with their titles and scholarly departments, has the effect of bolstering the academic strength of his book, lending it an authority and sense of reliability (as does the large-type PhD that reassuringly follows his name on the front cover of the book). His introduction is even more overt, claiming, 'This book is to help you understand what is going on and decide who is right' (1994, p. 17).

Contesting such claims are writers like Donald Wold who seeks to defend such texts from those whom he accuses of distorting and disabling the word of God (primary among them Bailey, Boswell, Horner and the Rev. Mel White), but also any who would 'try to strip the plain meaning from the text when it does not conform to their agenda' (1998, p. 208). Such publications reify the impression that scripture condemns homosexuality and promotes hetero-sexuality as the God-ordained proper orientation of human sexuality. They thus give weight to the notion that the scriptures themselves construct and uphold a homo–hetero binary. There are also publications that purport to give an objective study of scripture and the way it has been used and abused within current debate. Robert Gagnon's substantial work *The Bible and Homosexual Practice: Texts and Hermeneutics* (2001) is presented as such a work, though it has not and could not derive from an ivory tower of neutrality. It is a conservative text that uses a wealth of information, detailed study and apparent judicious discernment to convince the reader that the final word on the matter has been spoken, but its ideology is just as apparent as the ideology of those he criticizes.

In the present climate, the texts of terror are repeatedly invoked in religious and academic discourse. Whether or not they should be, the situation is that they are currently foundational for contemporary discussion and religious positional statements. The focus on these texts seems to reify the impression that humanity can be divided into homosexuals and heterosexuals and that the scriptures themselves recognize this division. The next section considers how far such an impression is understandable given the othering of same-sex practices in the scriptures, but ultimately refutes this notion and considers strategies whereby it can be contested.

The Othering of Same-Sex Practices in the Scriptures

As noted in the previous section, scholarly histories relating to early Israel, until relatively recently, took the Deuteronomist's account of Israelite origins largely at face value. Albright's (1940) readiness to interpret archaeo-logical evidence relating to the Late Bronze and Early Iron Ages in terms of an Israelite conquest of Canaan was very influential. His classic *From the Stone Age to Christianity* (1940, p. 281) reinforced a binary clearly present in the Hebrew scriptures: the purity and distinctiveness of the Israelite mono-theistic Yahwistic culture over and against the pre-existing Canaanite religion and culture. And, as is the nature of binary oppositions, one of the terms (Canaanite) carries a negative value. This binary opposition between

Israelite and Canaanite was carried forward in the work of his pupils with the influential John Bright describing Canaanite religion in no uncertain terms: 'Canaanite religion presents us with no pretty picture. It was in fact an extraordinarily debasing form of paganism . . . numerous debasing practices, including sacred prostitution, homosexuality and various orgiastic rites were prevalent' (1981, p. 118). Such a view can also be found in Woolff's commentary on Hosea (1974, p. 14).

However, there is a growing body of opinion that the material relating to Israelite origins is a historicized theological construct, providing an ideological portrait of a largely imagined past in order to put forward an agenda for an 'Israel' contemporary with a post-exilic writer. The significance of the debate for this chapter lies in its recognition that the references to Israelites versus Canaanites (or Amorites plus Hittites, Perizzites, Hivites, Jebusites or Egyptians) helps the writers create an 'us and them' mentality, drawing clear lines between Israel and those considered 'outside'. Thus, John van Seters, commenting on the ideological usage of the ancient names Amorite and Hittite, says they are representative of 'the primeval wicked nations whom God displaced in order to give Israel its land. Retention of the land . . . is dependent upon complete separation from the people and religious practices of the Amorites or their ideological counterpart' (1972, p. 78). G. Mitchell more recently argued that the references to Canaanites, Amorites and Hittites 'all serve as symbols of primordial opposition to YHWH . . . by the eighth-century BCE, they are virtually synonymous archaic terms for the inhabitants of Syria-Palestine' (1993, pp. 130f). Cast in the role of archetypal enemy, and representing all things debasing, pagan and undesirable, Lemche speaks of the Canaanites fulfilling a literary role as the 'bad guys' of the Hebrew scriptures (1994, p. 168). As literary foils, they provide temptation for Israel, which will in turn lead to apostasy; such apostasy will lead to justified punishment and eventually to exile from the land.

As I have noted elsewhere (Guest, 1997), it is interesting to note that the list of nations from which Israel must separate itself appears not only in Deuteronomy 7.1 and Judges 3.5, but also in Ezra 9.1: a text concerned with the horror of intermingling. In the Persian context that the Ezra text purports to describe, the use of ancient names helps to distinguish two groups that were contemporary with each other: the 'people of the land' and the 'sons of the exile'. The 'people of the land' are clearly and strongly othered, represented as the primordial archetypes of the non-Israelite. This indicates a concern to dissuade his own community from any contact with them, to distance his community from peoples who, in reality, may have been much more closely related. Using names of recognized, arche-typal enemies, the actual, closely related local peoples are tarred as 'evil' and separated off from the writer's community.

With this in mind we can now turn to two of those texts of terror: Leviticus 18.22 and 20.13. Both texts appear in a section of the holiness code framed by clear instructions to separate from surrounding peoples. Thus 18.22 is introduced by the deity's exhortation in 18.3: 'You shall not do as they do in the land of Egypt, where you dwelt, and you shall not do as they do in the land of Canaan, to which I am bringing you. You shall not walk in their statutes.' The frame concludes with the warning in verses 24–30 that the previous occupants of the land were vomited out because of their defiling practices and that the same will happen again if the land continues to be defiled by abominations. Similarly Leviticus 20.13 is introduced by 20.7–8: 'Consecrate yourselves, therefore, and be holy; for I am the Lord your God. Keep my statutes, and observe them; I am the Lord; I sanctify you.' It concludes in 20.23–26: 'You shall not follow the practices of the nation that I am driving out before you . . . You shall be holy to me; for I the Lord am holy, and I have separated you from the other peoples to be mine.' Within these framing verses there are lists of practices (including same-sex practices) that characterize the nations that are being driven or vomited out of the land. An Israelite identity is evidently being constructed partly in terms of sexual behaviour. By positing an Israel that is distinguishable by its repudiation of the sexual customs of non-Israelites, the scriptures do appear to construct a sexual binary. It does not date back to a Mosaic age but most probably reflects the anxieties of the Yehud community separated literally by Nehemiah's walls from the surrounding populace. The 'Canaan-ites' and 'Egyptians' mentioned at the beginning of Leviticus 18 thus serve as boundary peoples; required to highlight the distinctive place of Israel in the land, and to represent the ever-present dangers of assimilation. There could be no 'Israel' if it were not for these boundary peoples. The binary always needs both elements, the insider and the outsider, in order to func-tion. As noted earlier, the success of the writer in achieving this aim can be seen in the continued representation of Canaanite religion as sexually degenerate in the commentarial history and the presentation of Judaism as a faith practised by heterosexuals.

The othering of same-sex behaviour is also an inherent feature of the Christian scriptures where behaviours concomitant with people belong-ing to the kingdom of God are contrasted with behaviours that character-ize the excluded. This time there is no recourse to ancient symbolic ethnic labels; the authors of the various letters use the practices of their Greek and Roman contemporaries to distinguish a pure Jesus-following community from its contaminating surroundings. Paul and the authors of Jude, 2 Peter and 1 Timothy all appear to be reacting to the Hellenistic context in which they lived and are calling their respective audiences to make themselves identifiably different. In so doing, they represent same-sex activities as a phenomenon that belongs to the surrounding nations, and engage in an othering process that, somewhat ironically, was also emerging in the Roman world itself.[129]

The compilers of scripture thus distance themselves, and their communities, from any participation in same-sex practices, and give the impression that there is a hetero–homo binary running through the scriptures – a binary that Jewish and Christian discourse continues to uphold by repeated reference to these texts in any discussion of homosexuality. In order to disrupt that impression, a lesbian-identified hermeneutic needs to identify strategies that deal effectively with these texts of terror and find ways of problematizing the binary they appear to construct.

One strategy that is now fairly well established is to undertake a detailed exegetical study of the individual texts paying close attention to matters of translation and context. As Helminiak noted, there can be a considerable polemical spin given to the translation of Greek terms such as 1 Corinthians 6.9's *malakoi* and *arsevokoitai* (which the 1976 *Good News Bible* translated as 'homosexual perverts', while 'practising homosexuals' was the preferred translation of the *New American Bible* published in 1970). Given that Paul certainly did not have the word 'homosexual' in his vocabulary and could not have envisaged the western construction of the homosexual in the late nineteenth century, using 'homosexual' in any translation of any scriptural text is problematic. Studies that investigate the construction of sex-gender norms in the Mediterranean world of the first two centuries CE can help to identify the kind of relationships to which Paul and other scriptural writers refer. They also have the added bonus of demonstrating how sex-gender systems are products of particular cultures at particular times. This would help to disrupt naive assumptions about essential, universally present sexual orientation, or the cross-cultural existence of 'homosexuals' and 'heterosexuals' throughout history. Recognition that sexuality is

---

129 Judith Hallet ably demonstrates how tribadism is presented, in Latin sources, as 'a Greek practice, geographically and chronologically distanced from present-day Roman behaviour, and as abnormal and unreal, involving the use and possession of male sexual apparatus' (1989. p. 180).

constructed differently in different contexts and has no necessarily direct lineage to modern (and postmodern) sexual categories can help to disrupt the notion that a homo–hetero binary, as we would understand it today, permeates ancient scriptures.

In recent years some key studies have been published that address the context-specific organization of sex and gender categories in the ancient world and use their findings to reassess scriptures that were thought to refer to homosexuality. Such studies have, for example, helped rupture the association of Genesis 19's men of Sodom with homosexual desire. Gerhard von Rad's commentary on Genesis, the first part of which originally appeared in Germany in 1949, not only linked the sin of Sodom with same-sex desire aroused by the good looks of the divine messengers, but also followed the ideology of the Hebrew scriptures in locating such desire with the Canaanites bringing in references to Leviticus 18.22 and 20.13 to make the same-sex connection overt:

> Then, however at bedtime, the Sodomites, both young and old, surround the house in order to lay hands on the guests. One must think of the heavenly messengers as young men in their prime, whose beauty particularly incited evil desire . . . In Canaan, where civilization at that time was already old, sexual aberrations were quite in vogue. At any event the Canaanites seemed dissolute to the migrating Israelites, who were bound to strict patriarchal customs and commands. This was especially true of the Canaanite cult of the fertility gods Baal and Astarte, which was erotic and orgiastic at times. (Lev. 18.22ff.; 20.13–23, (1972, p. 217)

Studies by Ken Stone (1996), Martti Nissinen (1998) and Michael Carden (1999, 2001) have radically overhauled such views. Interpreted in the light of a social world governed by concepts of honour and shame, the attack upon Lot's guests is still understood as an act of power that humiliates the guests. However, far from being ancestors of modern-day homosexuals, Carden argues that the would-be penetrative males are best understood as heterosexually identified men wielding phallic aggression with the intent of humiliating Lot's household. As Martti Nissinen puts it:

> Gang rape of a man has always been an extreme means to disgrace one's enemies and put them in their place. Its purpose is to disgrace one's male honor . . . it is not a matter of exercising one's homosexual orientation or looking for erotic pleasure but simply of protecting or threatening one's masculinity. (1998, p. 48)

So contra von Rad and Gunkel (whose 1910 commentary on Genesis also suggests the men of Sodom felt erotic attraction for Lot's visitors), recent studies demonstrate that this text is to do with dominance and phallic power of assertion. Lot was about to be taught a harsh lesson about the place of a foreigner in the city of Sodom. Carden (1999), for example, argues that the men of Sodom are attempting to assuage their own anxieties, not of homosexuality but fear of the foreigner. And in order to distance themselves from the foreigner, they assert their superiority and power by raping the visitors. Once the threatened rape is interpreted in terms of a culture organized around distinct sex and gender norms, it can be seen that the rape would be deemed a direct attack upon one's honour as a man and would effectively feminize any man so penetrated. Nissinen had made a similar conclusion:

> it is misleading to speak of the 'author's antagonism towards homosexuality' or claim that 'he condemns homosexuality.' Male–male sex appears in the story of Sodom only as a hostile sexual aggression toward strangers. Other than that, the writer's attitude to same-sex interaction remains unknown. (1998, p. 49)

Such studies, which attend to the specific cultural construction of sex and gender categories and use this knowledge to inform the translation of Hebrew and Greek and the subsequent interpretation of the text, are helping to disrupt binaries.

A second strategy that characterized lesbian and gay studies to date has been to combine critical exegetical study of the texts of terror with a focus upon different texts that appear to present same-sex relationships in a positive light. This destabilizes the notion that scripture has only one (negative) view about same-sex relationships. The stories of David and Jonathan and Ruth and Naomi, Jesus and the Beloved Disciple, have lent themselves to such a strategy. An early study by Tom Horner (1978) argues that David and Jonathan's friendship could be understood as a homoerotic relationship typical of warrior friends. In response to the question did they love each other physically, Horner unequivocally replies yes, they did. 'There can be little doubt . . . except on the part of those who absolutely refuse to believe it, that there existed a homosexual relationship between David and Jonathan' (1978, p. 20). By stating his argument in these terms, the ideological import of his thesis is very clear. It is those who are *willing to believe* who decipher the text's signifiers in this manner. For all that the Gilgamesh epic provides a plausible background for understanding David and Jonathan's relationship as homoerotic, he still concedes that much depends on the horizon of the reader and his or her willingness/ability to see this dimension. The reader has to come to the text with this as a thinkable option, that one is prepared to put aside the 'fifteen hundred years of homophobia in Western culture' (1978, p. 36) and the resultant tendency of commentaries to pass off or ignore the homoerotic content.

Since Horner's book was published there has been plenty of subsequent discussion. Martti Nissinen, writing 20 years later, considers the ancient context in much greater detail than Horner and agrees that the references to Jonathan loving David like his own soul, Saul's condemnation of his son, David's appreciation of Jonathan's love which was more than that of a woman, their tears and tender farewell, all combine to 'make it conceivable to interpret David and Jonathan's relationship as homoerotic' (1998, p. 55). However, Nissinen points out that this is not necessarily the only readerly possibility – simple camaraderie, for example, could explain their words and actions. Saul's outburst at his son could be motivated by a threat to his power, and the innuendo implied in referring to Jonathan's shame (1 Samuel 20.30) simply an attempt to get his son's attention. The homoerotic aspect has to remain simply a possibility to be left 'to the reader's imagination' (1998, p. 56). Elizabeth Stuart (1995) had taken a similar line:

> I would not even want to guess whether David and Jonathan had or were thought to have had homosexual sex, but I think their relationship as portrayed was undoubtedly sexual in that it was passionate, intense and physically expressed ... The Hebrew text bristles with ambiguity, perhaps deliberate ambiguity, to express the fact that here we are in the presence of a significant relationship for which there are no established means of description. Indeed, the Hebrew could be said to convey just enough to make it obvious that there was a sexual element and not enough to enable us to be sure about the exact nature of the relationship. Therefore, we have to focus on the passionate quality of the relationship and cannot be diverted into discussion about 'genital acts'. (1995, pp. 135–6)

On the Ruth and Naomi story, a staple for lesbian-identified readings, Stuart suggests there is far less ambiguity. It is primarily, for Stuart, a story of women flouting conventions in order to engage in a friendship of 'mutuality, passion and justice ... Everything that should have kept them apart – different nationalities, different religions, different blood families – could not suffocate the affection between Ruth and Naomi' (1995, p. 136). Again it is not a matter of whether their relationship was sexually expressed;

rather she seeks to 'demonstrate that their relationships were passionate, bodily and therefore sexual in the wider sense of that term' (1995, p. 137). Here Stuart is avoiding getting caught in the Church's obsession with sexual acts. Attempting to clarify whether they 'did it' is ultimately, in her view, a lost cause: these texts

> have become a wrestling ring in which scholars who want to claim that David and Jonathan had a homosexual relationship, and those who want to claim they did not, lock each other in an unwinnable grip. It is unwin-nable because ultimately there is not enough explicit evidence to support either contention. (1995, p. 132)

I agree that there is insufficient evidence to know one way or the other. I also agree that engaging in such questions could play to the Church's game of distinguishing between a sexual orientation (which is acceptable) and acting upon it (which, in the case of homosexuality, is usually negatively evaluated). I do not, however, think that one should be too quick to place an emphasis upon a non-genital passionate friendship since to push the possibility of physically expressed sexual pleasure away from view could collude with the negative evaluation of such acts.

What is particularly useful in the above discussion of Stuart's work is the way she implicitly highlights how what is considered 'sexual' can differ from context to context. As discussed in Chapter 3, what counts as a sexual act can be culture-specific, and in many cases, women's physical love-making does not constitute 'sex' if it does not specifically include penetration by males. Highlighting the culture-specific ways in which sex-gender relation-ships are organized in the social worlds that produced the scriptures can help rupture any easy equation of their categories with modern categories.

This may be the place where Rich's lesbian continuum serves a useful role. Rich, as discussed more fully in Chapter 1, wishes to bring under the umbrella of the lesbian continuum a range of woman-identified experience that has existed throughout history. It may or may not have been genitally expressed but it has been characterized by 'forms of primary intensity between and among women, including the sharing of a rich inner life, the bonding against male tyranny, the giving and receiving of practical and political support' (1987, p. 52). If we consider the knee-jerk reactions of heterosexually identified persons who object to certain people/groups being included in such a continuum, one gets an insight into the political implications and strengths of Rich's approach. Why else would there be such a reaction if not for specific concerns about the edges of homo–hetero boundaries? The notion of the continuum causes discomfort precisely because it calls into question first, the permeability of sexual categories and second, the uncritical assumption that women are 'naturally' heterosexual ('an enormous assumption to have glided so silently into the foundations of our thought' 1987, p. 34). Commenting upon that assumption she writes:

> I doubt that enough feminist scholars and theorists have taken pains to acknowledge the societal forces which wrench women's emotional and erotic energies away from themselves and other women and from woman-identified values ... [which] range from literal physical enslavement to the disguising and distorting of possible options. (1987, p. 35)

As we have seen in Chapter 3, in scriptural terms the disguising/distorting of other options operates by the valorization of motherhood, the presentation of women as competitive rivals and the presentation of divinely ordained imperative to subject oneself to male sexual desire. In order to challenge the mechanisms of erasure and in order to challenge the homo–hetero boundaries, a lesbian-identified hermeneutic can incorporate scriptural characters into the continuum by focusing upon narratives where same-sex friendships appear primary: the loving commitment of Ruth to Naomi, the female partnerships of Tryphaena and Tryphosa (Romans 16.12), Euodia and Syntyche (Philippians 4.2), possibly the friendship of Mary and Martha (John 11/Luke 10.38–42) that catches Nancy Wilson's eye. The fact that women are predominantly attached to men in the scriptures is not a stumbling-block. Dependence upon male relations for economic security and protection meant that women, unless they numbered among the few capable of living independently, inevitably married. But marital status does not necessarily indicate that their relationships with other women were not significant, or primary. In Chapter 2, we noted how women in the Afro-Surinamese context can enjoy special relationships with other women, while being married and bearing children. In Mati-culture this is not unusual. Bearing in mind the caution that must be exercised when using an analogy between the ancient world and more recent history, it is instructive to read Lillian Faderman's (1985, 1995) work on the passionate and enduring romantic friendships from the Renaissance onwards, that survived the marriage of one of the parties. Despite their lives being so heavily circumscribed by the lack of financial, economic and social independence that relations with men secure, married women clearly found outlets for their *primary* affinities with their female companions and lovers. Hence the continuum could plausibly incorporate scriptural figures.

Given the hostility historically and currently periodically waged by religious figures who wield the Bible as an authority for discrimination, this focus upon affirmative stories is an understandable strategy. It counteracts the strike-force of the Bible, rendering it at least a double-edged sword. The focus on narratives where the family relationships are unconventional, such as the Naomi, Ruth and Boaz triangle, may be of especial use in Asian contexts where the social and political emphasis on traditional family norms and the establishment of familial harmony has had such a devastating impact on daughters and sons whose primary affections are directed to members of their own sex. In her paper on the Chinese context, Chou Wah-Shan speaks of 'the need to build up indigenous *tongzhi* politics that will not reproduce Anglo-American experiences and strategies of lesbigay liberation' (2001, p. 27).[130] Use of the term *tongzhi* signals a desire to 'integrate the sexual into the social and cultural' and facilitates the disruption of the homo–hetero binary since it doesn't invoke a boundary between those who love the same and the opposite sex. She likens it to the force that queer has in the West:

> but whereas queer politics confronts the mainstream by appropriating a formerly derogatory label *Tongzhi* harmonizes social relationships by taking the most sacred title from the mainstream culture. It is an indigenous strategy of proclaiming one's sexual identity by appropriating rather than denying one's familial-cultural identity. (2001, p. 28)

In such a context, the western focus on coming out is inappropriate, 'hinged' as it is 'upon notions of the individual as an independent, discrete unit segregated economically, socially and geographically from the familial-kinship network' (Chou 2001, p. 32). Coming 'out' indicates a moving away, whereas it would be preferable 'to articulate indigenous categories and strategies that can reclaim *tongzhi* voices not by denying one's family-cultural identity but by integrating *tongzhi* into the family and cultural context' (2001, p. 35). Therefore an alternative model of coming home (*hui jia*) is proposed, where *jia* means not only family and home but 'also a mental space which refers to the ultimate home and roots to which a person belongs' (2001, p. 35). By relocating same-sex relations within the family and encouraging

---

130 For a definition of *tongzhi*, see Chapter 2, n. 37.

social contact through meals and playing mah-jong, by using and accepting familial language such as half-sister/brother, or adopted son/daughter, the same-sex partner can be integrated into family-kinship groups and so break down the insider–outsider distinction. Chou gives examples of how relationships have been successfully negotiated not by explicitly telling parents, but by gently introducing their lover into the family grouping over time. A focus upon those scriptural stories that include reference to homosocial relationships, especially one where one woman's commitment to another is accommodated and celebrated (as in Ruth's commitment to Naomi), could be of value for such aims.

However, focus on apparently affirmative texts certainly has its pitfalls and some evaluation of a reclamation focus is necessary if its potential for disrupting binaries is to be fulfilled. 'Reclamation' is a term sometimes used to characterize the salvage work conducted by second-wave feminists seeking to discover information about the place and importance of scriptural women, bringing their stories back from oblivion, seeking out submerged traditions, putting the fragments together, rescuing them from their patriarchal context and reading their stories in a new light. However, there were difficulties inherent in such projects and the valid criticisms that have been raised are equally applicable here. For example, second-wave feminism spoke too often in the voice of a hegemonic 'we' and was insufficiently alert to the interaction of sexism with classism and racism. Moreover, second-wave feminism tended to concentrate on affirming the dominant women at the expense of characters like Zipporah. Mukti Barton rightly challenges the way in which white scholars concentrated on bringing Miriam's story to light while leaving Zipporah's story in the shadows. She warns:

> Unless White feminists are vigilant, their hermeneutics will reflect the politics of omission. In their biblical interpretation they will hear, recover, probe and scrutinize the voices they see as White women's voices. Unwittingly they will highlight Miriam and marginalize Zipporah, revealing that their feminism is really White feminism. (2001, p. 79)

Lesbian-identified interpretations need to beware of suppressing the voices of those who live in different contexts and have different experiences from which to speak, and need to think carefully about the narratives and characters they focus upon.

Related to this point is the way in which second-wave reclamation of women's lives and voices also fell foul of valorizing women without doing the double-thinking that necessarily questioned whether such valorization was actually playing straight into the hands of the patriarchal agenda. With the benefit of hindsight, Cheryl Exum looked back critically to her 1983 article on the women that played a role in Moses' birth and survival. The literary criticism applied in her original paper foregrounded the important role of the women in the story, but as she wrote two years later, despite this affirmation

> the narrative quickly and thoroughly moves from a woman's story to a man's story. While a feminist critique might want to seize onto the affirm-ative dimension . . . accenting the important consequences of women's actions for the divine plan, it must also acknowledge that being mothers of heroes . . . is not enough; acting behind the scenes is not enough. (1985, p. 82)

What was needed were reading strategies (later utilized in her 1993 and 1996 publications) which 'expose and critique the ideology that motivates the biblical presentation of women' (1996, p. 82), that recognizes how 'Honor and status . . . are rewards patriarchy grants women for assent to their sub-ordination and cooperation in it' (1996, p. 94). Affirming women already praised in the text is only reifying the (hetero)patriarchal agenda. This is an important caution. Several gay and lesbian-identified interpretations to date have reclaimed an ancestry in the scriptures, but a critical appraisal of the characters reclaimed is vital if one is to avoid revalorizing the already valorized.

Strategies for reclamation are discussed in detail in the next chapter and what will be noted there is that queer theory has a useful role to play. The application of queer theory provides a third strategy for disruption. How-ever, since queer readings of scriptural texts have already been discussed briefly in Chapter 1 and are considered further in Chapter 5, it will suffice at this point to simply note the significant and valuable part they can play in rupturing the homo–hetero binary.

Insofar as heterosexual and homosexual are late-nineteenth-century, western terms that carry connotations of innate sexual orientation, there can be no homo–hetero binary in the scriptures, but there is a distinction made between Israelites and Jesus-followers who do not engage in same-sex acts and surrounding nations who do. However, the significance and meaning that accrue to such acts as described in, say, Leviticus 18.22 or 1 Corinthians 6.9, has to be considered in the light of ancient contexts. There is no easy equation to be made between the ancient world portrayed in the scriptures and twenty-first-century same-sex relationships. The continuity that religious and some academic discourse encourages us to find is more to do with theological beliefs concerning the nature and authority of scripture and its continued relevance to our contemporary age. It is to do with the conflict between literalist and/or conservative views of how scripture should be interpreted and applied and the more liberal, often academic, perspectives on that issue. The topic of homosexuality is simply a convenient controversial and provocative scapegoat for that larger battle. This will be touched upon in the section below and more fully in Chapter 6.

Staying with the 'Texts of Terror' Debate

Elizabeth Stuart (2003) has recently suggested that attempts by gay and lesbian-identified theologians to engage with church traditionalists have reached a stalemate situation where participants on each side of the debate have lapsed into tired reiteration of their positions without getting anywhere. It could be argued that the scrapping over scriptural texts is in a similar quagmire. J. Michael Clark argued as much in 1989 when he spoke of the 'seemingly endless and circular arguments to justify gay/lesbian existence with biblical exegesis', which has been a demoralizing and futile 'drain upon gay and lesbian energies' (1989, p. 11). Richard Cleaver (1995, pp. 26–7) refers to the 'stalemate' position of haggling over the meaning of Greek and Hebrew words if there is no tackling of the larger question of how we read scripture in the first place. The latest critic of the wrangling has been Tim Koch who, while acknowledging the 'hunger for an effective strategy' to deal with anti-gay texts, refers to this battle as a pissing contest destined to be played out time and time again, ad infinitum, ad nauseam. He particularly objects to the ways in which parties to this contest make adjudications about what activities he, as a gay-identified man, 'may or may not "rightfully" engage in' (2001b, p. 171), about which kind of relationships (usually stable, monogamous and responsibly loving ones) are acceptable (2001b, p. 173), and about who his ancestors are (Koch is none too impressed at being asked to identify with eunuchs or with the sexually and socially marginalized/circumscribed – 2001b, p. 174). In his view, the texts of terror debate is given too much weight, too much authority to 'direct *my* behavior and the behavior of others, either in calling me to "high moral standards" of love and decency . . . or even in calling those who would exclude me now to include me, to make room for me at *their* table' (2001b, p. 174). For him, it is time to move on and his alternative approach – a cruising methodology – is discussed further in Chapter 5.

But is it indeed the case that we are in a stalemate position; that enough energy has already been expended on these texts? In a global context where the lesbian-identified individual remains criminalized by law and subject to a range of punitive actions, it would be irresponsible not to continue working on the reception of these texts. Those living in the West have the European Union and individual government parties that actively support the human rights agenda for gay, lesbian, bisexual and transgendered-identified individuals. But those living outside not only have few such political friends, but have governments that position themselves in opposition to such western 'decadence' and 'immorality'. Their othering and condemnation of homosexuality, particularly in parts of Africa, draws support from the numerically significant conservative and evangelical wings of the Church which use scripture to endorse their position.[131] It is true that the work of largely white, Transatlantic scholars has not, and is not likely to, convince their opponents that these texts of terror require reconsideration, but this does not mean that we have reached an immovable stalemate position. On the contrary, the texts of terror debate needs to deepen and widen.

It needs to be deepened by viewing the use of these texts in the light of postcolonial theory. More work on the othering process occurring within the scriptures themselves is required. And more attention to the rôle of anti-colonial sentiment in the continuing usage of these texts to denounce homosexuality would be fruitful given the depths of anti-colonial feeling that has been whipped up in several regions of the world. It is possible, for instance, to view events like the 1998 Lambeth Conference as a flexing of new-found muscle by delegates who were asserting their independent judgement, refusing to be cowed by the more liberal views of some western bishops. This does not indicate that such voices should be silenced. Rather, it is a call to consider the interacting complexities and the vital role of hermeneutics in the debate concerning homosexuality (where 'homosexuality' has become the battleground around which a larger war over hermeneutics and the authority of scripture is being fought).

---

131 Thus, at the 1998 Lambeth Conference, 224 of the 736 bishops were from Africa, 95 from Asia, while 316 were from the US, Canada and Europe. The strong presence from the two-thirds world made itself felt as bishops defended staunch views on the authority of scripture and their unyielding belief that scripture condemns homosexuality.

The texts of terror debate needs to be widened because the contributing voices thus far have been largely white and Euro-American. In a post-colonial climate this merely serves to fan the flames of the controversy. What is required is the contribution of those living in non-European-American parts of the world, voices from within rather than outside. The methods of historical-criticism used in the West, the (lower) view of scriptural authority that often prevails, the 'out and proud' tactics of queer activists, will not always sit comfortably in non-western situations. As Kelly Brown Douglas points out, while theologians in the West have usually been trained in methods of historical-critical exegesis (a heritage that encourages critical distance from any literalist interpretation of scripture), the young vibrant churches of the two-thirds world often have a high view of scriptural authority and are suspicious of western methods of exegesis. Appeals to historical-critical arguments will not necessarily carry any weight within these communities when such academic methods are perceived to be distorted by European and Euro-American bias. She concludes:

> it is going to take more than 'traditional' (White) biblical scholarship to persuade many in the Black community that homosexuality is not condemned by scripture. This mistrust of White people's handling of the Bible runs too deep for Black people, who, as a result, find it hard to accept White renderings of biblical texts on any matter, including sexuality. This means that the interpretation of certain texts (such as Lev. 18:22; 20:13; Gen. 19:1–9 and Rom. 1:26–27) will more likely reflect the homophobic understandings handed down in the Black oral/aural tradition than the exegetical findings of biblical scholars, especially since these traditions and understandings seem to have served Black people well. (1999, p. 95)

The way forward, in her view, is for Black biblical scholars to get involved in the debate and, first, demonstrate the connection between pro-slavery texts of terror and those used against gay and lesbian-identified persons. Second, question how such texts offend the life and freedom of all Black people so that 'certain offending texts will lose authority in the Black faith' (1999, p. 96). And third, 'find ways to communicate the complex and rich message of the scriptural witness on issues surrounding sexuality to Black people in a language and manner that maintains the integrity of the Black biblical oral/aural tradition' (1999, p. 96). Douglas is speaking predominantly of Black America, but she clearly recognizes how the view that homosexuality is unAfrican impacts upon the debate.

Her words find an echo in the contributors to Comstock's *A Whosoever Church* (2001). Rev. Dr Arnold Thomas, who has travelled a long way given the traditional perspectives he inherited from his conservative roots, believes that 'conservatives are better able to speak to other conservatives. People who have grown up in a conservative atmosphere who now think differently are better able to speak to other conservatives who are homophobic' (2001, p. 117). In particular, they will appreciate the high regard that conservatives have for the univocal and infallible voice of scripture. Thomas points his friends to examples where the Bible does not speak in one voice in order to bring his friends to the discussion table. The irony that entrenched conservative views may be the result of white influence rather than an indigenous Black perspective is not lost on Comstock. He refers to James Cone's recognition that Blacks who were segregated from white evangelicals did not develop such a literal mode of scriptural interpretation, but learned it from the influence of the conservative white evangelists who were also 'strongly anti-gay . . . literalist, fundamentalist types' (2001, p. 209). Comstock continues:

> White Christianity alienated African Americans from their own Black experience, and thus they are easily swayed to become virulently anti-gay. White conservatives point out things in the Bible that are anti-anything, except racism, and some Blacks go along and turn out to be far more reactionary than the White conservatives whom they join. That is largely due to their separatism from their own Black tradition of solidarity with the oppressed of any group. (2001, p. 210)

Douglas' call for Black ministers and scholars to get involved, and indeed any call upon those living in non-western contexts to add their voices to the discussion must recognize the personal dangers and risks involved for such contributors. It must also be prepared to listen to views that critique and challenge the way in which western scholars have handled these texts. It must be ready to shoulder responsibility for the West's historical contribution to anti-gay/lesbian legislation in those contexts. But if the debate can be deepened and widened in this way, there may be hope for a breakthrough that has, to date, been elusive.

This is not to concede that the debate in the West has been entirely without success. Consider the effect of 50 years' research by those who have sought to blunt the ability to use these verses naively and simply as anti-lesbian/gay proof texts. It seems as if there needed to be decades of time available to ponder the implication of Bailey's (and by this time, other scholars') work for change even to be considered. Change comes slowly, especially with institutions such as the Church. Lack of immediate change does not necessarily indicate a bankrupt, stalemate discussion, but rather is indicative of the length of time needed to make important tradition-breaking decisions. The wheels of change may turn very slowly, but half a century of research has had an impact. Commentaries now being published on Genesis, Leviticus, Romans, 1 Corinthians, and 1 Timothy have been acknowledging different perspectives, and the fact that scholars like Robert Gagnon have felt the need to produce such an encyclopaedic volume on *The Bible and Homosexual Practice* (2001) indicates the influence that lesbian and gay-identified scholarship has exerted.

The work of the past 50 years has, above all, given these texts a good airing. It has prompted fresh research into ancient cultural codes of masculinity, specifically codes of male honour and shame, and subsequently revisited interpretational presumptions. It has not, however, been able to convince everyone that the scriptural references have little relevance to the contemporary understanding of homosexuality. This is because there is no agreement on the hermeneutical basis of different interpretations and no agreement on the relevance of medical and scientific discourse. The continued, even dogged, focus upon these selected texts by the Church indicates the continued belief that God has revealed something universally and cross-culturally relevant: that same-sex practices, however understood, put one outside God's will for humanity. Thus, above all, the texts of terror debate has raised the issue of scriptural authority, or rather, the power to claim scriptural authority for one's beliefs – matters that are addressed in Chapter 6.

5

Reclamation: commitment to strategies of appropriation

At first glance one might easily conclude that there is not much to be gained from the scriptures for a lesbian-identified critic. On the one hand, they are permeated by a paucity of any references to female homoeroticism, while on the other they are full of images of women anxious to become wives and mothers. When one combines this with the injunctions to gender-conformity in terms of apparel, behaviour and submission to patriarchy, and the heterosexual imperative founded by the influential opening chapters of Genesis, one seems faced with the most unlikeliest material for lesbian-identified hermeneutics. However, lesbian-identified individuals find unexpected rewards from a range of unlikely sources and scholars have critically explored ways in which a lesbian-identified perspective can be applied to the most *straight*forward of cultural productions.

Accordingly the first section of this chapter notes the ways in which a lesbian-identified, and/or a queer gaze operates, using examples drawn from literature, music and film. These examples inform the second section of this chapter, which considers how the scriptures contain elements that come alive to lesbian and gay-identified readers and are subsequently interpreted in ways not conventionally explored. A third section considers the role of the critical imagination in any work of reclamation. Feminists have already recognized that the scriptures tell a partial and distorted story and that the existing academic tools of investigation cannot accommodate the reconstructive work required. This is not to say that critical imagination has not always played its part in historical critical exegesis and reconstruction; it has always been there but not necessarily openly. Feminists have been more forthright and frank about it and arguably bolder in their applications. Imaginative readings of scriptural stories have already been mentioned in Chapter 3's discussion of Maitland's reading of the Deborah and

Jael story. This section examines further the contribution such readings can make to this principle of reclamation.

Unexpected Pleasures: Viewing/Reading Queerly

In a range of studies that deal with the reception of cultural productions – be they in music, literature, art, TV or film – the transmutation capabilities of the lesbian gaze (or better, gazes, since any such gaze will be marked by the diverse range of individuals who occupy it) have been explored.[132] This section illustrates such transmutations in literature, music and film before reflecting upon the intellectual discussion they have provoked.

In Chapter 1 I mentioned Alison Hennegan's unwillingness to concede her favourite books to their heterosexual resolutions, noting her creative rearrangement of partnerships in classic novels such as *David Copperfield*, *Pride and Prejudice* and *Mansfield Park*. In her reflections upon her reading methods as an adolescent she discusses how she found her way 'round those elements I rejected whilst discovering a means of reading my way *to* the ones I needed and increasingly suspected must be there in *some* books, *somewhere*' (1988, p. 169). As a teenager she found surprisingly amenable sources in the Enid Blyton schoolgirl fictions that so many girls of her generation were given, such as *Malory Towers*. These stories, located in an all-girls boarding school, provided imaginative access to a community of women including strong, capable, independent, career-minded teachers and lively boarders. Their relationships and antics offered pleasures and fulfilled desires that would undoubtedly, for some parents who had supplied this reading matter, have been unexpected. In these texts, Hennegan says, there was nothing that she had to work hard at to ignore, she simply supplied her own gap-filling scenarios based on the information already supplied. Thus:

> Horse-mad Bill (short for Wilhelmina) and the equally horse-mad (but also bewitching auburn haired and green eyed) Clarissa obviously belonged together which is where I put them. And, for the rest, the six

---

132 The following references are indicative of such studies: Bad Object Choices (1991), Bourne (1996), Bradby (1993), Brett, Thomas and Wood (1994), Burston and Richardson (1995), Gever et al (1993), Hamer and Budge (1994), Jay and Glasgow (1990), Munt (1992), Russo (1987), Stacey (1994), Wilton (1995b), Zimmerman and McNaron (1996).

volumes . . . provided, provide, an endless supply of erotic variables. (1988, p. 176)[133]

Turning now to music, simply a change of singer can make quite a difference to the reception of lyrics. When Doris Day sang 'Once I had a secret love', it marked the transition point in the musical *Calamity Jane* when Calamity changed from the admirable deer-skinned, gun-slinging, straight-talking tomboy to one who accepted the love of Wild Bill Hickock. However, when George Michael released his *Songs from the Last Century* album shortly after publicly identifying himself as a gay man, the track 'Once I had a secret love' took on entirely different connotations, especially the refrain 'Now I shout it from the highest hill . . . my secret love's no secret any more'. Hardly any negotiation needs to take place; the change of singer and implied audience is sufficient to transform a song that once marked the place where Day eventually succumbed to heterosexuality, into a virtual coming-out song. Lesbian-identified critics have not been slow to spot the way scriptural texts are similarly transmuted by replacing the expected (male) audience. Thus when a lesbian-identified audience is exhorted not to lie with a man in the manner in which they would lie with a woman, they cannot but heartily concur with such an injunction![134]

Another musical genre consumed by a range of audiences is that of country music. Notwithstanding its somewhat camp presentation, country music is imbued with conservative heteronormative scripts and values, incorporating standards like 'Stand by your man', 'Ruby don't take your love to town', or 'Jolene'. Although consumption of its music by a lesbian-identified audience may never have been consciously envisaged, there are features within this genre that have nonetheless appealed. Its strong female leads, such as Tammy Wynette, Patsy Cline or Dolly Parton, embody creativity, independence of spirit, defiance and the acknowledgement that it's tough for women to make their own way successfully in the world. The lyrics, for all the emphasis on domesticity and men, typically contain references to loneliness, betrayal, unrequited love, yearning and passion. As Ainley and Cooper note:

> While problems with your tractor may not have an enormous relevance for the urban lesbian, infidelity, non-monogamy and general all-round

---

133 Sometimes an original text is actually rescripted and published. Michelle Martin's (1986) *Pembroke Park* clearly rewrites Jane Austin's *Pride and Prejudice*, transforming it by an overtly lesbian-identified perspective.

134 The denting of the power of Leviticus 18.22 by positing a different audience was brought to my attention by Monroe (2000).

heartbreak do. So when your girlfriend goes off with your best friend, what else can you play but 'She's got you' or '(I never promised you a) Rosegarden'? (1994, p. 53)

While Ainley and Cooper suggest that the appeal of country music has its 'disturbing' features, such as evidencing 'a lack of available culture for lesbians to own' (1994, p. 56), they acknowledge how many lesbian-identified fans of country music will take what they can via a process of filtering and sifting popular culture to locate their own meaning and significance.

Filtering and sifting processes have had to be more determinedly engineered by Black spectators in cinemas as they renegotiate the (often negative) images placed in front of them. As Jacqueline Bobo states: 'we understand that mainstream media has never rendered our segment of the population faithfully . . . Out of habit, as readers of mainstream texts, we have learned to ferret out the beneficial and put up blinders against the rest' (1988, p. 96). *Lesbian*-identified Black spectators do have 'more room to play' than one might imagine, according to Nataf. Queer audiences, she writes, are capable of 'blatant breaking of codes and rules, ignoring the law, discrediting the value and guaranteed position of the phallus, unfixing the point of identity to allow the subject to shift between multiple, even contradictory, points of identity' (1995, p. 62). This statement can be illustrated by Penny Florence's mention of the Black spectator 'who found in Whoopi Goldberg's screen presence in *Ghosts* (1990) an image of Black lesbianhood otherwise unavailable to her' (1993, p. 137). The complex manoeuvres of resistance and appropriation performed by marginalized spectators make it possible to 'gain pleasure against the grain of the representational and narrative structures' (1993, p. 127). 'Meanings', writes Florence, 'are not locked up in the can with the celluloid' (1993, p. 138).

Certainly, Hollywood films and stardom, permeated with heteronormative values, though not without their subversive elements (see Russo 1987), have nonetheless provided unexpected pleasure for lesbian-identified spectators who resist the programmed angle of view and find visual pleasure in stars like Katharine Hepburn, Lauren Bacall, Marlene Dietrich, Doris Day, Julie Andrews, Catherine Deneuve, Bette Davis, Jodie Foster, Whoopi Goldberg and Sigourney Weaver, among others. In some cases this may well be due to the ambiguity of the star's sexuality but in many cases, the stars are heterosexually identified in both cinematic and the 'real' world. It is thus more to do with the roles that they play as strong autonomous women that holds the attraction. Thus, Caroline Sheldon notes the popularity of Hollywood movies made in the 1930s and 40s 'when the needs of the patriarchy of capitalism to make war and money demanded that women be orientated away from home-making and into industry to replace men sent away as cannon fodder' (1980, p. 17). She accounts for the popularity of these films by their appeal to an audience looking for strong women who 'define themselves in their own terms' and who are 'comparatively independent of domestic expectations and of men'. She later adds:

> Most lesbians have been through a heterosexual phase, so the plot demand that the heroine be attracted to a man is not particularly disturbing (irritating maybe), and the explanation for the plot development could lie in the fact that there is no woman around of equal strength to attract the heroine. (1980, p. 17)

Speaking of 1960s Hollywood stars, Deborah Bright also notes how they shared features that appealed, such as 'supple, athletic bodies in tailored suits, strong facial features, dominant rather than subordinate body language, displays of superior intelligence and wit, and (by definition) roles that challenged conventional feminine stereotypes' (1991, p. 152). She goes on to point out that, despite being regulated by the heterosexual logic of the film narrative, these characters could come alive to a lesbian-identified audience in a way that disrupted that logic:

> reception is driven by desire and what many young, middle-class proto dykes 'saw' in these films in the early 1960s were concrete (if attenuated) suggestions of erotic possibilities that they could not name and that their own lived experience did not provide. (1991, p. 152)

Challenging Laura Mulvey's argument that the female spectator has to transvestite herself in order to identify with the angle of vision provided for a male gaze, Bright argues that a lesbian gaze can take what is on offer and transmute the material not only by fully appreciating and actively occupying what is thought to be a male-only gaze that lingers on the desirability of the female stars, but by providing imaginative alternative scenarios.[135]

---

135 Mulvey's (1975, 1981) work is also criticized by Cherry Smyth who argues that understanding a female spectator position in terms of unsexing herself 'robs the unfeminine, female, active lesbian spectator of a point of entry into the text that operates as desire for, not identified with the female hero' (1995, p. 126). Mulvey's description of transsexual identity 'suggests that the female spectator feels more "natural" in stereotypically feminine dress, and that clothes and gender can be conflated. It forecloses the options for the butch-dyke spectator ... whose masculinity in the world is not a "regressive" fantasy, but a constantly subversive reality' (Smyth 1995, p. 126). See also the criticisms raised by Wilton (1995c).

Bright's photographic series *Dream Girls* makes visibly evident the way such transmutations occur. Taking stills from well-known 1960s Hollywood movies, she imposes herself into the scene, sabotaging the heterosexual frame with an overt dyke figure who draws the attention of the female star. For example, by imposing an image of herself as the recipient of Jackson's engaging, concentrated gaze in a scene taken from *A Touch of Class* (1973) she interrupts the relationship between Glenda Jackson and George Segal. In so doing George Segal is left completely out in the cold, 'firmly locked out of the visual loop' (1991, p. 152). Likewise the imposition of the leather-jacketed figure into a still from *The Sound of Music* (1965), whose eyes engage and return Julie Andrews' gaze, makes Christopher Plummer's embrace look like an anxiety-provoked grasping of his property.[136] This visual sabotage demonstrates tangibly the 'different set of expectations about the action that took place and the resolution of these stories' that occurs to lesbian-identified viewers (1991, p. 153). She concludes:

> As the title *Dream Girls* suggests, my work is about fantasy. The lesbian subject roams from still to still, movie to movie, disrupting the narrative and altering it to suit her purposes, *just as I did when I first watched these films* . . . To the lesbian friends who've seen them, these *Dream Girls* have provoked a whoop of recognition and pleasure. (1991, p. 154, emphasis added)

In similar fashion, contributors to *A Queer Romance* are not so much looking for lesbians and gay men within the representations of popular culture, as locating 'queerness in places that had previously been thought of as strictly for the straights' (Burston and Richardson 1995, p. 1). One of their contributors demonstrates how a most stereotypical image such as the female vampire (a typical positioning of the lesbian in terms of animalistic, fatal, and 'other') can be appropriated and read against the grain as a 'powerful and empowering emblem of same-sex desire' (Krzywinska 1995, p. 100). Krzywinska, convinced that we *can* use the master's guns without shooting ourselves in the foot, is able to find liberating pleasure in the image, preventing the expected patriarchal resolution from taking place by allowing her 'queer desire [to] temporarily spring the vampire out of the function of rep-

---

136 These images can be seen both in her 1991 article and the scene from *A Touch of Class* can be accessed on line at: http://rcswww.urz.tu-dresden.de/~english1/photo/photo/photo_deconstruction_bright.htm

resenting male construction of "otherness"' (1995, p. 102). Referring to the work of Laplanche and Pontalis, who suggest we read in multiple, shifting ways, capable of defying the script, she argues that this

> model of multiple and shifting identifications is at work within the process of textual spectatorship . . . theoretical positions that argue that mainstream films are closed books that are not open to fantasy and differing mappings of desire are, I would argue, monolithic and, in originating from the institutions of patriarchy and compulsory heterosexuality, undermine sexual plurality and difference . . . Playfulness is perhaps the crucial tool of queer theoretical practice which allows barriers and thresholds to be crossed, sexual and gendered roles to be explored, and, importantly, the acknowledgment of the role of fantasy within different discourses. (1995, p. 103)

Many of these reading/viewing strategies derive from a basic desire: to make visible the absence of positive lesbian-identified representations in popular culture. Thus, writing of her enjoyment of mainstream cinematic representations, Cherry Smyth acknowledges:

> I want to take what could be mine from Hollywood, put myself in the picture as it were, reinvent the story of the gaze. Wish-fulfilment you may say, as I wrest the mono-subject from its cosy hetero-complacent form and make it the major discourse. Maybe so, but then reading against the grain began as a wish for inclusion by marginalized, under-represented people and ended up as a strategy essential for our survival. (1995, p. 123)

Faced, until very recently, with an utter dearth of such images, there is a thirst for representations of women who are open in their love for women whether this be in art, music, film, sport, literature, theology or any other area. Even while such representations will inevitably prove to be unrepresentative, be vigorously challenged, in danger of reifying images that are ultimately harmful, and especially of reinforcing rather than disrupting the category of 'lesbian'; seeing one's desires and affinities in these cultural media can be endorsing, legitimating and comforting.

But what is one to make, intellectually, of these viewing/reading strategies that have been applied to a range of cultural productions? The fear is, as Smyth acknowledges in her talk of wish-fulfilment, that they will be seen as faddish enterprises that carry little academic weight, violating as they seem to do the authorial intention of the producers and defying the conventional norms and frameworks of scholarly enquiry. Bonnie Zimmerman recognizes this concern. Writing an overview of lesbian feminist criticism (originally published in 1981), she notes that the lesbian critic's stance 'involves peering into shadows, into the spaces between words, in to what has been unspoken and barely imagined'; but goes on to acknowledge some discomfort with the way in which such lurking in the margins contrasts with her training as a literary critic: 'It is a perilous critical adventure, with results that might violate accepted norms of traditional criticism, but it may also transform our notions of literary possibility' (1985, p. 188). Further thought on how literary possibilities may be transformed can be found in her later essay which refers to lesbian-identified reading of texts as a wilfully perverse way of reading, these two terms chosen very particularly. 'Perverse', she notes, is defined by the 1975 *Random House College Dictionary* as 'wilfully determined not to do what is expected or desired', while 'will' is defined in terms of 'the faculty of conscious and particularly of deliberate action; the power of control the mind has over its own actions'. Accordingly 'a perverse reader is one highly conscious of her own agency, who takes an active role in shaping the text she reads in accordance with her perspective on the world' (1993, p. 139). Naming lesbian-identified criticism as perverse emphasizes her consciousness that this kind of reading does not conform to mainstream scholarly expectations. She speaks of the way in which she was trained to have respect for the text; trained to detach her own interests from her scholarly work; trained to see only what is there and avoid wild speculation. But crucially, she recognizes that her anxieties have less to do with inappropriate speculation and everything to do with a conventional academic training that has controlled what kind of questions can be put to texts and what counts as accepted research. Her academic education with its heterocentric norms simply did not have the space for the kind of research in which she was interested. As she writes: 'The very social context (heterosexualism) that my reading intends to challenge becomes a constraint upon the possibility of such a reading' (1993, p. 145). What she therefore recognizes is how difficult it is to theorize and problematize heteronormativity when the theories and methods of reading have themselves been formulated within a heterocentric frame of reference. Lesbian-identified criticism has to break the mould, change the framework and terms of academic enquiry and this will involve getting over the fear, shame or guilt inculcated within scholars for disobeying the rules. She expresses this in the following way:

The only way out of this circular prison, I believe, is to untrain the critical self, not by abandoning the techniques of criticism, but by abandoning the impersonal attitude that critical training cultivates. This means reading audaciously and often 'naively' – that is, as one reads privately but fears to do publicly. By doing so, lesbian critics have provided fresh and radical interpretations of literary texts, traditions, and even values ... The self-conscious lesbian reader sees or imagines other possible endings that expand opportunities not only for writers of texts but also for women actively creating their lives. Thus, lesbian critical readings are not only possible, but necessary to revitalize the conventions we find stale and meaningless. (1993, p. 145)

Writing in 1993, Zimmerman was contributing to a scholarly discussion taking place on the cusp of the lesbian/gay approaches of the mid to late twentieth century, and the appearance of queer theory which would prove to be less shy about its disobedience though, in its early days, no less self-conscious. Thus, Zimmerman's anxiety that a lesbian-identified reading might appear to be an unwarranted imposition, an unjustifiable (and unforgivable) eisegesis artificially imposed upon the cultural product under consideration, is also evident in Alexander Doty's work. But here it is less of an anxiety and more of an angry frustration. In his 1993 *Making Things Perfectly Queer* Doty strongly resisted any notion that queer readings are 'alternative', 'wishful', 'wilful' or 'reading too much into things', contrarily arguing that they 'result from the recognition and articulation of the complex range of queerness *that has been in popular culture texts and their audiences all along*' (1993, p. 16, emphasis added). He was adamant that this was not a 'closeted queerness'; insinuated and inevitably '*sub*-textual, *sub*-cultural', brought to the surface only by '*alternative* readings, or pathetic and delusional attempts to see something that isn't there' (1993, p. xii). Cultural productions may well be conventionally thought of as transmitting heteronormative norms and may traditionally be read 'straight' but Doty contended that they can equally validly be read queerly since queerness exists 'within, or alongside, what traditionally have been considered straight cultural forms and conventions' (1993, p. 33). This insistence is even more strident in his more recent publication *Flaming Classics*. He vigorously objects to suggestions that he is ' "recruiting" straight texts as part of some nefarious or misguided plan for a queer takeover of (supposedly) heterosexual popular culture', or 'trying to pull a fast one by "reading an externally 'straight' text as 'queer' " ' (2000, pp. 55–6), frustrated by the implication that his interpretations flout 'common sense' readings. The films he discusses are mainstream classics, viewed comfortably as conveying heteronormative values and conforming to heteronormative expectations. And no doubt this is one of the reasons why his queer readings provoke such reaction. For example, one of his students refused to attend his session on *The Wizard of Oz* because 'she didn't want to have *The Wizard of Oz* "ruined" for her by all my dyke talk about the film' (2000, p. 53). Another student who had asked Doty to name some gay cult stars pleaded not have Bette Davis taken away from her as Doty reeled off a few names.[137] This attempted ownership of people and of films reveals both the disturbance that queer readings can provoke and the staunch resistance to such reclamations. But for Doty it is not a matter of queer readings co-opting or appropriating films. He is adamant: films are 'as queer as they are straight' (2000, p. 15); for him, 'any text is always already potentially queer' (2000, p. 2). In fact, it might be time to

> drop the idea of 'queering' something . . . as it implied taking a thing that is straight and doing something to it. I'd like to see queer discourses and practices as being less about co-opting and 'making' things queer . . . and more about discussing how things are, or might be understood as, queer. (2000, p. 2)

Ownership, however, *is* an issue, whether Doty concedes this or not. Whatever one makes of his thesis that closeted directors and screen writers deliberately included 'gay material' in their work for the discerning viewer, Doty is staking a claim to a collection of mainstream films in the face of opposition to that claim. As he acknowledges, when he gives lectures, conference papers, or submits manuscripts, his work provokes rancorous controversies about authorial intention. Clearly a film like *The Wizard of Oz can* be read both 'straight' and queerly, for such readings exist. What is at stake for some participants in this discussion (but not Doty) is *the authority of one reading over another*. The rancour that Doty's work provokes, the talk of taking stars or films away from audiences, all reveal anxieties about who can rightly lay claim to a text/film/star. And the appeal to authorial intention posed by both he and his detractors is a strategy for establishing ownership. The problem is that widespread views of authorial intention are regularly and routinely conceived through a heterocentric frame of

---

137 A similar story is told by Glenn Burger, who describes how a contributor to the Chaucernet bulletin board expressed '"dismay" at the "need of some gay and lesbian critics to find homosexuality in the authors they are writing about"' (1994, p. 165, n. 8).

reference, and consensus opinions on what the author intended are far too easily conflated with what is actually 'the preferred reading that dominant culture sanctions' (2000, p. 4). Doty says he does not want to play this game. In his essay on woman–woman intensities in *The Wizard of Oz*, he states: 'I don't see the process of queer interpretation as an act of "taking" texts from anyone. Just because straight interpretations have been allowed to flourish publicly doesn't mean they are the most "true" or "real" ones' (2000, p. 53). In my view, he is playing the game, but not on the same terms. Doty seems to argue for co-ownership of these films where there is no privileging of different readings over one another.[138]

Cultural productions are received by audiences that are not all straight-identified, where members of the audience are not hemmed in by heterocentric expectations and who therefore see the same film as their straight-identified counterparts but can have a different viewing experience if they can make the break with the heterocentric expectations that are instilled from an early age. Doty acknowledges that this is not always easy. Reflecting on his thought that it would have been great if just one of the characters in *The Blair Witch Project* had been gay, lesbian or bisexual, he realized that he had fallen into the heterocentric trap of

> assuming that all characters in a film are straight unless labeled, coded, or otherwise obviously proven to be queer ... [for] this is the type of understanding we have been culturally trained and encouraged to come to when filling in the narrative blanks about a character's sexuality. (2000, pp. 2–3)

In recognizing this, Doty helpfully indicates how heteronormativity affects assumptions and expectations, naturalizing a set of heterocentric responses to narrative silences so that any readings to the contrary appear to be unnatural and/or appropriative. Accordingly one can imagine all too readily the aghast reactions to the image of 'Dorothy/Judy Garland being understood as a "fag-hag"-in-the-making, skipping down the road with her rather queer male friends' (2000, p. 54)!

A case for co-ownership can be made on at least two grounds. First, if cultural productions, consciously or unconsciously, inherently contain their queer elements, sometimes overtly (as Russo's many examples from *The Celluloid Closet* illustrate), sometimes less so, and at other times

---

138 Though he does argue that heterocentric readings of *The Wizard of Oz* actually are the more appropriative (2000, p. 53).

in their silences, then Doty's queering of the film canon is not an imposition of wish-fulfilling appropriations, but a collection of close readings of a product's pre-existing queer features. Second, while the majority of audiences conventionally read/view within the filter of a heterocentric reception framework, there are people who receive the same products and understand them '*without reference* to these dominant cultural readings' (2000, p. 6). Viewing/reading through a non-straight filter does, as the earlier examples of this section demonstrated, produce different reception experiences. This latter point picks up references in Doty's 1993 publication where queerness was said to be something negotiated between product and receiver: 'the queerness of most mass culture texts is less than an essential, waiting-to-be discovered property than the result of acts of production or reception' (1993, p. xi).

Zimmerman was also of the opinion that the elements for her readings lie in the product itself and that a perverse reading is not, therefore, guilty of alternative appropriation. But she places greater emphasis upon the role of the receiver in either bringing to the surface features that non-lesbian receivers have not recognized, and/or completing narrative silences in different ways:

> Let me emphasize that the lesbian resisting reader, reading perversely, is not merely demanding a plot or character study that the writer has not chosen to create. She is picking up on hints and possibilities that the author, consciously or not, has strewn into the text . . . The reader is simply bringing to the text an understanding of the world as *she* has learned to read and thus to know it. (1993, p. 144)

The final sentence of that quotation recognizes that some readers have a different set of expectations, a different ordering of society in their heads that is not inevitably and inexorably heterocentric. That different world-view contributes to a reading experience that is governed by expectations, knowledges and norms which raise other possible scenarios, particularly says Zimmerman, at those junctures where texts raise 'what if' moments; points in the 'narrative labyrinth' at which a text could go off in a different direction. Reading perversely involves recognizing those junctures as the point of departure for different scenarios and resolutions. In her words, the reader comes to 'a point in the narrative labyrinth where she simply cuts a hole and follows her own path' (1993, p. 139). The above discussion has already provided examples of such escape hatches (in the imaginings of

Alison Hennegan and Deborah Bright for example) and Zimmerman gives her own illustration of a 'what if' moment in the typically heteronormative American soap *Dallas* (for further discussion, see 1993, p. 143).

This is a rather different position from Doty's. Zimmerman's exploration of alternative scenarios where the text goes one way and the reader/viewer goes another, has to contend with the fact that the piece of literature or the film does actually conclude differently. Thus, for all that the character of Jamie Ewing in *Dallas* had attitudes, clothing and a friendship with Sueellen (*sic*) that could be decoded by a lesbian-identified audience as being some-where on a lesbian continuum, at the end of the day, 'J.R. breaks up the two women, precipitating Sueellen's (*sic*) decline into alcohol dependency . . . and Jamie's transformation into a spiteful, clinging, feminine stereotype' (1993, p. 143). Doty's readings find queer elements or opportunities for queer blank-filling activities *throughout* the films he discusses. He is not actually exploring alternative scenarios and 'what-if' junctures, but is reading what is already there queerly. Both critics, however, see their readings as being consistent with the recognition of literary and film critics that cultural products have always been read polyphonically, that there is no single, universal meaning that can be extracted once and for all and that a lesbian-identified or queer reading takes its rightful place amid that polyphony.

Again, it is worth reiterating that one does not have to 'be' queer to see queerness, though as Burston and Richardson suggest, sexual minority status 'lends one an outsider's viewpoint which, though not entirely predictable in its consequences, does make for different ways of seeing' (1995, p. 5). Zimmerman, noting that 'lesbianism' is a disputed concept, more specifically suggests (rightly, in my view) that 'perspective is something we acquire as a result of living in the world' (1993, p. 135), and that a lesbian-identified perspective may not be biologically determined but is certainly informed by the consciousness that evolves from living a life characterized by a passion for women. And notably for Zimmerman, that involves the distinctiveness of a sexual passion.[139] It leads to a lesbian-identified perspective honed by being positioned on the margins which helps the critic locate those elements of a text that speak to this consciousness. Thus, whereas feminist critics may run courses on 'images of women' which bring women

---

139 Thus, enquiring about the difference between a lesbian feminist and a heterosexual feminist perspective, she concludes that the difference lies in 'desire and passion . . . Lesbians not only *see* women, but desire and feel passion for them . . . Lesbian being-in-the-world is sexual; it is largely our sexuality that distinguishes us from other women' (Zimmerman 1993, p. 138).

to the centre of discourse, because such courses have predominantly considered 'women within the roles and institutions established by a male-centered perspective: that is, woman as wife, as mother, as seductress, as mistress, even as independent woman', they have retained, says Zimmerman, 'a basically heterosexual approach to literary criticism' (1993, p. 137). Zimmerman suggests four ways that will distinguish a lesbian-identified approach. First, it will place a gynocentric emphasis on female bonding and friendship. Second, it will not contribute to the erasure of passion between women but will 'see and emphasize the sexual, romantic, and/or passionate elements of this relation' (1993, p. 138). Third, it will focus on the 'primacy and duration' of women's relationships, and fourth, will 'look beyond individual relationships, to female communities that do not need or want men ... In a lesbian perspective, women are both necessary and sufficient' (1993, p. 139).

There are potential problems here in that the category 'women' remains stable and unproblematized. Zimmerman is no essentialist; she fully recognizes that just as the 'lesbian' label disguises a diverse range of experiences and positions, so too the category 'women' cannot ever be fully representative. Nevertheless, the binary opposition between women and men in her 1993 essay is fairly rigidly maintained. Moreover, the emphasis on a distinctive lesbian-identified perspective, though useful, is in danger of reifying the category in opposition to non-lesbian perspectives. As discussed in Chapters 1 and 4, a lesbian-identified hermeneutic needs to find ways of problematizing its own categories even while they are used for heuristic purposes.

Having seen how (what first appear to be) unlikely sources can be reclaimed by unexpected audiences, the scriptures may turn out to be more amenable to a lesbian-identified hermeneutic than previously thought. The application of such a hermeneutic will without doubt provoke the kind of hostile reactions to which Doty has become accustomed. If *The Wizard of Oz* is 'for millions of straight and queer people ... a sacred text of their childhood, and, therefore, one that is not to be sullied by discussions of sexuality – particularly queer sexuality' (2000, p. 56), how much more will the sacred and sacrosanct Jewish and Christian scriptures be considered despoiled, even blasphemed by lesbian-identified readings? However, when it comes to material as culturally important as the scriptures, reclamation strategies are vital. Read from a heterocentric perspective or, more significantly, a heterosexist perspective, they continue to provide ammunition to be fired at any person or institution that attempts to introduce welcoming, accepting attitudes, discourses and actions. We have seen in Chapters 2 and 4 how the scriptures are used to prevent progressive legislation being passed and how they are appropriated in the vehement anti-lesbian/gay rhetoric of statesmen. If, however, the scriptures are a double-edged sword as LGBT/Q readings make evident, then their destructive power can be combated and their damaging effects counteracted, though the effectiveness of that counteraction remains to be seen. Continuing to deal with the texts of terror despite the questions that have been raised about the usefulness of the claim and counter-claim struggle it entails remains vital, as we have seen, but combining that strategy with one that reclaims scriptural narratives will have an even greater impact and be especially useful for those who wish to remain within their confessional homes and find liberating texts within their scriptures.

As we have seen, the reclamation of cultural productions by LGBT/Q audiences often takes its cue from elements within those productions that attract attention or from silences that can be filled by non-heterocentric imaginings. Such readings do not necessarily run against the grain of the text so much as against the dominant history of reception that has taken place within a heterocentric frame of reference.[140] When considering the scriptures, it is certainly the case that the interpretive history of the past two centuries has taken place within a heterocentric framework. Although individual interpreters may have come from various positions on a sexual continuum, the academic work of exegesis, dominated as it has been by the historical-critical agenda, has been characterized by the supposed neutral objectivity and detachment of the exegete from his or her personal values. But for neutral, read androcentric, Eurocentric and heterocentric. Readings by non-whites, non-males, non-American-Europeans and non-straights have thus been perceived as advocacy or interested interpretations; as if historical-critical exegesis were miraculously impartial and non-committal, producing universally applicable interpretations of texts. Fortunately, the interested nature of historical-critical enquiry has been uncovered, particularly in the last two or three decades, and it no longer holds an authoritative sway over biblical hermeneutics.[141] It is still a useful umbrella term for

---

140 This is not to resort to a position that defends the text and criticizes a heteropatriarchal history of reception in the way that several second-wave feminist theologians and biblical scholars reclaimed the text and criticized the interpreters. The text itself is a problem, prescribing as it does the death penalty for same-sex activities, exhortations to accommodate male–female gender norms in terms of dress, demeanour, discourse and actions, together with injunctions to follow a heterosexual imperative.

141 See, for example, Clines (1998), Dobbs-Allsopp (1999), Patte (1995), Segovia and Tolbert (1995a, 1995b), Segovia (1999, 2000) and Watson (1994).

dominant methods of enquiry and without doubt it still has *local* uses. But the past three decades have demonstrated there are a number of valid ways in which a scriptural text can be approached and interpreted and lesbian-identified approaches are perhaps the most recent illustration of that fact.

So, what happens when one evades the heterocentric reading position and looks at scripture from a lesbian-identified reading position? Is it the case that the Jewish and Christian scriptures possess an already existing queer potential that can be identified, and if so, how far might this potential be used to disrupt the emphases that have obscured the topic of female homoeroticism?

Scoring Hits with the Scriptures

Just as Doty finds queer elements in film and Zimmerman her 'what if' moments in literature, some lesbian and gay-identified biblical scholars have already been scoring similar hits with scripture. This terminology of scoring hits derives from Tim Koch's proposals for a homoerotic approach to scriptural texts which he calls a 'cruising' method. A cruising methodology is one of encounter where a text is brought alive to the reader due to some correlation between it and one's own experience. Informally, it offers a scan of the scriptures by a fully operational gaydar that bleeps obligingly when a likely text is located.[142] For Koch, such encounters are not tangibly different from encounters 'along a roadside, in a bar, in an internet chatroom' (2001a, p. 21). In all such cases a cruising method is one grounded in the reader's erotic knowledge which allows him or her to pursue that which catches the eye. There are issues in Koch's essay that need to be addressed, not least the troubling implication that those who follow such a method do not need to concern themselves with offering their readings at the table of discussion and evaluation.[143] Notwithstanding, a cruising method may well have its use as an *initial* starting place for engaging with scripture. In fact, this kind of connection is probably where many of the existing LGBT/Q readings of scripture have their origins.

---

142 The popular notion of the gaydar was explained in Chapter 1.

143 Daniel Spencer in his response to the essays in *Queer Commentary*, where a slightly revised version of Koch's article appears, also says he is 'a little uneasy with Koch's somewhat individualistic and personalistic approach . . . which is largely devoid of political and historical context and meaning' (2001, p. 199).

Koch's cruising method usefully indicates several texts containing features which carry potential significance to a non-straight readership. He briefly identifies five examples: the association of Elijah with leather goatskins wrapped around his loins; Elisha's public show of mourning in reaction to the loss of Elijah; Jehu's hand-in-hand chariot ride with Jehonadab; Ehud's left-handed encounter with Eglon; and elements of Lydia's story as narrated in Acts 16.14–16. Since the latter is more open to a 'lesbian' connection I will focus upon this text. The features that provoked the hit were as follows. First, the reference to her being a seller of purple. The colours of purple, pink or lavender have traditionally been associated with lesbian and gay communities. When Betty Friedan objected to the way lesbianism was, in her view, smearing the women's movement, she infamously referred to lesbians as the 'lavender menace'. Such terminology builds on traditional associations. In Chapter 1, I noted how reference to lavender has been used as code for gay presence on the screen (see Russo 1987). The pink triangle was also the sign of a prisoner arrested for homosexuality in Nazi Germany. According to Judy Grahn the association has antecedents much further back in history, and she offers a highly speculative account that takes the association as far back as the poet Sappho (see Grahn 1984, pp. 10–11). A reference to Lydia's selling of purple thus scores a quick and easy hit that can then be followed up. Accordingly in his brief investigation Koch notes the overt lack of reference to any male relations, how she appears to be running her own business and household, how she goes out to join a group of women gathered at the riverside on the Sabbath and finally both he and Nancy Wilson (1995, p. 158) comment on the fact that the route from Troas to Samothrace, to Neapolis and then Philippi where this scene is located (Acts 16.11) lies in the immediate vicinity of the Isle of Lesbos. Koch declares: 'If this doesn't at least suggest (let alone scream) "dyke", what does?!' (2001a, p. 19).

Well, maybe it does, but such connections are loose and flimsy. While appreciating the commitment to find elements of texts that can be reclaimed for a lesbian-identified readership and fully realizing that these are features that appeal, they do not, at that level of discussion, convince. I am acutely reminded here of Doty's justifiable weariness of negative reactions to his work and the way in which he has to undertake close readings to demonstrate his points. This criticism of Koch's and Wilson's use of the Lydia narrative could be seen as collusion with these resisting reactions. However, highlighting the reference to purple, a gathering of women and the vicinity of Lesbos might be fun, spark an amused grin, and certainly brings unexpected new pleasures to old stories; but these flashes do need to be followed through if this is to be anything more than a playful disruption of convention. Koch's hits are thus a useful *starting point* for the encounter and perhaps this is what Koch intended.

The same is true of several other hits scored by Nancy Wilson. Again, hers is an individual record of connections, published in an autobiographical homiletic book written within and for the community she serves as pastor. Frustrated with her dialogues with other churches where compromise has been the order of the day, she declares that she has had enough with meeting people halfway. This is a book for people like her, people of her community; others can read on if they dare! It is on this basis that she highlights a range of stories that have resonance for her and the community she serves. Accordingly, Jesus' relationship with the beloved disciple, identified as Lazarus, is highlighted. Lazarus provides a cipher for a gay man called out of the tomb of closeted, deathly existence. Wilson readily concedes it is 'quite another thing even to begin to suggest or think that Lazarus might have been a homosexual' (1995, p. 143), but she raises the questions that might typify a midrashic approach to John 11, asking a range of 'what if' questions that are reminiscent of Zimmerman's approach outlined above: 'What if Lazarus could speak? In the traditions of Jewish midrash and of feminist biblical interpretation, it is fitting and necessary to let the silenced in the Bible find their voice. What do we imagine Lazarus felt, thought, and knew?' (1995, p. 143). What if Lazarus was 'secretly – or not so secretly – in love with his friend?' (1995, p. 144). 'What if Jesus raised Lazarus partly because he could not go through his last weeks without Lazarus' support, company, love and friendship?' (1995, p. 144). What if homoerotic friendships were one of the attractive but also controversial features of the Jesus movement, what if others were jealous of Jesus' special relationship with this disciple, what if the synoptics are covering up an early example of what is referred to today as queer-bashing? Such speculation continues as she considers the relationship between Jesus, Lazarus and the two sisters Mary and Martha. She questions whether Mary and Martha were necessarily blood sisters, asking whether they might have been distant cousins and/or possible lovers whose deep relationship has been covered over by the Gospel writers. She finds further hits with Mary Magdalene whose independent status is likened to the status of some lesbian-identified independent women throughout history. Her fourth chapter 'Outing the Bible' continues in this way, scoring potential hit after hit. Often her speculative hits strain credulity: the *magi*, for example, are reclaimed as distant ancestors without any real warrant. I'm not at all convinced that their forethought to bring gifts is the 'obvious gay clue' that Wilson suggests (1995, p. 131), though admittedly the thought of 'all those children in their fathers' bathrobes in Christmas pageants every year, trying to portray three queens in semidrag' does raise a smile.

Ultimately, Wilson's work leaves me with the same problem encountered with Zimmerman's proposals. Those 'what if' junctures are all very well but the texts, as they stand, do not pursue the avenues followed by Wilson's imagination and neither does conventional interpretation. So just as Zimmerman found herself straining against all her training as an academic, against all the rules of reading she had learned, I too find myself torn between a willingness to follow Wilson's own brand of wilfully perverse interpretation and the desire that interpretation be grounded in sound methodological principles. To her credit, Wilson confesses that she engages in much speculation and regales the guild's heterocentric framework which has meant that its members have not generally concerned themselves with, for example, the 'many unresolved issues about Jesus' home and family life', and rightly reminds scholars of the dangers of making uncritical and unfounded heterosexist assumptions about Jesus:

A monolithically heterosexual, or even asexual assumption has dominated the interpretation of Jesus' life, ministry, and personhood for too long. For too long Jesus, and other New Testament characters, in particular, have been portrayed as biblical versions of 'genitalia-free' Barbie and Ken dolls. (1995, p. 139)

She also implies that some of her readings have purposefully gone 'too far' since, in order for a lesbian-identified hermeneutic to come of age, the pendulum has to swing widely away from the heterocentric assumptions towards a homocentric perspective. Wilson is staking *her* claim to co-ownership of the Bible and deliberately attempting to shake the Bible free from the hands of those who use it as an instrument of punishment against those who identify as lesbian, gay, bisexual and transgendered:

In a culture that vilifies homosexuals as promiscuous, as unable to keep commitments, as faithless, these stories of committed faithful love, filled with risk taking, are moving, powerful biblical stories for gay and lesbian people. We must take them back . . .

Heterosexuals have ripped off our love stories for too long! I find myself fantasizing about going through every wedding liturgy in every Christian worship book with my ecu-terrorist scissors and cutting out Ruth's words to Naomi. *You can't steal them!*

... I have fantasies of interrupting poor, unsuspecting heterosexuals at their wedding with 'STOP, in the name of Ruth and Naomi, Jonathan and David! Stop stealing our stories while making *our* relationships illegal or characterizing them as immoral! (1995, pp. 156–7)

Despite the fact that Wilson and Koch provide only brief speculative encounters with the texts, whereas Doty provides close readings, there are a number of similarities between their approaches. They all identify elements in the texts that reverberate with connotations that register with readers/viewers who do not read/view via a heterocentric filter. Wilson, Koch and Doty are staking their claim to cultural classics and provoking anxious counter-responses from those who believe they have a rightful and authoritative ownership to defend. Their work provokes hostility and they, therefore, struggle against the negative reactions of readers for similar reasons: such readings are seen as undue, delusional appropriations of cultural classics whether these be film or scriptural canons. Like Zimmerman and Doty, Nancy Wilson is keenly aware of the controversies and hostility such an approach will provoke. See, for example, Wilson's account of an angry response from a student gathering and the letter received at UFMCC HQ from a member of the Central Committee of the World Council of Churches who makes accusations of heresy and blasphemy (1995, pp. 75, 67). I agree with her that when words like blasphemy and heretical are cast about these are being used as tools of heterocentrism and are about 'control and intellectual terrorism' (1995, p. 68).

If the connections made by Koch's cruising methodology and those already highlighted by Wilson are subject to the closer scrutiny that Doty demonstrates, then maybe these early first ideas or 'hits' can gain greater edge. Certainly this has already proved to be the case in a number of cases. I had also spotted the queer features within the Ehud-Eglon encounter before reading Koch's paper, though this actually turned out to be yet another text of terror rather than a positive 'hit' (see Guest, forthcoming). The oft-made hit between gay readers and the David and Jonathan narratives also rewards a close reading of the Samuel narratives. In his contribution to Stone's *Queer Commentary and the Hebrew Bible*, Ted Jennings undertakes a close reading of this text and reveals an unexpected but there-in-the-text homoerotic relationship not between David and Jonathan but between David and the deity. Using a cross-cultural frame of reference, Jennings notes how war leaders often have boy companions and that the relationship between the two is often homoerotic. In the Samuel narratives the war leaders Saul and

Jonathan both have their young armour-bearers but they too serve in that capacity before the deity who appears as 'the pre-eminent warrior chieftain' (2001, p. 43). As chieftain the deity chooses first Saul and then David as his 'armour-bearers' and youthful companions, motivated it seems by 'the astonishing physical beauty of the young men' (2001, p. 43). The youths, however, are not feminized by such positioning; they retain masculine qualities and are brave warriors.

Turning to David's near-naked dancing before the ark in the presence of his deity and the enraged Michal, Jennings suggests that David is publicly demonstrating his love for his new male lover, one with whom Michal can never compete. Michal's references to his shame in front of all the women, and David's response that they will conversely honour him given what they have seen, suggests to Jennings that what are exposed here are David's genitals. And when Michal is punished with childlessness, it is the penis that is again in view – the fact that she will never have it again. In Jennings' view, one needs to recall that Uzzah has just been killed by the Lord for reaching out to steady the ark and that David, in response, goes to Jerusalem without it 'in a sulk and lets Adonai stew out on the farm, presumably to recover from this testosteronic tantrum' (2001, p. 53). The place where the ark has been left begins to flourish which is seen as a more appropriate demonstration of the deity's fertility and virility. Rewarding the deity's good behaviour, David brings the ark to Jerusalem and cavorts semi-nakedly to renegotiate their relationships and in order that the love between them can be consummated:

> In the homoerotically suffused relations between David and YHWH . . . both have 'ephods' . . . David's maleness is coyly draped in linen. Adonai's is impressively sheathed in the ark. One is lover, the other beloved. But it is the lover, the erastes, who has had to learn to behave himself if he is to be near his beloved, trusted by his beloved, ecstatically welcomed by the beloved. For if in this tale Adonai is the top and David (as usual) plays the role of the bottom, it is by no means the case that the top is always in control or that the bottom is simply dominated. This is not, after all, rape. It is love. (2001, pp. 60–1)

Now that the union between Michal and David is ruled out, the relationship and consummation of the union between David and YHWH comes specifically into view. When David offers to build his deity a permanent house to try and win the 'faithfulness of this rather unpredictable lover'

(2001, p. 63), the roles are reversed and it is the deity who establishes a dynastic house for David, perhaps 'making clear just who is the top here and who the bottom' (2001, p. 62). Through Nathan, the deity asserts his rights as the lover in a discourse that is 'both stern and affectionate . . . David is being gently reminded that he does not have to be the active subject but may rely confidently on YHWH to carry this role in their relationship' (2001, p. 63). In so doing the deity asserts his steadfast love for David – a vow, a union that will be everlasting and he asserts that he will be as a father to David's son, Solomon. David consents and refers to the deity as 'my lord', a title he has also given to Jonathan at the point of great intimacy (1 Samuel 20.7–8).

There is greater depth to Jennings' essay than has been possible to represent in the above summary. However, enough has been said to demonstrate that the close reading of films that Doty undertakes have their counterparts in the kind of queer exegesis undertaken by Jennings. The scriptures do contain elements that can be accessed by readers who approach from a different angle from that of the heterocentric reader. It is surprising, but the queer elements, so keenly illuminated by the essayists, are evident. These close readings, and others found in the collections by Goss and Strongheart (1997), Goss and West (2000) and the forthcoming commentary on the entire Bible from queer perspectives, demonstrate that these are not delusional, wilful appropriations. Taking their cue from elements within the text, queer readers bring to the surface features that have not been conventionally explored. The reasons why conventional analysis has not recognized these features is probably due to several reasons. In part, it is due to the lack of a relevant discourse horizon. While 'being' queer is not a prerequisite for undertaking a queer reading, some contributors to the *Queer Commentary* do examine scriptural texts in the light of their own experience of being gay-identified, Koch in particular. Until recently, reading through the lens of being a gay man was simply not a recognized option. Now that more scholars are open about their sexuality the effect of their discourse horizon upon their reading strategies is being presented for discussion. Another reason why such features have not been widely recognized may also be due to previous inconceivability of juxtaposing discourses on such subjects as sadomasochism, pederasty, transgenderism and homoeroticism to a collection of texts revered as sacred scripture. A further reason may be that queer readings do not always comply with exegetical norms. Queer readings can and do flout conventional modes of exegesis and transgress the rules. Yet, now that these readings have appeared, the queerness of scriptural texts is apparent. In my view, it is the combination of this inherent queerness plus the act of reception by those who are interpreting without reference to the dominant heterocentric norms that generate such readings.

What one soon discovers, however, is that there appears to be much more material amenable to a gay-identified or queer reading strategy than one that is geared towards a lesbian-identified hermeneutic. This is unsurprising given the prominence of male characters and a male deity. Moreover, the outnumbering of women in the academy also contributes to the fact that many queer readings so far published are by men, many of which relate to issues of masculinity and male homoeroticism (not that these themes are uninteresting or irrelevant to a lesbian-identified scholar). However, Schneider rightly notes that the emphasis on the homoerotic relationship between the deity and Israel (and/or its king) makes the scriptures appear to be even more of a man's thing than ever before:

> Queer commentary, thus far looks like it primarily serves male fantasies of being made queer . . . in God's image. Who else but a latter-day queer would think to point out that keeping Moses locked in closed conference for forty days and nights on Mount Sinai just for the purpose of getting instructions for building and decorating the tabernacle indicates an interior-decorator god of the most anal-retentive, fruity, late-twentieth-century kind? And the amusing thing is, it does. In addition, placing Yhwh in the center (or on the top) of a young male beauty cult surely says as much about the longings of queer men for a god who desires them as it does about a god of a nation, or creator of a world. Or it says as much about older queer men who place on the deity their own desires to love young bucks who come at a high price (which usually is some kind of kingdom). (2001, p. 216)

She adds that YHWH, according to Jennings', Boer's, and possibly even Stone's readings is related 'so exclusively and erotically to men via male sexualities and Mediterranean European constructions of masculinity that "the chosen" really can come to suggest a misogynistic strain in the human-divine relationship' (2001, pp. 216–17).

Like Schneider, I recognize that such feminist concerns play their own part in reifying 'female' versus 'male' categories, binaries that feed the heterosexual contract and need to be disrupted. However, the will to disrupt these categories and binaries does not necessitate the abandonment of a feminist perspective. Far from it. Several queer theorists such as Stone, Carden and Goss acknowledge and utilize feminist theory substantially in their studies and demonstrate how its use can help break down binary formations. Such good practice needs to continue so that queer theory engages fully with feminist ethics, theory and principles, thus realizing its potential to be the breakthrough reading method for biblical studies that it promises to be. The reason why this publication outlines a *lesbian*-identified hermeneutic rather than queer lies precisely in the need to place feminist and lesbian-identified concerns at the heart of the enquiry.

Certainly, the scriptures are amenable to a lesbian-identified reading position but one has to look twice as hard and rely, to a greater extent, on narrative silences. Looking for agreeable texts and the possibility of reading them queerly, Schneider writes:

> The queerest stories of women in the Hebrew Bible may in fact be those about women who managed to have a voice at all, women who managed to survive and/or overcome with some kind of chutzpah their barrenness, widowhood, slavery, rape, virginity, abandonment, marriage, ugliness, or other signifiers of their male-derivative identity, economic dependency and status. (2001, p. 218)

Gerda Lerner (1986, pp. 193–8) has already suggested that the snake in Eden represents a powerful fertility goddess of Mesopotamia. If so, says Schneider,

> then Her seduction of Eve and promises of freedom She whispers to Eve when they are alone are exhilaratingly provocative, while Her humiliation and apparent defeat by Yhwh speak both to His ethnic triumphalism and misogyny and to the rise of patriarchy. (2001, p. 219)

Schneider also very briefly mentions a hit with 1 Kings 3.16–28's story of the two women who come before Solomon to adjudicate the rightful mother of the surviving child. Here is a text that does indeed bear further scrutiny. In this narrative, the narrator wishes to demonstrate the wisdom of Israel's new king. To do so, he brings a case which he has rendered very difficult to judge by having no corroborating witnesses to the event. But so intent is the narrator on having Solomon demonstrate wisdom, that in his need for a complete lack of witnesses he brings into existence the scenario of two women, apparently not blood-related, living together in one home, alone even during childbirth. This inadvertent testimony to the possibility of two women living with each other, independently, is offset by his description of the women as prostitutes (*zonōt*) and by having them display the typical characteristics of deceit, jealousy and hostility with which women's relationships have been tainted. As it stands, the tale glorifies Solomon, valorizes the mother prepared to offer her (male) child to another woman so that it may live, and encourages contempt for the one who would kill a child rather than let her rival claim him. But assuming that the narrator's introduction of a household of two female friends bringing up a family in which no man participates has some grounding in conceivable realities, he has troubled the dominant presentation of women's lives and given an indication that there were alternative possibilities. Insofar as Solomon's 'wisdom' does not entertain the possibility of both women nurturing the surviving child but rather divides the women from each other, thereby sanctioning and contributing further to the depiction of enmity between them, the text is ripe for an analysis of the suppression and resistance to female bonding. The narrator's reference to such women as prostitutes is also of interest given the long association between prostitution and lesbianism. This quick analysis is brief but it is evident that lesbian-identified or queer readers have material here with which they could work.

Rebecca Alpert scores other hits that could be followed through:

> why when Shifrah and Puah are mentioned do they always appear together? How did Miriam and Pharaoh's daughter know one another? What did Jephthah's daughter do when she went away with the women? Where did Dina go when she left the house of Shehem? (1997, pp. 51–2)

Certainly one is dealing here with narrative silences as opposed to close readings of texts, but this is not surprising. Given the substantial absence of women as leading players in scriptural narratives, limited as they are to being chorus girls on a larger stage, narrative silences will often be the elements that a lesbian-identified reading can most readily exploit, as the next section will demonstrate.

The Role of the Critical Imagination in Lesbian-Identified Hermeneutics

When feminists devised and deployed a hermeneutic of suspicion, they did so because of their recognition that the scriptures tell a partial, and therefore distorted story. Consciously or unconsciously, the existence and role of women has been suppressed and/or erased. Feminists, therefore, have long recognized the need for different tools, methods and questions than those conventionally used and asked within the academy. Thus, in the introduction to her work on *Gender and Difference in Ancient Israel*, Peggy Day (1989) cites Rosaldo: 'what we know is constrained by interpretative frameworks which, of course, limit our thinking; what we *can* know will be determined by the kinds of questions we ask' (1980, p. 390). Accordingly, Day argues that feminist historians need to distance themselves from the partial representations given in the text and approach the task of reconstruction from a different set of presumptions. Inquiring into women's activities without adopting the text's perspective on those activities

> is an appropriate and necessary task . . . Israelite women *did* exist in Israelite culture, and if we take that as our point of departure rather than grant the text the authority to speak on women's behalf, then we have every reason to try to ascertain, from a *female's* perspective, the realities of female existence. (1989, p. 5)

Day argues that one has to ask questions not previously raised and produce new reconstructions, though she carefully points out that this is not a remit for free flights of fancy. As a historian she is wary of any unwarranted use of the imagination if it produces reconstructions not grounded sufficiently in some kind of evidence, but nonetheless she does point out the need for new questions, new assumptions and perspectives. In an important article published two years previously, Phyllis Bird (1987) was perhaps more open to the considered and measured use of imaginative reconstruction. Bird argues that any investigation into the place of women in ancient Israelite religion has to find a way around the bias of scriptural texts which sideline (to say the least) women's involvement in the cult. It is not a matter of simply adding a chapter on 'women and the cult' to our existing Israelite religion textbooks; this only reifies the idea that women were periphery to Israelite religion, doing their own things in the margins. On the contrary, whatever the involvement of women was, and wherever it took place, it needs to be fully integrated into the wider context and this will mean rethinking entirely our reconstructions of the history of Israelite religion. However, because existing source material is so skewed and the material we would like to have is at best fragmentary, the lack of sources remains a problem impeding reconstructions from the outset. Therefore, the new interpretative model she advocates is one which not only presents the data we have but crucially also represents the missing data:

The blanks in the construct are as essential to the final portrait as the areas described by known data. They must be held open (as the boxes in any organizational unit) – or imaginatively filled – if the structure is not to collapse or the picture is not to be rendered inaccurate or unintelligible. *The primary means of filling the blanks is imaginative reconstruction informed by analogy.* (1987, pp. 399–400 emphasis added)[144]

When it comes to the Christian scriptures, feminists have to deal with the same problem. Thus, in order to reconstruct women's presence and roles in the early Christian movements, Elisabeth Schüssler Fiorenza has long been calling for a paradigm shift so that academic methods of enquiry are equipped to give voice to the silences inevitably built into androcentric narratives. To do this one needs

> to search for rhetorical clues and allusions that indicate the reality about which the texts are silent . . . to read their 'silences' as indications of the historical reality of women about which they do not speak directly . . . we have to read carefully the 'clues' of the text pointing to a different historical reality and to integrate them into feminist models of historical reconstruction in such a way that we can 'fill' out the silences and understand them as part of the submerged traditions of the egalitarian early Christian movement. (1985, p. 60)

Feminist research thus asks new questions and requires new methods that can incorporate narrative silences in one way or another, while simultaneously using the overt references plus clues and allusions to the existence and role of women. In such references, clues and allusions, scholars are at least able to locate tips of the submerged iceberg that their work seeks to bring to the surface. As we have seen, there are clues and allusions within scripture that lend themselves to a lesbian-identified gaze, but one has to work hard to find in these glimpses evidence of much more deeply submerged realities. If feminist studies to date have recognized the need for a paradigm change so that research takes into account the narrative suppressions and erasures, how much more thoroughgoing does this paradigm change need to be when considered from a lesbian-identified reading

---

144 The analogies she has in mind derive from the study of other ancient Near Eastern societies, bearing in mind that the extant source material from these will also be partial and biased, together with ethnographical studies of contemporary non-western societies.

position given the widescale erasure of female homoeroticism from the narrative storyworld?

The above writers suggest that the narrative silences be represented – either as silences or filled by other means – notably by the judicious use of analogy and the critical imagination. The possibilities of the former have already been explored in Chapter 3 where I noted how archaeology, sociological models and anthropological analogies can offset the images of women as competitive rivals and would-be wives and mothers. However, the emphasis upon the critical imagination also lends itself most readily to a lesbian-identified hermeneutic. As we have seen, imagination already plays a major role in the published lesbian-identified readings of scripture. At times, the imagination runs very freely and runs into Peggy Day's concerns about free flights of fancy. However, when one is talking about the *critical* imagination, informed by archaeology, cross-cultural analogies and experiential knowledge, one is not talking simply about speculation or creative writing. The critical imagination is an intellectual force that requires a great deal of contextual knowledge. Brooten, for example, points out how a researcher of women in the early Christian movement would need

a good understanding of social, political and economic conditions of the women of various classes in all parts of the Roman Empire; of women's participation in and the theology of other Greco-Roman religions, including Judaism; of first-century philosophical and religious thinking about women, of the laws affecting women in the various geographical regions; of women's participation in public life, including politics; sexual behavior and attitudes towards sexuality; and of the physical living conditions of women, that is, architecture, art, ceramics etc. One would want to know how many women could write, what women's education consisted of, what women wore, and what kinds of work slave women did. It would be necessary to note developments within women's history in the first century, tracing them back to and/or contrasting them with previous centuries. A study of first-century Christian women would also imply a study of first-century Christian men's theology and practice, as well as of such societal institutions as the family. All of this requires a new kind of synthesis, drawing upon New Testament and Jewish studies, classics, ancient history, archaeology, art history, papyrology, epigraphy, and anthropology. (1985, p. 80)

This is not to say that fictional writing does not have its place. The biblically themed novel or short story that lets the imagination run more freely should not be dismissed. Not only do such books provide an enjoyable alternative read, they can offer helpful contributions to contemporary scholarly debate by sparking thoughts about unexpected scenarios not conventionally considered, and by offering gap-filling ideas that do not derive from heterocentric assumptions. Thus, just as Doty had to correct himself when lamenting the absence of any gay character in *The Blair Witch Project* remembering that he had only assumed all the characters were straight, so one's assumptions about biblical characters can be challenged. It is assumed, for instance, that Sarah and Hagar's connections with Abraham and the rivalry that develops between them regarding sons indicates a mutually competitive hostility between heterosexually identified women. This scriptural presentation of the women's relationship has been subject to various feminist interpretations, but the antagonism and racism between the two women is still often taken as read. However, Sara Maitland's rereading of the Sarah, Hagar and Abraham triangle tells a different story.

Maitland's 'Triptych' tells the story from Hagar and Sarah's perspective. Abraham's story is one that she planned to write, but ultimately does not tell. She selects rather to offer some 'brief notes from the imaginary *S. L. Maitland Bible commentary*' which refer to 'two very serious errors' made by the compilers of the Genesis story. One is that they have conceded that it is Hagar who manages to see God and live, while the other is that 'in the face of their best efforts, *they dismally fail to write out, or suppress the abiding emotional reality of Sarah and Hagar*. At their every appearance the text vibrates, leaping, shining, buoyant, alive . . . Their vitality searing the pages across the long silences' (1988, p. 119 emphasis added).

As she tells Hagar's story, Maitland portrays a nurturing relationship between the young Hagar and the older Sarah who '[held] her in the night, in the women's tent, holding her against both their fears', who drowned out Ishmael's screams by leading 'Hagar away gently into the depths of the tent and covered her with a blanket and kissed her ears and eyes and mouth and genitals so that she would not have to hear the screams of her mutilated child' (1988, pp. 103, 105). In Sarah's story we witness again the love between the two women while 'neither of them love Abraham who pesters Hagar with his hot, but old, hands' (1988, p. 114). As with the Genesis narrative, the relationship degenerates but Maitland portrays this as the fault of a patriarchal system that both women are compelled to serve, with Sarah driven to distraction by Abraham's unwanted advances, pleading with Hagar to sleep with Abraham in order to 'get the old goat off both our backs' by producing an heir (1988, p. 106). Later, Sarah with 'black bruises' around the eyes and neck is compelled by Abraham to confirm that Hagar and her child should be expelled from the camp. There is a poignant silence while 'Every man who had known how they loved each other and had not liked it, every woman who had known and who had seen it as a sign of hope, had waited' (1988, p. 109). Beaten into submission, the hopes of those waiting women are dashed as Sarah reluctantly acquiesces and the women are forced apart.

Maitland's reading not only challenges the heterosexual matrix that dominates the Genesis story and its history of interpretation, but also heals to some extent the racial scars of the narrative, rightly highlighted by Trible (1984) and Weems (1988). Sarah's affliction of Hagar is not excused but is shown to be an affliction enforced by the narrator's heteropatriarchal agenda which uses class and race to provoke and naturalize wedges between the women. Maitland's reading has the benefit of not reproducing such a willing and naturalized enmity between them. Moreover, she finally finds joy for Hagar who is visited by the 'great black God' who 'strips her of her clothes and caresses her, kisses her sweeter than dreaming . . . [whose] great black smile . . . makes her laugh' (1988, p. 111). We leave Hagar 'dancing, dancing naked on the desert dancing floor, leaping and singing and laughing' making her way to the safe beaches of her homeland with her revived son, 'full of joy' (1988, p. 112).

Within this short story Maitland is able to centre the relations of the two women and imaginatively reconstruct relationships of mutual love and support that include loving, physical gestures of solidarity. Her fiction demonstrates that the heteronormative framework of the text can be disturbed when the presumptions of the reader are different. Reading with the grain of the text and the surrounding literature of the Hebrew scriptures, there has been a history of reception which has not paused to consider any real bonds of friendship between the two women. It has followed the rhetoric of the narrator who divides the women from each other. Feminists, employing a hermeneutic of suspicion, have noted how class and race issues have been used to drive a wedge between them, but have nevertheless succumbed to the assumption that these characters have little by way of mutual solidarity. Lesbian-identified hermeneutics, employing a hermeneutic of *hetero*-suspicion, credibly presupposes that female homoeroticism existed. Grounding the hermeneutic in the expectation that women were not always bitter rivals but could make each other's lives more bearable by co-operation and, in some cases, would find their primary passion and desires met in each other's company, means that the images of unco-operative, competitive, jealous and hostile relations between women now jar; they appear odd, are uncomfortable, appear out of the ordinary. Such portrayals are then more plainly seen as strategies used to thwart female friendship, to divide women from each other and to encourage jealous competitiveness. And because the images now grate against expectations it prompts questions from the reader such as: Why are the women imaged in this negative way? Why is female bonding located in contexts of doom? What is the threat that needed to be so fully suppressed? These questions will thereby prompt the exposure of the processes and operations that have motivated and maintained such suppression and, simultaneously, help critics locate subversive resistance to that suppression.

Maitland's fiction helps to bring these questions to light by its portrayal of conversations and activities that took place when the Genesis narrator was not looking. Occupying the silences and the gaps of his story, Maitland offers an imaginative account that runs in harness with that story, filling in its absences in an unexpected but no less implausible manner. Certainly as it stands her 'Triptych' is a piece of fiction; it is an imaginative retelling, something that could perhaps be seen as a flight of fancy. But when read in conjunction with the sociological and anthropological studies that attest that reality of female homoerotic relationships within the ancient Near East, the fiction is granted some kind of grounding. It is not that one is trying to prove that Hagar and Sarah historically had a homoerotic relationship – this is a complete red herring. These are most likely fictional characters in the larger mythical, fictional storyworld of Genesis. The narratives tell us far more about the post-exilic period in which they were most likely produced than the period in which they are set. Cross-cultural analogies are not called upon to verify that these particular literary women could have loved one another. Rather, the analogies are mentioned in order to broaden the worldview of the reader, bringing female homoeroticism into the realm of the thinkable and thereby disrupting the heterocentric filter through which we are all accustomed to reading and thinking. When one's worldview includes not only the possibility, but also the likelihood, that some women found their primary affinities oriented to members of their own sex, then Maitland's fiction seems less like a flight of fancy and more like the uncovering of suppressed elements of the women's stories left out of the Genesis story, itself also a fiction. As such, Maitland offers (whether she intended this or not) gap-filling material, restoring the lost dimension of female homoeroticism. Her short story exists between the lines of the Genesis text. She does not ignore or radically alter that text. She disrupts it by occupying its spaces and positing a bonding between the two women (complicated by Abraham) and a final resolution for Hagar that simply does not figure in the Genesis text. Unlike Zimmerman's occupation of 'what-if' junctures which is compromised by the fact that the actual texts have resolutions that are contrary to her musings, Maitland's reading can accompany the existing Genesis text from beginning to end, countering its centring of the male pair – Abraham and the deity – by her foregrounding of what goes on in the women's tents. What cannot be countered is the fact that the Genesis narrative is the one that is canonized and will therefore always be read as it stands without reference to such accompanying narratives as Maitland's, but this is the fate that confounds all those who would comment on scriptural texts and has troubled feminists for decades.[145]

As noted at the close of Chapter 3, Maitland's fictional work has its Jewish counterpart in women's writing of midrash. Noting the Mishnah's injunction 'turn it and turn it, for everything is in it' (*Avot* 5.25), feminist and lesbian-feminist Jews have already been occupying the narrative silences of Hebrew texts in order to bring their existing but erased presence to the foreground of these narratives. For Alpert this is nothing less than an obligation:

> Lesbians have had to read between the lines for centuries in Western cultures, looking for role models where all traces were hidden. For those of us women whose love of women has had no public acknowledgment, writing midrash has given us an opportunity to make our presence known and lend validity to our relationships. We must insist in our right to find hints of the existence of women like ourselves in the past where we can find them. Reading the stories of Ruth and Naomi, Eve and Lilith, and other texts in this way should be considered an obligation to our nameless ancestors, to give them too, an opportunity to speak. (1997, p. 52)

She considers, for example, Judith Plaskow's midrash on a far more ancient midrash: the story of Lilith, banished from the garden because of her refusal

---

145 Feminists who have dealt with texts that are profoundly damaging for readers offer various strategies of resistance, but have to contend with the fact that texts remain in their canonical form and are still read as sacred scripture in churches and synagogues without the attendant warnings that feminist articles offer. I once advocated tearing pages out of the canon (Guest, 1999), but now see this as an unrealistic and undesirable strategy since it removes the history of women's oppression, which needs to be recorded.

to acknowledge the superiority and control of Adam. Plaskow (1979) brings the two women – Lilith and Eve – together. They talk long and regularly, again and again they laugh, they cry, strengthening the bond between them. Alpert notes how this feminist midrash opens the possibility for a further *lesbian*-feminist midrash where an erotically charged relationship is developed further.

Alpert also provides her own midrash on the book of Ruth where Ruth's famous words of commitment to Naomi are newly infused with sexual desire. The resolution of the book, where Ruth marries Boaz and bears his child, does not prove to be an obstacle since marriages do not necessarily prevent the primary direction of women's affinity for another. In fact, as Alpert points out, the only references to lesbianism in the Jewish legal texts are those which forbid *married* women to engage in *mesolelot*, a term that seems to imply the non-penetrative rubbing of the genitals (see Rashi Yebamot 76a). Marriage has historically been an economically necessary arrangement; the fact that Ruth marries Boaz does not therefore necessarily indicate that there existed a primary passion between Ruth and Boaz, especially when the overt words of love and commitment that *are* spoken in this text are those from Ruth to Naomi. A lesbian-identified midrash can base itself upon this element, clearly present in the text, and centre it, demonstrating as Doty did with his reading of *The Wizard of Oz* that sometimes it is the heterocentric reading that appears to be the more appropriative. And yet, as Alpert notes, 'nonlesbian scholars and commentators . . . fail to see what we see . . . convinced that the important love relationship is the one between Ruth and Boaz' and the 'possibilities that the story of Ruth and Naomi could be read as a lesbian love story will certainly distress some readers' (1997, p. 51). Alpert, like Doty, like Zimmerman, casts her eye over her shoulder, knowing that some will see such readings as 'irrational and unnecessary, even amusing' (1997, p. 41). But she resists the pressure to read heterocentrically and her midrash reads between the lines of the existing text, filling in the gaps and taking her lead from the commitment between Ruth and Naomi already present within the text. Moreover, she is very aware that for gay or lesbian Jews who wish to remain within their religious homes and who 'feel compelled by the absolute authority and immutability of the Torah text', midrashic approaches, among others, help them 'to affirm both their gay and Jewish selves and helps them to feel whole' (1997, p. 41). Lesbian-identified midrash, such as her reading of the book of Ruth, is thus 'a way of welcoming lesbians into the contemporary Jewish community' (1997, p. 51).

One of the benefits of midrash is that it has a closer, more organic connection with the scriptural texts on which it is based, since Jewish readers are far more accustomed to considering midrashic readings as part of usual interpretative praxis. Midrash is an esteemed traditional practice. It plays a vital role in Jewish life in a way that fictional readings such as Maitland's will never find within Christian circles. Perhaps it is the recognition of the usefulness of midrash and its capacity to enhance non-straight interpretation that has led to the borrowing of this approach by non-Jewish queer writers. Michael Carden, for example, draws on Jewish commentaries in his queer midrash on the destruction of Sodom. Using commentaries which speak of rebellious daughters acting compassionately in this context (Genesis Rabbah 49.6.3 and Sanh. 109b), he asks whether it is 'too much to imagine an underground sorority of tribades, frictrices, lesbians in the cities of the plain who are in ongoing conflict with the laws of their fathers?' (2001, p. 57). I fear that it probably is asking rather a lot, but it is an entertaining account especially when Carden engages Marcel Proust's *Sodome et Gommorrhe* as a further intertext, whose angels positioned at the gates of Sodom allow any sufficiently penitent citizen to leave before the catastrophe engulfs them. Carden likes to imagine

> that the shade of Pelotit[146] comes on the eve of Sodom's doom and spirits away everyone in those tribadic/fairy sororities/fraternities ... So rather than a site of queer genocide, I can imagine a Sodom and Gomorrah that are doomed for homophobia and become a site of miraculous queer deliverance. (2001, p. 159)

Carden's midrash goes with the text of Genesis 19; the city is still destroyed as punishment for its sin. However, as he has argued elsewhere (1999), it is a certain strand within the history of interpretation that is revoked. He argues that the sin is one of inhospitality and xenophobia that manifests itself in the attempted male rape of Lot's visitors. His queer midrash offers a further imaginative way of detoxifying the homophobic readings of this text still further by filling in the gaps of the account with scenarios not conventionally considered, especially in Christian circles.

At the beginning of this section four feminists were cited, all of whom recognize that the existing storyworlds of the scriptures that purport to tell

---

146 Pelotit is the name given, in Jewish tradition, to Lot's other daughter who is burned for smuggling food to a beggar in Sodom.

of the birth of Israel and its subsequent history and the origins of the Jesus movement and its development, are all partial. The literary representations are largely, if not entirely, male-authored accounts that have consistently neglected, suppressed and/or erased the details of women's companionships and social lives and the role that they have played. Given how culturally influential the scriptures have been for determining what part actual women can and cannot play in the world, these erasures carry a significance far greater than is usually due to literary representations of the past. This is one of the reasons why the call to represent the blanks in any reconstruction of that past is so necessary. On the whole, feminists have not, however, recognized that one of those gaping blanks obliterates a most important aspect of women's social lives – their relationships with each other, including the sustaining erotically charged relationships. If these are to be reclaimed, then use of the critical imagination has to play an important role in any reconstruction.

Conclusion

The principle of reclamation needs to be used in conjunction with all the other principles. Chapter 3 investigated the principle of resistance and the above discussion has demonstrated how it interacts with the principle of reclamation. The principle of resistance exposes the issue of erasure and problematizes absence. It recognizes 'the radical lack of our knowledge about women in antiquity', that the story 'is nearly entirely missing', that the material we *do* have is an account of 'what men thought about women' not a representation of women's authentic lives (Brooten 1985, pp. 67, 65). Accordingly, the researcher needs different tools and methods, a different paradigm which will include the use of archaeology, the analogies offered by anthropological studies, the models made available through sociological studies, consideration of non-textual remains such as artistic representations, funerary reliefs and inscriptions. Chapter 3 demonstrated how such studies can be used to problematize absence and subvert strategies of erasure. The principle of resistance can thereby provide an enriched discourse horizon. Based on the knowledge that female homoeroticism was an ancient reality, it inculcates a broader worldview, disrupting the hegemonic heteronormativity that has dominated historical research. This broadened horizon is then taken up in the principle of reclamation helping to ground the reading strategies discussed in this chapter. The two operate in harness with each other, informing each other, before engaging further with the third and fourth principles of rupture and re-engagement discussed in Chapters 4 and 6.

6

Re-engagement: commitment to making a difference

This publication has been written at a time when lesbian-identified persons probably face unprecedented levels of tolerance and acceptance in those parts of the world where legislation to protect them from discrimination has been established and where the right to have their relationships formally recognized in marriage and civil partnerships now exists. It is written at a time when their existence is beginning to be recognized in the cultural media – not as doomed tragic cases or as freakish creatures to be documented and analysed (though this still occurs) – but as part of the diversity of human life. It is written at a time when it is the homophobe who is being scrutinized and criticized rather than the women who identify as lesbian. Notwithstanding, although many girls may now grow up without being verbally, mentally or physically bullied and/or abused, this publication is simultaneously written at a time where some lesbian-identified women continue to face a range of abusive treatments ranging from being called names or spat at in the street to arrest, imprisonment, rape and in dire circumstances death; at a time where the membership and ordination of lesbian-identified congregants in churches and synagogues remain hotly disputed issues; and at a time when Jewish and Christian scriptures continue to be referenced by speakers in governmental positions across the world in order to block anti-discriminatory legislation.

The focus in this book has been on the worst of times in order to demonstrate the historical social, political and religious climate in which this lesbian-identified hermeneutic is grounded. In my view, one cannot fully understand why a lesbian-identified approach to reading scripture is necessary, or why it might operate according to the principles outlined and the strategies advocated, without appreciating the historical contexts from which it derives. Patricia Hill Collins argues that the special relationship between Black intellectuals and the community of African-American women 'frames the contours of Black feminist thought' (1991, p. 30). The lived realities of Black existence raise the issues for intellectual consideration, and the academic discourse then returns its contribution to the community in a merging of theory and practical action. As an interested project, a responsible lesbian-identified approach is likewise informed by the lived realities of those positioned as lesbians, its agenda driven by the issues of those grassroots communities, the theorizing bearing a responsibility to those communities if publications such as this one are to make a difference.

In the emphasis I place upon context – both global and local – this development of a lesbian-identified hermeneutic resides in the company of those liberation theologies and approaches to scripture that overtly acknowledge the relevance of scholarship to contemporary issues. To date, lesbian-identified readings of scriptural texts have demonstrated this commitment insofar as they have taken up and addressed a range of contemporary personal and social issues – though it has to be acknowledged that most of the publications to date derive from Transatlantic contexts and reflect the immediate concerns facing those who live in North America and the United Kingdom. The comparative absence of scriptural interpretations by women in other parts of the world is immediately evident. Facilitating their ability to publish and negotiate their own principles and strategies for interpretation needs to be a priority if a lesbian-identified hermeneutic is going to be relevant to the needs of diverse local contexts. For the present, examples of how lesbian-identified readings have been interested projects will have to be drawn from existing essays.

Irene Travis, an African-American womanist who had no one to consult about her 'postadolescent lesbianism', no 'role models for establishing a lesbian-headed Christian family' (2000, p. 39), addresses the continued exclusion of practising gays and lesbians from the Church, or church attempts to cure them and marry them off. Using a hermeneutic of suspicion she approaches the text with the presumption that women found ways of mutually relating and staying close to each other despite pressures to do otherwise. She notes how resourceful women have always created ways to remain together and believes that even the married women of the Hebrew Bible may have been women attracted primarily to women, who despite their commitment to husband and children, would find 'comfort in one another's very close company' (2000, p. 38). Using the stories of Ruth and Naomi, Mary and Martha, Travis finds ways to reclaim scriptures for herself and those like her. Her essay engages directly with the contemporary issue of lesbian parenting and advocates a way of reading scripture that enables us to value rather than condemn these families of choice.

Mona West's reading of the Exodus story addresses the issue of coming out. The Egyptian oppression of the Hebrews is likened to the closeted existence of 'queers' who are oppressed by the dominant culture for being different. The search for the gay gene is likened to Pharaoh's planned infanticide. The wilderness wanderings with the moaning, rebellions and painful deliberations are compared with the ways that coming out can be traumatic, initiating in some cases years of therapy as one moves through a gamut of emotions trying to reconcile oneself to the new sense of self and accommodating that within one's religious heritage. The covenant made in the wilderness is likened to gaining a sense of peace with God and a move from being alienated from God to being covenant partners, often within new accepting denominations. This therapeutic use of scripture offsets the ways in which scripture has traditionally been used as a weapon with which to harangue lesbian-identified people. Her essay on Lamentations, published in Stone's *Queer Commentary*, similarly uses its imagery and poetry to speak to a community ravaged by AIDS, suggesting that 'Lamentations gives the queer community the gift of a voice to speak the unspeakable about AIDS' (2001, p. 142).

As a woman living in both Jewish and lesbian worlds, the substantial contributions made by Rebecca Alpert engage with a variety of contemporary predicaments lesbian-identified Jewish women find themselves in. Her work has addressed, among other issues, those of lesbian motherhood (1992), the celebration of lesbian unions (1994), coming out (1997, 2000), the need to find new sacred texts (1997) and issues faced by a first generation of lesbian rabbis (2001). Above all, her work can be seen as an attempt to transform the Jewish tradition for, as she says, even if the international Jewish community began welcoming and supporting its lesbian and gay members there would remain a residual problem with the scriptures themselves which are hugely influential, whether or not 'we read these texts, share these beliefs, or observe these practices' (1997, p. 6). Scriptural injunctions can be used to bolster contemporary political statements and thereby foster homophobic activity, for assumptions that are based on the legacy of the Torah 'find their way into newspapers, movies, and television' (1997, p. 18). No matter how reformed or liberal, Jews, like Christians, 'claim a connection to a culture whose sacred texts incorporate ideas that exclude and hurt us' (1997, p. 7). In order to

make it possible for lesbians to participate fully, as lesbians, in Jewish life

... not only Jews but Judaism and its sacred texts must be transformed from a lesbian perspective. This transformation must incorporate new readings of ancient texts, an effort to find or rediscover Jewish texts from other eras that incorporate a lesbian sensibility and the creation of new sacred texts that are affirmatively Jewish and lesbian. (1997, pp. 7–8)

If things cannot be changed, there is the likelihood that many Jews will simply abandon their tradition. Her approach is geared towards finding ways of negotiating that tradition, finding opportunities 'to reinterpret and transform these rules and prohibitions as well as to reject specific ones if necessary and build on a new foundation' (1997, p. 13).

These few examples demonstrate the situatedness of current readings. One of the reasons that this publication was conceived was because the shift away from lesbian and gay to queer studies appears to have brought with it a parallel shift away from this direct engagement with grassroots concerns. It is true that many of the readings noted above appear in *Take Back the Word* – a book that carries the subtitle *a queer reading of the Bible*. But there is a tangible difference between readings that use queer as an umbrella label for all sexual outlaws, whereby a lesbian or transgender or bisexual reading is de facto a 'queer reading'; and those that apply queer theory that has been honed in the academy in a more sustained critical way. I was therefore not surprised to read Spencer's comment that Mona West's essay in Stone's *Queer Commentary* is unlike the other essays insofar as it is more of a 'queer *appropriation* and *application* of the text to queer experience' (2001, p. 201). Other essays in *Queer Commentary* are more theoretically based and do not address grassroots concerns in such a clear and direct way.

Perhaps to some extent this is due to the different location of contributors to such publications. The essays cited above from *Take Back the Word* mostly have their origins in, or connections to, lay situations. Irene Travis described herself as a retired school teacher working in full-time ministry and an African-American pastor at the largest gay and lesbian church – the Cathedral of Hope, Dallas. Mona West, biblical studies lecturer at Austin College, Texas and Anderson College, South Carolina, academic dean at Samaritan Institute of Religious Studies, was also then working at the Cathedral of Hope as Pastor of Spiritual Life. Rebecca Alpert is the co-director of the women's studies program and assistant professor of religion and women's studies at Temple University. She is also an ordained rabbi and her work clearly demonstrates her interest in practical issues that affect Jews who identify as lesbian, gay, bisexual and/or transgendered. The involvement of these women in the worshipping lives of Jews and Christians lends their work a practical, applied edge that is not immediately obvious in essays that derive from those rooted solely, or mainly, within academia. That statement, however, has to be immediately qualified since there are authors of queer readings who engage with the Bible as an influential cultural artefact while owning no personal religious allegiance to it whatsoever. Notwithstanding, I would still suggest that essays written primarily within an academic context – where one is expected to utilize contemporary critical theory, where, in the UK at least, the lurking shadow of the research assessment exercise is never far away, where there has been a long-standing tradition and emphasis upon dispassionate enquiry and supposed objectivity, where getting politically involved with contemporary issues can be deemed suspect and have a detrimental effect upon one's reputation and indeed tenure – are inevitably affected by such concerns. This may well contribute to anxieties about producing academic work that is committed to the principle of making a difference. After all, it was not so long ago that writers in secular lesbian and gay studies told of their experience of being advised to choose areas of study that would not be so 'dangerous' for their reputation and careers, of seeing members of the department 'grasping a file cabinet for support' when being told of research topics and being asked if they realized how far they were jeopardizing their careers (see D'Emilio 1992, p. 141). Indeed, as modules on lesbian and gay issues, queer theory and theology begin to emerge within theology and religious studies departments, a spate of similar reactions can be noted. Scholars do still talk about the negative responses received when they mention their research interests. Kelly Brown Douglas, who does not identify as lesbian, but was according to Comstock 'the first scholar to address in a systematic and thorough way sexuality and homophobia in the Black Church' (2001, p. 232), had to put up with students spreading rumours that she was a lesbian and leaving her classes. Meanwhile the comments of colleagues such as 'oh, better you than me', 'glad *you're* doing it', or 'you're sticking out your neck now' (Comstock 2001, p. 233), indicate the risks commonly believed to be associated with such research. Within theology departments it can even be a dangerous pursuit since some colleagues have faced overt personal attack from students. Robert Goss (2002) tells of how his university office was broken into, how biblical quotations were posted around together with words like faggot, how rotting meat was pushed between the covers of his *Jesus Acted Up* publication. Research on lesbian and gay topics can still be dismissed as 'labours of love' or an unnecessary 'baring of the soul' that is slightly embarrassing and best left to the private sphere; it can be considered a 'faddish, transitory' enterprise, not quite part of the intellectual pursuit, a soft project rather than part of a good, solid, recognized field of research. Some post-doctoral students doing good research in this area, who have published significant books and papers, still cannot obtain academic posts.

In such a climate, a shift towards applying queer theory, honed within the academy and somewhat ironically becoming a respectable academic discourse, is arguably a safer option. Its theorists are more fully integrated into the academy than the previous generation of lesbian and gay scholars. It is not ghettoized as lesbian and gay studies tended to be (due to the latter's strong association with scholars who identified as lesbian or gay), but can be applied by trendy straight-identified academics to bring a new dimension to their modules.[147] It now has its introductory textbooks and, due to its ability to cut across disciplinary boundaries, is finding its way into a variety of subject areas. Despite the potential threat of a theory designed to expose and undermine the sex and gender binaries that have held sway certainly in the western world, and despite its playful, form-breaking style, queer theory finds a home within the academy because it simultaneously (and ironically) conforms to important establishment needs: it revitalizes flagging courses on interpretative methods by opening up a new category of analysis; its practitioners bring in research funding; it serves the needs of publishing houses by opening a new subject area; it is conducive to the poststructuralist climate in which we work; and it conforms to the high standards of critical theorizing expected of academic discourse (but which might be entirely unintelligible to the lay person whose life is affected by being positioned as a lesbian).

The location of queer theory in the academy is welcome for it can certainly be used effectively to disrupt heteronormative discourse. If, as Alpert suggests, the goal of queer theory is 'to eradicate fundamental social distinctions based on sex, gender, and sexual orientation and also to do away with the power relations that accrue according to those categories' (1997, p. 11), it is also a vital tool to have in the lesbian hermeneutical workshop. However,

---

147 Walters thus notes that her straight-identified colleague applying queer theory in his English classes 'is in a *structurally* different place than I am' (1996, p. 841). She continues: 'It is not to say that I (as a lesbian) can speak the "truth" of lesbian life more than he can; it is to say that this difference needs to be acknowledged and reckoned with in the course of academic life. This means not only being explicit about the different risks implied in our positions but also acknowledging the different ways we know and present this knowledge and the effects that may have on our students' (1996, p. 841).

if the consequences of queer theorists' work are not developed and applied then the tool is a blunt instrument, its incisive potential left too often to the imagination. Indebted to its feminist roots, the lesbian-identified hermeneutic proposed here is one that is committed to liberative engagement, committed to making a difference. It will thus be critical of the way queer readings are emerging within biblical studies if their critical cutting edge is being enhanced and sharpened at the expense of the practical engagement that has characterized the preceding lesbian and gay approaches. Consider for example the way that Ted Jennings articulates the difference between a queer reading strategy and the traditional strategies of lesbian and gay approaches. Jennings agrees that the latter's attention on texts of terror have won 'significant gains' but argues that it is limited; remaining 'basically defensive in character' (2001, p. 36). Tellingly, he points out that a queer reading is not involved in

> contesting homophobia directly or of legitimating same-sex practice or relationships through the discovery of canonical precedents. Instead it simply presupposes that queerness exists, at least in readers, and that this provides a way of illuminating the texts. (2001, p. 37)

The queer option does broaden the scope as Jennings indicates. No longer do we have to look for a text's explicit reference to same-sex relationships, for a queer reading can analyse any text for the way in which it is implicated in socially constructed sex-gender regimes and the maintenance of heteronormativity. But does it not remain vitally important to 'contest homophobia directly' if one is to have an impact upon contemporary political and religious discourse? It is understandable that the application of queer theory will find a more amenable home within an academy which does not desire to be engaged in the casualty-littered battleground of the anti and pro-lesbian/ gay reading of texts that range between religious conservatives and liberals, between institutions such as the Lesbian and Gay Christian Mission and the Christian Institute and, indeed, finds any such engagement anathema to its purposes. Queer readings that retain critical distance, that in the case of Jennings' essay disassociate themselves from any comments on YHWH as he 'really is', could imply that they do not want to be caught up in any subsequent religious debate (though I do not believe that this is Jennings' intention). While treating the text as a literary storyworld occupied with characters and plot is something that many academics do (myself included), one's findings will have ramifications for faithful readers who see in these characters, plots and storyworlds revelatory spirit-inspired expressions of God's relationship with humanity. Academics cannot be called upon to apply their work to the religious and/or theological lives of believers, but they can be asked at least to acknowledge their position; for one's religious perspective, or perspective on religion, does inevitably inform one's work. Scholars who no longer, or perhaps never had any allegiance to these scriptures, who approach the Bible as a cultural artefact rather than a religious object, may consider themselves unable to apply their readings, but they are not excused. When this has been the case within feminist approaches, there has still been a willingness to engage with contemporary concerns so that the capacity of these texts to shape sex and gender norms can be exposed (see Exum's *Fragmented Women* for an example).

It is probably the case that queer theory will be applied to scriptural texts by those who have no interest in its direct application for communities of faith, who leave such applications to be made by the communities concerned. Such readings remain valuable, for the implications of these readings *can* be drawn out by those interested in making applied connections. Ultimately, what is important to me is that the insights of a queer reading are, *at some point*, made to engage with the contemporary world where homoeroticism remains criminalized and where lesbian/gay/bisexual/transgender-identified persons are at best discriminated against and at worst imprisoned. This is why I develop a feminist-informed, lesbian-identified hermeneutic and not one that simply goes by the name of 'queer' and why the first section of this chapter considers how far it is the ethical responsibility of scholars within the academy to recognize and address the effects and consequences of their exegesis for contemporary contexts.

One matter that is continually elided in queer readings and in some lesbian and gay readings of scripture is that of scriptural authority, yet this is one of, if not *the* most difficult issue facing lesbian-identified women who are also practising Jews or Christians. It is all very well enjoying the illuminating essays in *Queer Commentary* or in *Take Back the Word*, but where do they leave the reader who has to face the same scriptures being wielded against them in the pulpit on the Sabbath/Sundays or by well-meaning institutions and authoritative figures? A commitment to making a difference needs to confront the issue of scriptural authority and consider how a lesbian-identified hermeneutic negotiates the question of authority. Accordingly, the second section of this chapter examines how various lesbian and gay-identified writers position themselves vis-à-vis the scriptures, ranging from suggestions that we call a halt to attempts to soften texts that are, at root, irredeemable, to the arguments put forward by those who call for a renewal of the tradition, and covering the views of those who think a shift away from organized institutional Judaism or Christianity is required.

The final section of this chapter puts forward my own view that a lesbian-identified hermeneutic that is committed to making a difference, grounded in local contexts and theorized within the academy, would find a welcoming and thriving home in the *métissage* – an umbrella space for those committed to social, political, economic and religious justice and transformation.

The Responsible Academy

In a refreshing, personal reflection upon her own career and the situation of women's studies and feminism within the academy, Alice Bach speaks of how she struggles between the desire for activism and the picture of herself as a 'cosy reader' who faces the insistent question: 'As an academic do I fight to change the condition of women, or is my job solely to interpret the condition of women?' (2002, p. 389). She notes the conventional wisdom among feminists 'that success in academe mutes the activist voice. In the process of making it in academia, feminists become spectators, commentators on the arenas of activism' and it is but 'cold comfort that we have planted deep the bulbs of feminist thought and they shall continue to bloom in the terrain of higher education' (2002, pp. 389–90). She admires the way womanists have been the ones able to 'keep their passion even as they become academics' (2002, p. 390). She does not elaborate on why this might be, but notes Gloria Anzaldúa's explanation that 'women of color have a need for theories that not only explain "what goes on between inner, outer, and peripheral I's within a person and within the personal I's and the collective 'we' of our ethnic communities"' (2002, p. 390 citing Anzaldúa 1990, pp. xxxv–vi). Bach sees, rightly, how white feminists can learn from this. The future for feminists in the academy lies in the reclamation of, rather than critical distance from, the lived realities of women throughout the world via the embracing of 'an ethic of personal accountability' (2002, p. 390). As Bach says, if feminism is going to survive as a thriving, developing, transformative mode of analysis, feminists

> will have to accept the mantle of radicalist and place their feminism within a theoretical context of demanding social, political, and institutional change. This activist model differs from the girl in the guild model by its

level of discomfort. Women as a topic of academic concern is necessary but certainly no longer sufficient. (2002, pp. 390–1)

Discomfort, in my view, is indeed a useful measure of how far one's analysis is transformative. Discomfort is aroused when boundaries are crossed, established norms destabilized, existing positions disturbed, expectations confounded. Bach notes how students can be discomforted by the presence of the engaged academic in the classroom:

Trying to combine the roles of scholar and activist in the classroom, I find some students unsettled by my bias. On the one hand advocacy scholarship keeps me rooted in the social movement from which many of us spring; to others it threatens the bland security of 'objective' scholarship. (2002, pp. 392–3)

With insight, she suggests that it is the suppression of a radical practical agenda that constitutes the new backlash against feminism:

In the old backlash feminism was bad. Now feminism is fine so long as it is confined to theory, and precious little praxis. This manoeuvre lets men feel progressive and broad-minded, and it lets women feel that the most militant thing they can do is forget about all those pillow-talk spoilers like job discrimination and the Hyde amendment. (2002, p. 392)

Near her conclusion, she calls for a feminism that, among other things, goes 'back to the streets' (2002, p. 394). Lesbian-identified approaches, however, have not yet (at least within biblical studies) deserted the streets. As noted in the introductory section, such approaches *have* been driven by contemporary issues affecting lesbian-identified women at grassroots levels. But it is important to take note of Bach's cautionary call, written as it is after the assimilation of feminist theory into the academic guild, for it warns against complacency, against the temptation to establish one's academic credentials at the expense of one's engagement with contemporary concerns, against letting the fear of breaking with academic norms dictate levels of permitted, tolerated engagement.

When it comes to lesbian-identified approaches within biblical studies, the contemporary relevance of what we do in the classroom certainly becomes very clear and the fact that biblical studies is lagging behind other disciplines where lesbian critical studies are more prominent may not be due to the usual case of theology/religious studies departments playing 'catch-up' with developing fields within other disciplines. Ken Stone overtly speculates that 'the relative scarcity' of lesbian, gay or bisexual-identified readings 'may be due in part to professional and ecclesial factors that discourage biblical scholars from self-identifying as lesbian, gay, or bisexual or from working on gay-related projects' (1999a, p. 433). Creating space for lesbian, gay, bisexual and transgender engagements with scripture has an obvious contemporary relevance that is not always evident for other readerly approaches within biblical studies. As I have recently argued (2001), scholars cannot write commentaries on books that include well-known texts of terror (such as Leviticus, Romans, 1 Corinthians) without being aware of the import their words will have for contemporary debate. When certain Jewish and Christian faith communities and their leaders are outlawing practising lesbian Christians/Jews from churches and synagogues, when politicians are using scripture in the Houses of Commons and Lords to uphold discriminatory laws, it is clear that scripture is a significant weapon to wield in social, political and religious debates. An approach to scripture that affirms the value of reading scripture through lesbian-identified eyes, that legitimates the existence of the lesbian-identified Christian, Jew (or Muslim), that criticizes the heteropatriarchy of the scriptures and their history of reception, demonstrates clearly how academic research has considerable practical implications. The kind of attention given to these texts by the tutors in the classroom will carry significance for students, particularly those who identify as lesbian or gay whether openly or not. As Jacquelyn Grant notes:

> The way a professor responds to a question or a comment that comes from a student who thinks that homosexuals are going to hell says a lot about how the other students may begin to feel about their own attitudes and beliefs about homosexuals. (in Comstock 2001, p. 131)

The academy is not a disinterested party. Although they are writing in a more general context, Daniel Patte (1995) and David Clines (1995, 1997, 1998) both point out that academics involved in biblical studies have a duty to consider the ethical effects of reading the Bible and explore our complicity in those effects. As Clines puts it:

> If there is one place that biblical studies needs to move to in the coming century, it is – as I see it – from the essentially antiquarian question of original meaning to questions of our own existence, *to the question of the effects of the texts we are so devotedly preserving, to the question of our complicity*

with their unloveliness as well as with their values. (1998, pp. 289–90 emphasis added)

The academy is inextricably connected to prevailing cultural norms and values and its scholars, whether they acknowledge it or not, are affected by their personal interests, values and context:

> universities are not ivory towers where individuals engage in the disinterested, dispassionate, and detached pursuit of knowledge and truth. Rather, universities are intimately connected to the society of which they are a part. They are capable of producing change, to be sure, but they can also reflect, and reproduce, the dominant values, beliefs, habits, and inequalities of their society. Everything we do – the research questions we formulate; the research process itself; where we publish our results; the courses we decide, or are told, to teach; the books and articles we assign – represents choices that individuals make. These choices reflect a particular view of the world, of our society and of how things ought to be. (D'Emilio 1992, p. 162)

A responsible lesbian-identified hermeneutic is one that shows the way forward in this regard. It does not hide beneath a costume of dispassionate analysis, but takes its rightful place within an ongoing history of scriptural interpretation that has regularly, but covertly, addressed the contemporary issues of the day.[148] This brings a lesbian-identified hermeneutic into engagement with the inevitable issue of scriptural authority. Currently, most of the lesbian and gay-identified approaches to scripture have been published by writers who retain a sense of allegiance to their Christian or Jewish faiths, often seeking to renegotiate this allegiance in the light of their experience of having the scriptures of those faiths wielded against

---

148 When Schüssler Fiorenza wrote her entry on 'Feminist hermeneutics' for the *Anchor Bible Dictionary* (1992b), she noted how such a label inferred that there was an objective norm of hermeneutic of which 'feminist' was a distinct branch. She contested such a notion and suggested that other entries should be labelled – perhaps as masculine hermeneutics or as white, western, male hermeneutics. By so doing, she reminded readers that all hermeneutics derive from particular contexts. Some practitioners own this while others conceal or are simply not aware of their bias. However, the myth that historical criticism, for example, provides objective exegesis has been exposed, as the reality of its value-laden presuppositions derived from western enlightenment and humanism become clear.

them. As will be demonstrated in the next section, it is sometimes an uneasy allegiance as individuals contend with scriptures that appear to condemn their loving relations and exclude them from God's kingdom. Occasionally, a writer surrenders the battle and moves away from the squabble with scripture towards a spirituality based on alternative traditions. This next section considers how lesbian and gay-identified scholars position themselves vis-à-vis the scriptures, what methodological mechanisms are used to reconcile their sense of self-dignity as sexual beings within a Christianity or Judaism that has historically been oppressive, and the reasons given for both reclaiming one's religious tradition and for moving away from it.

Scripture, Inner Conviction and Questions of Authority

In the (largely western) published collections of coming-out stories, there is usually an existential moment that occurs when individuals describe the realization that their primary affinities lie with members of their own sex. If those individuals have also been brought up in a religion tradition to which they may or may not have given their allegiance, there is an additional crunch moment. Isn't passionate desire for one's own sex a 'sin'? Don't the scriptures indicate that such passion is 'unnatural' or an 'abomination'? Haven't religious leaders and laypersons been televised declaring the baseness of homosexuality and God's hatred of this lifestyle? Such thoughts have been sufficient to drive some to self-hatred and self-harm,[149] to the arms of waiting 'healing' ministries where their desires can apparently be expelled and their repentant selves reconciled to a loving deity. In the pre-Stonewall days, when images of homosexuals were often of doomed, tragic individuals whose passions were consummated in the dingy depths of underground clubs, unfit to be seen in the life-giving light of the day, such disastrous destinies were to some extent

---

149 Virginia Mollenkott who was adolescent during the 1940s and 50s recalls how someone read Romans to her when she was 13 years of age, 'telling me that if I continued to love women I would prove I was "without God in my mind" and "worthy of death." Being a compliant type and passionately devoted to God, I did try to kill myself, as so many queer teenagers do. But worse than that attempt were the years of living death in marriage to a man who was convinced that I was divinely created to clean up after him' (2000, p. 14).

inevitable.[150] In parts of the world where homosexuality is still pushed underground as unspeakable, where there has not been an active gay liberation movement, despair and suicide remain chosen options. In her unpublished MA thesis on the situation in Korea, where the Church of Korea is implacable in its opposition to homosexuality, Hanna Kim mentions the 2003 suicide of Okoodang, a 19-year-old Catholic whose will bemoaned the cruel discrimination he had faced.

However, in North America and the UK, the post-Stonewall context facilitated a lesbian and gay theology that fought back. Early writers such as Sally Gearhart and Bill Johnson, Malcolm Macourt, Jim Cotter, Giles Hibbert, John J. McNeill, John E. Fortunato, Chris Glaser, Craig O'Neill and Kathleen Ritter provided liturgies, theologies and scriptural interpretations that began to prioritize the authority of inner conviction over traditional church teaching. Believing themselves to be both lesbian and/or gay *and* loved by God, such writers affirmed lesbian or gay orientation as a distinctive spiritual gift, encouraged and identified the coming-out process as a spiritual milestone, began an engagement with scripture that both tackled the texts of terror while reclaiming stories of same-sex love, and renewed dialogue with the churches. Published in the first phase of lesbian and gay studies, such work inevitably bears the hallmarks of its period, based as it is in notions of stable sexual identities and orientation that have since been justifiably criticized. But what is notable for the purposes of this chapter is the emphasis placed on the value of inner conviction as a yardstick for judging what the scriptures have to say about 'homosexuality' and God's relationship to 'homosexuals'.

An air of optimism permeated these early publications. In the 'gay is good' climate of the 1970s, traditional ideas about homosexuality as an immoral evil were vigorously contested. The overwhelming 'yes' that the gay liberation movements gave to the emerging communities nurtured an inner core of belief that to identify as lesbian or gay was not necessarily going to invoke the wrath of God. As with 1970s feminist approaches to scripture and with Black readings, there emerged an unwillingness to accept blindly what various authorities had to say about one's existence and one's choices, a refusal to accept traditional understandings and applications of scripture, and an emphasis upon trusting in one's own sense of dignity and self-worth. The

---

150 I use the word 'disastrous' since suicide bids are potentially disastrous and because attempts to cure homosexuality via exorcism, prayer, religious-based guilt inducement or other religious means have been largely unsuccessful. See Ritter and O'Neill (1989), Haldeman (1994), Morrow (2003) and Mills (1999).

consciousness-raising groups that had facilitated the widespread adoption of feminist ideas and practices were echoed in the various branches of gay liberation movements that sprang up including lesbian and gay support networks within Christianity and Judaism. The first gay and lesbian Jewish organizations were formed in London and Los Angeles in 1972 and New York in early 1973. By 1975, lesbian and gay Jewish organizations were also active in San Francisco, Boston, Washington DC, Philadelphia and Miami. In 1976, the first formal international meeting of gay and lesbian Jewish organisations was held in Washington DC and by 1980 the World Congress (now the World Congress of Gay, Lesbian, Bisexual and Transgender Jews) was officially established. Within Christianity, the Roman Catholic support group Dignity emerged in the late 1960s, and during the 1970s several denominational and ecumenical movements arose: the Friends Homosexual Fellowship in 1973, Integrity (a support group for Episcopalians) in 1974, Evangelicals Concerned in 1975, the Lesbian and Gay Christian Movement (then under the label of the Christian Gay Movement, and focused on Anglican issues though open to members of all denominations) in 1976. Affirmation, a Mormon support group, has its origins in the late 1970s, and in 1979 the Evangelic Fellowship for Lesbian and Gay Christians was founded. There were interdenominational networks such as the Open Church Group in 1975 and the ground-breaking new church that addressed the specific needs of lesbian, gay, bisexual and transgender congregants – the United Fellowship of the Metropolitan Community Church – was established in Britain in 1973. Such supportive networks reinforced the sense of self-worth being promulgated more widely by the secular 'gay is good' campaign, encouraged members to value their authentic experience as people loved by God, and thereby facilitated a positive, if somewhat confrontative, relationship with one's religious tradition. The activism of these groups prompted their host religious organizations to revisit their positional statements on homosexuality. It was no longer possible to ignore the fact that members of their congregations identified as lesbian or gay and no longer believed this represented a contradiction. The 'homosexuality as sin' model had to be reconsidered and key to this discussion would be the interpretation and application of scripture. Several texts appear to declare God's unambiguous opposition to same-sex practices and Christian and Jewish institutions were faced with the conundrum discussed in Chapter 4: how to negotiate these texts if they were to welcome and accept practising lesbian and gay-identified members of their congregations?

In this early period of lesbian and gay theology/biblical studies one sees the beginnings of an emphasis upon the adjudicating role of experience over and against traditional church teaching. One also finds a willingness to exonerate the Bible so that lesbian and gay-identified Christians are positioned in a battle with its *interpreters* rather than forced into an unpalatable squabble with the scriptures per se.

Exonerating the scriptures

Early publications engaged in the 'texts of terror' debate in order to blunt apparent scriptural condemnations of homosexuality. This, as we have seen in Chapter 4, was achieved largely by emphasizing authorial intention (Genesis 19 was never intended to be a diatribe against homosexuality but is rather a condemnation of inhospitality); by emphasizing historical context (Paul did not know of the condition of inversion or of mutual consenting same-sex relationship enjoyed in the modern world and his criticisms were directed against the unequal practice of pederasty); and by focusing upon matters of translation (the terms *malakos* and *arsenokoitai* cannot justly be translated as 'homosexual perverts'). Such emphases upon historical context helped distance readers in the twenty-first century from the ancient past represented in the scriptures and encouraged a questioning of how relevant these texts are for today. As noted in Chapter 4, this introduces the question of interpretation. Arguments premised on 'the Bible says . . .' could be countered by questioning existing translations and by suggesting that when an author's intention is considered in the light of his historical context, the Bible actually is not saying what we have thought it said.

In such a debate the Bible itself appears to be exonerated by all sides. It is the history of commentarial tradition and translation that is criticized. Recognizing that political and religious opposition to lesbian and gay-identified persons is founded upon these texts, that Christians and Jews who identify as lesbian or gay themselves find these texts difficult, one aim of the debate had been to clarify the meaning of the texts. If it could be demonstrated by so doing that the Bible is actually the *friend*, not the foe, of lesbian and gay-identified people, then that was all to the good. Some studies set about the task with the overt desire to achieve the latter result and in some cases this has led to strained argument, special pleading and unconvincing analyses (which itself is an indicator of the overwhelming desire to render the Bible an ally rather than an enemy). Overall, the approach has been generally apologetic and has enhanced the status of the

Jewish and Christian Bibles as vehicles of revelation and authority. It has played the game on the territory of those who would use the Jewish and/or Christian Bibles to oppose and condemn, blunting their capacity to kill by arguing it is the interpretation of the scriptures, not the scriptures themselves that have been condemnatory.

The 'Bible is good news' approach had other strategies in addition to blunting the texts of terror. As with other advocacy readings, there was often an emphasis upon the liberative traditions within scripture such as the exodus story, the prophetic call to practise social justice, a reclamation of affirming narratives such as the Ruth and Naomi, David and Jonathan stories, and a strong emphasis on Jesus' life and ministry. The aim was to transform Judaism's and Christianity's oppositional stance to one that is welcoming and accepting of lesbian and gay-identified Jews and Christians. The strength to do so appears to have largely derived from the inner conviction that God did not condemn. Thus John Fortunato, echoing the 'gay is good' slogan of the secular liberation movements, opened his book with the sentence 'Gay and Christian. Cornerstones of who I am. And, though it hasn't always been so, I've come to believe that both are good' (1982, p. 1). The voice of inner belief, of inner authority, thus makes itself heard, and as we shall see it is this conviction that becomes louder as the relationship with scripture becomes more strained.

Wrestling with scripture

In the 1980s and early 1990s scripture itself came under greater scrutiny. This was a period marked by the AIDS crisis, a backlash against the progress of gay liberation movements and the failure to make substantial progress with religious institutions. The deep hurt, anger and resentment provoked by the negative secular and religious response to AIDS, especially the inflammatory comments of the religious right in America that associated AIDS with God's wrath and judgement, is reflected in approaches to scripture and theology that are more radical. Faced with continued oppression and influenced by the change of tactics in the secular lesbian and gay communities to more direct, ACT-UP strategies,[151] gay and lesbian-identified theologians/scriptural scholars began taking a confrontative rather than an apologetic stance. In this context, the emphasis upon the authority of

---

151 ACT-UP is an acronym for AIDS Coalition to Unleash Power.

experience and inner conviction deepens and begins to be prioritized not only over the traditional interpretation of scripture but over scripture itself. A new motif – that of being in exile from the traditional worshipping community – emerges. For some, such as McNeill, the time spent in exile can be a time of temporary atheism, a necessary therapeutic period of healing and gaining strength which will ultimately enable a return to the Church to transform it from within. For others, the crisis initiates serious consideration of the view that the truly liberative action is to abandon one's religious institutions, and in some cases the scriptures, in order to find a positive spiritual space.

We begin with McNeill. Originally published in 1988, his *Taking a Chance on God* draws on the psychoanalytical concept of the 'Keeping-Mother-Good' syndrome; the tendency to heap blame upon and ascribe badness to oneself in order to absolve the Mother figure from suspicion of cruelty. Were one to contemplate that 'Mother' might not be all-good, then the impact may drive one into withdrawal from a reality so unpalatable that it could provoke psychological breakdown. Moreover, when the child is subject to excessive demands and expectations while opportunities for developing autonomy are curtailed, then the results are seen in passive obedience or rebellion. If God or God-inspired scriptures are given the role of superparent, or 'referee' in McNeill's terms, then this can similarly be experienced as an unrelenting judgemental presence from which one rebels or to which one conforms. McNeill encourages his readers to be mature, healthy individuals with a strong sense of self-dignity, a willingness to stand one's ground, alert to the inner voice of conviction sanctioned by the voice of the spirit: 'We can refuse to believe that the God whose love we experience daily can be sadistic' (1996, p. 79), we can choose to listen to 'what God is saying to us directly' (1996, p. 79), we can see ourselves 'as persons with divine dignity and responsibility, to see our gayness itself as a blessing and not as a curse, a blessing for which we should be grateful to God. We must learn as gay persons to celebrate our existence' (1996, p. 80). On this basis, he envisages a move to a critical, rather than apologetic, stance:

> We gay and lesbian Christians must strive to become loving critics and critical lovers of the Church. We must learn to be appropriately angry over the injustices we experience without being apologetic. We must continue to state clearly the ideals we stand for . . . Our anger over the injustices will remain neurotic as long as we want and experience something from the Church authorities that they cannot or will not give us.

... [We must be] self-centered in a healthy way so that we are able to take responsibility before God and our fellow humans for our choices and our lives. We must learn that we cannot live our lives to meet the expectations of others. The primary way of letting go of our anger at our parents and the Church, as we have seen, is to heal the wounds they have inflicted on us. We must be a therapeutic community. If we can heal the wounds of self-hatred and self-rejection, then we can let go of the neurotic anger we feel towards those we see as having inflicted the wounds. (1996, p. 184)

McNeill thus gives a positive interpretation of the time spent in exile. Taking time out from the church or synagogue, or from God by entering a period of atheism, is seen as a healthy reaction to the experience of religious oppression. Indeed, as a counsellor he acknowledges that many of his clients find that recourse to atheism is not temporary. 'Large numbers' feel that their only realistic option is to abandon religious faith altogether (1996, pp. 37–8). However, it was McNeill's hope that denominational gay and lesbian support networks or the Metropolitan Community Church would provide safe spaces for the healing of wounds and the development of resilience so that one is strengthened to renegotiate one's relationship with God and the church or synagogue. Faced with conflicting opinions of what the scriptures mean and how they should be applied, the individual emerging from the therapeutic time of exile will make their decisions on the basis of inner conviction and personal authority:

We must ask ourselves which of the Church's values we continue to want, respect, and love; which values are compatible with who we are and are not destructive of our dignity as persons. The basis of the communal discernment ... is the premise that whatever is psychologically destructive must be bad theology. Our discernment will thus perform an important service for the Church, helping it to separate purely human and destructive traditions from the authentic word of God. (1996, p. 185)

This manoeuvre – one familiar within feminist and Black studies – manages to keep an authoritative place for scripture generally, but not all scriptures specifically. Often the separation of authentic and inauthentic words of God is described as the creation of a 'canon within a canon', but it is probably more appropriately viewed as a canonical approach which permits the offsetting and privileging of one text against another. In practice, this approach has resulted in an emphasis upon liberative traditions within scripture (such as the exodus tradition and for Christian commentators an emphasis upon Jesus' life and ministry), while taking a harder stance against texts that do not contribute to the dignity and well-being of lesbian and gay-identified readers.

This is often accompanied by a second manoeuvre, again mirrored in feminist theology: the identification of an authentic core of Judaism or Christianity that can be privileged over the oppressive practices of religious institutions that have lost touch with these roots. In the theology of Carter Heyward (1984, 1989a, 1989b) for example, her feminist convictions operate as a tool for uncovering an authentic Christianity from its historical distortions, as she locates her agenda as an extension of Jesus' agenda. In so doing she claims the ground of an orthodox Christian woman and a traditionalist calling Christianity back to its original commitment to social justice. In *Jesus Acted Up* Goss emphasizes the social and political revolutions that accompanied the ministry of Jesus, whose solidarity with the humiliated, marginalized, oppressed, persecuted and outcast bespoke resistance to 'the domination politics of first-century C.E. Palestine' (1993, p. 73). He indicates that the experience of being marginalized and oppressed will mean that queer readers have a particular identification with 'the nonperson in first-century Palestine ... the leper, the homeless Jewish peasant ... the woman caught in adultery, the Samaritan, the prostitute, the poor, the hungry, the shunned' (1993, p. 105). There will be an identification with the 'band of fugitive Israelite slaves ... the hopes of liberation of the conquered Jewish people, and the liberation hopes of the nascent Jesus movement against the background of Jewish nationalist and Roman politics of domination' (1993, p. 105). The resurrection is central since it provides God's 'yes' to Jesus' programme of resistance. The risen Christ is thus free to become the Queer Christ – a symbol of solidarity with those who suffer such oppression. He continues this theme in *Queering Christ* where he again highlights the crucifixion as an example of Jesus' solidarity with the oppressed, and the resurrection as God's 'yes': 'God came out for justice-love for all oppressed peoples. Easter thus communicated God's erotic and compassionate solidarity with queers and their sufferings' (2002, p. 26). The Bible thus, for all its texts of terror, is a liberative empowering resource for justice and liberation. Both Heyward and Goss privilege God's option for the oppressed and draw strongly on the scriptures that represent God as one who sides with them.

The ability to discern between authentic Christianity/Judaism, between revelatory and non-revelatory texts, lies ultimately in personal conviction. Goss argues it is the experienced struggle against injustice that forms the framework for interpretation:

> With the help of historical criticism and the primacy of their own struggles as lesbians and gay men, they transform any particular story into a narrative amplification of their own struggles. They imaginatively release the elements of struggle and resistance within the text into their lives. (1993, p. 110)

Rather than exonerating scripture, this approach is more accurately described as one that wrestles with scripture where one's inner conviction plays a pivotal role in discerning the priorities of the scriptures. This enables one to maintain one's religious allegiances and demonstrate to non-Christians (who justifiably wonder why anyone retains such a commitment given the texts of terror and history of religious opposition) that God is not necessarily involved in the negative experiences but found in the liberating interpretations of scripture that gay and lesbian-identified readers provide.

This change of mood can be well illustrated by Gary Comstock's *Theology Without Apology* – a book that tells of his own acceptance of Levitical condemnation and his lengthy struggle to overcome his own internalized homophobia during the years spent living with and exploring the gay communities in San Francisco. His story echoes the readiness to 'keep-Mother-good' as described by McNeill insofar as he speaks of a 'lingering desire to regard the Bible as a parental authority from which I wanted and needed approval and permission', which led him to be 'more willing to apologize for it than to criticize it' (1993, p. 11). However, Comstock does not remain in this position but works out a new relationship to the Bible. The Bible is personified as 'one to whom I have made a commitment and in whom I have invested dearly, but with whom I insist on a mutual exchange of critique, encouragement, support, and challenge' (1993, p. 11). Supportive, encouraging narratives are found in the traditions of the exodus and the account of Jesus' death and resurrection. In his view, the norm that emerges from these two narratives is that the infliction of pain or suffering upon another human is unacceptable. These two significant narratives are privileged and permitted to counter any anti-gay/lesbian statements. He readily concedes that there are such statements and that attempts to prove otherwise are unconvincing. Commenting upon the hermeneutical strategies found in Bailey, Boswell, Scroggs, Horner and Edwards, he says

in the interest of convincing ourselves and the Church that the Bible does not condemn us, we have brought our own bias to our reading of it. We have tended to overlook the danger and hostility that lurk in the very passages with which we have tried to become friends. We have not been sufficiently sceptical of the patriarchal framework within which these passages occur. I would suggest that our approach to the Bible become less apologetic and more critical – that we approach it not as an authority from which we want approval, but as a document whose shortcomings must be cited. (1993, p. 39)

Scripture is no longer exonerated as the unambiguous revealer of God's will. Comstock faces the possibility that they do not contain good news for those who enjoy same-sex relationships. Thus, on Romans 1, he continues:

I am not convinced or soothed by claims that the letter targets a particular kind of homosexuality or that Paul attacks other kinds of sins, not just homosexuality, with the same enthusiasm . . . Not to recognize, critique, and condemn Paul's equations of godlessness with homosexuality is dangerous. To remain within our respective Christian traditions and not challenge these passages that degrade and destroy us is to contribute to our own oppression . . . Those passages will be brought up and used against us again and again until Christians *demand their removal from the biblical canon or, at the very least, formally discredit their authority to prescribe behavior.* (1993, p. 43 emphasis added)

Comstock understands his approach as 'an act of independence, not rebellion' (1993, p. 108) and it seems to match McNeill's model of the mature individual who has used their time as an exile profitably and has returned to renegotiate the covenant. But this criticism of earlier apologetic strategies is something new. Comstock's first suggestion – that we remove pages from the canon – is one that I also once advocated (Guest, 1999), but in hindsight regard as unrealistic and arguably short-sighted, since a good case can be made for retaining such texts for their value in tracing the histories of oppression. The 'encounter approach', as described by Alpert, has its place here. This is where one faces texts of terror square on, willing to 'encounter the text directly with our emotions and our self-knowledge' (Alpert 1997, p. 38). There are several testimonies to such 'encounters' but one of the most moving that I have read is that of Orthodox rabbi, Steve Greenberg, whose words deserve citation in full:

In the years of my painfully slow coming out, I was fitfully able to face myself as a gay man, but it was becoming much harder to face God. While I had begun to feel more at ease about myself, I began to feel terribly out of place in synagogue. The worst was Yom Kippur.

Every Yom Kippur gay Jews who attend services are faced with a dilemma... In the afternoon services of Yom Kippur... the portion from Leviticus delineating the sexual prohibitions is read: 'And with a male you shall not lie the lyings of a woman, it is an abomination.'

I cringed to hear my shame read aloud on the Day of Atonement. The emotions accompanying the reading have changed through the years. At first, what I felt was guilt and contrition. Later, I felt a deep sadness for being caught up in gay desire and I would petition heaven for understanding. At other times, I would sob in my corner seat of the shul, acknowledging the pain of those verses upon my body and spirit. I have tried to connect myself with Jews of countless ages; listening in shul, their deepest feelings of love and desire turned abhorrent, ugly, and sinful. Finally, listening has become, in addition to all else I might feel, a protest.

During this entire period, I never missed the afternoon service on Yom Kippur. Never did I leave the synagogue for this gut-wrenching reading. It never dawned upon me to walk out. Over the years, I developed a sort of personal custom to stand up during the reading. I have always spent Yom Kippur in the seriously prayerful Orthodox environments. No one ever noticed me wrapped in my Kittel (a white cotton robe worn all day on Yom Kippur and in which pious Jews are buried when they die) with my tallit over my head, standing up for a single portion of a Torah reading, and crying. (2002, p. 41)

The encounter approach deliberately lowers one's defences and allows oneself to be moved by the text; to tears, to anger, but always eventually to action:

We imagine the untold damage done to generations of men, women, and children who experienced same-sex feelings and were forced to cloak or repress them. We reflect on those who acted on those feelings and were forced to feel shame and guilt and to fear from their lives. We remember how we felt when we first heard those words and knew their holy source. And we get angry – at the power these words have had over our lives, at the pain we have experienced in no small part because of these words. (Alpert 1997, p. 44)

This idea of making space for anger and protest is healthy. Several gay-affirmative books on raising self-esteem, counselling, aiding spiritual well-being, or matters pertaining to gay/lesbian people in health and social care settings, contain chapters on counteracting the effects of one's religious upbringing. What is of interest is the way such literature points to the urgent need for clients to express their hurt and their anger since this represents an important stage in coming to terms with the way their scriptures and their deity has been mobilized against them. In a forthcoming essay I suggest ways in which the book of Lamentations could be used as a resource, providing a public, canonically sanctioned opportunity to give voice to human pain and to address God.[152] Distress, anger, rage, protest are all appropriate reactions to the texts of terror and, as Alpert notes, there are ways of using this anger creatively:

> If we can, we grow beyond the rage. We begin to see these words as tools with which to educate people about the deep-rooted history of lesbian and gay oppression. We begin to use these very words to begin to break down the silence that surrounds us. (1997, p. 44)

This is more consistent with Comstock's second idea of discrediting the authority of such texts to prescribe the behaviour of twenty-first-century people. Certainly, the encounter approach can lead to revised notion of scriptural authority. Speaking, for example, about various contemporary Jewish responses to Leviticus 18.22, Mark Solomon notes that the options leave little leeway for the gay-identified Jew who can opt to live with a guilty conscience, avoid anal intercourse, or reject the commandment as being 'utterly incompatible with the nature of God whom I love and worship' (1995, p. 81). This latter option leads Solomon to a revision of his concept of the Torah as the 'unmediated revelation of God's immutable will' to one where he sees Torah as 'an early record of the sustained encounter of our people with God, at times expressing the highest wisdom, beauty and goodness of which inspired humanity is capable, at others reflecting the prejudices and fallacies of a primitive and patriarchal society' (1995, p. 82). This led to a renegotiation of a positive relationship with God. In Sweasey's *From Queer to Eternity*, Solomon says, 'When I didn't have to keep apologizing to God for existing, our relationship improved immeasurably' (1997, p. 42).

---

152 'Lamentations' in *Queer Bible Commentary*, edited by Robert Goss, Mona West, Tom Bohache and myself, Continuum, forthcoming.

Ultimately, the approaches discussed above are geared towards the goal of enabling lesbian and gay-identified Jews and Christians to remain within their confessional homes. Comstock, like many other writers, believes there may be advantages to staying with one's tradition, primarily that of being able to transform that tradition from within, a view he confirmed in a later publication that draws upon his interviews with several pastors within the Black churches in North America. Many of these pastors believe it is good for lesbian and gay-identified people to make themselves known in the Black churches for, although it may provoke controversy, it will facilitate progress and transformation. This may well be a costly path for those attempting to effect the transformation. Emilie Townes, for example, notes how it is hard to stay within a church where one is 'getting an onslaught of nastiness every week either in the worship service or in some of the other activities of the church' (Comstock 2001, p. 226). Irene Monroe also acknowledges this and admits that she personally finds it difficult at times, but she believes that amid the 'bigotry' and the 'railing and ranting about homosexuality' there is something liberative going on (Comstock 2001, p. 68). Other contributors make similar comments: Chip Murray, senior pastor at First AME Church, LA, talks about the need for gays and lesbians to spearhead the revolution while Rev. Altagracia Perez speaks of lesbians and gays as the pioneers who will move the church and society forward. Rev. Arnold Thomas looks forward to a transformed, inclusive church and says that the acceptance of gays, lesbians and bisexuals will be part of making that happen (Comstock 2001, p. 122). Robert Goss had taken a similar line in his 1993 *Jesus Acted Up* where he argued that effective progress can be made if one stays in the Church as an out-of-the-closet individual. In fact, the voice for change is the only thing that justifies remaining with the Church, in his view.

However, Comstock is also aware that the costliness of this choice may be too much. In his keynote address given before the national meeting of the United Church of Christ's Lesbian and Gay Coalition on 5 July 1985, entitled 'Aliens in the Promised Land?' he described the Church as a place where

> I feel defensive and least encouraged to share the meaningful and intimate parts of my life. The Church remains for me the place where the lump still tightens in my throat, where my stomach still knots in anticipation of rejection and difficulty, where I find myself ill at ease. (cited in McNeill 1996, p. 195)

The idea of moving permanently into exile has also been taken up since by Goss who finds that even churches that have advertised themselves as 'welcoming' do not offer full inclusion, but only 'token assimilation' (1998, p.190). He therefore asks, is it time to move out 'into exile and create a space that is more welcoming?', a space that he refers to as a 'queer post-denominational church' (1998, pp. 190, 191). He has continued to uphold the usefulness of the 'loyal resistance' model, noting how such groups as Dignity, Integrity, Affirmation, etc. do important work not only in their local denominational constituencies, but by combining their strength at the religious round table to combat the religious right. But a multi-pronged approach is needed and he talks affirmatively of post-denominational religious organizations such as Other Sheep with its ministry to sexual minorities in Latin America and with networks in Cuba, Africa and India; the Jonathan and David communities that have emerged in Europe bringing Protestant and Catholic translesbigays together; the cross-denominational LGCM in the UK and, of course, the Metropolitan Community Church which is the largest queer church with over three hundred churches in 17 countries.

Goss personally still hopes that a new Christianity, one that 'escapes from its heritage of violence', can emerge, but he does engage with Mary Daly's critique of Christianity and acknowledges that, for some, the idea of doing lesbian or gay-identified biblical studies/theology is akin to 'rearranging the deck chairs on the Titanic' (1998, p. 192) and that such people might legitimately choose to reject the authority of the scriptures in toto. Thus we come to a position where all significance is placed upon one's inner convictions where the scriptures no longer carry any authoritative weight for how one understands and organizes one's life.

Rejecting the scriptures as authoritative

Within feminist theology there has been a long-standing debate regarding the compatibility of feminism and religious allegiance. Naomi Goldberg (1979), Mary Daly (1986) and Daphne Hampson (1990, 1996) found that commitment to their feminist principles and inner convictions meant that they could no longer hold to the religious beliefs in which they had been nurtured. In individual ways, each has pioneered an exodus from their religious roots and raised at least two critical questions: (1) Is the continued effort to engage with scripture and one's religious tradition ultimately tantamount to collusion? (2) Would one's interests be better served by gaining the courage to leave, defined by Mary Daly as 'virtue enabling women to depart from all patriarchal religion and other hopeless institutions, springing from deep knowledge of the nucleus of nothingness which is at the core of these institutions' (1988, p. 69).

Elizabeth Stuart cautions against such a move, arguing that one cannot fully escape the influence of religion for it permeates contemporary life whether or not one owns any allegiance to it. In her view, in a context where religious influence is so deeply embedded, the absence of a 'queer voice' would 'hand over huge amounts of power to the oppressors . . . and leave the area wide open to be controlled and manipulated by those who seek to do us harm' (1997, p. 15). She holds out hope for the transformation of a Christianity which, she reminds her readers, is a dynamic, living tradition, capable of being transformed:

> What has been represented as universal Christian truth has actually been the reflection of a small number of men . . . Those of us who remain within Christianity often do so because we believe that although rooted in a historical event and tradition the Christian faith is not a finished, static, mono-dimensional 'package', but a living, fluid, changing and diverse system and story, constantly in the process of deconstruction and reconstruction. We believe, against all the odds and outward appearances, that it can be redeemed from oppressiveness, because from the beginning it has had some inbuilt resistance to what has been made of it and there have always been Christians even in the darkest of days who have picked up on this liberating strand. (1997, p. 15)

However, Stuart rightly recognizes the need for all individuals to consider their options, to be free to make their own decision and have it respected. For women such as Goldberg, Daly, Hampson and Starhawk, a shift into postchristianity, or in Starhawk's case into Goddess spirituality, may be the only option by which individuals can retain their sense of integrity. These figures come to mind because they have published accounts of their spiritual journeys. There may be a large number of lesbian-identified people who have also taken this option but, because they have not been in a position, or desired, to publish an account of their journey, they remain unknown. Obviously, once one has taken this step, there is no compunction to spend any more energy engaging with the scriptures and thus it is difficult to find material for incorporating their perspective within a lesbian-identified hermeneutic for interpreting scripture. Nevertheless, as Robert Goss notes, one should keep in touch with their exploration of new spiritualities since these may be 'foundational for reformulating and reenvisioning imaginative Christian queer theologies' (2002, p. 249).

A gay-identified scholar whose journey has taken him from Methodist minister to member of the loyal opposition, to exile, and then beyond, is John Michael Clark. Rather than considering what the Bible has to say about homosexuality, Clark argued that one needs to grant homosexuality the privileged status and use it as a lens to scrutinize scripture. In his early work he argued that there was an

> increasing awareness that the seemingly endless and circular arguments to justify gay/lesbian existence with biblical exegesis, to achieve ordination in traditional denominations, and on the part of the MCC, to receive recognition by and membership in the National Council of Churches, all together have become a futile, Kafkaesque drain upon gay and lesbian energies. The institutional religious system clearly functions so as to diffuse our efforts, keeping us waiting and negotiating for a positive response which is unlikely ever to come. Such apologetic efforts . . . are proving a demoralizing dead end . . . Rather than expending all our energies in such futile pursuits, gay men and lesbians need, instead, to lay an assertive and righteous claim upon the religious traditions and heritage into which we were born . . . Gay people must make a commitment to be a force to be reckoned with . . . by claiming and assuming our right to theologize and to speak prophetically. (1989, p. 11)

Clark's *Place to Start* was prepared to put existing religious allegiances on the line. It encouraged readers to enquire 'whether gay theology will be something distinctly different from or unique to, Judaism and Christianity, or simply a gay perspective brought to those traditions' (1989, p. 6). As articulated in 1989, this fresh start rejected assimilationist strategies as unworkable, partly because scriptures can never be fully redeemed to the extent that their capacity to harm is closed off forever ('in the popular consciousness, at least, no contextual exegesis can undo either Leviticus' demand for death to homosexual men or Romans' vehement homophobia' – 1989, p. 12). Yet Clark remained open to using scriptures to critique that judgement via an emphasis upon the prophetic strand that demands justice. In this, he drew specifically on Rosemary Radford Ruether's belief that while 'we must confront the fact that scripture and theology have contributed to these very evils that trouble us . . . we discover within [them] essential resources to unmask these very failures of religion' (Ruether 1983, p. 5). Clark was thus at this stage, like other lesbian and gay-identified theologians, privileging one biblical strand over another so as not to lose contact with Jewish and Christian roots altogether.

However, his confidence dwindles. In his 1992 conversation with Ron Long he points out the danger of the wrestling with God/scripture approach that 'keeps the faithful in an argumentative mode and does nothing to facilitate action' (Long and Clarke 1992, p. 24). And some eight years on from his 1989 work, writing from the perspective of one wrestling theologically with the reality of his HIV-positive status, he opts to avoid using the Bible as a resource, now referring to himself as a 'scripture-phobe'. One of the reasons given for abandoning the Bible as a primary source for engagement is due to its oppressive power:

> I am painfully aware of the extent to which the Bible has been used, over and over again, as a tool of oppression and even terrorism, as the ideological justification not only for excluding gay men and lesbians, but also for blaming the victim in the AIDS health crisis and for engaging in acts of antigay/antilesbian violence. (1997, p. 10)

He concedes that the attempt to stand within the tradition and privilege the voice of prophetic critique was all well and good, but the minority communities that use this strategy have 'little efficacy against the oppressive, majoritarian status quo' (1997, p. 11), and he begins to wonder 'whether the scriptures really have much of positive value to say to gay and lesbian experience' (1997, p. 11). Even the reinterpretations of Genesis 19 that were bearing fruit do not give him hope since

> average churchgoers and mainstream white middle-Americans are likely to remain unconvinced . . . Similarly, in the New Testament, we may find a variety of ways to contextualize, explain, or otherwise mitigate Paul's exclusion of gay male *and* lesbian sexuality, but I do not believe we ever will find a way to clearly make the Pauline corpus progay! Granted, we do find certain possibly homoerotic images in the Bible, such as the same-sex love of David and Jonathan, or Ruth and Naomi, or even Jesus and John the Beloved. However comforting these images may be at some level, they nevertheless seem incidental, artifactual, and merely conveniently comforting asides for gay men and/or lesbians, but asides with no particular message or authority. (1997, p. 12)

While he identifies four authoritative resources that include scripture and canon, the community of faith, the institutions of such communities and their traditions, and the experience of those oppressed by religious expression and praxis, he argues that the latter resource

> virtually undermines any authoritativeness in the other three ... In other words, particularly for those of us who are gay men and lesbians in the primarily Christian West, our experience of oppression by much of the canon, scriptural interpretation and tradition, and church and synagogue becomes our authoritative standpoint for appraising all of the other basic resources. (1997, p. 10)

His reflections lead him to conclude that 'the scriptures are neither authoritative nor particularly informative for gay/lesbian being, relationships, or liberation' (1997, p. 12). What is required is a radical decentring where scriptural authority is dismantled as one admits other texts and other experiences into the discussion on an equal footing. To this end, he speaks of studiously avoiding the Bible and preferring 'an ever-expanding canon of feminist, profeminist, and gay-affirmative books and articles which I believe to be the most reliable resources for my work in post-Christian and profeminist gay theology and ethics' (1997, p. 9).

Several other writers have spoken about the usefulness of extra biblical resources. Gary Comstock (1993, p. 109) speaks of assembling his own scriptural non-canonical texts (such as E. M. Forster's *Maurice*, Hermann Hesse's *Siddhartha*, Toni Morrison's *Sula*, Audre Lord's *Sister Outsider* and Beth Brant's *Mohawk Trail*). In them he finds himself accepted and he can share their vision; they also challenge him to find new ways of living in the world. Rebecca Alpert considers the ways that contemporary fiction helps lesbian-identified Jews to see Judaism through a lesbian lens. Thus, the *mikveh* in Alice Bloch's *The Law of Return* 'is transformed into a potentially erotic site of women bathing and bonding together over a shared experience of pleasure in their bodies' (Alpert 1997, p. 153). The erotic encounter between Sophie and Muffin in Sarah Schulman's novel *The Sophie Horowitz Story* takes place behind the *mehizah*, thereby infusing sacred Jewish space with a lesbian presence, and transforming it. This literature facilitates a transformation of tradition as the fictional characters reinterpret old texts in a new lesbian light in a way that is both critical and optimistic. For Alpert, however, this use of fiction does not come about after a rejection of scripture, but as a way of helping readers engage with scripture from a lesbian-identified perspective:

260

As skeptics we can stand apart from that life and with good humor and insight bring a critique of the texts, looking at them from a perspective that has up till now been silenced. And as prophets, we can imagine the possibilities for change inherent in the traditions and texts of our people and our relationship to them. (1997, p. 161)

Unlike Clark, for these writers the inclusion of contemporary literature helps them to find a critical lens through which to interact with scripture. It does not constitute a move away from scripture but facilitates an engagement with it; not from a position where one's lesbian or gay status is the issue under scrutiny, but from a place where one's lesbian or gay, bisexual or transgendered perspective scrutinizes the scriptures.

Such a move is characteristic of queer readings of scripture. Drawing on David Halperin's understanding of Foucault's notion of reverse discourse, Ken Stone encourages readers to shift away from an approach where homosexuality is the object of scrutiny to the position of queer subjectivity. This privileged angle of vision does not derive from any inherent biologically wired homosexual orientation. Queer subjectivity derives from one's being positioned as a category of person and using that positionality to construct resistant discourse and thereby initiate self-transformation. Applying such thinking to biblical studies means that queer subjectivity could function 'as a "legitimate condition of knowledge" *about* the Bible' rather than asking what the Bible has to say about homosexuality (1999b, p. 19 citing Halperin 1995, pp. 60–1). As noted previously, queer readings are amenable to those who do not own confessional allegiances. Indeed, as Laurel Schneider notes, they 'seem to depend on a kind of distance from the text-as-Scripture (in the sense of Scripture-as-Revelation)' (2001, p. 215). I have criticized them for not being sufficiently engaged in contemporary politics, not for their critical distance from the text. Insofar as *some* queer readings are offered by scholars who do not appear to have any personal investment in religion, or who perhaps have made their own journey into space beyond institutional Judaism or Christianity, queer represents a valuable way of continuing to engage with scriptures that continue to exert an influence upon the contemporary world while not personally owning any commitment to them. And for those who *do* retain confessional interests, a queer subjectivity, with its focus on textual elements that sustain heteronormativity, can 'authorize a kind of return fire against those who commandeer the entire weight of Scripture against contemporary gay, lesbian, bisexual, transgendered and other "queer" persons' (Schneider 2001, p. 222) – a potential that regrettably currently remains under-explored.

The clarity and honesty with which the above scholars write is welcome. Their presentations give the reader a clear sense of why they continue, or opt not to continue, wrestling with scripture. They also indicate openly where the authority for the interpretation resides. Without being overtly prescriptive they present their views and leave readers to make their own informed decision about what they will do with these scriptures. Such openness and flexibility is not a major characteristic of the work of their detractors. As noted in Chapter 4 and in Guest (2001), opposition to gay, lesbian, or queer-identified interpretation is usually grounded in sincere claims to be honourably defending scriptural norms and values and their unchanging universal relevance to global humanity. In the earnest desire to shore up scriptural authority and values there is little room for flexibility and apparently no place for personal convictions since these could be the product of a corrupt fallen humanity. Thus Wold advocates 'sound' exegesis that expounds the 'plainest meaning of the text' (1998, p. 81); one that does not fall foul of temptations 'to twist the biblical data' (1998, p. 21) and make the scriptures conform to *our* contemporary ethics and norms. In such publications what rarely comes under the spotlight is the way their personal convictions and ideologies are also fully active. In presenting their perspective as normative and scriptural, they naturalize heterocentric ideology as neutral, objective, common sense and decent, thus implicitly presenting the lesbian-identified exegete as the radical, the distorter, the indecent (a positioning that queer ironically plays straight into the hands of).

However, one of the most significant contributions of Marcella Althaus-Reid's *Indecent Theology* is her reminder that exegesis and theology can never be liberative while its practitioners hide behind a smokescreen of 'decency'. Her questioning and deconstructing of liberation theology from the perspective of 'a woman from the Port of Buenos Aires' (2001, p. 2) indicates how all theology has been implicated in a culture that separates sexuality into categories of decent and indecent, natural and unnatural, privileged and unprivileged. She unveils the fact that theology and biblical studies have always been *sexual projects*: 'Based on sexual categories and heterosexual binary systems, obsessed with sexual behaviour and orders, every theological discourse is implicitly a sexual discourse, a decent one, an accepted one' (2001, p. 22). She calls for an out-of-the-closet theology where heterosexual, lesbian, gay, bisexual, transgender and queer-identified writers acknowledge the sexual interests that drive and underpin their production of commentaries, theologies and positional statements.

This encouragement to put heterocentric-driven studies under the same scrutiny as LGBT/Q-identified studies is welcome not least for its potential to expose the ideological commitments underlying all sides to the debate. This project should keep many of us occupied for the next few years and will keep the issue of how one constructs and upholds authority at the forefront of a lesbian-identified hermeneutic that is committed to making a difference for those who are implicated in such debates.

Making a Difference in the Métissage

In this chapter, as in the book as a whole, I have made it clear that my own hope for a lesbian-identified approach is that it will be one committed to making a difference. An ethically responsible approach, it will keep in view the global ways in which lesbian-identified persons are positioned and thereby oppressed; it will keep in touch with the concerns of grassroots communities as it takes up and theorizes those concerns in ways that are ethically accountable to those communities. Informed by feminist principles and strategies it will be committed to social, political, economic and religious justice and transformation. This vision is a personal one and while I hope that the principles and strategies identified in this publication are in keeping with these goals, it will inevitably have its blind spots. Accordingly, the suggestions made in this publication are offered for rigorous discussion and debate and open to being expanded by those who work within different cultural and/or religious communities. Within theological circles we are fortunate to have a round table virtual community that is already committed to developing and nurturing contributions such as this, a space that was initiated by Elisabeth Schüssler Fiorenza's calling into being of the *ekklēsia gynaikōn*.

When Fiorenza coined this phrase, she understood *ekklēsia* to indicate the ideal of a public assembly of free Greek citizens of the *polis* who gathered as equal citizens and equal participants in government in order to determine their own and their children's communal, political and spiritual well-being. In practice, boundaries were drawn around who could count as a free and equal citizen so that 'only a very few freeborn, propertied, educated Greek male heads of households actually exercised democratic government' (1994, p. 15). Adding *gynaikōn* allowed Fiorenza to stress that neither the *polis* nor the Church is a democratic assembly unless women are fully included. The deliberate oxymoron thus points to the ideal for which one works and the jarring reality in which one stands. However, the qualifier *gynaikōn* is misunderstood if it is taken as an indicator of female-only space. Fiorenza's spelling of wo/men is a way of encompassing all marginalized and oppressed women and men in the *ekklēsia*, and also a tangible indication of her desire to disrupt the category itself. The new spelling indicates that 'women are not a unitary social group but rather are fragmented and fractured by structures of race, class, religion, heterosexuality, colonialism, age and health' (1994 pp. 24–5) and recognizes that 'woman' is a socially constructed gender position, a script, neither divinely ordained nor biologically inevitable, but one whereby women are implicated into hegemonic discourses of power. The *ekklēsia gynaikōn* is thus an umbrella space occupied by those committed to resisting kyriarchal (master-centred) discourses and practices.[153] Women too can speak and act in kyriarchal ways by being racist, classist, heterosexist, colonialist, and men can be the victims of kyriarchal discourses. So although the phrase *ekklēsia gynaikōn* places a deliberate emphasis upon women, refusing to marginalize and erase yet again the presence of women, Fiorenza attempts to locate this community outside the sex-gender system so that it can 'demystify that system, naming it as a cultural discourse of domination' (1992a, p. 104). It is thus a site where the logic of identity is replaced with the logic of democracy, and where the privileged voices are those that speak from the experience of multiplicative oppression. The cement that holds its participants together is not gender, but the struggle for justice and transformation. This desire – to work outside sex/gender frameworks and find an alternative space that will facilitate exposure of the sex-gender system itself while not losing sight of women – is certainly amenable to a lesbian-identified approach which shares this goal.

In her critical review of Fiorenza's work, J'annine Jobling registers some concerns with this terminology and approach. Jobling agrees that the abandonment of a sex/gender framework is desirable given its tendency to reify binary logic and identity and agrees with the abandonment of essentialism in favour of accepting radical plurality in terms of race, gender, economics and sexuality. However, she is concerned that Fiorenza's approach runs the risk of promoting a 'feminism without women'. Jobling therefore returns to sexed bodies, not essentialized but discursively constructed. Using a logic of equity, she counters Monique Wittig's argument that woman is a male-determined construct by saying this is only so if we

---

153 For a useful extended discussion of kyriarchy, see Schüssler Fiorenza (2001, pp. 118–24).

work on their terms. Within her logic of equity, the category 'becomes a radically undetermined category within which heterogeneity flourishes' (2002, p. 154, n. 22). She concedes that woman is 'a biologically constituted condition' that kyriarchy has positioned as Other to man (2002, pp. 154–5), but if we commit ourselves to a view of fluid identities then the category can serve as a heuristic rallying point for those who choose to acknowledge their common interests and positioning within society. She concludes:

> given the kyriarchal ordering of current conditions, it is expedient to recognize commonalities in the position of women within this system as a basis for political action. This could be deemed a form of 'strategic essentialism' . . . however, in fact, it operates in a different key: it recognizes commonalities in the causes of women which are not reducible one to another but which nevertheless offer a basis for a shared but differentiated ground for speaking. This model mirrors that of the *métissage*, as a knotwork of differences which are nevertheless woven together. This 'knotting together' is an important move because it disrupts and dislodges the dominant order by letting one of its repressed others 'speak', which might allow space for an equitable order to emerge. That, of course, is the ultimate goal of the *ekklēsia*. (2002, p. 157)

Fiorenza was not unaware of the risk of operating a 'feminism without women'. In fact, she directly addressed this problem. In *Jesus, Miriam's Child* she wrote: 'I do not think that feminists can relinquish the analytic category "woman" entirely and replace it with the analytic category "gender" if we do not wish to marginalize or erase the presence of women in our own feminist discourses' (1994, pp. 24–5), and she referred the reader to Tania Modleski's *Feminism Without Women* (1991). She does retain a commitment to women and in particular to those 'who live at the bottom of the kyriarchal pyramid and who struggle against multiplicative forms of oppression' (1994, p. 14). It is her desire to be inclusive and her recognition that certain men too can find themselves at the lower strata of the pyramid, that leads to her shift away from an approach that is entirely women-centred. Jobling's question – where is the feminist solidarity in this? – is a good one, and her focus on differentiated commonalities takes the discussion in an interesting direction. Of course, Fiorenza and Jobling are not alone in addressing such questions. The question of how one locates a shared basis of solidarity and action which does not obliterate difference has been perplexing feminists for the past few decades. It is not within the remit of this chapter to enter into a detailed discussion of this issue; it must be sufficient to note that this ongoing debate has a relevance to lesbian-identified hermeneutics.

Another criticism raised by Jobling relates to the association that *ekklēsia gynaikōn* has with Christianity. It is clear that Fiorenza herself works from within her Roman Catholic heritage, even while she clearly prioritizes feminist principles over scriptural and church tradition. Thus, while Fiorenza's notion of the *ekklēsia* 'is not co-extensive with the "patriarchal" Church, nor co-opted into it', Jobling believes it 'inhabits a site both umbilically and critically related to it' (2002, p. 53). It is clearly not Fiorenza's intention to use *ekklēsia* as a 'churchy' concept but, in Jobling's view, there is a 'distinctly Christian context to Schüssler Fiorenza's vision' (2002, p. 49) and the *potential* for 'an unnecessary act of Christian colonization' (2002, p. 51, n. 78). Uncomfortable with a term so heavily loaded with Christian significance, Jobling suggests that those working primarily within a Christian framework might find the *ekklēsia gynaikōn* a suitable forum for their work, but that this can be seen as a branch of a larger forum that embraces those working from different cultural and/or religious (or non-religious?) backgrounds. Thus *ekklēsia* would represent a 'radically democratic movement within Christianity' as a 'movement within a differently named broader movement incorporating a diverse spread of such "localized" movements' (2002, p. 50). The name she offers for this broader movement is the *métissage*. She believes that if the *métissage* is located as a 'central site of community, as a community of feminist communities' and acts according to the four principles outlined by Linda Hogan (1993), it has the potential to be a place where diversity can thrive.[154] The *métissage* will be a place committed to 'polyphonic and open enquiry and dialogue' while not aiming 'monolithically to solicit agreement and consensus' (2002, p. 161). It will be a 'justice-seeking community of communities, constituted by a feminist emancipatory interest, pragmatically grounded in particular embodied experiences, praxis and thinking' (2002, pp. 161–2).

I believe this proposal is helpful. I continue to work with the terminology of *ekklēsia gynaikōn* because my own work inevitably is marked by my Christian heritage and theological framework, even while I personally identify as postchristian.

---

154 The four principles are: first, 'pragmatic' rather than ontological foundations, based in the 'positionality of women in networks are shifting power relations' (Jobling 2002, p. 160); second, the centrality of community as a negotiating forum; third, embodied thinking which recognizes that truth claims are contextual products and not eternal universals; and fourth, universal accountability that takes into account the 'particular experiences of others and the impact of our own practices upon them' (2002, p. 161).

As a postchristian, there is a place for my contribution within the *ekklēsia gynaikōn* for it can still be a helpful meeting place for those who have acted upon their conviction to move into postchristian space. Fiorenza, while not travelling that path herself, is not averse to our presence. For her, the *ekklēsia* provides a feminist public space 'that attempts to keep communication between its various "denominations" (womanist, *mujerista*, Asian, Africana, lesbian, differently abled, gender-feminist, liberationist feminist, etc.) and its various religious audiences (Jewish, Muslim, Christian, Goddess, atheist, agnostic) "open"' (1998, p. 134). I suspect that it would be those who have moved out of their religious affiliations who would query whether they should spend their energies belonging to and addressing such a com-munity. However, what I have often found when meeting with other postchristian colleagues and students is that we sometimes share a sense of being in the wilderness; a difficulty in knowing how to find each other to form supportive networks; a bewilderment about how to negotiate and communally practise a postchristian spirituality. Insofar as Fiorenza's *ekklēsia* offers a community that embraces those who find their home in the Church and those who move out of the churches into other spiritualities, it provides a forum by which we can keep in touch with each other and learn from each other. However, Jobling's proposal that the *ekklēsia* be a forum within a larger forum that hears from Buddhist, Sikh, Hindu, Jewish, Muslim, atheist and agnostic voices, seems to be a sensible move.

Conclusion

In arguing that a lesbian-hermeneutic should be committed to making a difference I am aware that this will be a costly endeavour. Making the application of one's work overtly relevant may not be deemed consistent with the standards of dispassionate enquiry in which many western academics have been trained. It may not sit comfortably with research assessment boards. Fiorenza cautions that her work and activism have rendered her a 'troublemaker' in the academy and she has paid a price for her rigorous and relentless advocacy of this role.[155] She describes herself as a 'resident alien';

---

155 Her significant work on Christian origins (1983) and attempt to make a paradigm shift in biblical studies have been neglected and/or ignored by academics due to the appearance of 'feminist' or 'women' in several of her titles. Despite being tenured in a prestigious Ivy League university, she sees herself as a token white member of staff and writes of being drained by the (unconscious) displays of misogyny and blatant disrespect in meetings (see Bach 1999).

resident insofar as she operates within academic structures, but alien insofar as she chooses to operate outside its kyriarchal practices as far as possible. She warns that when one enters the academy, one enters a masculine world and in order to participate, one has to learn the master's tools and become socialized into the 'entire constellation of beliefs, values, techniques, shared worldviews, and systems of knowledge' that govern the scholarly community (1992a, p. 181) – i.e. socialized into an alien culture. Fiorenza reminds feminists that they need to beware of 'mastering' the requirements only by repressing their own experiences and interests and thereby becoming honorary men. Such women

> often resent women faculty and students who question the patriarchal academic system on feminist terms. These students, among them white middle-class women especially, are often too happy to become 'good daughters' of their theological or spiritual 'fathers' in order to participate in the scholarly discourses of 'the fathers'. They conform to traditional norms of being a 'good girl' or 'good wife' who must not be too aggressive and self-assertive but must provide emotional and intellectual support by silently doing 'shadow work' for the 'great men' in their lives. (1992a, p. 182)

Feminists need to make a strategic collaboration with the patriarchal academy if their work is to be taken seriously and if they are to survive professionally, but they/we 'must not forget that we are strangers in a land whose language, constitution, history, religion, and culture we did not create' (1992a, p. 185). Feminists cannot look to the academy for their grounding roots. Rather, the grounding of a feminist hermeneutic lies in women's movements for overcoming dehumanizing structures, discourse and practices, deriving its questions and issues from women's movements and being accountable to those movements: 'in my opinion we are able to bring about change only if our work remains a part of a movement of solidarity and struggle'; only then can we continue to speak as 'insiders-outsiders, as resident aliens of Church and academy' (Fiorenza 1994, p. 11). It will be costly for lesbian-feminists to follow her lead, but if an ethically responsible lesbian-identified hermeneutic is going to make a difference, its practitioners who are located in privileged academic settings need to be prepared to pay that price.

Conclusions

Throughout this publication I have been able to draw upon a limited number of lesbian-identified readings of scripture that derive predominantly, if not entirely, from western contexts. If a lesbian-identified hermeneutic is, as I hope, going to develop and expand then we need to hear the voices of those situated in non-Transatlantic contexts, or who live in marginalized communities within those contexts. This may well involve the contestation of key terms used in this publication, such as 'lesbian', and 'feminist', and may involve a lively debate concerning the principles and strategies that have been advocated, but this is welcome. The project needs to be broadened and deepened as participants work out strategies that will work best in their local contexts. Locating the project in the *métissage* signals my intent to provide an open arena for further debate and discussion, rather than presenting a universally relevant, ready-made hermeneutic.

There is much further work to be done, several avenues to be pursued, as identified at various stages throughout the preceding chapters. The strategies I have identified for resisting the erasure of female homoeroticism, for disrupting sex/gender binaries, for reclaiming texts, all need to be tested and applied in a more thoroughgoing way than has been possible within the remit of this publication. The applied nature of a lesbian-identified hermeneutic means that it must keep step with movements in the political, social, economic and religious realms, analysing how scripture and the authority of scripture is called upon to support future legislation and institutional discourse. This will also mean that the complicity of the academy in such discourse has to be kept in focus. The practical effects of scriptural interpretation need to be borne in mind as academics take ethical responsibility for the effects of their exegesis. The relationship between a lesbian-identified hermeneutic and a queer reading, which I believe to be one of critical friendship, also needs to be further developed. As I have already argued, I believe queer theory can be a very useful analytical tool for a lesbian-identified approach, rather than the ultimate home of a superseded lesbian-identified hermeneutic. However, further discussion will no doubt illuminate the potential strengths and weaknesses of this relationship.

Ultimately, it is my hope that feminist, womanist and *mujerista* interpretations of scripture, in particular, will be enhanced by the development of a lesbian-identified angle of vision. But I also hope that biblical hermeneutics, more generally, will find in a lesbian-identified critique an approach that reminds all practitioners of their personal involvements and commitments that drive the act of interpretation.

Bibliography

Margrete Aarmo, 1999, 'How Homosexuality Became "un-African": The Case of Zimbabwe', in Evelyn Blackwood and Saskia E. Wieringa (eds), *Same-Sex Relations and Female Desires: Transgender Practices Across Cultures*, New York: Columbia University Press, pp. 255–80.

Sidney Abbott and Barbara Love, 1972, *Sappho Was a Right-On Woman: A Liberated View of Lesbianism*, New York: Stein and Day.

Lila Abu-Lughod, 1985, 'A Community of Secrets: The Separate World of Bedouin Women', *Signs* 10/4, pp. 637–57.

—— 1990, 'The Romance of Resistance: Tracing Transformations of Power through Bedouin Women', in Peggy Reeves Sanday and Ruth Gallagher Goodenough (eds), *Beyond the Second Sex: New Directions in the Anthropology of Gender*, Philadelphia: University of Pennsylvania Press, pp. 311–37.

—— 1993, *Writing Women's Worlds: Bedouin Stories*, Berkeley and Oxford: University of California Press.

Susan Ackerman, 1993, 'The Queen Mother and the Cult in Ancient Israel', *Journal of Biblical Literature*, 112, pp. 385–401.

—— 1998, *Warrior, Dancer, Seductress, Queen: Women in Judges and Biblical Israel*, The Anchor Bible Reference Library, New York, London, Toronto, Sydney, Auckland: Doubleday.

Rosa Ainley and Sarah Cooper, 1994, 'She Thinks I still Care: Lesbians and Country Music', in Diane Hamer and Belinda Budge (eds), *The Good, the Bad and the Gorgeous*, London and San Francisco: Pandora, pp. 41–56.

R. Albertz, 1992, *Religiongeschichte Israels in alttestamentlicher zeit*, Göttingen: Vandenhoeck and Ruprecht.

William F. Albright, 1940, *From the Stone Age to Christianity: Monotheism and the Historical Process*, Baltimore: Johns Hopkins Press.

Rebecca Alpert, 1992, 'Challenging Male/Female Complementarity: Jewish Lesbians and the Jewish Tradition', in Howard Eilberg-Schwartz (ed.), *People of the Body: Jews and Judaism from an Embodied Perspective*, Albany: State University of New York Press, pp. 361–77.

—— 1994, 'Finding Our Past: A Lesbian Interpretation of the Book of Ruth', in Judith A. Kates and Gail Twersky Reimer (eds), *Reading Ruth: Contemporary Women Reclaim a Sacred Story*, New York: Ballantine, pp. 91–6.

—— 1997, *Like Bread on the Seder Plate: Jewish Lesbians and the Transformation of Tradition*, New York: Columbia University Press.

—— 2000, 'Do Justice, Love Mercy, Walk Humbly: Reflections on Micah and Gay Ethics',

271

in Robert E. Goss and Mona West (eds), *Take Back the Word: A Queer Reading of the Bible*, Cleveland, Ohio: The Pilgrim Press, pp. 170–82.

Rebecca T. Alpert, Sue Levi Elwell and Shirley Idelson (eds), 2001, *Lesbian Rabbis: The First Generation*, New Brunswick, New Jersey and London: Rutgers University Press.

Rachel Alsop, Annette Fitzsimons, Kathleen Lennon and Rosalind Minsky, 2002, *Theorizing Gender*, Oxford: Polity Press.

Robert Alter, 1992, *The World of Biblical Literature*, London: SPCK.

Dennis Altman, 1971, *Homosexual Oppression and Liberation*, London: Allen Lane.

—— 1982, *The Homosexualization of America*, Boston: Beacon Press.

Dennis Altman, Carole Vance, Martha Vicinius and Jeffrey Weeks (eds), 1989, *Homosexuality, which Homosexuality? International Conference on Gay and Lesbian Studies*, London: Gay Men's Press.

Amnesty International, 1999, 'The Louder We Will Sing', ACT 79/03/99, London: Amnesty International Publications. http://web.amnesty.org/library/index/engact790031999

—— 2001, 'Crimes of Hate, Conspiracy of Silence: Torture and Ill-Treatment Based on Sexual Identity', ACT 40/016/2001, Oxford: The Alden Press. http://web.amnesty.org/library/Index/engact400162001?opendocument&of=&of=THEMES%5CTORTURE

G. W. Anderson, 1966, *The History and Religion of Israel*, Oxford: Oxford University Press.

J. C. Anderson, 1991, 'Mapping Feminist Biblical Criticism: The American Scene, 1983–1990', in Society of Biblical Literature (eds), *Critical Review of Books in Religion*, Atlanta: Scholars Press, pp. 21–44.

Gloria Anzaldúa, 1990, *Making Face, Making Soul: haciendo caras*, San Francisco: Aunt Lute Books.

—— 1991, 'To(o) Queer the Writer: loco escrito y chicana', in Betsy Warland (ed.), *InVersions: Writings by Dykes, Queers and Lesbians*, Vancouver: Press Gang, pp. 249–63.

The Associates, 2000, 'Count me in', Brighton: Spectrum. http://www.spectrumbrighton.com/countmein/

Alice Bach, 1993, 'Reading Allowed: Feminist Biblical Criticism Approaching the Millennium', *Currents in Review: Biblical Studies* 1, pp. 191–215.

—— 1999, 'Elisabeth Schüssler Fiorenza: An Interview', *Biblicon*, 3, pp. 27–44.

—— 2002, 'Alice's Adventures in Wonderland: A Girl in the Guild', in Alastair G. Hunter and Philip R. Davies (eds), *Sense and Sensitivity: Essays on Reading the Bible in Memory of Robert Carroll*, JSOTSS 348, London and New York: Sheffield Academic Press, pp. 385–94.

Bad Object Choices (eds), 1991, *How Do I Look? Queer Film and Video*, San Francisco: Bay Press.

Derrick Sherwin Bailey, 1955, *Homosexuality and the Western Christian Tradition*, London, New York, Toronto: Longmans Green and Co.

M. Bal, 1988, *Death and Dissymmetry: The Politics of Coherence in the Book of Judges*, Chicago: University of Chicago Press.

Christine Balka and Andy Rose (eds), 1989, *Twice Blessed: Being Gay or Lesbian and Jewish*, Boston, MA: Beacon Press.

Ian Barnard, 1999, 'Queer Race', *Social Semiotics*, 9/2, pp. 199–212.

Mukti Barton, 2001, 'The Skin of Miriam Became as White as Snow: The Bible, Western Feminism and Colour Politics', *Feminist Theology* 27, pp. 68–80.

Bibliography

Evelyn Torton Beck (ed.), 1989, *Nice Jewish Girls: A Lesbian Anthology*, revised and updated edition, Boston: Beacon Press.

Anthony Bendall and Tim Leach (eds), 1995, *'Homosexual Panic Defence' and Other Family Values: Forum on the Homosexual Panic Defence*, Darlinghurst, New South Wales: Lesbian and Gay Anti-Violence Project.

Peter L. Berger and Thomas Luckmann, 1966, *The Social Construction of Reality*, New York: Doubleday.

Martha Dickinson Bianchi, 1924, *The Life and Letters of Emily Dickinson*, Boston: Houghton Mifflin.

Tilde Binger, 1997, *Asherah: Goddesses in Ugarit, Israel and the Old Testament*, JSOTSS 232, Sheffield: Sheffield Academic Press.

Phyllis Bird, 1974, 'Images of Women in the Old Testament', in Rosemary Radford Ruether (ed.), *Religion and Sexism: Images of Women in the Jewish and Christian Traditions*, Copenhagen International Seminar 2, New York: Simon and Schuster, pp. 41–88.

—— 1987, 'The Place of Women in the Israelite Cultus', in P. D. Miller, P. D. Hanson and S. D. McBride (eds), *Ancient Israelite Religion: Essays in Honor of Frank Moore Cross*, Philadelphia: Fortress Press, pp. 397–419.

Evelyn Blackwood and Saskia E. Wieringa (eds), 1999, *Same-sex Relations and Female Desires: Transgender Practices Across Cultures*, New York: Columbia University Press.

Rudi C. Bleys, 1996, *The Geography of Perversion: Male-to-Male Sexual Behavior Outside the West and the Ethnographic Imagination 1750–1918*, London and New York: Cassell.

John Boardman and Eugenio La Rocca, 1975, *Eros in Greece*, Milan: Arnoldo Mondadori.

Roland Boer, 2001, 'Yahweh as Top: A Lost Targum', in Ken Stone (ed.), *Queer Commentary on the Hebrew Bible*, JSOTSS 334, London and New York: Sheffield Academic Press, pp. 75–105.

Jacqueline Bobo, 1988, 'The Color Purple: Black Women as Cultural Readers', in E. Deidre Pibram (ed.), *Female Spectators: Looking at Film and TV*, London: Verso, pp. 90–109.

John Boswell, 1980, *Christianity, Social Tolerance and Homosexuality*, Chicago: University of Chicago Press.

—— 1990, 'Revolutions, Universals, and Sexual Categories', in M. Duberman, M. Vicinus and G. Chauncey, Jr (eds), *Hidden from History: Reclaiming the Gay and Lesbian Past*, New York: Meridian, pp. 17–36.

—— 1994a, *Same Sex Unions in Premodern Europe*, New York: Villiard Books.

—— 1994b, 'Homosexuality and Religious Life: A Historical Approach', in James B. Nelson and Sandra P. Longfellow (eds), *Sexuality and the Sacred: Sources for Theological Reflection*, London: Mowbray and Louisville: Westminster/John Knox Press, pp. 361–73.

Stephen Bourne, 1996, *Brief Encounters: Lesbians and Gays in British Cinema 1930–1971*, London: Cassell.

Barbara Bradby, 1993, 'Lesbians and Popular Music: Does it Matter Who Is Singing?', in Gabriele Griffin (ed.), *Outwrite: Lesbian and Popular Culture*, London and Boulder, Colorado: Pluto Press, pp. 148–72.

Athalya Brenner, 1985, *The Israelite Woman: Social Role and Literary Type*, The Biblical Seminar 2, Sheffield: JSOT Press.

—— 1997, *The Intercourse of Knowledge: On Gendering Desire and "Sexuality" in the Hebrew Bible*, Biblical Interpretation Series 26, Leiden and New York: Brill.

Bibliography

Philip Brett, Gary C. Thomas and Elizabeth Wood (eds), 1994, *Queering the Pitch: The New Gay and Lesbian Musicology*, New York: Routledge.

Deborah Bright, 1991, 'Dream Girls', in T. Boffin and J. Fraser (eds), *Stolen Glances: Lesbians Take Photographs*, London: Pandora Press, pp. 144–55.

John Bright, 1981, *A History of Israel*, third edition, London: SCM Press.

Karen J. Brison, 1992, *Just Talk: Gossip, Meetings, and Power in a Papua New Guinea Village*, Studies in Melanesian Anthropology 11, Berkeley: University of California Press.

Bernadette J. Brooten, 1985, 'Early Christian Women and Their Cultural Context', in Adela Yarbro Collins (ed.), *Feminist Perspectives on Biblical Scholarship*, Atlanta: Scholars Press, pp. 65–91.

—— 1996, *Love Between Women: Early Christian Responses to Female Homoeroticism*, The Chicago Series on Sexuality, History, and Society, Chicago and London: University of Chicago Press.

Elsa Barkley Brown, 1992, '"What Has Happened here": The Politics of Difference In Women's History and Feminist Politics', *Feminist Studies*, 18/2, pp. 295–312.

Charlotte Bunch, 1975, *Passionate Politics: Feminist Theory in Action: Essays 1968–1986*, New York: St Martin's Press.

Glenn Burger, 1994, 'Queer Chaucer', in *English Studies in Canada*, 20/2, pp. 153–70.

Paul Burston and Colin Richardson (eds), 1995, *A Queer Romance: Lesbians, Gay Men and Popular Culture*, London: Routledge.

Judith Butler, 1990, *Gender Trouble: Feminism and the Subversion of Identity*, London: Routledge.

—— 1991, 'Imitation and Gender Insubordination', in Diana Fuss (ed.), *Inside/out Lesbian Theories, Gay Theories*, New York and London: Routledge, pp. 13–31.

M. Callaway, 1986, *Sing, O Barren One: A Study in Comparative Midrash*, Atlanta: Scholars Press.

Beatrix Campbell, 1980, 'A Feminist Sexual Politics: Now You See it, Now You don't', *Feminist Review*, 5, pp. 1–18.

Hazel Carby, 1992, 'Policing the Black Woman's Body in the Urban Context', *Critical Inquiry*, 18, pp. 738–55.

Michael Carden, 1999, 'Homophobia and Rape in Sodom and Gibeah: A Response to Ken Stone', *Journal for the Study of the Old Testament*, 82, pp. 93–6.

—— 2001, 'Remembering Pelotit: A Queer Midrash on Calling Down Fire', in Ken Stone (ed.), *Queer Commentary on the Hebrew Bible*, JSOTSS 334, London and New York: Sheffield Academic Press, pp. 152–68.

Nina Beth Cardin, 1999, *Tears of Sorrow, Seeds of Hope: A Jewish Spiritual Companion for Infertility and Pregnancy Loss*, Woodstock: Jewish Lights Publications.

James V. Carmichael, Jr, 1998, 'Introduction: Makeover Without a Mirror – A Face for Lesbigay Library History', in James V. Carmichael, Jr (ed.), *Daring to Find Our Names: The Search for Lesbigay Library History*, Westport and London: Greenwood Press, pp. 1–23.

Edward Carpenter, 1914, 'The Intermediate Sex', in Edward Carpenter, *Love's Coming of Age*, London: Methuen, pp. 114–34.

Terry Castle, 1993, *The Apparitional Lesbian: Female Homosexuality and Modern Culture*, New York: Columbia University Press.

Helen (charles), 1993, 'Queer Nigger: Theorizing "white" Activism', in Joseph Bristow and Angelina R. Wilson (eds), *Activating Theory: Lesbian, Gay, Bisexual Politics*, London: Lawrence and Wishart, pp. 97–106.

Bibliography

George Chauncey, Jr, 1982–3, 'From Sexual Inversion to Homosexuality: Medicine and the Changing Conceptualization of Female Desire', *Salmagundi*, 58–59, pp. 114–46.

—— 1984, *Gay New York: Gender, Urban Culture and the Making of the Gay Male World 1890–1940*, New York: Basic Books.

Kittredge Cherry and Zalmon Sherwood (eds), 1995, *Equal Rites: Lesbian and Gay Worship, Ceremonies, and Celebrations*, Louisville: John Knox Press.

Chou Wah-Shan, 2001, 'Homosexuality and the Cultural Politics of *Tongzhi* in Chinese Societies', in Gerard Sullivan and Peter Jackson (eds), *Gay and Lesbian Asia: Culture, Identity, Community*, New York: Harrington Park Press, pp. 27–46.

The Christian Institute, 2002a, 'Counterfeit Marriage: How "Civil Partnerships" Devalue the Currency of Marriage', Newcastle-upon-Tyne: The Christian Institute. http://www.christian.org.uk/pdfpublications/counterfeit-marriage.pdf

—— 2002b, 'Squeezing Churches Into a Secular Mould: How Planned Government Employment Laws Threaten Religious Liberty', Newcastle-upon-Tyne: The Christian Institute. http://www.christian.org.uk/pdfpublications/employ_regs_leaflet_dec 2002.pdf

—— 2003, 'Implementing the EU Employment Directive', Newcastle-upon-Tyne: The Christian Institute. http://www.christian.org.uk/directive2003/seminar.pdf

Church of England House of Bishops, 1991, *Issues in Human Sexuality: A Statement by the House of Bishops of the General Synod of the Church of England*, London: Church House Publishing.

—— 2003, *Some Issues in Human Sexuality: A Guide to the Debate: A Discussion Document from the House of Bishops' Group on Issues in Human Sexuality*, London: Church House Publishing.

John Michael Clark, 1989, *A Place to Start: Towards an Unapologetic Gay Liberation Theology*, Dallas: Monument Press.

—— 1997, *Defying the Darkness: Gay Theology in the Shadows*, Cleveland, Ohio: Pilgrim Press.

Wendy Clark, 1987, 'The Dyke, the Feminist and the Devil', in Feminist Review (eds) *Sexuality: A Reader*, London: Virago Press, pp. 201–15.

Richard Cleaver, 1995, *Know My Name: A Gay Liberation Theology*, Louisville: Westminster John Knox Press.

David J. A. Clines, 1995, *Interested Parties: The Ideology of Writers and Readers of the Hebrew Bible*, Gender, Culture, Theory 1, JSOTSS 205, Sheffield: Sheffield Academic Press.

—— 1997, *The Bible and the Modern World*, The Biblical Seminar 51, Sheffield: Sheffield Academic Press.

—— 1998, 'The Postmodern Adventure in Biblical Studies', in David J. A. Clines and Stephen D. Moore (eds), *Auguries: The Jubilee Volume of the Sheffield Department of Biblical Studies*, JSOTSS 269, Sheffield: Sheffield Academic Press, pp. 276–91.

Cathy J. Cohen, 2003, 'Black Gay Identities and the Politics of AIDS', in Robert J. Corber and Stephen Valocchi (eds), *Queer Studies: An Interdisciplinary Reader*, Malden, MA, Oxford, Melbourne, Berlin: Blackwell Publishing, pp. 46–60.

Jane Fishburne Collier, 1974, 'Women in Politics', in Michelle Zimbalist Rosaldo and Louise Lamphere (eds), *Women, Culture, and Society*, Stanford: Stanford University Press, pp. 89–96.

Bibliography

Adela Yarbro Collins (ed.), 1985, *Feminist Perspectives on Biblical Scholarship*, Scholarship in North America 10, Chico, California: Scholars Press.

Patricia Hill Collins, 1991, *Black Feminist Thought: Knowledge, Consciousness, and the Politics of Empowerment Perspectives on Gender*, New York: Routledge.

—— 2002, 'The Sexual Politics of Black Womanhood', in Christine L. Williams and Arlene Stein (eds), *Sexuality and Gender*, Blackwell Readers in Sociology 7, Oxford: Blackwell Publishing, pp. 193–206.

Ralph Colson, 1941, *Philo*, 10 vols, 2 suppl. vols, Loeb Classical Library, Cambridge, MA: Harvard University Press.

The Combahee River Collective, 2000, 'The Combahee River Collective Statement', in Barbara Smith (ed.), *Home Girls: A Black Feminist Anthology*, New York: Kitchen Table/ Women of Color Press, pp. 264–74.

Gary D. Comstock, 1993, *Gay Theology Without Apology*, Cleveland, Ohio: Pilgrim Press.

—— 2001, *A Whosoever Church: Welcoming Lesbians and Gay Men Into African American Congregations*, Louisville, Kentucky: Westminster John Knox Press.

Gary D. Comstock and Susan E Henking (eds), 1996, *Que(e)rying Religious Studies: A Critical Anthology*, New York: Continuum.

Blanche Cooke, 1979, 'The Historical Denial of Lesbianism', *Radical History Review*, 20, pp. 60–5.

Robert J. Corber and Stephen Valocchi, 'Introduction', in Robert J. Corber and Stephen Valocchi (eds), *Queer Studies: An Interdisciplinary Reader*, Malden, MA, Oxford, Melbourne, Berlin: Blackwell Publishing, 2003, pp. 1–20.

Paul Crane, 1992, *Gays and the Law*, London: Pluto.

Rob Cover, 2002, 'Strategic Subjects: The Sexual Binary, Transgression and the Ethics of Strategic Essentialism', *Colloquy: Text Theory Critique*, 6, http://www.arts.monash.edu. au/others/colloquy/

Margaret Cruikshank, 1996, 'Foreword', in Bonnie Zimmerman and Toni A. H. McNaron (eds), *The New Lesbian Studies: Into the Twenty-First Century*, New York: The Feminist Press, pp. xi–xii.

Rosemary Curb and Nancy Manahan, 1985, *Lesbian Nuns: Breaking Silence*, Florida: Naiad Press.

Mary Daly, 1986, *Beyond God the Father: Toward a Philosophy of Women's Liberation*, London: The Women's Press.

—— 1988, *Webster's First New Intergalactic Wickedary of the English Language Conjured by Mary Daly in Cahoots with Jane Caputi*, London: Women's Press.

Mary Rose D'Angelo, 1997, 'Women Partners in the New Testament', in Gary D. Comstock and Susan E. Henking (eds), *Que(e)rying Religion: A Critical Anthology*, New York: Continuum, pp. 441–55.

Dominic Davies, 1996, 'Homophobia and Heterosexism', in Dominic Davies and Charles Neal (eds), *Pink Therapy: A Guide for Counsellors and Therapists Working with Lesbian, Gay and Bisexual Clients*, Buckingham and Philadelphia: Open University Press, pp. 41–65.

Peggy Day, 1989, *Gender and Difference in Ancient Israel*, Minneapolis: Augsburg Fortress.

John D'Emilio, 1992, *Making Trouble: Essays on Gay History, Politics and the University*, New York and London: Routledge.

William G. Dever, 1984, 'Asherah, Consort of Yahweh?', *Bulletin of the American Schools of Oriental Research*, 255, pp. 21–38.

Bibliography

Anita Diamant, 2001, *The Red Tent*, London: Macmillan.

Joanne DiPlacido, 1998, 'Minority Stress Among Lesbians, Gay Men, and Bisexuals: A Consequence of Heterosexism, Homophobia and Stigmatisation', in Gregory M. Herek (ed.), *Stigma and Sexual Orientation: Understanding Prejudice Against Lesbians, Gay Men, and Bisexuals* (Psychological Perspectives on Lesbian and Gay Issues, volume 4), Thousand Oaks, London, New Delhi: Sage Publications, pp. 138–59.

F. W. Dobbs-Allsopp, 1999, 'Rethinking Historical Criticism', *Biblical Interpretation: A Journal of Contemporary Approaches*, 7/3, pp. 235–72.

Jack Donnelly, 2003, *Universal Human Rights in Theory and Practice*, second edition, Ithaca and London: Cornell University Press.

Emma Donoghue, 1993, 'Imagined more than Women: Lesbians as Hermaphrodites, 1671–1766', *Women's History Review*, 2/2, pp. 199–216.

Alexander Doty, 1993, *Making Things Perfectly Queer: Interpreting Mass Culture*, Minnesota and London: University of Minnesota Press.

—— 2000, *Flaming Classics: Queering the Film Canon*, New York and London: Routledge.

Kelly Brown Douglas, 1999, *Sexuality and the Black Church: A Womanist Perspective*, New York: Orbis Books.

Peter Drucker (ed.), 2000, *Different Rainbows*, London: Millivres-Prowler Group Ltd.

Musa W. Dube, 2000, *Postcolonial Feminist Interpretation of the Bible*, St Louis: Chalice Press.

—— (ed.), 2001, *Other Ways of Reading: African Women and the Bible*, Atlanta: Society of Biblical Literature.

Martin Duberman, 1993, *Stonewall*, New York: Dutton.

M. Duberman, M. Vicinus and G. Chauncey, Jr (eds), 1990, *Hidden from History: Reclaiming the Gay and Lesbian Past*, New York: Meridian.

Hadar Dubowsky, 2002, 'Jewish Dyke Baby-Making', in David Shneer and Caryn Aviv (eds), *Queer Jews*, New York and London: Routledge, pp. 44–54.

Lisa Duggan, 1998, 'The Theory Wars, or, Who's Afraid of Judith Butler', *Journal of Women's History*, 10/1, pp. 9–19.

—— 2003, 'The Trials of Alice Mitchell: Sensationalism, Sexology, and the Lesbian Subject in Turn-of-the Century America', in Robert J. Corber and Stephen Valocchi (eds), *Queer Studies: An Interdisciplinary Reader*, Oxford: Blackwell Publishing, pp. 73–87.

Lisa Duggan and Nan D. Hunter, 1995, *Sex Wars: Sexual Dissent and Political Culture*, London: Routledge.

Celena M. Duncan, 2000, 'The Book of Ruth: On Boundaries, Love, and Truth', in Robert E. Goss and Mona West (eds), *Take Back the Word: A Queer Reading of the Bible*, Cleveland, Ohio: The Pilgrim Press, pp. 92–102.

Gillian A. Dunne, 1997, *Lesbian Lifestyles: Women's Work and the Politics of Sexuality*, Basingstoke: Macmillan Press.

Chris Dunton and Mai Palmberg, 1996, *Human Rights and Homosexuality in Southern Africa*, Current African Issues 19, Uppsala: The Nordic Africa Institute.

Daisy Dwyer, 1978, 'Ideologies of Sexual Inequality and Strategies for Change in Male–Female Relations', *American Ethnologist*, 5, pp. 227–40.

Alice Echols, 1984, 'The New Feminism of Yin and Yang', in Ann Snitow, Christine Stansell and Sharon Thompson (eds), *Desire: the Politics of Sexuality*, London: Virago Press, pp. 62–81.

Bibliography

Alice Echols, 1989, *Daring to Be Bad: Radical Feminism in America 1967–1975*, Minneapolis: University of Minnesota Press.

Elizabeth Edwards, 1995, 'Homoerotic Friendships and College Principals, 1880–1960', *Women's History Review*, 4/2, pp. 149–63.

Havelock Ellis, 1894, 'The Study of Sexual Inversion', *Medico-Legal Journal*, 12, pp. 148–57.

—— 1895, 'Sexual Inversion in Women', *Alienist and Neurologist*, 16/2, pp. 141–58.

—— 1936, *Studies in the Psychology of Sex*, vol. 1, part IV, New York: Random House.

Marc Epprecht, 1998, 'The "Unsaying" of Homosexuality Among Indigenous Black Zimbabweans: Mapping a Blindspot in an African Masculinity', *Journal of Southern African Studies*, 24/4, pp. 631–51.

—— 2000, 'Africa: Precolonial Sub-Saharan Africa', in George E. Haggerty (ed.), *Gay Histories and Cultures: An Encyclopedia*, volume II, New York and London: Garland Publishing Inc., pp. 16–19.

Steven Epstein, 1987, 'Gay Politics, Ethnic Identity: The Limits of Social Construction-ism', *Socialist Review*, 93/94, pp. 9–54.

J. Escoffier, 1990, 'Inside the Ivory Closet: The Challenges Facing Lesbian and Gay Studies', *Out/Look: National Lesbian and Gay Quarterly*, 10, pp. 40–8.

J. Cheryl Exum, 1983, '"You Shall Let Every Daughter Live": A Study of Exodus 1:8–2:10', in Mary Ann Tolbert (ed.), *The Bible and Feminist Hermeneutics*, Semeia 28, Decatur, GA: Scholars Press, pp. 63–82.

—— 1985a, '"Mother in Israel": A Familiar Figure Reconsidered', in Letty Russell (ed.), *Feminist Interpretation of the Bible*, Philadelphia: Westminster Press, pp. 73–85.

—— 1985b, 'Deborah', in P. J. Achtemeier (ed.), *Harper's Bible Dictionary*, San Francisco: Harper and Row, p. 214.

—— 1993, *Fragmented Women: Feminist (Sub)versions of Biblical Narratives*, JSOTSS 163, Sheffield: Sheffield Academic Press.

—— 1995, 'Feminist Criticism: Whose Interests Are Being Served?', in Gale Yee, *Judges and Method: New Approaches in Biblical Studies*, Minneapolis: Fortress Press, pp. 65–90.

—— 1996, *Plotted, Shot, and Painted: Cultural Representations of Biblical Women*, JSOTSS 215, Gender Culture Theory 3, Sheffield: Sheffield Academic Press.

—— 2000, 'Feminist Study of the Old Testament', in A. D. H. Mayes (ed.), *Text in Context: Essays by Members of the Society for Old Testament Study*, Oxford: Oxford University Press, pp. 86–115.

Lillian Faderman, 1982, 'Who Hid Lesbian History?', in Margaret Cruikshank (ed.), *Lesbian Studies Present and Future*, New York: The Feminist Press, pp. 115–21.

—— 1985, *Surpassing the Love of Men: Romantic Friendship and Love Between Women from the Renaissance to the Present*, London: The Women's Press.

—— (ed.), 1995, *Chloe plus Olivia: An Anthology of Lesbian Literature from the Seventeenth Century to the Present*, New York: Penguin.

—— 1997, 'Afterword', in Dana Heller (ed.), *Cross Purposes: Lesbians, Feminists, and the Limits of Alliance*, Bloomington: Indiana University Press, pp. 221–9.

Frantz Fanon, 1967, *Black Skin, White Masks*, trans. Charles Lam Markman, New York: Grove Press.

Annabel Faraday, 1988, 'Lesbian Outlaws: Past Attempts to Legislate Against Lesbians', *Trouble and Strife: A Radical Feminist Magazine*, 13, pp. 9–16.

Margaret A. Farley, 1985, 'Feminist Consciousness and the Interpretation of Scripture',

Bibliography

in Letty M. Russell (ed.), *Feminist Interpretation of the Bible*, Philadelphia: Westminster Press, pp. 41–51.

Marilyn R. Farwell, 1996, *Heterosexual Plots and Lesbian Narratives*, The Cutting Edge: Lesbian Life and Literature, New York and London: New York University Press.

Ann Ferguson, 1990, 'Is there a Lesbian Culture?', in Jeffner Allen (ed.), *Lesbian Philosophies and Cultures*, New York: State University of New York Press, pp. 63–88.

Ann Ferguson, Jacquelyn Zita and Kathryn Addelson, 1981, 'On "Compulsory Heterosexuality and Lesbian Existence": Defining the Issues', *Signs*, 7/1, pp. 158–99.

Danna Nolan Fewell, 1998, 'Judges', in Carol A. Newsom and Sharon H. Ringe (eds), *Women's Bible Commentary*, second edition, Louisville, KY: Westminster/John Knox Press, pp. 73–83.

Danna Nolan Fewell and David M. Gunn, 1990, 'Controlling Perspectives: Women, Men and the Authority of Violence in Judges 4 and 5', *Journal of the American Academy of Religion*, LVIII/3, pp. 389–411.

Lynn Y. Fletcher and Adrien Saks (eds), 1990, *Lavender Lists*, Boston: Alyson.

Penny Florence, 'Lesbian Cinema, Women's Cinema', in Gabrielle Griffin (ed.) *Outwrite: Lesbian and Popular Culture*, London, Boulder: Pluto Press, 1993, pp. 126–47.

G. Fohrer, 1973, *History of Israelite Religion*, London: SPCK.

Carol R. Fontaine, 1999, 'A Heifer from thy Stable: On Goddesses and the Status of Women in the Ancient Near East', in Alice Bach (ed.), *Women in the Hebrew Bible: A Reader*, London: Routledge, pp. 159–78.

J. E. Fortunato, 1982, *Embracing the Exile: Healing Journeys for Gay Christians*, San Francisco: Harper and Row.

Michel Foucault, 1978, *The History of Sexuality. Volume 1: An Introduction*, translated by Robert Hurley, London: Penguin.

Trisha Franzen, 1993, 'Differences and Identities: Feminism and the Albuquerque Lesbian Community', *Signs*, 18/4, pp. 891–906.

D. N. Freedman, 1987, 'Yahweh of Samaria and his Asherah', *Biblical Archaeologist*, 50/4, pp. 241–9.

Ernestine Friedl, 1967, 'The Position of Women: Appearance and Reality', *Anthropological Quarterly*, 40, pp. 97–108.

Marilyn Frye, 1982, 'A Lesbian Perspective in Women's Studies', in Margaret Cruikshank (ed.), *Lesbian Studies Present and Future*, New York: The Feminist Press, pp. 194–8.

—— 1990, 'Lesbian "Sex"', in Jeffner Allen (ed.), *Lesbian Philosophies and Cultures*, New York: State University of New York Press, pp. 305–15.

Esther Fuchs, 2000, *Sexual Politics in the Biblical Narrative: Reading the Hebrew Bible as a Woman*, JSOTSS 310, Sheffield: Sheffield Academic Press.

Diana Fuss (ed.), 1991, *Inside/out: Lesbian Theories, Gay Theories*, New York and London: Routledge.

Robert A. J. Gagnon, 2001, *The Bible and Homosexual Practice: Texts and Hermeneutics*, Nashville: Abingdon.

Linda Garber, 2001, *Identity Poetics: Race, Class, and the Lesbian-Feminist Roots of Queer Theory*, New York: Columbia University Press.

Noel I. Garde, 1964, *Jonathan to Gide: The Homosexual in History*, New York: Vintage.

Linda Garnets and Douglas Kimmel (eds), 1993, *Psychological Perspectives on Lesbian and Gay Male Experiences*, Columbia University Press.

Bibliography

S. Gearhart and W. R. Johnson (eds), 1974, *Loving Women/Loving Men: Gay Liberation and the Church*, San Francisco: Glide Publications.

Erhard S. Gerstenberger, 1996, *Yahweh the Patriarch: Ancient Images of God and Feminist Theology*, Minneapolis: Fortress Press.

—— 2002, *Theologies in the Old Testament*, translated by John Bowden, London and New York: T and T Clark.

Martha Gever, Pratibha Parmar and John Greyson (eds), 1993, *Queer Looks: Perspectives on Lesbian and Gay Film and Video*, London: Routledge.

Edward Gibbon, 1929, *The Decline and Fall of the Roman Empire*, volume 4, edited by J. B. Bury, London: Methuen.

Joan Gibbs and Sara Bennett (eds), 1980, *Top Ranking: A Collection of Articles on Racism and Classism in the Lesbian Community*, Brooklyn: February Third Press.

Margaret Gibson, 1997, 'Clitoral Corruption: Body Metaphors and American Doctors. Constructions of Female Homosexuality, 1870–1900', in Vernon A. Rosario (ed.), *Science and Homosexualities*, New York and London: Routledge, pp. 122–4.

Paula Giddings, 1992, 'The Last Taboo', in Toni Morrison (ed.), *Race-ing Justice, En-gendering Power: Essays on Anita Hill, Clarence Thomas and the Construction of Social Reality*, New York: Pantheon.

Sean Gill (ed.), 1998, *The Lesbian and Gay Christian Movement. Campaigning for Justice, Truth and Love*, London and New York: Cassell.

Chris Glaser, 1990, *Come Home! Reclaiming Spirituality and Community as Gay Men and Lesbians*, San Francisco: Harper and Row.

Naomi Goldberg, 1979, *Changing of the Gods: Feminism and the End of Traditional Religions*, Boston: Beacon Press.

J. C. Gonsiorek, 1991, 'The Empirical Basis for the Demise of the Illness Model of Homosexuality', in J. C. Gonsiorek and J. D. Weinrich (eds), *Homosexuality: Research Implications for Public Policy*, Newbury Park, CA: Sage, pp. 115–36.

Robert E. Goss, 1993, *Jesus Acted Up: A Gay and Lesbian Manifesto*, New York: HarperSanFrancisco.

—— 1996, 'Insurrection of the Polymorphously Perverse: Queer Hermeneutics', in J. Michael Clark and Robert E. Goss (eds), *A Rainbow of Religious Studies*, Texas: Monument Press, pp. 9–31.

—— 1998, 'Sexual Visionaries and Freedom Fighters for a Sexual Reformation: From Gay Theology to Queer Sexual Theologies', in Sean Gill (ed.), *The Lesbian and Gay Christian Movement: Campaigning for Justice, Truth and Love*, London and New York: Cassell, pp. 187–202.

—— 2002, *Queering Christ: Beyond Jesus Acted Up*, Cleveland, Ohio: Pilgrim Press.

Robert E. Goss and Amy Squire Strongheart (eds), 1997, *Our Families, Our Values: Snapshots of Queer Kinship*, New York and London: Harrington Park Press.

Robert E. Goss and Mona West (eds), 2000, *Take Back the Word: A Queer Reading of the Bible*, Cleveland, Ohio: Pilgrim Press.

Laura Gowing, 1997, 'History', in Andy Medhurst and Sally R. Munt (eds), *Lesbian and Gay Studies: A Critical Introduction*, London and Washington: Cassell, pp. 53–66.

Judy Grahn, 1984, *Another Mother Tongue: Gay Words, Gay Worlds*, Boston: Beacon Press.

Beverly Greene, 1996, 'Lesbians and Gay Men of Color: The Legacy of Ethnosexual Mythologies in Heterosexism', in Esther D. Rothblum and Lynn A. Bond (eds),

Bibliography

Preventing Heterosexism and Homophobia, California, London and New Delhi: Sage Publications, pp. 59–70.

J. Grant, 1989, *White Woman's Christ, Black Woman's Jesus: Feminist Christianity and Womanist Response*, Atlanta: Scholars Press.

David F. Greenberg, 1988, *The Construction of Homosexuality*, Chicago and London: University of Chicago Press.

Steve Greenberg, 2002, 'A Gay Orthodox Rabbi', in David Shneer and Caryn Aviv (eds), *Queer Jews*, New York and London: Routledge, pp. 36–43.

Gabriele Griffin (ed.), 1993, *Outwrite: Lesbian and Popular Culture*, London, Boulder: Pluto Press.

Gabriele Griffin and Sonia Andermahr (eds), 1997, *Straight Studies Modified: Lesbian Interventions in the Academy*, London and Washington: Cassell.

Elizabeth Grosz, 'Experimental Desire: Rethinking Queer Subjectivity', in J. Copcec (ed.), 1994, *Supposing the Subject*, London: Verso, pp. 133–57.

P. Deryn Guest, 1997, 'Dangerous Liaisons in the Book of Judges', *Scandinavian Journal for the Study of the Old Testament*, 11/2, pp. 241–69.

—— 1999, 'Hiding Behind the Naked Woman: A Recriminative Response', *Biblical Interpretation: A Journal of Contemporary Approaches*, VII/4, pp. 413–48.

—— 2001, 'Battling for the Bible: Academy, Church and the Gay Agenda', *Theology and Sexuality*, 15, (2001), pp. 66–93.

—— 2003, 'Judges', in James D. G. Dunn and John W. Rogerson (eds), *Eerdmans Commentary on the Bible*, Grand Rapids: Eerdmans, pp. 190–207.

—— forthcoming, 'Judges', in Deryn Guest, Mana West, Robert E. Goss and Tom Bohache (eds), *Queer Bible Commentary*, London, Continuum.

Hermann Gunkel, 1910, *Genesis*, third edition, Göttingen: Vandenhoeck and Ruprecht.

David M. Gunn, 1978, *The Story of King David: Genre and Interpretation*, JSOTSS 6, Sheffield, JSOT Press.

David M. Gunn and Danna Nolan Fewell, 1993, *Narrative in the Hebrew Bible*, Oxford: Oxford University Press.

J. A. Hackett, 1987, 'Women's Studies and the Hebrew Bible', in R. E. Friedman and H. G. M. Williamson (eds), *The Future of Biblical Studies – the Hebrew Scriptures*, Atlanta: Scholars Press, pp. 141–64.

Judith M. Hadley, 2000, *The Cult of Asherah in Ancient Israel and Judah: Evidence for a Hebrew Goddess*, University of Cambridge Oriental Publications 57, Cambridge: Cambridge University Press.

Judith 'Jack' Halberstam and Del LaGrace Volcano, 1999, *The Drag King Book*, London: Serpent's Tail.

D. C. Haldeman, 1994, 'The Practice and Ethics of Sexual Orientation Conversion Therapy', *Journal of Consulting and Clinical Psychology*, 62/2, pp. 221–7.

M. Hall, 1986, 'The Lesbian Corporate Experience', *Journal of Homosexuality*, 12/3–4, pp. 59–75.

John (Marguerite) Radclyffe Hall, 1928, *The Well of Loneliness*, New York: Sun Dial Press.

Judith Hallett, 1989, 'Female Homoeroticism and the Denial of Roman Reality in Latin Literature', *Yale Journal of Criticism*, 3, pp. 209–27.

David M. Halperin, 1990, *One Hundred Years of Homosexuality and Other Essays on Greek Love*, New York and London: Routledge.

Bibliography

David M. Halperin, 1995, *Saint Foucault: Towards a Gay Hagiography*, Cambridge, MA: Harvard University Press.

Diane Hamer and Belinda Budge (eds), 1994, *The Good, the Bad and the Gorgeous*, London and San Francisco: Pandora.

Barbara Hammer, 'The Politics of Abstraction', in Martha Gever, Pratibha Parmar and John Greyson (eds), 1993, *Queer Looks: Perspectives on Lesbian and Gay Film and Video*, London: Routledge, pp. 70–5.

Evelynn Hammonds, 1994, 'Black (W)holes and the Geometry of Black Female Sexuality', *Differences*, 6/2–3, pp. 126–45.

Daphne Hampson, 1990, *Theology and Feminism*, Signposts in Theology, Oxford: Blackwell Publishers.

Daphne Hampson, 1996, *After Christianity*, London: SCM Press.

Karen V. Hansen, 1995, '"No Kisses Is Like Youres": An Erotic Friendship Between Two African-American Women During the Mid-Nineteenth Century', *Gender and History*, 7/2, pp. 143–82.

Susan Harding, 1975, 'Women and Words in a Spanish Village', in Rayna R. Reiter (ed.), *Toward an Anthropology of Women*, New York: Monthly Review Press, pp. 283–308.

R. Harris, 1963, 'The Organization and Administration of the Cloister in Ancient Babylonia', *Journal of the Economic and Social History of the Orient*, 6/2, pp. 121–57.

—— 1969, 'Notes on the Babylonian Cloister and Hearth: A Review Article', *Orientalia*, 38, pp. 133–45.

Dana Heller (ed.), 1997, *Cross Purposes: Lesbians, Feminists, and the Limits of Alliance*, Bloomington: Indiana University Press.

D. O. Helly and S. M. Reverby (eds), 1992, *Gendered Domains: Rethinking Public and Private in Women's History*, Ithaca: Cornell University Press.

Daniel A. Helminiak, 1994, *What the Bible Really Says About Homosexuality*, San Francisco: Alamo Square Press.

L. Henderson, D. Reid, F. Hickson, S. McLean, J. Cross and P. Weatherburn, 2002, *First, Service: Relationships, Sex and Health among Lesbian and Bisexual women*, University of Portsmouth: Sigma Research. http://www.sigmaresearch.org.uk/downloads/report02a.pdf

Alison Hennegan, 1988, 'On Becoming a Lesbian Reader', in Susannah Radstone (ed.), *Sweet Dreams: Sexuality, Gender and Popular Fiction*, London: Lawrence and Wishart, pp. 165–90.

Gregory M. Herek (ed.), 1998, *Stigma and Sexual Orientation: Understanding Prejudice Against Lesbians, Gay Men, and Bisexuals*, Psychological Perspectives on Lesbian and Gay Issues, volume 4, Thousand Oaks, London, New Delhi: Sage Publications.

Carter Heyward, 1984, *Our Passion for Justice: Images of Power, Sexuality and Liberation*, New York: Pilgrim Press.

—— 1989a, *Touching Our Strength: The Erotic as Power and the Love of God*, San Francisco: Harper and Row.

—— 1989b, *Speaking of Christ: A Lesbian Feminist Voice*, edited by Ellen C. Davies, New York: Pilgrim Press.

Evelyn Brooks Higginbotham, 1992, 'African-American Women's History and the Metalanguage of Race', *Signs*, 17/2, pp. 251–74.

Bibliography

Renée Hill, 1997, 'Who Are We for Each Other? Sexism, Sexuality and Womanist Theology', in Paul Germond and Steve de Gruchy (eds), *Aliens in the Household of God: Homosexuality and Christian Faith in South Africa*, Cape Town and Johannesburg: David Philip Publishing, pp. 146–52.

Darlene Clark Hine, 1989, 'Rape and the Inner Lives of Black Women in the Middle West: Preliminary Thoughts on the Culture of Dissemblance', *Signs*, 14/4, pp. 915–20.

Richard Davenport Hines, 1990, *Sex, Death and Punishment: Attitudes to Sex and Sexuality in Britain since the Renaissance*, London: Collins.

Linda Hogan, 1993, 'Resources for a Feminist Ethic: Women's Experience and Praxis', *Feminist Theology*, 3, pp. 82–99.

Mona Holmlund, 1999, *Women Together: Portraits of Love, Commitment and Life*, Philadelphia: Running Press.

bell hooks, 1981, *Ain't I a Woman: Black Women and Feminism*, Boston: South End Press.

Tom Horner, 1978, *Jonathan Loved David: Homosexuality in Biblical Times*, Philadelphia: The Westminster Press.

Gloria Hull, Patricia Scott and Barbara Smith (eds), 1982, *All the Women are White, All the Blacks are Men, but Some of Us are Brave: Black Women's Studies*, New York: Feminist Press.

Human Rights Watch and the International Gay and Lesbian Human Rights Commission, 1998, 'Public Scandals: Sexual Orientation and Criminal Law in Romania', New York, London, Brussels: Human Rights Watch and IGLHRC. http://www.hrw.org/reports97/romania/

—— 2003, 'More than a Name: State-Sponsored Homophobia and its Consequences in Southern Africa', New York, London, Brussels: Human Rights Watch and IGLHRC. http://www.hrw.org/reports/2003/safrica/

Margaret Hunt, 1990, 'The De-Eroticization of Women's Liberation: Social Purity Movements and the Revolutionary Feminism of Sheila Jeffreys', *Feminist Review*, 34, pp. 23–46.

Mary E. Hunt, 1994, 'Lovingly Lesbian: Towards a Feminist Theology of Friendship', in James B. Nelson and Sandra P. Longfellow (eds), *Sexuality and the Sacred: Sources for Theological Reflection*, London: Mowbray and Louisville: Westminster/John Knox Press, pp. 169–82.

M. Jackson, 1994, *The Real Facts of Life: Feminism and the Politics of Sexuality c1850–1940*, London: Taylor and Francis.

Peter A. Jackson, 2001, 'Pre-Gay, Post-Queer: Thai Perspectives on Proliferating Gender/Sex Diversity in Asia', in Gerard Sullivan and Peter Jackson (eds), *Gay and Lesbian Asia: Culture, Identity, Community*, New York: Harrington Park Press, pp. 1–25.

Stevi Jackson, 1999, *Heterosexuality in Question*, London, Thousand Oaks, New Delhi: Sage Publications.

Annamarie Jagose, 1996, *Queer Theory*, Victoria: Melbourne University Press.

Karla Jay and Joanne Glasgow (eds), 1990, *Lesbian Texts and Contexts*, New York and London: New York University Press.

Sheila Jeffreys, 1984, 'Does it Matter if They Did it?', *Trouble and Strife: A Radical Feminist Magazine*, 3, pp. 25–9.

—— 1994, 'The Queer Disappearance of Lesbians: Sexuality in the Academy', *Women's Studies International Forum*, 17/5, pp. 459–72.

Bibliography

Sheila Jeffreys, 2003, *Unpacking Queer Politics: A Lesbian Feminist Perspective*, Cambridge: Polity Press.

Theodore W. Jennings, Jr, 2001, 'YHWH as Erastes', in Ken Stone (ed.), *Queer Commentary on the Hebrew Bible*, JSOTSS 334, London and New York: Sheffield Academic Press, pp. 36–74.

Ulla Jeyes, 1983, 'The Naditu Women of Sippar', in Averil Cameron and Amélie Kuhrt, *Images of Women in Antiquity*, London and Canberra: Croom Helm, pp. 260–72.

J'annine Jobling, 2002, *Feminist Biblical Interpretation in Theological Context: Restless Readings*, Ashgate New Critical Thinking in Theology and Biblical Studies, Aldershot: Ashgate.

Susan E. Johnson, 1990, *Staying Power: Long Term Lesbian Couples*, Tallahassee: Naiad Press.

T. Johnson and T. Ward (eds), 1958, *The Letters of Emily Dickinson*, Cambridge: Harvard University Press.

Jonathan Ned Katz, 1976, *Gay American History*, New York: Thomas Y. Crowell.

—— 1983, *Gay/Lesbian Almanac*, New York, London, Mexico City, São Paulo, Sydney: Harper and Row.

Martin F. Kilmer, 1993, *Greek Erotica on Attic Red-Figure Vases*, London: Duckworths.

Celia Kitzinger, 1996, 'Heteropatriarchal Language: The Case Against "homophobia"', in Lilian Mohin (ed.), *An Intimacy of Equals: Lesbian Feminist Ethics*, London: Onlywomen Press, pp. 34–42.

Lillian Klein, 1994, 'Hannah: Marginalized Victim and Social Redeemer', in A. Brenner (ed.), *A Feminist Companion to Samuel and Kings*, The Feminist Companion to the Bible 5, Sheffield: Sheffield Academic Press, pp. 77–92.

Rochelle L. Klinger, 1996, 'Lesbian Couples', in Robert P. Cabaj and Terry S. Stein (eds), *Textbook of Homosexuality and Mental Health*, Washington and London: American Psychiatric Press Inc., pp. 339–52.

Tim Koch, 2001a, 'Cruising as Methodology: Homoeroticism and the Scriptures', *Theology and Sexuality*, 14, pp. 10–22.

—— 2001b, 'Cruising as Methodology: Homoeroticism and the Scriptures', in Ken Stone (ed.), *Queer Commentary on the Hebrew Bible*, JSOTSS 334, London and New York: Sheffield Academic Press, pp. 169–80.

Ross S. Kraemer, 1989, 'Monastic Jewish Women in Greco-Roman Egypt: Philo Judaeus on the Therapeutrides', *Signs*, 14/2, pp. 342–70.

Tanya Krzywinska, 1995, 'La Belle Dame sans Merci?', in Paul Burston and Colin Richardson (eds), *A Queer Romance: Lesbians, Gay Men and Popular Culture*, London: Routledge, pp. 99–110.

Louise Lamphere, 1974, 'Strategies, Cooperation and Conflict Among Women in Domestic Groups', in Louise Lamphere and Michelle Zimbalist Rosaldo (eds), *Women, Culture, and Society*, Stanford: Stanford University Press, pp. 97–112.

Teresa de Lauretis, 1994, *The Practice of Love: Lesbian Sexuality and Perverse Desire*, Bloomington and Indianapolis: Indiana University Press.

Leeds Revolutionary Feminist Group, 1982, 'Political Lesbianism: The Case Against Heterosexuality', in Mary Evans (ed.), *The Women Question: Readings on the Subordination of Women*, London: Fontana, pp. 63–72.

Niels Peter Lemche, 1988, *Ancient Israel: A New History of Israelite Society*, The Biblical Seminar, Sheffield: JSOT Press.

Bibliography

Niels Peter Lemche, 1993, 'The Old Testament – A Hellenistic Book?', *Scandinavian Journal of the Old Testament*, 7/2, pp. 163–93.

—— 'Is it Still Possible to Write a History of Ancient Israel?', *Scandinavian Journal of the Old Testament*, 8/2, pp. 165–90.

Gerda Lerner, 1986, *The Creation of Patriarchy*, Oxford: Oxford University Press.

Lesbian and Gay Christian Movement, 2000, *Christian Homophobia – The Churches' Persecution of Gay and Lesbian People*, London: LGCM.

Lesbian History Group, 1996, *Not a Passing Phase: Reclaiming Lesbians in History 1840–1985*, London: The Women's Press.

Tat-Siong Benny Liew, 2001, '(Co)responding: A Letter to the Editor', in Ken Stone (ed.), *Queer Commentary on the Hebrew Bible*, JSOTSS 334, London and New York: Sheffield Academic Press, pp. 182–92.

Ronald E. Long and J. Michael Clark, 1992, *AIDS, God, and Faith: Continuing the Dialogue on Constructing Gay Theology*, Las Colinas, Texas: Monument Press.

Audre Lorde, 1981, 'The Master's Tools Will Never Dismantle the Master's House', in Cherríe Moraga and Gloria Anzaldúa (eds), *This Bridge Called My Back: Writings by Radical Women of Color*, Watertown, MA: Persephone Press, pp. 98–101.

—— 1984, *Sister Outsider: Essays and Speeches*, New York: Crossing Press.

—— 1996, *The Audre Lorde Compendium: Essays, Speeches and Journals. Introduced by Alice Walker*, London: Pandora.

B. Lynch, 1996, 'Religious and Spirituality Conflicts', in Dominic Davies and Charles Neal (eds), *Pink Therapy: A Guide for Counsellors and Therapists Working with Lesbian, Gay and Bisexual Clients*, Buckingham and Philadelphia: Open University Press, pp. 199–208.

Lee Lynch, 1990, 'Cruising the Libraries', in Karla Jay and Joanne Glasgow (eds), *Lesbian Texts and Contexts*, New York and London: New York University Press, pp. 39–48.

M. Macourt (ed.), 1977, *Towards a Theology of Gay Liberation*, London: SCM Press.

Sara Maitland, 1983, *Telling Tales*, London: Journeyman Press.

—— 1988, 'Triptych', in Sara Maitland, *A Book of Spells*, London: Methuen, pp. 101–19.

Christof Maletsky, 1998, 'Government Planning to Criminalize Gays', *Namibian*, 9 November.

—— 2001, '"Madness on the Loose" says Nujoma', *Namibian*, 23 April.

Harriet Malinowitz, 1993, 'Queer Theory: Whose Theory?', *Frontiers*, 13, pp. 168–84.

—— 1996, 'Lesbian Studies and Postmodern Queer Theory', in Bonnie Zimmerman and Toni A. H. McNaron (eds), *The New Lesbian Studies: Into the Twenty-First Century*, New York: The Feminist Press, pp. 262–8.

Kathryn S. March and Rachelle L. Taqqu, 1986, *Women's Informal Associations in Developing Countries*, Women in Cross-Cultural Perspective, Boulder: Westview Press.

Rodney Mariner, 1995, 'The Jewish Homosexual and the Halakhic Tradition: A Suitable Case for Treatment', in Jonathan Magonet (ed.), *Jewish Explorations of Sexuality*, Providence and Oxford: Berghahn Books, pp. 83–93.

C. J. Martin, 1999, 'Womanist Biblical Interpretation', in John H. Hayes (ed.), *Dictionary of Biblical Interpretation*, vol. 2, Nashville: Abingdon Press, pp. 655–8.

Eric Martin, 1993, *Making History: The Struggle for Gay and Lesbian Rights, an Oral History 1945–1990*, New York: Harper Perennial.

Michelle Martin, 1986, *Pembroke Park*, Tallahassee: Naiad Press.

Linda McFarlane, 1998, *Diagnosis: Homophobic: The Experiences of Lesbians and Gay Men and Bisexuals in Mental Health Services*, London: Project for Advice, Counselling and Education.

Mary McIntosh, 1968, 'The Homosexual Role', *Social Problems*, 16/2, pp. 186–92.

—— 1993, 'Queer Theory and the War of the Sexes', in Joe Bristow and Angela R. Wilson (eds), *Activating Theory: Lesbian, Gay, Bisexual Politics*, London: Lawrence and Wishart, pp. 30–52.

Heather A. McKay, 1997, 'On the Future of Feminist Biblical Criticism', in Athalya Brenner and Carole Fontaine (eds), *A Feminist Companion to Reading the Bible: Approaches, Methods and Strategies*, The Feminist Companion to the Bible, Sheffield: Sheffield Academic Press, pp. 61–83.

Alan McKee, 1999, '"Resistance is Hopeless": Assimilating Queer Theory', *Social Semiotics*, 9/2, pp. 235–50.

Toni A. H. McNaron, Gloria Anzaldúa, Lourdes Arguëlles and Elizabeth Lapovsky Kennedy, 1993, 'Editorial', *Signs*, 18/4, pp. 757–63.

J. J. McNeill, 1976, *The Church and the Homosexual*, Kansas City: Sheed, Andrews and McMeel.

—— 1996, *Taking a Chance on God: Liberating Theology for Gays, Lesbians, and their Lovers, Families and Friends*, Boston: Beacon Press.

Carol Meyers, 1978, 'The Roots of Restriction: Women in Early Israel', *Biblical Archaeologist*, 41/3, pp. 91–103.

—— 1988, *Discovering Eve: Ancient Israelite Women in Context*, New York and Oxford: Oxford University Press.

—— 1991, 'Of Drums and Damsels: Women's Performance in Ancient Israel', *Biblical Archaeologist*, 54, pp. 16–27.

—— 1999a, 'Mother to Muse: An Archaeolmusicological Study of Women's Performance in Ancient Israel', in Athalya Brenner and Jan Willem van Henten (eds), *Recycling Biblical Figures: Papers Read at a NOSTER Colloquium in Amsterdam 12–13 May 1997*, Studies in Theology and Religion 1, London: Deo Publishing, pp. 50–77.

—— 1999b, 'Guilds and Gatherings: Women's Groups in Ancient Israel', in P. M. Williams, Jr and T. Hiebert (eds), *Realia Dei: Essays in Archaeology and Biblical Interpretation in Honor of Edward F. Campbell Jr at His Retirement*, Durham: Duke University Press, pp. 154–84.

—— 1999c, '"Women of the Neighborhood" (Ruth 4.17): Informal Female Networks in Ancient Israel', in A. Brenner (ed.), *Ruth and Esther: A Feminist Companion to the Bible*, The Feminist Companion to the Bible (Second Series) 3, Sheffield: Sheffield Academic Press, pp. 110–27.

Evalyn Jacobson Michaelson and Walter Goldschmidt, 1971, 'Female Roles and Male Dominance Among Peasants', *Southwest Journal of Anthropology*, 27, pp. 330–52.

Jacob Milgrom, 1993, 'Does the Bible Prohibit Homosexuality?', *Bible Review*, 9, p. 11.

—— 2000, *Leviticus 17–22: A New Translation with Introduction and Commentary*, The Anchor Bible, New York, London, Toronto, Sydney, Auckland: Doubleday.

Neil Miller, 1995, *Out of the Past: Gay and Lesbian History from 1869 to the Present*, New York: Vintage.

Pamela J. Milne, 1997, 'Towards Feminist Companionship: The Future of Feminist Biblical Studies and Feminism', in Athalya Brenner and Carole Fontaine (eds), *A Feminist Companion to Reading the Bible: Approaches, Methods and Strategies*, The Feminist Companion to the Bible, Sheffield: Sheffield Academic Press, pp. 39–60.

Bibliography

Kim Mills, 1999, 'Mission Impossible: Why Reparative Therapy and Ex-Gay Ministries Fail', http://www.csufresno.edu/StudentOrgs/usp/resources/flyers/missionimpossible.htm

G. Mitchell, 1993, *Together in the Land: A Reading of the Book of Joshua*, JSOTSS 134, Sheffield: Sheffield Academic Press.

Tani Modleski, 1991, *Feminist Without Women: Culture and Criticism in a 'Postfeminist' Age*, London: Routledge.

Virginia Ramay Mollenkott, 2000, 'Reading the Bible from Low and Outside: Lesbitransgay People as God's Tricksters', in Robert E. Goss and Mona West (eds), *Take Back the Word: a Queer Reading of the Bible*, Cleveland, Ohio: The Pilgrim Press, pp. 13–22.

Irene Monroe, 2000, 'When and Where I Enter, then the Whole Race Enters with Me: Que(e)rying Exodus', in Robert E. Goss and Mona West (eds), *Take Back the Word: a Queer Reading of the Bible*, Cleveland, Ohio: The Pilgrim Press, pp. 82–91.

Henrietta L. Moore, 1989, *Feminism and Anthropology*, Minneapolis: University of Minnesota Press.

Cherríe Moraga and Gloria Anzaldúa (eds), 1981, *This Bridge Called My Back: Writings by Radical Women of Color*, Watertown, MA: Persephone Press.

L. Morgan and N. Bell, 2003, 'First out … Report of the Findings of the Beyond Barriers Survey of Lesbian, Gay, Bisexual and Transgender People in Scotland', Glasgow: Beyond Barriers FMR. http://www.beyondbarriers.org.uk/docs/First_Out_PDF-Report.pdf

Pam Morris, 1993, *Literature and Feminism: An Introduction*, Oxford: Blackwells.

Deana F. Morrow, 2003, 'Cast Into the Wilderness: The Impact of Institutionalized Religion on Lesbians', *Journal of Lesbian Studies*, 7, pp. 109–23.

Jenny Mouzos and Sue Thompson, 2000, 'Gay-Related Homicides: An Overview of Major Findings in New South Wales', Issues Paper No. 155, Australian Institute of Criminology.

Laura Mulvey, 1975, 'Visual Pleasure and Narrative Cinema', *Screen*, 16/3, pp. 6–18.

—— 1981, 'Afterthoughts on "Visual Pleasure and Narrative Cinema" Inspired by King Vidor's *Duel in the Sun* (1946)', *Framework*, 15–17, pp. 12–15.

Sally Munt (ed.), 1992, *New Lesbian Criticism: Literary and Cultural Readings*, New York: Columbia University Press.

Nancy Myron and Charlotte Bunch (eds), 1975, *Lesbianism and the Women's Movement*, Baltimore: Diana Press.

Z. Isiling Nataf, 1995, 'Black Lesbian Spectatorship and Pleasure in Popular Cinema', in Paul Burston and Colin Richardson (eds), *A Queer Romance: Lesbians, Gay Men and Popular Culture*, London: Routledge, pp. 57–80.

Cynthia Nelson, 1974, 'Public and Private Politics: Women in the Middle Eastern World', *American Ethnologist*, 1, pp. 551–63.

Joan Nestle, 1981, 'Butch-Fem Relationships: Sexual Coming of Age in the 1950s', *Heresies*, 3/12, pp. 21–4.

—— 1987, *A Restricted Country: Documents of Desire and Resistance*, London: Pandora.

Joan Nestle, 1993, *The Persistent Desire: A Femme-Butch Reader*, Boston: Alyson.

Susan Niditch, 1989, 'Eroticism and Death in the Tale of Jael', in Peggy Day (ed.), *Gender and Difference in Ancient Israel*, Philadelphia: Fortress Press, pp. 43–57.

Bibliography

Martti Nissinen, 1998, *Homoeroticism in the Biblical World: A Historical Perspective*, trans. Kirsi Stjerna, Minneapolis: Augsburg Fortress Publishers.

Rictor Norton, 1997, *The Myth of the Modern Homosexual: Queer History and the Search for Cultural Unity*, London and Washington: Cassell.

Rictor Norton, 2003, 'The Nature of Lesbian History', *Lesbian History*, 1, 2003, www. infopt.demon.co.uk/lesbians.htm

Saul Olyan, 1996, '"And with a Male You Shall not Lie Down the Lying Down of a Woman": On the Meaning and Significance of Lev. 18.22 and 20.13', in Gary D. Comstock and Susan E. Henking (eds), *Que(e)rying Religious Studies: A Critical Anthology*, New York: Continuum, pp. 398–414.

Barbara Omolade, 1984, 'Hearts of Darkness', in A. Snitow, C. Stansell and S. Thompson (eds), *Desire: The Politics of Sexuality*, London: Virago, pp. 361–77.

Alison Oram and Annmarie Turnbull, 2001, *The Lesbian History Sourcebook: Love and Sex Between Women in Britain from 1780 to 1970*, London: Routledge.

Robert Padgug, 1979, 'Sexual Matters: On Conceptualising Sexuality in History', *Radical History Review*, 20, pp. 3–23.

Daniel Patte, 1995, *Ethics of Biblical Interpretation: A Re-Evaluation*, Louisville: Westminster John Knox Press.

Cindy Patton, 1993, 'Tremble, Hetero-Swine!', in M. Warner (ed.), *Fear of a Queer Planet: Queer Politics and Social Theory*, Minneapolis: University of Minnesota Press, pp. 143–77.

Lynn Pearce, 1996, 'Lesbian Criticism', in Sara Mills and Lynn Pearce, *Feminist Readings Feminists Reading*, second edition, London, New York, Toronto, Sydney, Tokyo, Singapore, Madrid, Mexico City, Munich: Prentice Hall/Harvester Wheatsheaf, pp. 225–56.

Angela Pears, 2004, *Feminist Christian Encounters: The Methods and Strategies of Feminist Informed Christian Theologies*, Aldershot: Ashgate.

Shane Phelan, 1993, '(Be)Coming out: Lesbian Identity and Politics', *Signs*, 18/4, pp. 765–90.

Steven D. Pinkerton and Paul R. Abramson, 1997, 'Japan', in Donald J. West and Richard Green (eds), *Sociolegal Control of Homosexuality: A Multi-Nation Comparison*, New York and London: Plenum Press, pp. 67–86.

Judith Plaskow, 1979, 'The Coming of Lilith: Toward a Feminist Theology', in Carol P. Christ and Judith Plaskow (eds), *Womanspirit rising: A Feminist Reader in Religion*, San Francisco: Harper and Row, pp. 198–209.

Kenneth Plummer, 1975, *Sexual Stigma*, London: Routledge.

—— (ed.), 1981, *The Making of the Modern Homosexual*, London: Hutchinson.

M. H. Pope, 1976, 'Homosexuality', in K. Crimm, R. R. Bailey, V. P. Furnish and E. S. Bucke (eds), *The Interpreter's Dictionary of the Bible: An Illustrated Encyclopedia*, Supplementary Volume, Nashville: Abingdon, pp. 514–17.

Nancy Sorkin Rabinowitz, 2002a, 'Introduction', in Nancy Sorkin Rabinowitz and Lisa Auanger (eds), *Among Women: From the Homosocial to the Homoerotic in the Ancient World*, Austin: University of Texas Press, pp. 1–33.

—— 2002b, 'Excavating Women's Homoeroticism in Ancient Greece: The Evidence from Attic Vase Painting', in Nancy Sorkin Rabinowitz and Lisa Auanger (eds), *Among Women: From the Homosocial to the Homoerotic in the Ancient World*, Austin: University of Texas Press, pp. 106–66.

Radicalesbians, 1997, 'The Woman-Identified Woman', in Mark Blasius and Shane Phelan (eds), *We Are Everywhere: A Historical Sourcebook of Gay and Lesbian Politics*, London: Routledge, pp. 396–9.

Janice Raymond, 1991, *A Passion for Friends: Towards a Philosophy of Female Affection*, London: The Women's Press.

Adele Reinhartz, 1997, 'Feminist Criticism and Biblical Studies on the Verge of the Twenty-First Century', in Athalya Brenner and Carole Fontaine (eds), *A Feminist Companion to Reading the Bible: Approaches, Methods and Strategies*, The Feminist Companion to the Bible, Sheffield: Sheffield Academic Press, pp. 30–8.

Adrienne Rich, 1980, 'Toward a Woman-Centered University', in Adrienne Rich, *On Lies, Secrets and Silence: Selected Prose 1966–1978*, London: Virago, pp. 125–55.

——1987, 'Compulsory Heterosexuality and Lesbian Existence', in Adrienne Rich, *Blood, Bread and Poetry: Selected Prose 1979–1985*, New York: W. W. Norton and Co., pp. 23–75.

B. Ruby Rich, 1986, 'Review Essay: Feminism and Sexuality During the 1980s', *Feminist Studies*, 12/3, pp. 525–62.

Dell Richards, 1990, *Lesbian Lists*, Boston: Alyson.

Helmer Ringgren, 1966, *Israelite Religion*, Philadelphia: Fortress Press.

Y. Y. Ritter and C. W. O'Neill, 1989, 'Moving Through Loss: The Spiritual Journey of Gay Men and Lesbian Women', *Journal of Counseling and Development*, 68, pp. 9–15.

Shelly Roberts, 1996, *Roberts' Rules of Lesbian Living*, Duluth: Spinsters Inc.

Gillian Rodgerson, 2003, 'Ugandan Lesbian Refused Asylum in Britain', *Diva*, 86, July, pp. 18, 25.

Susan C. Rogers, 1975, 'Female Forms of Power and the Myth of Male Dominance: A Model of Female/Male Interaction in Peasant Society', *American Ethnologist*, 2, pp. 727–56.

Michelle Z. Rosaldo, 1980, 'The Use and Abuse of Anthropology: Reflections on Feminism and Cross-Cultural Understanding', *Signs*, 5/3, pp. 389–417.

Sasha Roseneil, 2002, 'The Heterosexual/Homosexual Binary: Past, Present and Future', in Diane Richardson and Steven Seidman (eds), *Handbook of Lesbian and Gay Studies*, London, Thousand Oaks, New Delhi: Sage Publications Ltd, pp. 27–43.

Lori Rowlett, 2001, 'Violent Femmes and S/M: Queering Samson and Delilah', in Ken Stone (ed.), *Queer Commentary on the Hebrew Bible*, JSOTSS 334, London and New York: Sheffield Academic Press, pp. 106–15.

Fang-Fu Ruan, 1997, 'China', in Donald J. West and Richard Green (eds), *Sociolegal Control of Homosexuality: A Multi-Nation Comparison*, New York and London: Plenum Press, pp. 57–66.

Kathy Rudy, 1996, 'Queer Theory and Feminism', in J. Michael Clark and Robert E. Goss (eds), *A Rainbow of Religious Studies*, Texas: Monument Press, pp. 81–101.

Sonja Ruehl, 1983, 'Sexual Theory and Practice: Another Double Standard', in Sue Cartledge and Joanna Ryan (eds), *Sex and Love: New Thoughts on Old Contradictions*, London: The Women's Press, pp. 210–23.

Rosemary Radford Ruether, 1983, *Sexism and God-talk: Towards a Feminist Theology*, London: SCM Press.

Rosemary Radford Ruether, 1985, 'Feminist Interpretation: A Method Of Correlation', in Letty M. Russell (ed.), *Feminist Interpretation of the Bible*, Philadelphia: Westminster Press, pp. 111–24.

Bibliography

Letty M. Russell (ed.), 1985, *Feminist Interpretation of the Bible*, Philadelphia: Westminster Press.

Vito Russo, 1987, *The Celluloid Closet: Homosexuality in the Movies*, revised edition, Perennial Library, New York: Harper and Row.

Leigh W. Rutledge, 1987, *The Gay Book of Lists*, Boston: Alyson.

—— 1989, *The Gay Fireside Companion*, Boston: Alyson.

Katharine Doob Sakenfeld, 1982, 'Old Testament Perspectives: Methodological Issues', *Journal for the Study of the Old Testament*, 22, pp. 13–20.

—— 1985, 'Feminist Uses of Biblical Materials', in Letty M. Russell, *Feminist Interpretation of the Bible*, Philadelphia: Westminster Press, pp. 55–64.

Eric Savoy, 1994, 'You Can't Go Homo Again: Queer Theory and the Foreclosure of Gay Studies', *English Studies in Canada*, 20/2, pp. 129–52.

Laurel C. Schneider, 2001, 'Yahwist Desires: Imagining Divinity Queerly', in Ken Stone (ed.), *Queer Commentary on the Hebrew Bible*, JSOTSS 334, London and New York: Sheffield Academic Press, pp. 210–27.

Elisabeth Schüssler Fiorenza, 1983, *In Memory of Her: a Feminist Reconstruction of Christian Origins*, London: SCM Press.

—— 1984, *Bread not Stone: The Challenge of Feminist Biblical Interpretation*, Edinburgh: T and T Clark.

—— 1985, 'Remembering the Past in Creating the Future: Historical-Critical Scholarship and Feminist Biblical Interpretation', in Adela Yarbro Collins (ed.), *Feminist Perspectives on Biblical Scholarship*, Chico, California: Scholars Press, pp. 43–63.

—— 1992a, *But She Said: Feminist Practices of Biblical Interpretation*, Boston: Beacon Press.

—— 1992b, 'Feminist Hermeneutics', in D. N. Freedman (ed.), *The Anchor Bible Dictionary*, vol. 2, New York: Doubleday, pp. 783–91.

—— 1994, *Jesus: Miriam's Child, Sophia's Prophet: Critical Issues in Feminist Christology*, London: SCM Press.

—— 1998, *Sharing Her Word: Feminist Biblical Interpretation in Context*, Edinburgh: T and T Clark.

—— 2001, *Wisdom Ways: Introducing Feminist Biblical Interpretation*, Maryknoll: Orbis Books.

Fernando F. Segovia, 1999, 'My Personal Voice: The Making of a Postcolonial Critic', in Ingrid Rosa Kitzberger, *The Personal Voice in Biblical Interpretation*, London and New York: Routledge, pp. 25–37.

—— 2000, *Decolonizing Biblical Studies: A View from the Margins*, Maryknoll: Orbis Books.

Fernando F. Segovia and Mary Ann Tolbert (eds), 1995a, *Reading from this Place: Social Location and Biblical Interpretation in the United States*, vol. 1, Minneapolis: Fortress Press.

—— (eds), 1995b, *Reading from this Place: Social Location and Biblical Interpretation in the United States*, vol. 2, Minneapolis: Fortress Press.

Steven Seidman, 1993, 'Identity and Politics in a "Postmodern" Gay Culture: Some Historical and Conceptual Notes', in M. Warner (ed.), *Fear of a Queer Planet: Queer Politics and Social Theory*, Minneapolis: University of Minnesota Press, pp. 105–42.

—— (ed.), 1996, *Queer Theory/Sociology*, Oxford: Blackwell Publishing.

Seo Dong-Jin, 2001, 'Mapping the Vicissitudes of Homosexual Identities', in Gerard Sullivan and Peter Jackson (eds), *Gay and Lesbian Asia: Culture, Identity, Community*, New York: Harrington Park Press, pp. 65–80.

Bibliography

J. Sharistanian (ed.), 1987, *Beyond the Public/Private Dichotomy: Contemporary Perspectives on Women's Public Lives*, Contributions to Women's Studies 78, Westport: Greenwood Press.

Caroline Sheldon, 1980, 'Lesbians and Film: Some Thoughts', in Richard Dyer (ed.), *Gays and Film*, London: British Film Institute.

Ronnie Simson, 1984, 'The Afro-American Female: The Historical Contexts of the Construction of Sexual Identity', in A. Snitow, C. Stansell and S. Thompson (eds), *Desire: The Politics of Sexuality*, London: Virago, pp. 243–9.

Barbara Smith, 1982, 'Toward a Black Feminist Criticism', in Gloria Hull, Patricia Scott and Barbara Smith (eds), *But Some of Us Are Brave*, New York: Feminist Press, pp. 157–75.

—— 2000, 'Introduction', in Barbara Smith (ed.), *Home Girls: A Black Feminist Anthology*, New York: Kitchen Table/Women of Color Press, pp. xxi–lviii.

Carroll Smith-Rosenberg, 1975, 'The Female World of Love and Ritual: Relations Between Women in Nineteenth Century America', *Signs*, 1, pp. 1–29.

Cherry Smyth, 1992, *Lesbians Talk Queer Notions*, London: Scarlet Press.

—— 1995, 'The Transgressive Sexual Subject', in Paul Burston and Colin Richardson (eds), *A Queer Romance: Lesbians, Gay Men and Popular Culture*, London: Routledge, pp. 123–43.

Dawn Snape, Katarina Thompson and Mark Chetwynd, 1995, *Discrimination Against Gay Men and Lesbians: A Study of the Nature and Extent of Discrimination against Homosexual Men and Women in Britain Today*, London: Social and Community Planning Research.

Mark Solomon, 1995, 'A Strange Conjunction', in Jonathan Magonet (ed.), *Jewish Explorations of Sexuality*, Providence and Oxford: Berghahn Books, pp. 75–82.

Dawn B. Sova, 1998, *Passion and Penance: The Lesbian in Pulp Fiction*, New York: Faber and Faber.

Daniel T. Spencer, 2001, 'A Gay Male Ethicist's Response to Queer Readings of the Bible', in Ken Stone (ed.), *Queer Commentary on the Hebrew Bible*, JSOTSS 334, London and New York: Sheffield Academic Press, pp. 193–209.

Jackie Stacey, 1994, *Star Gazing: Hollywood Cinema and Female Spectatorship*, London: Routledge.

Arlene Stein, 1992, 'Sisters and Queers: The Decentering of Lesbian Feminist', *Socialist Review*, 22/1, pp. 33–55.

Edward Stein (ed.), 1992, *Forms of Desire: Sexual Orientation and the Social Constructionist Controversy*, New York and London: Routledge.

Catherine Stimpson, 1981, 'Zero Degree Deviancy: The Lesbian Novel in English', *Critical Enquiry*, 8, pp. 363–80.

Elizabeth C. Stone, 1982, 'The Social Role of the Naditu Women in Old Babylonian Nippur', *Journal of the Economic and Social History of the Orient*, XXV/1, pp. 50–70.

Ken Stone, 1996, *Sex, Honor and Power in the Deuteronomistic History*, JSOTSS 234, Sheffield: Sheffield Academic Press.

—— 1999a, 'Gay/Lesbian Interpretation', in John H. Hayes, (ed), *Dictionary of Biblical Interpretation*, Nashville: Abingdon Press, pp. 432–4.

—— 1999b, 'Safer Text: Reading Biblical Laments in the Age of AIDS', *Theology and Sexuality*, 10, pp. 16–27.

—— 2000, 'The Garden of Eden and the Heterosexual Contract', in Robert E. Goss and

Mona West (eds), *Take Back the Word: A Queer Reading of the Bible*, Cleveland, Ohio: The Pilgrim Press, pp. 57–70.

—— 2001a, 'Introduction', in Ken Stone (ed.), *Queer Commentary on the Hebrew Bible*, JSOTSS 334, London and New York: Sheffield Academic Press, pp. 11–34.

—— 2001b, 'Homosexuality and the Bible or Queer Reading? A Response to Martti Nissinen', *Theology and Sexuality*, 14, pp. 107–18.

Susan Stryker, 2001, *Queer Pulp: Perverted Passions from the Golden Age of the Paperback*, San Francisco: Chronicle Books.

Elizabeth Stuart, 1995, *Just Good Friends: Towards a Lesbian and Gay Theology of Relationships*, London and New York: Mowbray.

Elizabeth Stuart, 2000, 'Camping Around the Canon: Humor as a Hermeneutical Tool in Queer Readings of Biblical Texts', in Robert E. Goss and Mona West (eds), *Take Back the Word: A Queer Reading of the Bible*, Cleveland, Ohio: The Pilgrim Press, pp. 23–34.

—— 2003, *Gay and Lesbian Theologies: Repetitions with Critical Difference*, Aldershot: Ashgate.

Elizabeth Stuart with Andy Braunston, Malcolm Edwards, John McMahon, Tim Morrison, 1997, *Religion is a Queer Thing: A Guide to the Christian Faith for Lesbian, Gay, Bisexual and Transgendered People*, London and Washington: Cassell.

Andrew Sullivan, 1996, *Virtually Normal: An Argument About Homosexuality*, London: Picador.

Gerard Sullivan and Peter Jackson (eds), 2001, *Gay and Lesbian Asia: Culture, Identity, Community*, New York: Harrington Park Press.

Nikki Sullivan, 2003, *A Critical Introduction to Queer Theory*, Edinburgh: Edinburgh University Press.

Peter Sweasey, 1997, *From Queer to Eternity: Spirituality in the Lives of Lesbian, Gay and Bisexual People*, London and Washington: Cassell.

Jay Taverner, 2001, 'Long Term Lovers', *Diva*, 63 (August), pp. 10–13.

Jennifer Terry, 1991, 'Theorizing Deviant Historiography', *Differences: A Journal of Feminist Cultural Studies*, 3/2, pp. 55–74.

Stephen Tomsen, 1998, ' "He Had to Be a Poofter or Something": Violence, Male Honour and Heterosexual Panic', *Journal of Interdisciplinary Gender Studies*, 3/2, pp. 44–57.

Valerie Traub, 2002, *The Renaissance of Lesbianism in Early Modern England*, Cambridge Studies in Renaissance Literature and Culture, Cambridge: Cambridge University Press.

Irene S. Travis, 2000, 'Love Your Mother: A Lesbian Womanist Reading of Scripture', in Robert E. Goss and Mona West (eds), *Take Back the Word: A Queer Reading of the Bible*, Cleveland, Ohio: The Pilgrim Press, pp. 35–42.

Phyllis Trible, 1978, *God and the Rhetoric of Sexuality*, Overtures to Biblical Theology 2, Philadelphia: Fortress Press.

—— 1984, *Texts of Terror: Literary-Feminist Readings of Biblical Narratives*, Philadelphia: Fortress.

Una Troubridge, 1973, *The Life of Radclyffe Hall*, New York: Citadel.

Onunwa Udobata, 1988, 'The Paradox of Power and "Submission" of Women in African Traditional Religion and Society', *Journal of Dharma*, 13, pp. 31–8.

Alan Unterman, 1995, 'Judaism and Homosexuality: Some Orthodox Perspectives', in Jonathan Magonet (ed.), *Jewish Explorations of Sexuality*, Providence and Oxford: Berghahn Books, pp. 67–74.

Urvashi Vaid, 1997, 'Let's Put Our Own House in Order: Speech to the National Lesbian Conference, Atlanta, Georgia 1991', in Mark Blasius and Shane Phelan (eds), *We Are Everywhere: A Historical Sourcebook of Gay and Lesbian Politics*, London: Routledge, pp. 798–802.

John van Seters, 1972, 'The terms "Amorite" and "Hittite" in the Old Testament', *Vetus Testamentum*, 22, pp. 64–82.

—— 1983, *In Search of History: Historiography in the Ancient World and the Origins of Biblical History*, New Haven and London: Yale University Press.

Carole S. Vance (ed.), 1984, *Pleasure and Danger: Exploring Female Sexuality*, London: Pandora.

—— 1989, 'Social Construction Theory: Problems in the History of Sexuality', in Dennis Altman, Carole Vance, Martha Vicinius, Jeffrey Weeks (eds), *Homosexuality, which Homosexuality? International Conference on Gay and Lesbian Studies*, London: Gay Men's Press, pp. 13–34.

Del LaGrace Volcano, 2000, *Sublime Mutations*, Tübingen: Konkursbuchverlag.

Gerhard von Rad, 1972, *Genesis*, Old Testament Library, London: SCM Press.

Alice Walker, 1983, *In Search of Our Mother's Gardens: Womanist Prose*, London: The Women's Press.

F. Watson, 1994, *Text, Church and World: Biblical Interpretation in Theological Perspective*, Edinburgh: T and T Clark.

Barry G. Webb, 1987, *The Book of Judges: An Integrated Reading*, JSOTSS 46, Sheffield: Sheffield Academic Press.

Chris Weedon, 1999, *Feminism, Theory and the Politics of Difference*, Oxford and Malden: Blackwells.

Jeffrey Weeks, 1977, *Coming Out: Homosexual Politics in Britain, from the Nineteenth Century to the Present*, London, Melbourne, New York: Quartet Books.

—— 1996, 'The Construction of Homosexuality', in Steven Seidman (ed.), *Queer Theory/Sociology*, Oxford: Blackwells, pp. 41–63.

—— 2000, *Making Sexual History*, Cambridge: Polity Press.

Renita Weems, 1988, *Just a Sister Away: A Womanist Vision of Women's Relationships in the Bible*, California: San Diego.

R. Weems, 1991, 'Reading Her Way through the Struggle: African American Women and the Bible', in Cain Hope Felder (ed.), *Stony the Road We Trod: African American Biblical Interpretation*, Minneapolis: Fortress Press, pp. 57–80.

Gloria Wekker, 1993, 'Mati-ism and Black Lesbianism: Two Idealtype Expressions of Female Homosexuality in Black Communities of the Diaspora', in John P. de Cecco and John P. Elia (eds), *If You Seduce a Straight Person, Can You Make Them Gay? Issues in Biological Essentialism versus Social Constructionism in Gay and Lesbian Identities*, New York: The Haworth Press, pp. 145–58.

Donald J. West, 1969, *Homosexuality*, second edition, London: Harmondsworth.

Donald J. West and Richard Green (eds), 1997, *Sociolegal Control of Homosexuality: A Multi-Nation Comparison*, New York and London: Plenum Press.

Donald J. West and Andrea Wöelke, 1997, 'England', in Donald J. West and Richard Green (eds), *Sociolegal Control of Homosexuality: A Multi-Nation Comparison*, New York and London: Plenum Press, pp. 197–220.

Gerard O. West and Musa W. Dube (eds), 2000, *The Bible in Africa: Transactions, Trajectories, and Trends*, Leiden, Boston, Köln: Brill.

Mona West, 1997, 'The Book of Ruth: An Example of Procreative Strategies for Queers', in Robert E. Goss and Amy Adams Squire Strongheart (eds), *Our Families, Our Values: Snapshots of Queer Kinship*, New York: The Harrington Park Press, pp. 51–60.

—— 2000, 'Outsiders, Aliens, and Boundary Crossers: A Queer Reading of the Hebrew Exodus', in Robert E. Goss and Mona West (eds), *Take Back the Word: A Queer Reading of the Bible*, Cleveland, Ohio: The Pilgrim Press, pp. 71–81.

—— 2001, 'The Gift of Voice, the Gift of Tears: A Queer Reading of Lamentations in the Context of AIDS', in Ken Stone (ed.), *Queer Commentary on the Hebrew Bible*, JSOTSS 334, London and New York: Sheffield Academic Press, pp. 140–51.

Kath Weston, 1996, *Render Me, Gender Me: Lesbians Talk Sex, Class, Color, Nation, Studmuffins ...*, Between Men-Between Women, New York: Columbia University Press.

Karl von Westphal, 1869, 'Die konträre sexualempfinding', *Archiven für Psychiatrie und Nervenkrankheiten*, 2, pp. 73–108.

Helena Whitbread (ed.), 1992a, *I Know My own Heart: The Diaries of Anne Lister 1791–1840*, New York: New York University Press.

—— (ed.), 1992b, *No Priest but Love: The Journals of Anne Lister from 1824–1826*, Otley: Smith Settle Ltd.

Deborah Gray White, 1987, *Ar'n't I a Woman? Female Slaves in the Plantation South*, New York and London: W. W. Norton and Co.

Nancy Wilson, 1995, *Our Tribe: Queer Folks, God, Jesus, and the Bible*, New York: HarperSanFrancisco.

Tamsin Wilton, 1995a, *Lesbian Studies: Setting an Agenda*, London: Routledge.

—— (ed.), 1995b, *Immortal Invisible: Lesbians and the Moving Image*, London: Routledge.

—— 1995c, '"On not Being Lady Macbeth": Some (Troubled) Thoughts on Lesbian Spectatorship', in Tamsin Wilton (ed.), *Immortal Invisible: Lesbians and the Moving Image*, London: Routledge, pp. 143–62.

—— 1996, *Finger-Licking Good: The Ins and Outs of Lesbian Sex*, London: Cassell.

—— 2000, *Sexualities in Health and Social Care: A Textbook*, Buckingham and Philadelphia: Open University Press.

Jeanette Winterson, 1985, *Oranges Are Not the Only Fruit*, London, Sydney, Wellington: Pandora.

Monique Wittig, 1992, *The Straight Mind and Other Essays*, New York, London, Toronto, Sydney, Tokyo, Singapore: Harvester Wheatsheaf.

Donald J. Wold, 1998, *Out of Order: Homosexuality in the Bible and the Ancient Near East*, Grand Rapids: Baker Books.

Margery Wolf, 1974, 'Chinese Women: Old Skills in a New Context', in Michelle Zimbalist Rosaldo and Louise Lamphere (eds), *Women, Culture, and Society*, Stanford: Stanford University Press, pp. 157–72.

Women and Equality Unit Department of Trade and Industry, 2003, 'Civil Partnership: A Framework for the Legal Recognition of Same-Sex Couples' London: WEU Publications.

Virginia Woolf, 1929, *A Room of One's Own*, London: The Hogarth Press.

G. E. Wright, 1955, *The Old Testament Against its Environment*, London: SCM Press.

Gale A Yee, 2003, *Poor Banished Children of Eve: Woman as Evil in the Hebrew Bible*, Minneapolis: Fortress Press.

Bibliography

Jaye Zimet, 1999, *Strange Sisters: The Art of Lesbian Pulp Fiction, 1949–1969*, New York: Viking Penguin Inc.

Bonnie Zimmerman, 1985, 'What Has Never Been: An Overview of Lesbian Feminist Criticism', in Gayle Green and Coppélia Kahn (eds), *Making a Difference: Feminist Literary Criticism*, London and New York: Routledge, pp. 177–210.

——1993, 'Perverse Reading: The Lesbian Appropriation of Literature', in Susan J. Wolfe and Julia Penelope (eds), *Sexual Practice, Textual Theory*, Oxford: Blackwells, pp. 125–34.

—— 1996, 'Placing Lesbians', in Bonnie Zimmerman and Toni A. H. McNaron (eds), *The New Lesbian Studies: Into the Twenty-First Century*, New York: The Feminist Press, pp. 269–75.

Bonnie Zimmerman and Toni A. H. McNaron (eds), 1996, *The New Lesbian Studies: Into the Twenty-First Century*, New York: The Feminist Press.

Subject Index

Affirmation 245, 256
Afghanistan 65n41, 65n42
Algeria 67
Angola 65n41
Anti-lesbian/gay 48, 66–104, 161, 164, 166, 193, 209
Asia 60–1, 64, 65n41, 79–81, 191n131
Authority, experiential 243–63
  scriptural 227–42

Bahrain 65n41
Bangladesh 65n41, 67
Barbados 65n41
Barrenness 131–2, 141, 218
Benin 65n41
Black churches 31n18, 63–4, 99n85, 165–6, 235, 255
  lesbians 21–4, 29, 31–2, 53–4, 73, 198
  readings of scripture 59–60, 63–4, 157, 192–3, 244
Blackness, authentic 21, 63, 165–6, 67, 72
Brunei 65n41
Burundi 65n41

Cameroon 65n41
Canaanites 176–82, 125, 166–9, 171

Cape Verde 67
Catholic church, opposition to homosexuality 94, 97–8, 174–5
Celibacy 35, 98, 101, 103, 135–9
Cetiner, Marianne 64, 77–8
Chechen Republic 65n41, 65n42
Critical imagination 154–6, 195, 219–30
China 24, 61, 79–81, 187–8
Christian Institute, opposition to civil partnership 94–100
  opposition to sexual discrimination law 101–4
  influence of 94–5
Civil partnership legislation 64, 83–5, 94–100, 147, 231
Co-wives 129, 142–6
Combahee River Collective 21–2, 35n22
Coming Out 32, 39, 89, 187–8, 197, 233, 243–4, 253
Commission on Christian Homophobia 102–4
Complimentarity 98, 130, 146–55
Congregation for the doctrine of the faith 97n80, 98, 174

Daughters of Bilitis 46, 60
Deborah 152–5, 195–6

Delilah 43–4
Deuteronomistic history 43, 142, 166
Dignity 245, 256
Dinah 129, 133–4
Djibputi 65n41

Ekkēlsia gynaikōn, purposes 263–7
Encounter approach 252–4
Essentialism 15–19, 37–8, 56, 73, 98–9, 108, 111, 117–23, 159, 161, 164, 172, 181, 264–5
Ethiopia 65n41
Evangelicals Concerned 245
Exile from worshipping communities 248–9, 252, 256, 258
Eurocentrism 60, 81, 123, 192, 209
European Union 76, 78, 191

Family 71–2, 74, 79–81, 84–5, 87, 89, 93–7, 100, 104, 117, 140–2, 147, 149, 187–8, 213, 219, 222, 232
Female homoeroticism 61, 124–9, 142–6, 167, 221–30
suppression of 111–23, 124–7, 130–56, 221–2
Feminism and activism 36–9, 50, 59, 239–43, 267
second wave 5, 19–38, 116, 157, 188, 209n140
Friends Homosexual Fellowship 245

GALZ 72, 92
Gay is good 39, 244, 245, 247
Gay Liberation Front 46, 60

Gaydar 17, 210
Gender Nonconformity 3, 13–14, 28, 153
Gloucester report 170
Grenada 65n41
Guinea Conakry 65n41, 67

Hannah 131–2, 140, 142–3
Hermeneutic of hetero-suspicion 124–30
Heterocentrism 107–10, 148, 214, 209–10, 213–17, 225, 227, 262
Heteronormativity 25, 27, 37, 39–42, 45, 50, 52, 57, 75, 81, 100, 143, 146, 148, 155, 163, 197–8, 202–5, 207, 224, 229, 236, 261
Heteropatriarchy 48, 241
Heterosexism 21, 27, 46, 108, 130, 135, 140, 208, 213, 264
Holocaust 64–5
Homo-hetero binary 28, 38–43, 52, 57–8, 61n37, 62n38, 158–9, 163–94
Homophobia, see anti-lesbian/gay
Homosexuality, death penalty 209n140, 93, 167, 231, 258
illegal 65–6
western phenomenon 57, 60–2, 71–4, 80–1, 122, 181, 187–9, 191–3
Hui jia 187

Indecent, homosexual acts as 75, 262
Indecent Theology 262
Integrity 245
Inversion 10–15, 162, 168–9, 246

Israelite religion, women's roles in
220–1, 137–9
Intersex 11n5
Iran 65n41, 65n42

Jael 128n100, 154–5
Japan 79–80
Jephthah's daughter 129, 219
Jesus, sexuality of 212–13, 259

Korea 79, 80, 244

Lavender/purple 17, 211
Lavender menace 20
Lebanon 65n41
Leeds revolutionary Feminist
Group 22
Lesbian, ancestry 16, 26, 73, 119–
20, 189
earliest references to 11n3
continuum 10, 23–36, 96–7,
138–9, 185–7,
sensibility 10, 15–19, 234
pulp fiction 113
rabbis 233
western signifier 60–2
Lesbian sex, integral to definition
28–35, 122–3, 185, 207
undefined 30, 74, 79, 122, 123n97,
185–6
condemned by religious
discourse 98–102,
Lesbian and Gay Christian
Movement 102, 165, 245,
256
Lesbian and gay, theology 162,
244–6
Lesbian and gay research, risks
of 193, 235–6

Lesbianism, silencing/erasure of in
history 48, 111–23,
221–2, 229
in scripture 124–56, 229
political choice 22
Lesbians, isolation of 80, 112–16
LGBT/Q 62n38
Liberia 65n41, 67
Libya 65n41
Lister, Ann 11n3, 13–31

Malawi 65n41, 67
Male rape 66, 228
Mati culture 60, 123
Mattachine society 45, 60
Mauritania 65n41, 65n42
Mauritius 65n41
Métissage 266
Metropolitan community church
16, 245, 249, 256
Michal 132, 215
Midrash 140, 155, 212, 226–9
Morocco 65n41, 67
Motherhood, lesbian 139–41
valorized 130–42
Mothers, imaged as competitive
rivals 142–6
Musla-Uganda 70

Naditu 135–8
National Organization of Women
20
New lesbian criticism 56
Nicaragua 65n41

Oman 65n41
Open church 245
Order of virgins 139
widows 139

Osborne report 170
Othering 146–54

Pakistan 65n41, 65n42, 67
Postchristian 5, 257–8, 266–7
Postcolonial 72–3, 81, 191–2
Puerto Rico 65n41

Qatar 65n41
Queer Theory 10, 41–52, 159,
    163, 189, 195–210, 218,
    234–7
    applied to scripture 43–4,
      47–52, 210–19
    lesbian-feminist critique of
      45–7, 50–1, 217–18, 236–7

Radicalesbians 20–2
Romania 76–8
Romantic friendship 13, 19–20,
    28–31, 186–7, 208
Ruth and Naomi 108, 139–41,
    142n111, 152, 183–4, 186–7,
    188, 213–14, 226–7, 232, 247,
    259

Saint Lucia 65n41
Salvation Army 4, 98–100, 149
Samson 43–4
Saudi Arabia 65n41, 65n42
Section 28 64, 84–5, 93, 100
Senegal 65n41, 67
Sex wars 54
Sexologists 9–15, 19, 20, 169, 172
Sexual Offences Act 168
Social constructionism 117–23
Solomon 216, 218–19
Solomon islands 65n41, 67
South Africa 76, 157

Stonewall, event 59–60, 118, 151,
    243
    organization 83, 87, 95
Sudan 65n41, 65 n42
Swaziland 65n41

Texts of terror 6, 149, 152, 164,
    167, 174, 177–8, 180–94, 109,
    214, 237, 241, 244, 246–7,
    250–4
Thailand 61
Therapeutrides 137–8
Theology, lesbian and gay 27–8,
    158, 161–3, 244–5, 250–2,
    258–60
    queer 161–3, 258
Tobago 65n41, 67
Togo 65n41
Tongzhi 61, 81, 187
Tribade 11n3, 11n5, 126–7, 228
Trinidad 65n41, 67
Tunisia 65n41

United Arab Emirates 65n41,
    65n42

Virginity 139, 218

Western Samoa 65n41
Wolfenden Committee 167–8
Woman-identified-woman 22–3
Womanism 21, 25, 54, 107n88,
    107, 109, 123–4, 232, 239, 267,
    270
Wo/men 49, 264
Woolf, Virginia 114–16

Yemen 65n41, 65n42

Zambia 68, 91–2
Zilpah 133
Zimbabwe 72–5, 92–3

Name Index

Aarmo, Margrete 72–4, 93
Abu-Lughod, Lila 143–5
Alpert, Rebecca 148–50, 219, 226–7, 233–4, 236, 252–4, 260–1
Altman, Dennis 40, 118n93
Anzaldúa, Gloria 47, 239

Bach, Alice 107n88, 109, 129, 239–40, 267n155
Bailey, Derrick Sherwin 15, 168–9, 171–5, 178
Bal, Mieke 152
Beck, Evelyn Torton 165
Bird, Phyllis 131n101, 134, 137n108, 220
Blackwood and Wieringa 61, 123n97
Boer, Roland 44
Boswell, John 118, 120n96, 135, 136n106, 177, 178, 251
Brenner, Athalya 131n101, 132–3, 142n112,
Bright, Deborah 199–200, 207
Brooten, Bernadette J. 11n3, 11n5, 126–8, 222, 229
Butler, Judith 40n24, 50, 150–1

Carden, Michael 49, 175, 182–3, 217, 228

Chou, Wah-Shan 61, 80, 187, 188
Clark, John Michael 190, 258–9, 261
Collins, Patricia Hill 31, 157n120, 160, 231
Comstock, Gary D. 173, 193, 235, 241, 251, 252, 255, 260

D'Angelo, Mary Rose 25–6
Day, Peggy 220
Doty, Alexander 203–5, 208, 210, 214, 216, 223, 227
Douglas, Kelly Brown 31n18, 192, 193, 235
Duncan Celena M 140

Ellis, Havelock 11, 12n6, 14, 20
Epprecht, Marc 73–5, 93
Exum, J. Cheryl 107n88, 108, 131n101, 132n103, 142, 146n117, 152, 188

Faderman, Lillian 20, 28, 29, 82n60, 112, 116, 117
Faraday, Annabel 82n60
Farwell, Marilyn R. 10, 38, 46n29
Fortunato, J.E. 161n121, 244, 247
Foucault, Michel 118n93
Frye, Marilyn 123n97, 149

Fuchs, Esther 108–9, 131n101

Gagnon, Robert A. J. 193, 178
Goss, Robert E. 50n33, 162,
    174n124, 216, 217, 235, 250–1,
    254n152, 255, 256, 257–8
Grahn, Judy 17, 112, 119, 211
Guest, P. Deryn 153, 177, 179, 214,
    226n145, 252, 262

Halperin, David M. 45n28,
    118–19, 261
Helminiak, Daniel A. 174–7, 181
Hennegan, Alison 18, 114, 196, 207
Heyward, Carter 250
Horner, Tom 178, 183–4, 251
Hunt, Mary E. 27–8

Jeffreys, Sheila 31, 33, 46n29
Jennings Jr., Theodore W. 214–16,
    237
Jobling, J'annine 264–6

Katz, Jonathan Ned 11n4, 11n5, 12,
    13, 14, 40, 118n93
Kitzinger, Celia 66n43
Koch, Tim 158, 190–1, 210,
    211–12, 214, 216

Lauretis, Teresa de 37
Lerner, Gerda 218
Liew, Tat-Siong Benny 47
Lorde, Audre 32, 35n22, 39n23, 54
    55, 60, 158
Lynch, Lee 113–14, 116

Maitland, Sara 154, 223–6
McNeill, J.J. 161n121, 244, 248–9,
    251, 255
Meyers, Carol 131, 135–7, 145, 147–8

Milgrom, Jacob 125, 127
Mollenkott, Virginia
    Ramay 243n149
Monroe, Irene 197n134, 255
Munt, Sally 9, 19, 56, 196n132

Nestle, Joan 28n12, 32–4, 53n34, 54
Nissinen, Martti 125, 128, 182–4

Olyan, Saul 127

Phelan, Shane 55–6
Plaskow, Judith 227

Rabinowitz, Nancy Sorkin 122–3,
    126
Rich, Adrienne 22–6, 33, 35, 36, 51,
    54n35, 128, 129, 138, 146, 160, 185
Rowlett, Lori 43–4
Rudy, Kathy 45
Russo, Vito 17, 18n8, 196n132, 198,
    211

Schneider, Laurel C. 44, 47,
    217–18, 261
Schüssler Fiorenza, Elisabeth 49,
    108, 124, 221, 242n148, 263–8
Seo, Dong-Jin 79–80
Smith, Barbara 21, 157n120
Smith-Rosenberg, Carroll 28n13
Smyth, Cherry 46n29, 199n135, 201
Solomon, Mark 165, 254
Spencer, Daniel T. 44, 210n143
Stone, Ken 45, 49, 150, 182, 217, 241,
    261
Stuart, Elizabeth 152, 161, 184–5,
    190, 257

Terry, Jennifer 10n2, 41–3, 48

Travis, Irene S. 232–4

Weems, Renita 107n88,
    158n120, 224
Wekker, Gloria 60
West, Mona 49, 50n33, 140–1, 234,
    254n152
Wilson, Nancy 15–17, 26, 211, 212,
    214

Wilton, Tamsin 48, 54, 90, 111,
    196n132, 199n135
Wittig, Monique 36–8, 150

Yee, Gale A. 142–5, 147–8

Zimmerman, Bonnie 31, 51–2,
    196n132, 202–3, 206–8, 210, 213,
    214, 227

Bible Reference Index

Genesis

1—3 104, 128, 147–9, 164–5, 172

1.27–8 146, 149

2.24 100, 148–9

3.16 150

19 164, 168, 171, 173, 174, 182–3, 228, 246, 259

Leviticus

18.3 166

18.22 164–5, 167–8, 173–4, 180, 182, 189, 197 n134, 254

20.13 164–5, 167–8, 173–4, 180, 182

Deuteronomy

7.1 179

23.17–8 169, 173

Ruth 140, 152, 183–7, 214, 226, 227, 232, 247, 259

Judges

1 166

3.5 179

4—5 128 n100, 152, 153–5

11 129

13—16 44

17.6 166

21.25 166

1 Samuel

20.7–8 216

20.30 184

2 131, 140, 142–3

2 Samuel

6.23 132

1 Kings 169

3.16–28 218–9

Proverbs

30.17 131

Jeremiah

31.15 140

Ezra

9.1 179

Matthew

19.45 100

22 151

Luke

1.46–55 131

10.38–42 26, 186

John

11 26, 186, 212

Acts

16, 11, 14–16 211

Romans

1.26–7 124, 126, 151, 164, 168, 169, 173, 174, 252, 258

16.12 186

16.17 139

2 Corinthians
6.9   164, 168,
           169, 173,
           174, 176,
           177, 181, 189,
           241

Ephesians
5.12   169
5.21–33   151

Philippians
4.2   26, 139, 186

1 Timothy
1.9–10   164, 168,
           169, 173,
           174, 177

2 Peter   181

Jude   181

Revelation
21.8   169
22.15   169

Lightning Source UK Ltd.
Milton Keynes UK
UKHW021340030921
389835UK00005B/1327